Heritage and History in the China–Australia Migration Corridor

Crossing Seas

Editors: Henry Yu (University of British Columbia) and Elizabeth Sinn (University of Hong Kong)

The Crossing Seas series brings together books that investigate Chinese migration from the migrants' perspective. As migrants travelled from one destination to another throughout their lifetimes, they created and maintained layers of different networks. Along the way these migrants also dispersed, recreated, and adapted their cultural practices. To study these different networks, the series publishes books in disciplines such as history, women's studies, geography, cultural anthropology, and archaeology and prominently features publications informed by interdisciplinary approaches that focus on multiple aspects of the migration processes.

Books in the series:

Chinese Diaspora Charity and the Cantonese Pacific, 1850–1949
Edited by John Fitzgerald and Hon-ming Yip

Heritage and History in the China–Australia Migration Corridor
Edited by Denis Byrne, Ien Ang, and Phillip Mar

Locating Chinese Women: Historical Mobility between China and Australia
Edited by Kate Bagnall and Julia T. Martínez

Returning Home with Glory: Chinese Villagers around the Pacific, 1849 to 1949
Michael Williams

Searching for Sweetness: Women's Mobile Lives in China and Lesotho
Sarah Hanisch

Heritage and History in the China–Australia Migration Corridor

Edited by Denis Byrne, Ien Ang, and Phillip Mar

Hong Kong University Press
The University of Hong Kong
Pok Fu Lam Road
Hong Kong
https://hkupress.hku.hk

© 2023 Hong Kong University Press

ISBN 978-988-8805-62-4 (*Hardback*)

All rights reserved. No portion of this publication may be reproduced or transmitted in any form or by any means, electronic or mechanical, including photocopying, recording, or any information storage or retrieval system, without prior permission in writing from the publisher.

This hardcover edition by Hong Kong University Press is not for sale in Australia and New Zealand.

British Library Cataloguing-in-Publication Data
A catalogue record for this book is available from the British Library.

Digitally printed

Contents

List of Figures	vii
Acknowledgements	ix
Introduction	1
Ien Ang and Denis Byrne	

Part 1: Connections, Flows, Identities

1. Villages of the Fragrant Hills	25
Michael Williams	
2. A Heritage of Lifelines in the Migration Corridor	52
Denis Byrne	
3. (Un)making Transnational Identities: Migration and Chineseness	75
Ien Ang	
4. Diaspora Tourism and Homeland Travel	106
Alexandra Wong	

Part 2: Sites in the Heritage Corridor

5. Making Heritage: The Mar Family and Sha Chong	133
Glenn Mar and Phillip Mar	
6. Remittance Houses in Zhongshan	154
Denis Byrne	
7. From Ancestral Halls to Modern Schools: Diaspora-Funded Education in Zhongshan	185
Christopher Cheng and Phillip Mar	
8. Zhongshan in Sydney's Chinatown	215
Ien Ang and Alexandra Wong	
9. Making Heritage in the Migration Corridor	240
Denis Byrne	

Glossary	263
List of Contributors	267
Index	269

Figures

Figure 0.1:	Map of the Pearl River Delta	3
Figure 0.2:	Map of Zhongshan showing villages which sent migrants to Australia	5
Figure 0.3:	A street in Caobian village (曹邊村), Zhongshan, remittance houses shown on the right	14
Figure 1.1:	Map of counties in the Pearl River Delta	27
Figure 1.2:	Map of Long Du (隆都) and Liang Du (良都) villages	40
Figure 2.1:	Stanley Hunt's truck	64
Figure 2.2:	Mashan School (馬山小學)	66
Figure 2.3	Map at Mashan School	66
Figure 2.4:	Jang Tim's tools	70
Figure 3.1:	Gordon Mar's ancestral mansion, Sha Chong village (沙涌村)	95
Figure 3.2:	Kam Louie's family home, Dutou village (渡頭村)	97
Figure 4.1:	Mansion built by Denise Ma's great-grandfather	113
Figure 4.2:	Ma clan photo (馬氏家族合照), Sha Chong village, 1917	115
Figure 4.3:	Descendants of Ma Joe Young (馬祖容), Sydney, 2019	115
Figure 4.4:	William Lee and his mother Doris at Yet Shing & Co. (日昇公司)	116
Figure 4.5:	Shop owned by Lee Chee Win (李紫雲) in Shekki (石岐)	118
Figure 4.6:	Mabel Lee (陳順妍) and her sisters	119
Figure 4.7:	Sung-Sun Hall of Learning, Mashan School (馬山小學崇信教學樓), 2017	121
Figure 5.1:	Managers of Wing Sang & Co. (永生果欄), including Mar See Poy (馬社培)	136
Figure 5.2:	Wong Shee Ping (黃樹屏), 1920	139
Figure 5.3:	Mar Family at Sha Chong village gate (沙涌牌坊)	143
Figure 5.4:	James Mar (馬啟華) at house in Sha Chong (沙涌村)	146
Figure 5.5:	Child's bike, Sha Chong house	148

Figure 5.6: Toy gun, Sha Chong house	148
Figure 5.7: Another family's photos, Sha Chong house	148
Figure 6.1: Type 1 house, Caobian village (曹邊村)	159
Figure 6.2: Type 2 house, Caobian village (曹邊村)	161
Figure 6.3: Detail of an interior panel painting in Type 2 house, Caobian village (曹邊村)	161
Figure 6.4: A bed compartment and panel paintings, Type 2 house, Caobian village (曹邊村)	163
Figure 6.5: Type 3 portico-balcony house, Hou Tau village (濠頭村)	164
Figure 6.6: Art Deco mansion built by the Kwok brothers in Chuk Sau Yuen village (竹秀園 Zhuxiuyuan)	167
Figure 6.7: Ground floor of 'Kwok mansion' (沛勳堂), with 'lattice screen' style doors and stained-glass window	168
Figure 6.8: A watchtower house (碉樓 *diaolou*) in Jinjiangli village, Kaiping County (開平縣錦江里村)	170
Figure 7.1: Map of Australian diaspora-funded schools (僑捐學校) in Zhongshan	187
Figure 7.2: Sketch of the Ma ancestral hall (馬氏大宗祠) in Sha Chong (沙涌村)	194
Figure 7.3: Foundation stone of Liangdu Church (良都堂), laid in 1918	194
Figure 7.4: Chuen Luk School (全祿學校), Dachong, Zhongshan, completed in 1991	203
Figure 7.5: Former Sha Chong School 沙涌學校 (舊址) in a dilapidated condition, used as a factory building	205
Figure 7.6: Rooftop cupola of former Sha Chong School 沙涌學校 (舊址)	205
Figure 7.7: Interior courtyard of the former Caobian school 曹邊學校 (天井)	207
Figure 8.1: The Kwong War Chong building (廣和昌) in Dixon Street (德信街), 1910	225
Figure 8.2: The Wing Sang building (永生果欄), Sussex and Hay Streets, circa 1910	232
Figure 8.3: The Emperor's Garden Restaurant (皇冠海鮮酒樓), Sydney Chinatown	235
Figure 9.1: Ou Saek (烏石 Wushi) villager holding photograph of Cheng (Henry) Fine Chong's (鄭番昌) house	249
Figure 9.2: A villager in Ou Saek (烏石), reminiscing	251
Figure 9.3: Inspecting renovations of a shrine at the Choy ancestral hall (蔡氏大宗祠), Ngoi Sha (外沙 Waisha), Zhuhai	257

Acknowledgements

This book stems from multidisciplinary research carried out between 2017 and 2022 on which all the authors collaborated. The project, to research the transnational dimension of the migration corridor between Zhongshan, in China, and Australia during the period between the 1840s and 1940s, was funded by the Australian Research Council (grant DP170101200).

As the editors of this volume, our first thanks go to all the descendants of migrants from Zhongshan, most of whom were living in Sydney at the time of our research, for agreeing to be interviewed for the project. In many cases their participation in the research included sharing with us the results of their own endeavours in researching the history of their forebears' lives both in Australia and in China. They helped make it possible for us, during our fieldwork in Zhongshan, to locate and document ancestral houses, lineage halls, and other buildings in their ancestral villages to which they have direct or indirect links. Without their help we would not have been able to reconstruct the individual migration narratives contained in the book and those narratives would not have taken on for us the vividness which they did, a vividness we hope we have been able to do justice to here.

In Sydney, we are thankful for the generous support we have received from the Chung Shan Society of Australia, as well as the Chinese Australian Historical Society, which provided us with an opportunity to present our research to a receptive audience in the early stages of this project. Many people have been generous in supporting us throughout the project, including King Fong, Douglas Lam, William and Nancy Lee, Mabel Lee, Kam Louie, Daphne Lowe-Kelley, Denise Ma, Glenn Mar, Gordon Mar, Brad Powe, and Howard Wilson.

In Queensland, Christopher Cheng would especially like to thank Joe and Judy Leong, and Dr Sandi Robb (historian) of Townsville; Julia Volkmar, Mary Low, and Chan Lai Chu of Cairns; and Felicia Seeto (née Leung) of Brisbane.

In Zhongshan, thanks are due to the numerous people who generously assisted with information and guidance, particularly in regard to the built heritage of those who migrated to Australia. These include King Chow of the Zhongshan branch of the Bureau of Chinese Overseas Affairs, Chen Diqiu (historian and former employee of the Bureau), Gan Jianbo (former Zhongshan museum curator), and Anthony

Leong (historian), all of whom were as generous with their specialist knowledge as they were with their hospitality.

Some of the stories and images related to the China–Australia heritage corridor which this project has compiled can be found on our website, www.heritagecorridor. org.au. The website includes a link to an interactive database of relevant people and places using the Heurist data management platform (http://database.heritagecorridor.org.au). Thanks are due to Ian Johnson and Michael Falk for guiding us in the development of the Heurist research database.

Finally, we want to acknowledge and thank the Institute for Culture and Society at Western Sydney University, of which all but one of the authors of the book's chapters are either members or associates, for the numerous forms of practical support which made the research possible. The collegial intellectual environment provided by the Institute has played an essential role in the development of our thinking about migration corridors as social-historical fields and as transnational spheres of material heritage.

Last but not least, we wish to thank the staff at Hong Kong University Press for their efficient and knowledgeable editorial guidance.

Introduction

Ien Ang and Denis Byrne

This book presents a series of articles that view the history and heritage of Chinese migration to Australia through a transnational lens.[1] It focuses on a particular strand of transnational migration that, from the mid-nineteenth century to the mid-twentieth century, involved the departure for Australia of thousands of people, mainly males, from Zhongshan (中山, also spelt Chung Shan),[2] a county located in the Pearl River Delta region of Guangdong in southern China (Figure 0.1). The book examines this migration as an historical phenomenon and as a legacy, or heritage, that is embodied in the lives of the migrants' descendants today, impelling many of them to retrace their forebears' steps back to Zhongshan from Australia and playing into the construction of their hybrid Chinese Australian identities. It is also a legacy that, as we will show, has a very physical dimension in the form of material traces of Chinese migration, such as old buildings, located in Australia as well as in the home villages of the migrants in Zhongshan.

Most of those who left Zhongshan for Australia were destined for New South Wales or Queensland, with many of them ending up in Sydney, which from the turn of the twentieth century developed into the largest urban hub for Chinese Australian networks.[3] As the chapters in the book detail, the legacy of the migration corridor that connects Zhongshan and Sydney remains alive to this day, both in Zhongshan itself and in Sydney and other parts of Australia where Zhongshan migrants once passed through.

Migration from Zhongshan to Australia was anything but one-way. In the foreground of the transnational approach that we take in this book are the ongoing bi-directional flows of people, ideas, objects, and money that, stimulated by initial acts of migration, moved along a spatially confined passageway or corridor that

---

1. Traditional Chinese characters have been used throughout this book. Pinyin has been used for romanising Mandarin Chinese terms. For romanisations of Cantonese and other dialect names and terms, see information in parentheses throughout the book.
2. See glossary for variations in place names.
3. John Fitzgerald, *Big White Lie: Chinese Australians in White Australia* (Sydney: UNSW Press, 2007), 54.

irrevocably links Zhongshan and Australia. What is especially significant to us is that these flows occurred between particular nodes of Zhongshanese settlement in Australia and particular villages in Zhongshan (Figure 0.2). This geographic specificity has manifested at many levels. It means, for example, that individual migrants often used money they earned in Australia to build houses in their ancestral village that, while providing accommodation for those left behind, also acted as placeholders for them in the villages and as a base for return visits and, for many of them, eventual retirement. Simultaneously, the emotional and economic investment of these migrants in their home villages meant that the villages came to assume a certain symbolic presence in Australia that has continued to resonate up to the present. It is this level of directed interconnectivity that leads us to frame this book around the corridor metaphor and to propose the concept of a China–Australia heritage corridor.

From Migration Corridor to Heritage Corridor

In our use of the corridor metaphor, both in the book's title and throughout the chapters, we home in on the cross-border flows just mentioned. The metaphor has broad currency in migration discourse – the term 'remittance corridor' is, for example, widely used in the banking sector. The Zhongshan–Australia corridor is one of a number of distinct migration corridors that emerged in the mid-nineteenth century between southern China and key ports around the Pacific Rim.[4] Sydney was one such port, and just as we focus on Zhongshan county as a locus of emigration in the Pearl River Delta, at the Australian end our attention is primarily on Sydney. As Michael Williams notes, at times in the first half of the century, from 20 to 40 per cent of Sydney's Chinese population was from Zhongshan.[5]

In Philip Kuhn's conceptualisation, a migration corridor is 'a channel of connections that keep the migrant in a meaningful relationship with the old country (or old village, lineage, or province)',[6] a connection reproduced from generation to generation. Although such corridors have a spatial aspect, Kuhn argues that they are 'best thought of as social and economic organisms', where 'the income, the kinship links and the social structure of the *qiaoxiang*[7] exist in a special zone that is neither fully part of the homeland nor fully part of the adopted land of the émigrés'.[8] Migrants in the destination locale and the kin they left behind coalesce as a transnational community in which the well-being of those in each locale depends

---

4. Elizabeth Sinn, *Pacific Crossing: California Gold, Chinese Migration and the Making of Hong Kong* (Hong Kong: Hong Kong University Press, 2012), 9.
5. Michael Williams, *Returning Home with Glory* (Hong Kong: Hong Kong University Press, 2018), 5.
6. Philip A. Kuhn, *Chinese Among Others: Emigration in Modern Times* (Lanham, MA: Rowman and Littlefield, 2008), 49.
7. The term '*qiaoxiang*' 僑鄉, pronounced in Mandarin, refers to ancestral localities in China transformed by emigration, namely overseas remittances, and new buildings.
8. Kuhn, *Chinese Among Others*, 49–50.

Figure 0.1: Map of the Pearl River Delta (珠江三角洲)

on the continued back-and-forth flow of people, money, goods, information, ideas, and culture between them.

As this border-crossing traffic through the migration corridor has been reproduced over time, it can also be said to have in a sense 'solidified' into things that retrospectively may be construed as material heritage – hence our coinage of the term 'heritage corridor'. This concept embodies for us the idea that the built environment of migrants is stretched between their origin and destination locales and that it emerges out of the agency of people and objects in collectives dispersed across the corridor.[9] The houses constructed by migrants in their home villages were, for example, a product of remittance flows, and while they are spatially grounded in emigrant villages – their foundations are sunk in village soil – they are things that have taken form in the dreams of those whose labour at the destination end of the migration corridor has paid for them. For all the attention given in this book to the various aspects of the material world of Chinese migration, we are, however, careful not to reify the heritage corridor as a 'thing' – it remains for us a metaphor, a useful way of conceptualising the spatially distributed material traces of transnational flows.

Two related aspects of these flows are salient in our use of the corridor metaphor. The first is their two-way character, seen for example in the way the traffic of goods flowing from China to Australia, which included incense sticks, chopsticks, dried seafood, and ceramic jars containing preserved vegetables, was matched by a traffic of goods flowing in the other direction, including gold dust and gold ingots sent as remittances in the late nineteenth century, and the clothing, woodworking tools, and gifts of various kinds carried by migrants from Australia on return visits to their home villages. The goods flowing outward and inward along the China–Australia migration corridor passed by each other, so to speak, on their respective oceanic journeys. The second salient aspect of cross-border connectivity is its ongoing nature, the way it persisted after the initial act of migration. This is evident in the way that so many migrants made regular return visits to their families and friends in China over the years and in the way that, while in Australia, so many of them remained deeply involved in the affairs of their homeland, an involvement exemplified in the educational sphere. Most early Chinese migrants left their homeland with little or no formal education, but they took with them the high moral value placed on education in Chinese society, and, once in Australia and achieving even a modest degree of wealth, often this valuation translated into a flow of donations back to China for the building of the first modern schools in their home villages.[10]

---

9. Denis Byrne, 'Heritage Corridors: Transnational Flows and the Built Environment of Migration', *Journal of Ethnic and Migration Studies* 42, no. 14 (2016): 2360–78, https://doi.org/10.1080/1369183X.2016.1205805.

10. Christopher Cheng, 'Beacons of Modern Learning: Diaspora-Funded Schools in the China–Australia Corridor', *Asian and Pacific Migration Journal* 29, no. 2 (2020): 139–62, https://doi.org/10.1177/0117196820930309. See also Chapter 7 of this volume.

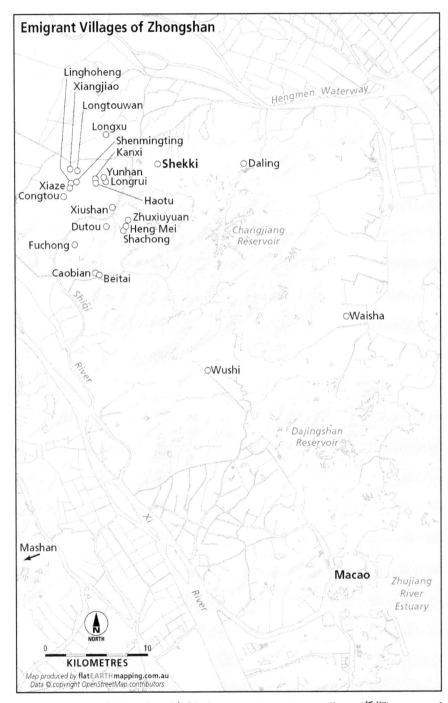

Figure 0.2: Map of Zhongshan (中山) showing main emigrant villages (僑鄉) connected to Australia

The corridor metaphor is particularly apt in the case of Chinese transnational migration in the period between the 1840s and the 1940s. This is due to the way overseas migration was institutionalised at the level of the family in the migrant-sending villages of the Pearl River Delta, the origin place of the great majority of those who went to Australia. Glen Peterson describes how such families were structured around the principle that their working-age males would be based overseas, earning money to be channelled back to the family.[11] This 'household strategy' – he borrows the term from Immanuel Wallerstein – meant stretching the household transnationally, but with the understanding that its centre of gravity remained in China.[12] Peterson observes that the 'accumulation of ancestral land and houses in China served as the material embodiment of the patriline, whose preservation and ritual honouring was a central focus of Chinese life and often the primary motivation for emigrating in the first place.[13] Williams's account of this household strategy as it applied to families in the emigrant villages of Zhongshan county describes it as a pattern of labour migration dating back to the Ming dynasty (1368–1644), a pattern that developed into a distinctive transnational lifestyle that blurred the distinction between the villages and the destination locales.[14] It was a cross-border way of life which, in heritage terms, meant that sites associated with these migrants in places such as Australia – their dwellings, the shops they operated, the market gardens they laboured in – were closely networked to the sites of the family estate in China, including to remittance-built houses, family graves, and ancestral halls. Indeed, we maintain that whichever end of the migration corridor they are situated in, these places simply do not make sense *as* heritage sites except in relation to the sites at its other end.

The transnational household strategy could and did extend across generations, often with two or more generations of males being absent from the family at any one time.[15] Not infrequently, those overseas ended up putting down roots there, many of them maintaining a 'family at both ends' (兩頭家, *liangtoujia* in Mandarin), but even when this occurred it was common for their wives or partners overseas and the children from these relationships to spend periods of time with the family back in China, again underlining the appropriateness of the corridor metaphor.[16] With the Japanese occupation of Guangdong from 1938 to 1945, followed by civil war and the 1949 Communist Revolution, many members of these transnational households found themselves stranded overseas in places such as Australia and forced to settle there. Nevertheless, as the chapters in the book describe, this transnational history of the migration corridor has continued to reverberate in the lives and orientations

---

11. Glen Peterson, *Overseas Chinese in the People's Republic of China* (London: Routledge, 2012).
12. Peterson, *Overseas Chinese*, 37.
13. Peterson, *Overseas Chinese*, 28.
14. Williams, *Returning Home with Glory*, 74–75. Williams refers to this as a *huaqiao* strategy. See also Steven B. Miles, *Chinese Diasporas: A Social History of Global Migration* (London: Routledge, 2020), 20–36.
15. Williams, *Returning Home with Glory*, 74.
16. Williams, *Returning Home with Glory*, 74–75.

of contemporary generations of descendants of early migrants, some of whom undertake to resume the connection by making the journey back to their ancestral village. In so doing, they contribute to a lasting mutual entanglement of Australia and China that belies the sanctity of nation-centric narratives of national identity and history.

While we use the word 'family' in unqualified terms in the book, it is important to note that, under the circumstances of transnational migration, the structure of the traditional Chinese family changed. Building on Aihwa Ong's concept of 'flexible citizenship' and Pierre Bourdieu's notion of 'practical kinship', Anne-Christine Trémon proposes the term 'flexible kinship' to describe these changes, which included a weakening of the patriarchal extended family and clan, a corresponding increase in the importance of the 'uterine' family, and a growing equalisation between men and women.[17] While, in Zhongshan, women effectively became the head of the household in families with male members abroad,[18] in Australia, Chinese Australian women's involvement in charitable work for religious and civic organisations played a key role in fostering Chinese connections with Anglo Australians.[19] Migration engendered diversity in family formations, as seen in the liaisons and marriages formed between Chinese men and Anglo Australian women and in the interfolding of these relationships and the offspring of them with conjugal families based in China. We also note that non-heteronormative sexualities, including what are today known as queer or homosexual, existed in the migration context, as they did in traditional Chinese culture.[20]

A Transnational Lens on Migration and Heritage

With its focus on the China–Australia migration and heritage corridor, this book contributes to the broader 'transnational turn' in migration studies since the turn of the century. Attention to border-crossing phenomena has become prominent in this field as a response to intensifying global population movement and migrant mobilities in what has been called 'the age of migration'.[21] Recognising the

---

17. Anne-Christie Trémon, 'Flexible Kinship: Shaping Transnational Families among the Chinese in Tahiti', *Journal of the Royal Anthropological Institute* 23 (2016): 42–60.
18. Williams, *Returning Home with Glory*, 74–77.
19. Mei-fen Kuo, 'The "Invisible" Work of Women: Gender and Philanthropic Sociability in the Evolution of Early Chinese Australian Voluntary Organizations', in *Chinese Diaspora Charity and the Cantonese Pacific 1850–1949*, ed. John Fitzgerald and Hon-ming Yip (Hong Kong: University of Hong Kong Press, 2020), 154–72.
20. Miles, *Chinese Diasporas*, 47; Alex Bayley, 'The Story of Ah Chew, Convicted and Flogged for Attempted Sodomy: A Tale of Chinese Homosexuality on the Victorian Goldfields', blog post, 2019, https://alexbayley.id.au/blog/; Yorick Small, 'Queer Pleasure: Masculinity, Male Homosexuality and Public Space', *Queensland Historical Atlas*, 2019, https://www.qhatlas.com.au/content/queer-pleasure-masculinity-male-homosexuality-and-public-space#.
21. Hein de Haas, Stephen Castles, and Mark J. Miller, *The Age of Migration: International Population Movements in the Modern World*, sixth edition (London: Red Globe Press, 2020).

irreducible significance of these border-crossing processes has been a key rationale for asserting the importance of applying a transnational lens to migration.[22] In this development, migration is generally recognised as a transformative force, not just for the migrants themselves but also for the societies they move between: both their countries of origin and the countries in which they settle, either temporarily or permanently. Migration, which – depending on perspective – involves both emigration and immigration, disrupts the vision of the world as consisting of self-contained, bounded nation-states; it involves processes that irrevocably interconnect countries and highlight the porousness of their borders.

For most of the twentieth century, scholarship on migration primarily focused on how immigrants adapted to their host societies, implicitly taking the perspective of the migrant-receiving nation-state as the normative starting point for examination. For example, a long tradition of American sociological scholarship, beginning with the Chicago School in the 1920s, has focused on the assimilation or integration of migrants in their new social environment in the United States, which is known as a long-established immigration society.[23] In Australia, twentieth-century migration scholarship broadly reflected the evolution of government immigration policy from assimilation to multiculturalism, articulating an admission of the importance of ethnic identity maintenance for migrants and the impossibility of full-blown assimilation.[24] What these lines of scholarship share is a methodological nationalism,[25] which tends to neglect the fact that immigrants are also emigrants: they concentrate exclusively on the national context of the migrant presence and its impacts, forgetting that the impacts on the countries these migrants come from may be equally significant and worth examining. Migrant-sending countries are often relatively poor and less developed – which is an important reason for emigration in the first place, as migrants are compelled to seek opportunities to support their livelihoods elsewhere – and, in these cases too, research tends towards a methodological nationalism that focuses on the impact of emigration, and particularly remittances, on the economic development of the migrant-sending country.[26] What this methodological nationalism produces is a conceptual and empirical separation

---

22. Steven Vertovec, *Transnationalism* (Abingdon: Routledge, 2009).

23. Mirna Safi, 'Immigrant Assimilation Theory: Insights from American Sociology', *Sociologie* 2, no. 2 (2011): 149–64, https://doi.org/10.3917/socio.022.0149; Alejandro Portes and Min Zhou, 'The New Second Generation: Segmented Assimilation and Its Variants', *The Annals of the American Academy of Political and Social Science* 530, no. 1 (1993): 74–96, https://doi.org/10.1177/0002716293530001006.

24. Christine Inglis, 'Some Recent Australian Writing on Immigration and Assimilation', *International Migration Review* 9, no. 3 (1975): 335–44, https://doi.org/10.1177%2F019791837500900304; Stephen Castles, Mary Kalantzis, Bill Cope, and Michael Morrissey, *Mistaken Identity: Multiculturalism and the Demise of Nationalism in Australia* (Annandale: Pluto Press, 1988).

25. Andreas Wimmer and Nina Glick Schiller, 'Methodological Nationalism, the Social Sciences, and the Study of Migration: An Essay in Historical Epistemology', *International Migration Review* 37, no. 3 (2003): 576–610.

26. See, for example, J. Edward Taylor, Joaquín Arango, Graeme Hugo, Ali Kouaouci, Douglas S. Massey and Adela Pellegrino, 'International Migration and National Development', *Population Index* 62, no. 2 (1996): 181–212, https://doi.org/10.2307/3646297; Samuel Munzele and Dilip Ratha, eds, *Remittances: Development Impact and Future Prospects* (Washington, DC: The World Bank 2005).

of migrant-receiving and migrant-sending nation-states, overlooking the fact that the movement between nation-states undertaken by migrants brings about transformative changes on both sides, resulting not only in their inescapable interconnectedness but also in the permeability of their social and cultural, if not physical, boundaries. Moreover, as Andreas Wimmer and Nina Glick Schiller point out, by naturalising the nation-state as the unit of analysis, methodological nationalism cements the presumption that 'every move across national frontiers becomes an exception to the rule of sedentariness within the boundaries of the nation-state',[27] effectively rendering the migrant a marginal, anomalous figure whose activities and experiences are relegated to the periphery of the nation-state.

The turn to transnationalism was a critical response that aimed to overcome this methodological nationalism by developing 'a new analytical optic which makes visible the increasing intensity and scope of circular flows of persons, goods, information and symbols triggered by international labour migration'.[28] Key to this new analytical optic is a centring of the perspective of the migrant: for migrants, immigration and emigration are not two totally separate processes but are intimately connected, like two sides of a coin. The very act of migrating brings (at least) two places symbolically together, and many migrant practices are characterised by more or less organised efforts to bridge the physical distance through the establishment and sustenance of cross-border ties, linkages, exchanges, and mobilities. These are transnational practices that fundamentally transcend the apparent fixity of nation-states and destabilise the static disjunction between migrant-receiving and migrant-sending societies. In the turn to transnationalism, as Steven Vertovec argues, the goal is 'to examine empirically, and to analyse, transnational activities and social forms along with the political and economic factors that condition their creation and reproduction'.[29] One important indication of the rise of a transnational paradigm in migration studies is the upsurge in the use of the term 'diaspora' in referring to migrant communities since the 1990s. As Khachig Tölölyan, founder of the journal *Diaspora*, has remarked, 'diasporas are the exemplary communities of the transnational moment'.[30] Diasporas by definition are communities formed by a simultaneous attachment to 'home' and 'away'. To put it differently, it is through their diasporic connections that migrants become transnational actors circulating in various ways in the corridor space that spans their place of origin and place of settlement, as well as the places in between.

This book adopts the transnational paradigm to focus on the historical experience of migration from China to Australia. It does so in order to advance a

---

27. Wimmer and Glick Schiller, 'Methodological Nationalism', 585.
28. Ayse Caglar, 'Constraining Metaphors and the Transnationalisation of Spaces in Berlin', *Journal of Ethnic and Migration Studies* 27, no. 4 (2001): 607, http://dx.doi.org/10.1080/13691830120090403.
29. Vertovec, *Transnationalism*, 29.
30. Khachig Tölölyan, 'The Nation-State and Its Others: In Lieu of a Preface', *Diaspora: Journal of Transnational Studies* 1, no. 1 (1991): 3, https://doi.org/ 10.1353/dsp.1991.0008.

perspective on heritage that, the book hopes to show, requires an equivalent trans-national lens if we are to do full justice to the cultural and material legacy of this migration history.[31] While 'authorised' discourses of heritage have defined what counts as 'heritage' overwhelmingly in nationalist terms (typically by sanctioning collective memories of the past that promote a unified and grandiloquent histori-cal understanding of the nation),[32] we argue that valuing the heritage of migration, and the world-making practices, places, and identities migrants have engendered, can only be achieved through a transnational perspective that not only transcends, but also actively unsettles, the isolationist certitudes of competing nation-centric narratives.[33]

Chinese Australian Migrant Transnationalism

The chequered history of the Chinese diaspora exemplifies the fact that robust trans-nationalism is by no means a recent phenomenon but has been a defining feature of the Chinese migration experience from the mid-nineteenth century onwards, when thousands of Chinese labourers spread out from their villages in Guangdong and Fujian provinces in search of work and gold in white settler colonies in Australia as well as California, Canada, Hawai'i, and elsewhere, mostly recruited by European colonists who were desperate for mass labour to develop the colonies.[34] Over the course of the following decades a distinctively transnational pattern of Chinese migration developed which has been called the 'sojourner' pattern, referring to the well-documented practice of Chinese migrants returning to their home vil-lages after years of work and having accumulated sufficient wealth, although many others did stay put, by force or by preference.[35] In Australia and elsewhere, the perception that the Chinese were sojourners, not settlers, was deployed in white anti-Chinese discourses to legitimise Chinese exclusion because they tended to stick to a Chinese way of life and supposedly lacked a commitment to contribute

---

31. There is voluminous scholarship on the history of Chinese migration to many corners of the world (including Australia). For a global history, see Kuhn, *Chinese Among Others*.
32. Laurajane Smith, *Uses of Heritage* (London: Routledge, 2006); Gregory Ashworth, Brian Graham, and John Tunbridge, *Pluralising Pasts: Heritage, Identity and Place in Multicultural Societies* (London: Pluto Press, 2007).
33. Ien Ang, 'Unsettling the Nation: Heritage and Diaspora', in *Heritage, Memory and Identity*, ed. Helmut Anheier and Yudhishthir Raj Isar (London: SAGE, 2011), 84–94; Byrne, 'Heritage Corridors'.
34. Adam McKeown, 'Conceptualizing Chinese Diasporas, 1842–1979', *Journal of Asian Studies* 58, no. 2 (May 1999): 306–37, https://doi.org/10.2307/2659399. We should add that Chinese emigration to Southeast Asia commenced much earlier in the sixteenth century, and that Southeast Asia today is still where the largest percentage of descendants of Chinese people live.
35. Yuen-fong Woon, 'The Voluntary Sojourner among the Overseas Chinese: Myth or Reality?', *Pacific Affairs* 56, no. 4 (Winter 1983–1984): 673–90, https://doi.org/10.2307/2758597; Anthony Reid, ed., *Sojourners and Settlers: Histories of Southeast Asia and the Chinese* (Sydney: Allen & Unwin, 1996).

to the nation.[36] During the period from the 1910s to the 1940s, large contingents of migrant Chinese self-identified as *huaqiao* (華僑, pronounced in Mandarin), meaning 'Chinese temporarily residing overseas' – a term impressed on them by China-based nationalists who wished to enlist the Chinese diaspora in the cause of building a strong Chinese nation.[37] The *huaqiao* discourse was controversial because, linked with the sojourner discourse, it dramatised Chinese diasporic fealty to China, at the expense of an orientation to their country of residence. Mobo Gao stresses the defensive nature of the *huaqiao* outlook in the early twentieth century as it was informed by a desire to fortify Chinese nationalism in a time when China was under attack from European and Japanese imperialists.[38] Williams, meanwhile, emphasises the cultural dimension of the *huaqiao*'s homeland orientation as motivated by a wish for 'returning home with glory' (滿載榮歸).[39] By contrast, in his broadside against the racism of the White Australia policy, John Fitzgerald highlights Chinese migrants to Australia as dedicated settlers who were committed to Australian values and citizenship.[40]

Whatever the case, this book does not seek to expound on the politicised dimensions of the *huaqiao* and sojourner discourses, which are controversial only if one takes the primacy of competing nationalist perspectives – Australian or Chinese – for granted. The more important fact to emphasise is that the Chinese migration experience, from its early days, has been quintessentially transnational, characterised by a constant to-and-fro traversing of the China–Australia migration corridor, which transcends the bounded territorial entities of both China and Australia. As Gao notes, for early Chinese migrants, 'home was in China, but home was also in the colony'. Political, socio-economic, and individual circumstances often made it difficult for migrants to decide where home was: 'home was ambiguous and was a space that spanned different continents'. In this regard, Gao adds, 'those uneducated Chinese peasants were actually post-modern because they anticipated transnationalism a century ahead of time'.[41] It is the legacy of this long-standing Chinese transnationalism that this book aims to explicate, focusing on the history and heritage of the Zhongshan–Sydney/Australia migration corridor.

Adam McKeown was one of the first to take the lens of methodological transnationalism in this field seriously when he argued that:

---

36. Mobo Gao, 'Early Chinese Migrants to Australia: A Critique of the Sojourner Narrative on Nineteenth-Century Chinese Migration to British Colonies', *Asian Studies Review* 4, no. 3 (2017): 389–404, https://doi.org/10.1080/10357823.2017.1336747.

37. Wang Gungwu, 'The Origins of Hua-Ch'iao', in his *Community and Nation: China, Southeast Asia and Australia* (St Leonards, NSW: Allen & Unwin, 1992), 1–10.

38. Gao, 'Early Chinese Migrants', 395–96.

39. Williams, *Returning Home with Glory*.

40. Fitzgerald, *Big White Lie*.

41. Gao, 'Early Chinese Migrants', 401.

an understanding of Chinese migration and of ethnic Chinese needs to incorporate an historical perspective other than just those shaped by nation states. We need to direct attention to the roles played by transnational institutions, flows and connections, as well as to the way that local transformations are embedded in larger, global processes.[42]

For over a century, McKeown argues, Chinese migration served as a viable and self-reproducing economic strategy and a stable system for the circulation of goods, people, information, and profit through the creation of transnational networks which 'were remarkable for their strength, scale, and resilience', and which 'not only facilitated and directed movement, but also depended on the continued generation of movement as a source of profit'.[43] For example, a central component of the operation of these transnational networks were the so-called Gold Mountain firms (金山莊, *jinshanzhuang* in Mandarin), many based in Hong Kong, which acted as transnational banking institutions, transmitted goods from China to importers abroad, and distributed letters and remittances back to the villages from which the migrants hailed.[44] These firms also provided profitable services to smooth the movement of people through the organisation of steamer tickets, false identities, access to consuls and visas, successful medical exams, customs formalities, information about changing immigration procedures and employment opportunities abroad, and so on.[45] It is through the activities of such commercial firms that the transnational migrant networks were able to expand throughout the world. From a global perspective, as McKeown puts it, 'we can imagine Hong Kong as a hub from which rays spread out in one direction to South China villages, and in the other to locations around the world, further branching out from secondary nodes in places like San Francisco and Singapore' (and, one might add, Sydney).[46]

From the perspective on the ground, however, that of the individual migrants themselves and the villages they came from, transnationalism takes the form less of entry into an expansive globalising network than of participation in more spatially confined corridors within that network, which links particular migrant-sending villages with specific parts of the world through a process of chain migration bolstered by kinship relationships, lineage membership, and native-place connections. McKeown observes that the networking of emigrant villages in China to specific overseas countries and towns 'could crystallize into inflexible, self-reproducing grooves'. These grooves were migration corridors that represented 'a transnationalism made possible through parochialism: local specialization in international

---

42. McKeown, 'Conceptualizing Chinese Diasporas', 331.
43. McKeown, 'Conceptualizing Chinese Diasporas', 317.
44. Madeline Hsu, 'Trading with Gold Mountain: *Jinshanzhuang* and Networks of Kinship and Native Place', in *Chinese American Transnationalism: The Flow of People, Resources, and Ideas between China and America during the Exclusion Era*, ed. Sucheng Chan (Philadelphia, PA: Temple University Press, 2005), 22–33.
45. McKeown, 'Conceptualizing Chinese Diasporas', 320.
46. McKeown, 'Conceptualizing Chinese Diasporas', 321.

movement',[47] while still being part of the larger global diasporic network. As McKeown continues, '[e]ven though individual migrants travelling through single grooves may have had no subjective awareness of a larger diaspora, none of those grooves could have existed without the more extensive complex of institutions and activities that brought them together as a larger bundle integrated into the world economy.'[48]

Diasporic Heritage-Making

In this book we use a broad definition of heritage, one that encompasses objects and sites that constitute the material heritage of the China–Australia (or Zhongshan–Sydney) migration corridor as well as the archival and oral history records relating to it. Taken together, all these elements constitute an archive of information that can be used to construct accounts of how this migration occurred and how it was experienced by those involved, amounting to what can be called diasporic heritage-making. This archive can also be used to construct a picture of the physical and social settings in which migration occurred. On the materialities front, for example, our research on the built environment of emigrant villages in Zhongshan county in the late nineteenth and early twentieth centuries allows an account to be given of the emergence there of architecturally distinct houses that were built with funds remitted by Chinese migrants in Australia (Figure 0.3).[49] But we are also very much concerned with what the collective archive – architectural, documentary, mnemonic – means to people in the present. The ways in which it is drawn upon and reconfigured by migrants' descendants in constructing the histories of their 'migrant' families can, as Sophie Couchman and Kate Bagnall observe, help provide a way of overcoming Australia's 'national forgetting' of the transnational dimension of the heritage of Chinese migration.[50] These diasporic heritage-making endeavours involve descendants in projects in which they retrieve and assemble surviving letters and photographs, information held in government archives, and recollections passed on orally in families. Often these are supplemented by journeys of discovery undertaken to ancestral villages in China during which descendants expand and deepen their knowledge of their forebears' lives. Such visits can entail

---

47. Such narrow migration grooves or corridors have occurred in other contexts in more recent times as well. For example, Peggy Levitt, in her study of the emigrant village of Miraflores in the Dominican Republic, found that nearly two-thirds of households have relatives living in the greater Boston area and receive their income from the United States. There are such close social and economic ties to one another that community life seems to take place in the two settings. Peggy Levitt, *The Transnational Villagers* (Berkeley: University of California Press, 2011).
48. McKeown, 'Conceptualizing Chinese Diasporas', 322.
49. See Chapter 6 of this volume.
50. Sophie Couchman and Kate Bagnall, 'Memory and Meaning in the Search for Australian-Chinese Families', in *Remembering Migration: Oral Histories and Heritage in Australia*, ed. Kate Darian-Smith and Paula Hamilton (London: Palgrave Macmillan, 2019), 333.

Figure 0.3: A street in Caobian village (曹邊村), Zhongshan, remittance houses on the right

emotional encounters with place that fit what Waterton and Gayo refer to as personal, vernacular, or everyday genres of heritage.[51]

This book is informed by the understanding that heritage is something made or 'assembled' in the present rather than something we simply inherit as a legacy. There is no question that the letters written by a migrant ancestor that have survived into the present exist in their own right as objects with their own discreet integrity, but for a descendant of that ancestor to regard them as part of their heritage is to give them a meaning they never originally had, and it is also suggestive of them being woven into a present context – a family narrative, for instance – in a process that profoundly recontextualises them. Heritage is always, in this sense, that which is retrieved from the past to be reworked for present purposes.

What is true of letters or photographs is also true of more materially weighty objects, such as a family house in the ancestral village. The house may change through time as it decays or undergoes renovation, but as it enters the theatre of heritage, multiple versions of it are likely to come into existence. A local government heritage

---

51. Emma Waterton and Modesto Gayo, 'The Elite and the Everyday in the Australian Heritage Field', in *Fields, Capitals, Habitus: Australian Culture, Inequalities and Social Division*, ed. Tony Bennett, David Carter, Modesto Gayo, Michelle Kelly, and Greg Noble (London: Routledge, 2020), 66. See also Chapters 7 and 8 of this volume.

agency in China may treat the house as a relic of the area's history of emigration that can be woven into a state narrative of ongoing diaspora involvement in the homeland.[52] A quite different version of the house emerges from the heritage-making activity of the descendants of the migrant who constructed and/or occupied it, as seen in the case of the ancestral house in Sha Chong village (沙涌村), Zhongshan, which Glenn and Phillip Mar describe in Chapter 5. To take another case of something from the past being brought forward into the present, Zheng Si-Hang (鄭思航), who as a young woman lived in the house her grandfather built in his home village in Zhongshan, spent several years trying to discover her grandfather's final resting place in Queensland.[53] In 2015 she located his unmarked grave in a Cairns cemetery and she and her husband erected a headstone over it, giving it renewed visibility in the landscape of present-day Queensland and installing it as a site in her family's own array of heritage places that spans Australia and China. Like thousands of migrant descendants globally, she was engaged in the kind of heritage-making project in which 'being there' is crucial.

Diasporic heritage-making projects, whether they involve compiling family genealogies, visiting ancestral villages, or locating lost graves, can be seminal to processes of identity formation among migrants and their descendants, as explored in Chapters 3 and 4 of the book. In this regard, identity is something that tends to be actively contemplated rather than taken as given – it is something that tends to be *made* rather than simply inherited, involving intimate engagement with what otherwise would be just a foreign country. Migration tends to unsettle identities, even after many generations, encouraging a transnational sense of belonging and a diasporic identity that is distributed, to varying degrees, across the heritage corridor rather than being rooted firmly in either nation.

As both Ien Ang and Cangbai Wang have argued, adopting a diasporic perspective on cultural heritage unsettles the restrictive nation-state framework that has long dominated the heritage field.[54] At the same time, diasporic heritage itself can take on ambiguous and 'ambivalent' meanings. As Wang notes, 'embedded in a complicated history and constructed in transnational spaces, the value, ownership, and uses of diasporic heritage are highly contested, subject to constant negotiations among various parties involved and between the past and the present.'[55] The chapters in this book testify to these multiple negotiations across time and space in the heritage corridor. In short, as this book aims to demonstrate, adopting a transnational lens not only on migration but also on heritage brings to light the

---

52. See Chapter 9 of this volume for a discussion of migrant heritage in relation to China's 'diaspora strategies'.
53. For an account of Zheng Si-Hang's quest, see Chapter 2 of this volume.
54. Ang, 'Unsettling the Nation'; Cangbai Wang, 'Ambivalent Heritage: The Im/Possibility of Museumifying the Overseas Chinese in South China', *Modern China* 46, no. 3 (2019): 1–26, https://doi.org/10.1177%2F0097700419878801.
55. Wang, 'Ambivalent Heritage', 20.

16 Introduction

heterogeneity, ambiguity, and contested nature of the legacy of migration, intrinsically transgressive of the territorial and cultural boundaries of the nation.

Research Basis and Structure of the Book

This book draws on research conducted by the authors as part of an Australian Research Council Discovery grant project entitled 'The China–Australia heritage corridor' (DP170101200), which set out to develop a transnational approach to the heritage of Chinese migration to Australia. Until the 1960s, most Chinese who arrived in Australia came from the migrant-sending counties of the Pearl River Delta, Zhongshan county being one of the most prominent origin places of those sojourning or settling in New South Wales and Queensland. We chose Zhongshan, rather than one of the other migrant-sending localities of the delta, for this reason, but also because one of us, Michael Williams, had carried out historical doctoral research there in the late 1990s and early 2000s and had continued his scholarly involvement with the region in the years following.[56] Ien Ang and Denis Byrne brought to the project and to this book the perspectives of their specialist fields – cultural studies and Chinese diaspora studies on the part of Ien Ang, who is of Chinese Indonesian descent; and archaeology and heritage studies on Denis Byrne's part. As a research assistant on the project and a recent migrant from Hong Kong, Alexandra Wong's contributions to the book reflect her research interests in Sydney's Chinatown and in diaspora tourism in China. Christopher Cheng (as a doctoral candidate attached to the project), Glenn Mar and Phillip Mar all have ancestral links to Zhongshan – their contributions to the book reflect both their research interests and their personal stake in Zhongshan. The book thus represents both a trans-disciplinary endeavour and, on the part of four of our contributors, a trans-generational one.

The insights we have gained into the enduring cross-generational links that migrants and migrant descendants in Australia maintain with Zhongshan come from a series of semi-structured interviews we conducted in Sydney in 2017 and 2018.[57] The interviewees were approached on the basis of either being already known to us, by word of mouth, or being recommended to us by the Chung Shan Society of Australia in Sydney. They consisted of 21 men and six women, the majority of whom were either first-generation Zhongshan migrants or second- or third-generation descendants, and most were middle-aged or elderly. In most cases, the interviewees told us what they knew about their forebears, showed us copies of archival documents and photographs relating to them, and provided us with

---

56. Williams, *Returning Home with Glory*.
57. This does not include the numerous people in Zhongshan and Australia interviewed by Christopher Cheng for his doctoral study of schools built and or supported by members of the Zhongshan diaspora in Australia (see Chapter 7 of this volume).

information on their own migration history and their links to people and places in Zhongshan, past and present. In the course of our research, we carried out fieldwork in Zhongshan on a number of occasions between 2017 and 2020. This was mainly devoted to visiting the villages to which our interviewees in Australia had ancestral connections as well as visiting, or attempting to locate, the houses that their migrant forebears had built there with money earned in Australia. While in Zhongshan, we also spoke with relatives of some of our interviewees and numerous elderly villagers who knew them or knew of them, as well as with representatives of a range of local organisations. In navigating Zhongshan, we were assisted by the Zhongshan Foreign and Overseas Chinese Affairs Bureau (中山市外事僑務局).

Today's Zhongshan is a very different place to what it was a century ago or more, when emigration to Australia first began. High levels of urbanisation and demographic change as a consequence of internal migration in the past few decades have transformed Zhongshan into a modern city, engulfing many of the old villages that used to make up the county. Nevertheless, remnants of the latter, including inhabitants with deep links to the past, still remain, though they are rapidly disappearing. This book is therefore timely, as it captures some of the living legacy of this past while it is still possible to do so.

The book is arranged in two parts: 'Connections, Flows, Identities' and 'Sites in the Heritage Corridor'. In the first, we address the dynamics of the China–Australia heritage corridor as a whole but focus our attention on that strand of it which linked Zhongshan county and Australia, in particular Sydney.

In Chapter 1, Michael Williams examines the history of migration from Zhongshan to Australia, situating it in the broader history of China and of Chinese overseas migration. Since almost all those who emigrated from the counties of the Pearl River Delta came from agricultural villages, an understanding of village life is essential to understanding the migration corridor, not least because emigrants remained members of village society, often channelling the bulk of their overseas earnings back there; building houses for their families there; funding schools, clinics, and transport infrastructure; and, in the case of many of those who died abroad, ensuring that their bones were repatriated for internment in the village cemetery. For such people, there is a sense in which they never definitively left the village. Put differently, emigrant villages became transnational entities.

Denis Byrne, in Chapter 2, takes up this theme in examining the material heritage that migration generated at both ends of the migration corridor. He explores the reasons why the built heritage of Chinese migration actually has more visibility in the home villages of those who left for Australia than it does in the landscape of Australia itself. Tim Ingold's 'meshwork' theory is drawn upon to propose a way for heritage practitioners and scholars to give due weight to the heritage implications of forms of transnational connectivity and cross-border mobility.

In Chapter 3, Ien Ang elucidates the diasporic identities that have evolved from the legacy of Chinese migration to Australia, the making of which has been influenced strongly by the changing political circumstances in both China and Australia over the course of the twentieth century. In particular, the turmoil caused by the radical Mao years in the People's Republic of China disrupted the transnational flows and links that were central to the heritage corridor's vivacity, with major impacts on the lives of migrants and their families. Ang focuses on the experiences of four men who either migrated from Zhongshan or are descendants of Zhongshan migrants, and now live in Sydney. Although they are all fully settled in Australia and consider themselves 'Australian', each of them has maintained – in different ways – an identification with 'Chineseness', testifying to a continuing lived transnationalism, which is expressed in a desire to rediscover and reconnect with their family's Chinese past, including physical return visits to the ancestral village in Zhongshan.

This theme is picked up in Chapter 4 by Alexandra Wong, who sheds light on the diverse ways in which Chinese Australian descendants of ancestors who migrated from Zhongshan in the late nineteenth century have experienced their 'return' to their ancestral villages in China, a phenomenon that has been termed 'diaspora tourism'. Featuring three cases of such homeland visits, the chapter focuses on these descendants' encounters with their family's material heritage and social relations through an 'embodied transnational' lens and traces the impact of their visits on their place attachment and self-identity. Taken together, Chapters 3 and 4 demonstrate that the China–Australia heritage corridor is populated by diverse and heterogeneous diasporic identities, and that transnationalism can be a more or less prominent dimension of the Chinese Australian experience.

The second part of the book, 'Sites in the Heritage Corridor', focuses on the material heritage that has emerged at specific sites and spaces, both in China (in particular Zhongshan) and in Australia (particularly Sydney). Chapter 5, by brothers Glenn and Phillip Mar, augments Alex Wong's stories of 'return' visits of Chinese Australians as often problematic struggles with identity and place. This chapter focuses on the brothers' 'return' to their ancestral home in Sha Chong village (沙涌村) and presents two insider perspectives on the intricacies of migrant heritage and inheritance. Glenn Mar tells of the long processes of discovering hidden connections to not one but two lost grandfathers, while Phillip Mar examines the affective dimensions of the Mar family's visit to Sha Chong in search of their 'roots' and ancestral home. The chapter emphasises that the making of heritage does not simply entail a backward-looking discovery of the past but involves a live engagement with a place in the present.

In Chapter 6, Denis Byrne presents a typology of remittances houses in the emigrant villages of Zhongshan, showing how the earliest examples, built in the last decades of the nineteenth century, represent little more than a modest enlargement of pre-existing vernacular houses, but how, moving into the early twentieth century, grander houses in a hybrid neoclassical style emerged that were eloquent statements of the overseas-earned wealth and the aspirant social status of their migrant builders. Byrne argues against regarding the houses as inert physical things, seeing them instead as vibrant structures where the human and non-human interfolded – structures which, at the level of affect and emotion, were intimately entangled in the lives of their owners.

In Chapter 7, Christopher Cheng and Phillip Mar shed light on the significant social and material legacy of the Australian Chinese diaspora in building and maintaining schools in Zhongshan, arguing that schools were an essential part of the transnational migration ecology, equipping young villagers from rural backgrounds to engage with modern and increasingly mobile realities. The chapter presents an account of the two intensive periods of diaspora school-building, the 1920s to the 1930s and the post-1978 years, which were separated by a period of difficult political circumstances that inhibited access and exchange within the China–Australia corridor.

In Chapter 8, Ien Ang and Alexandra Wong turn their attention to the Australian end of the heritage corridor and focus on Sydney's Chinatown, a key site where many early migrant entrepreneurs from Zhongshan made their mark in setting up businesses, some catering primarily to their compatriots, such as the Kwong War Chong general store and trading company (廣和昌), while others expanded their commercial ventures to wider regional and transnational networks (such as the Wing Sang banana and fruit company 永生果欄). The chapter describes how such businesses have put a defining stamp on the social and material fabric of the area which continues to exist to this day.

In the book's final chapter, Denis Byrne describes Australia's multiculturalist framing of migrant heritage as one based on a narrative of migrant arrival and settlement that excludes the history of ongoing engagement by migrants in the life of their origin countries. This is compared with China's interpretation of the many old buildings constructed by 'overseas Chinese' in their home villages and towns as representing their enduring loyalty to China. He argues that both approaches are limited by their fundamentally nationalist orientation. The book's framing of migration heritage in terms of cross-border flows in a transnational heritage corridor is offered as a more open-ended, cosmopolitan alternative.

Bibliography

Ang, Ien. 'Unsettling the Nation: Heritage and Diaspora'. In *Heritage, Memory and Identity*, edited by Helmut Anheier and Yudhishthir Raj Isar, 84–94. London: SAGE, 2011.

Ashworth, Gregory, Brian Graham, and John Tunbridge. *Pluralising Pasts: Heritage, Identity and Place in Multicultural Societies*. London: Pluto Press, 2007.

Byrne, Denis. 'Heritage Corridors: Transnational Flows and the Built Environment of Migration'. *Journal of Ethnic and Migration Studies* 42, no. 14 (2016): 2360–78. https://doi.org/10.1080/1369183X.2016.1205805.

Caglar, Ayse. 'Constraining Metaphors and the Transnationalisation of Spaces in Berlin'. *Journal of Ethnic and Migration Studies* 27, no. 4 (2001): 601–13. http://dx.doi.org/10.1080/13691830120090403.

Castles, Stephen, Mary Kalantzis, Bill Cope, and Michael Morrissey. *Mistaken Identity: Multiculturalism and the Demise of Nationalism in Australia*. Annandale: Pluto Press, 1988.

Cheng, Christopher. 'Beacons of Modern Learning: Diaspora-Funded Schools in the China–Australia Corridor'. *Asian and Pacific Migration Journal* 29, no. 2 (2020): 139–62. https://doi.org/10.1177/0117196820930309.

Couchman, Sophie, and Kate Bagnall. 'Memory and Meaning in the Search for Australian-Chinese Families'. In *Remembering Migration: Oral Histories and Heritage in Australia*, edited by Kate Darian-Smith and Paula Hamilton, 331–46. London: Palgrave Macmillan, 2019.

De Haas, Hein, Stephen Castles, and Mark J. Miller. *The Age of Migration: International Population Movements in the Modern World*. Sixth edition. London: Red Globe Press, 2020.

Fitzgerald, John. *Big White Lie: Chinese Australians in White Australia*. Sydney: UNSW Press, 2007.

Gao, Mobo. 'Early Chinese Migrants to Australia: A Critique of the Sojourner Narrative on Nineteenth-Century Chinese Migration to British Colonies'. *Asian Studies Review* 4, no. 3 (2017): 389–404. https://doi.org/10.1080/10357823.2017.1336747.

Hsu, Madeline. 'Trading with Gold Mountain: *Jinshanzhuang* and Networks of Kinship and Native Place'. In *Chinese American Transnationalism: The Flow of People, Resources, and Ideas between China and America during the Exclusion Era*, edited by Sucheng Chan, 22–33. Philadelphia, PA: Temple University Press, 2005.

Inglis, Christine. 'Some Recent Australian Writing on Immigration and Assimilation'. *International Migration Review* 9, no. 3 (1975): 335–44. https://doi.org/10.1177%2F019791837500900304.

Kuhn, Philip A. *Chinese Among Others: Emigration in Modern Times*. Lanham, MD: Rowman and Littlefield, 2008.

Kuo, Mei-fen. 'The "Invisible" Work of Women: Gender and Philanthropic Sociability in the Evolution of Early Chinese Australian Voluntary Organizations'. In *Chinese Diaspora Charity and the Cantonese Pacific 1850–1949*, edited by John Fitzgerald and Hon-ming Yip, 154–72. Hong Kong: University of Hong Kong Press, 2020.

Levitt, Peggy. *The Transnational Villagers*. Berkeley: University of California Press, 2011.

McKeown, Adam. 'Conceptualizing Chinese Diasporas, 1842–1979'. *Journal of Asian Studies* 58, no. 2 (May 1999): 306–37. https://doi.org/10.2307/2659399.

Miles, Steven B. *Chinese Diasporas: A Social History of Global Migration*. London: Routledge, 2020.

Munzele, Samuel, and Dilip Ratha, eds. *Remittances: Development Impact and Future Prospects*. Washington, DC: The World Bank, 2005.

Peterson, Glen. *Overseas Chinese in the People's Republic of China*. London: Routledge, 2012.

Portes, Alejandro, and Min Zhou. 'The New Second Generation: Segmented Assimilation and Its Variants'. *The Annals of the American Academy of Political and Social Science* 530, no. 1 (1993): 74–96. https://doi.org/10.1177/0002716293530001006.

Reid, Anthony, ed. *Sojourners and Settlers: Histories of Southeast Asia and the Chinese*. Sydney: Allen & Unwin, 1996.

Safi, Mirna. 'Immigrant Assimilation Theory: Insights from American Sociology'. *Sociologie* 2, no. 2 (2011): 149–64. https://doi.org/10.3917/socio.022.0149.

Sinn, Elizabeth. *Pacific Crossing: California Gold, Chinese Migration and the Making of Hong Kong*. Hong Kong: Hong Kong University Press, 2012.

Smith, Laurajane. *Uses of Heritage*. London: Routledge, 2006.

Taylor, J. Edward, Joaquín Arango, Graeme Hugo, Ali Kouaouci, Douglas S. Massey, and Adela Pellegrino. 'International Migration and National Development'. *Population Index* 62, no. 2 (1996): 181–212. https://doi.org/10.2307/3646297.

Tölölyan, Khachig. 'The Nation-State and Its Others: In Lieu of a Preface'. *Diaspora: Journal of Transnational Studies* 1, no. 1 (1991): 3–7. https://doi.org/10.1353/dsp.1991.0008.

Trémon, Anne-Christine. 'Flexible Kinship: Shaping Transnational Families among the Chinese in Tahiti'. *Journal of the Royal Anthropological Institute* 23 (2016): 42–60. https://rai.onlinelibrary.wiley.com/doi/epdf/10.1111/1467-9655.12543.

Vertovec, Steven. *Transnationalism*. Abingdon: Routledge, 2009.

Wang, Cangbai. 'Ambivalent Heritage: The Im/Possibility of Museumifying the Overseas Chinese in South China'. *Modern China* 46, no. 3 (2019): 1–26. https://doi.org/10.1177%2F0097700419878801.

Wang, Gungwu. 'The Origins of Hua-Ch'iao'. In *Community and Nation: China, Southeast Asia and Australia*, 1–10. St Leonards, NSW: Allen & Unwin, 1992.

Waterton, Emma, and Modesto Gayo. 'The Elite and the Everyday in the Australian Heritage Field'. In *Fields, Capitals, Habitus: Australian Culture, Inequalities and Social Division*, edited by Tony Bennett, David Carter, Modesto Gayo, Michelle Kelly, and Greg Noble, 66–82. London: Routledge, 2020.

Williams, Michael. *Returning Home with Glory*. Hong Kong: Hong Kong University Press, 2018.

Wimmer, Andreas, and Nina Glick Schiller. 'Methodological Nationalism, the Social Sciences, and the Study of Migration: An Essay in Historical Epistemology'. *International Migration Review* 37 no. 3 (2003): 576–610. http://www.jstor.org/stable/30037750.

Woon, Yuen-fong. 'The Voluntary Sojourner among the Overseas Chinese: Myth or Reality?' *Pacific Affairs* 56, no. 4 (Winter 1983–1984): 673–90. https://doi.org/10.2307/2758597.

Part 1

Connections, Flows, Identities

1
Villages of the Fragrant Hills

Michael Williams

Introduction

The link between Australia and China predates European invasion and encompasses connections on many levels.[1] The most enduring, complex, and deep connection is undoubtedly that with the Pearl River Delta (珠江三角洲) county now called Zhongshan (中山), which was known as Heung San in Cantonese (香山, Xiangshan in Mandarin) before 1925.[2] The small county of Zhongshan, located in South China's Pearl River Delta region of Guangdong (廣東) province not far from Hong Kong (香港), is a place of origin, return, education, nostalgia, memory and heritage for a great many Australians of Chinese background (see Figure 1.1).[3] In order to understand how a Zhongshan–Sydney migration and heritage corridor emerged, along with a now 180-year-old historical link with Australia, it is necessary to look at the broader provincial context of Guangdong, as well as that of the global 'Chinese diaspora', before focusing on Zhongshan itself. This broader scope will, among other things, assist to bypass the white colonial nation-state narrative through which much of the history of Chinese people in Australia has been narrowly interpreted to date. Another advantage of seeing beyond the nation-state perspective is that the tendency to see many aspects of Chinese people in Australia as 'exceptional' or even

---

1. This includes the trepang trade. For a general discussion of Australia's pre-European links with China, see Frank Farrell, 'Who Discovered Australia?', in *Themes in Australian History: Questions, Issues and Interpretation in an Evolving Historiography* (Kensington: UNSW Press, 1990), 1–21. Dutch records from the eighteenth century report a 'Chinese trader' returning from a trip to the south of 'five days sailing before the wind and two days and nights having drifted', who reported visiting a land of people 'very black and the hair woolly'. The Timor Resident believed this to have been the 'mainland coast of the Southland'. See 'Extract from a Letter of the Resident of Timor, September 20, 1751', in Willem Robert, *The Dutch Explorations, of 1605–1756, of the North and Northwest Coast of Australia* (Amsterdam: Philo Press, 1973), 146–49.
2. The city and district of Zhongshan, or Chung Shan (中山), was renamed in 1925 from Heung San/Xiangshan (香山, lit. fragrant hills) to honour its favourite son, Sun Yat-sen (孫逸仙), or Sun Zhongshan (孫中山). To avoid confusion, this county will be referred to as Zhongshan throughout this book. See glossary for variations in place names.
3. See Figure 1.1 for the location of this and other Pearl River Delta counties long associated with Australia.

'exotic' within an Australian context, usually based on ignorance of Chinese culture and certainly strong stereotyping, can be more easily avoided.[4]

The county's capital, Zhongshan City, a modern, prosperous metropolis surrounded still by rice fields and traditional villages, albeit with a shrinking traditional presence, is now linked across the Pearl River Delta to Hong Kong by bridge.[5] However, the many villages and families of Zhongshan, both city and county, have long enjoyed links with Southeast Asia, the Pacific region, Hong Kong, Shanghai, and most significantly with Australia, particularly Queensland, New South Wales, and of course Sydney. The county's most famous son, for example, Sun Yat-sen, and the political movement he founded which helped China overthrow its last imperial dynasty and found its first republic, was intimately connected with this overseas network originating from Zhongshan and other nearby counties. Sun Yat-sen received his early education in Hawai'i, where his elder brother's business was located and where large numbers of people from Zhongshan relocated starting in the mid-nineteenth century. Political support for Sun Yat-sen, both before and after the 1911 revolution, drew heavily on people from the Pearl River Delta living and working around the Pacific, who constituted what the same movement characterised as the 'overseas Chinese' (華僑, *huaqiao* in Mandarin).

However, long before the Chinese overseas began supporting movements to overthrow the Qing dynasty or the new ruling Kuomintang (國民黨, lit. Nationalist Party), this South China region had been developing 'overseas' links since at least the fifteenth century and the Ming dynasty. These were links and associated patterns of behaviour founded on sending (mostly) men overseas to seek earnings and remit money back to their families in the villages of Zhongshan and other districts around the province of Guangdong. It is this broad context and long-standing history through which we must understand the evolution of the heritage corridor that has been established between Zhongshan and Sydney, and more broadly with many other parts of Australia as well as Hong Kong and Shanghai. This chapter provides an historical overview of Zhongshan, which has been closely connected to Australia, and Sydney in particular, for over 180 years. This is a link stretching from many but by no means all of its hundreds of villages to Sydney, as well as to Hong Kong and Shanghai, and back to the villages, in a complex interchange of people, money, jobs, influence, ideas, and generational change.

---

4. These range from negative – opium smokers, to positive – hard working, and much in-between. Comparative analysis with the labour migration patterns of other cultural groups would indicate that the Chinese are perhaps only exceptional in being more intense and persistent in patterns that, broadly speaking, are common to many groups. See, for example, Michael Williams, 'Sojourners & Birds of Passage: Chinese and Italian Migrants in Australia and the United States in Comparative Perspective, 1871–1914', *Journal of the European Association for Studies on Australia* 11, no. 2 (2020): 2–16.
5. Formerly 'Shekki' in Cantonese (石岐, Shiqi in Mandarin), Zhongshan city is the capital of Zhongshan county. The Hong Kong–Zhuhai–Macao Bridge or HZMB (港珠澳大橋), a 55-kilometre bridge–tunnel system, opened in 2018.

For most Australians, the most obvious explanation for the origins of the Zhongshan–Australia heritage corridor discussed in this book lies in the colonial gold rushes of the mid-nineteenth century. However, to leave it at that runs a risk that is a commonplace of nation-state histories such as Australia's, namely the assumption that the main motivations and features that found and shape the history are to be found in the nation-state itself. In terms of Chinese Australian history, this is most often articulated by a focus on racism and discrimination with a consequent neglect of agency on the part of those who travelled back and forth along this corridor long before it achieved heritage status. It is an ironic feature of many post-colonial histories that seek to condemn the perceived unfairness and

Figure 1.1: Map of counties of the Pearl River Delta (珠江三角洲)

domination of colonialism and its white settler Australian variation that they often simply continue this domination, albeit by condemning it, rather than acknowledging agency on the part of the assumed 'victims'.[6] This narrow preferencing of white colonial agency and its continuing victim narrative is best balanced by a deeper understanding of the history of labour migration and sojourning among migrants from the Pearl River Delta counties, dating back as it does some 300 years before the Australian gold rushes. From this can be identified patterns of behaviour that long pre-date arrival in Australia. This is not to say that Australian conditions did not have specific influences and contributions, but this longer historical context enables these contributions to be more clearly discerned and understood.

History and Geography

Zhongshan county was created as an official district in the thirteenth century,[7] and the various areas into which Zhongshan was subdivided, such as Long Du (隆都) and Liang Du (良都), may have been for the purpose of military garrisons.[8] While the history of labour migration in the Pearl River Delta stretches back at least to the Ming dynasty, it was also throughout this period that Zhongshan itself was literally growing from the 'sands' (沙田, *shatian* in Mandarin) of the Pearl River Delta by a process of land reclamation sponsored by landlords of the neighbouring county of Shunde (順德).[9] The higher and relatively less fertile districts within Zhongshan of Long Du and Liang Du, which became particular centres of the migration movements, may have existed before this process as islands and were gradually surrounded by fertile fields, perhaps owned by absentee landlords.

Related to this process is that socially Zhongshan, like many of the districts of the Pearl River Delta, was divided into '*shatianqu*' (沙田區, pronounced in Mandarin) and '*mintianqu*' (民田區). This division roughly coincided with the most fertile, sandy, rice-growing lands of the northwest and southeast of the district (*shatian* literally means sandy fields) and the hillier, drier areas of the county's centre. Long Du and Liang Du were *mintian* areas. A recognised division between these two types of areas was that it was the *mintian* that provided the bulk of those who travelled to other provinces and overseas. *Shatian* people were generally looked down upon as poorer, ill-educated, and likely to be a source of bandits. Housing was also distinctive with the *shatian* living in 'grass' houses, usually a combination of reeds and bark, while *mintian* people could build with brick. *Shatian* people were

---

6. For a general discussion of this as it relates to museums, see Karen Schamberger, 'Whose Stories Are We Telling? Chinese Australian History in New South Wales and Victorian Museums', *Australian Historical Studies*, 52, no. 4 (2021): 567–90, https://doi.org/10.1080/1031461X.2021.1926521.
7. Much of this early history of Zhongshan was first published in Michael Williams, *Returning Home with Glory: Chinese Villagers around the Pacific, 1849 to 1949* (Hong Kong: Hong Kong University Press, 2018).
8. See map of Long Du and Liang Du, Figure 1.2.
9. For an account of the methods used, see Helen F. Siu, *Agents and Victims in South China: Accomplices in Rural Revolution* (New Haven, CT: Yale University Press, 1989), 24–26.

largely tenants or landless labourers while landlords and those with commercial interests were more likely to be found in the *mintian* areas. Another feature that distinguishes Long Du but not Liang Du or other Zhongshan districts is that its people speak a non-Cantonese language, one that has helped them to re-enforce a sense of distinctness and fellowship both within Zhongshan and among Long Du communities overseas.[10]

These districts also found themselves on the route from the Portuguese enclave of Macao (澳門), carved in the sixteenth century from Zhongshan, to the provincial capital Canton (廣州, also known as Guangzhou), including the European trading factories that were well established by the mid-eighteenth century. In the early nineteenth century these districts also found themselves in close proximity to the new British-controlled port of Hong Kong and its European shipping links with the also recently established white settler colonies around the Pacific. All this was to bring many opportunities which the Pearl River Delta peoples were in a prime position, due to both their historical practices and their geographic location, to take up, particularly those of the county of Zhongshan.

Premodern History

In the long history of China as a unified state stretching back to at least the Qin dynasty of the fifth century BC, the South China region we know today as Guangdong is of relatively late incorporation. And within this province dominated by speakers of the Cantonese (粵, Yue in Mandarin) language among several others, the county of Zhongshan is of even more recent origin. This is a history that not only has made South China distinctly different from the north of China, but that also has seen waves of migrations from the north that have left their mark in a diverse pattern of languages, dialects, customs, and cuisines. For districts such as Zhongshan, this history also includes intensive multigenerational patterns of labour migration both within and outside China itself.

It was the collapse of the Northern Song dynasty in the twelfth century that brought some of the most significant waves of migration into southern China, and it is from this period that many families, lineages, and villages in and around the Pearl River Delta trace their origins. While these origins are generally traced to an official or general forced to flee south, the reality was perhaps not always so elite. Nevertheless, elite or not, the result was the cultural incorporation of Guangdong into the Chinese imperial state and a legacy of diversity, both cultural and linguistic, ranging from the scattered Hakka (客家, lit. guest people) to the people of the Zhongshan district of Long Du (隆都). The latter is a small cluster of villages in the

---

10. Long Du and Liang Du were so closely associated that many Liang Du people were familiar with the language of Long Du as their mothers were very often from Long Du villages.

midst of Cantonese-speaking Zhongshan using a language related to the Fujianese of the province directly to the north of Guangdong.[11]

The significance to the overseas Chinese in general, and to the heritage corridor in particular, of this dialect and language diversity, including the special case of Long Du, will be discussed later. Here the contribution of the diverse geographical context will be considered. The province of Guangdong lies within easy reach of the province of Guangxi (廣西) to the west and near to what is now Vietnam to the south. Until the Ming dynasty of the thirteenth and fourteenth centuries, both these areas were part of the Ming Empire and both were what can be considered frontier areas. The significance of this is that many people of Guangdong could and did use their skills, capital, and enterprise to establish extensive trade networks by sending male members of families into these frontier regions for years at a time. The trope of men yearning for home and of women yearning for their absent menfolk became such a common one that it was celebrated in poetry, song, and, in one case, the topography of the region.[12]

These long-distance income-earning activities of people from the region extending up the West River and south into Vietnam in the Ming period featured two major characteristics that can be recognised in Chinese Australian history. These were the remittance of money back to the families and its use to build up the family fortunes in the villages of origin, and support for those away from home for long periods through organisations based on dialect and district of origin. By the fall of the Ming and its replacement with the Qing dynasty of the invading Manchu in the seventeenth century, Vietnam had regained its independence while Guangxi was more fully incorporated within the imperial system. Nevertheless, the people of Guangdong continued to travel to seek income in both Guangxi and Vietnam as well as to what became known as the Nanyang (南洋, lit. south seas) or Southeast Asia, where they established long-standing trading centres characterised by inter-marriage and settlement.[13]

Colonialism

Guangdong was not the only province to take advantage of trading opportunities with the south seas. The province of Fujian (福建), immediately to the north along

---

11. Li Zhaoyong 李兆永, 'Longduhua, Nanlongcunhua yuan shi Fuzhouhua' 隆都話，南朗村話原是福州話 [Long Du and Nam Long dialects origins in Fujian dialect], *Zhongshan wenshi* 中山文史 [Zhongshan Cultural History] 31 (1994): 229–30.

12. '[M]any diasporic or transnational practices that scholars of overseas Chinese identify for the modern era seem closely related to the practises of Cantonese West River migrants in the preceding three centuries.' A rock formation overlooking the West River is said to resemble a wife looking out for her returning spouse. Steven B. Miles, *Upriver Journeys: Diaspora and Empire in Southern China, 1570–1850* (Harvard-Yenching Institute Monograph Series 106, 2017), 242–43, https://doi.org/10.2307/j.ctv47wbkq.

13. See, for example, Wang Gungwu, *Short History of the Nanyang* (Singapore: Eastern Universities Press, 1959).

China's coast, was also strongly represented overseas. As a result, these two alone of China's many provinces were to find themselves in close connection not only with the people of Southeast Asia but also with the new arrivals in the region beginning in the sixteenth century – peoples from Europe. While primarily interested in trade, the Europeans also used their power to gradually establish a political dominance that greatly transformed both trading and labour relationships. This was a transformation that took place in what is now called Southeast Asia both in the nature of the links with Guangdong and Fujian, and in the role and status of Chinese people.[14]

This change in the nature of the links included the opening up of opportunities for much larger numbers of people to travel and earn an income as labourers (albeit often indentured) as well as traders and merchants. These links under colonialism broadly continued the patterns that had previously been established. However, the increased numbers of unskilled or initially impoverished workers, often exploited under a variety of labour conditions sometimes amounting to slavery, made the remitting of money, the support or establishment of families, and even return, difficult or even impossible for some. The various conditions under which people travelled to the Nanyang ranged from the harsh, including kidnapping and misleading and exploitative contracts; to milder forms of 'credit-ticket', which entailed paying debts to agents or family members; to simple free movement utilising personal or family capital.[15] Some form of contract or debt was most common, and this was in part responsible for the relative discipline and focused nature of labour from China, which was both respected and feared depending on its perception as cheap labour to be exploited or as competition for scarce income.

It was under these conditions of developing colonialism that the first connections between Zhongshan and the colonial port of Sydney were made. The variation of colonialism established in the Colony of New South Wales with Sydney as the main port was of the 'white settler' type, under which the indigenous population was totally expropriated. But as in all forms of colonialism, the need for a large and subservient labour force was fundamental. These two coastal provinces of China, with their established histories of labour migration, were able to supply this form of labour under a variety of circumstances and conditions.

Both Chinese and Europeans in Southeast Asia imported labour from Guangdong and Fujian to work in mines, plantations, and stores and to perform other tasks. But it was the defeat in 1842 of the Qing during the First Opium War and the establishment of the 'Treaty Port' system that allowed large-scale importation of labour to begin, including to the Colony of New South Wales. The people of

---

14. See, for example, P. C. Emmer, ed., *Colonialism and Migration: Indentured Labour before and after Slavery* (Dordrecht: Martinus Nijhoff, 1986).
15. For an account that clearly explains the difference between indenture and credit-ticket, see Wang Sing-wu, *The Organisation of Chinese Emigration 1848–1888: With Special Reference to Chinese Emigration to Australia* (San Francisco: Chinese Materials Centre, 1978).

the county of Zhongshan in this period were the first to become involved with the new British port at Hong Kong, first occupied during this war and then ratified by the Treaty of Nanjing, to which they were among the closest counties.[16] But it was through the more northerly Fujian port of Amoy (廈門, also known as Xiamen) that Chinese people in any numbers first began to enter the British colony on the Australian continent. They were recruited by European merchants under indentures to work as shepherds, mainly in a period when the cessation of transportation caused employers to seek out a cheap labour source other than the convicts they had been accustomed to relying upon.[17]

Gold Rush

This situation was transformed after 1849 with the discovery of gold, first in California, then a few years later in the Colony of New South Wales, and subsequently in the recently established Colony of Victoria carved from that of New South Wales. The people of the Pearl River Delta soon took up the opportunity to search for gold around the Pacific which the new port of Hong Kong now gave them.[18] They did so under a variety of local and family debt arrangements that enabled thousands of men to purchase passage and set up on distant goldfields. The methods were such that very often the people of the Pearl River Delta villages were organised in groups both to travel and to begin the search for gold.[19] In addition, there were many individuals with sufficient capital and business experience to sell supplies rather than dig for gold, and so stores and other support enterprises ranging from fish curing to opera also accompanied these gold seekers.[20]

The earliest identifiable evidence of Zhongshan people specifically in Australia comes from a record of bones being sent to China in 1862.[21] These are from the New South Wales goldfields and indicate almost certainly that Zhongshan people were

---

16. Williams, *Returning Home with Glory*, 47–48.
17. Maxine Darnell, 'The Chinese Labour Trade to New South Wales, 1783–1853' (PhD thesis, University of New England, 1997). In fact, Tasmania seems to have been the first colony to receive a small group of indentured Chinese carpenters in 1830, possibly recruited through Singapore. This also appears to be the first, though by no means the last, time the argument of a threat to wages is mentioned: 'they will be very likely to reduce the prices of cabinet work', *Launceston Advertiser*, 26 July 1830, 2.
18. See Figure 1.1 for the counties involved. While the indentured workers from Fujian, known as Amoy people, already in Australia readily took up gold mining, they seemingly never established links back to their villages of origin and either returned permanently or married and settled in the Australian colonies.
19. See the *Bathurst Free Press and Mining Journal*, 30 July 1856, 2, for an interesting description of the arrival of 150 well-organised Chinese gold seekers (the second such group) who brought fans and other items to sell to the locals. It is not known if these were from Zhongshan or another county, but that they were all from the same county is certain.
20. For the fishing industry, see Michael Williams, *Chinese Settlement in NSW: A Thematic History* (Sydney: Heritage Office of NSW, 1999), 26; and for opera, see Michael Williams, 'Smoking Opium, Puffing Cigars, and Drinking Gingerbeer: Chinese Opera in Australia', in *Opera, Emotion, and the Antipodes*, ed. Jane W. Davidson, Michael Halliwell, and Stephanie Rocke (Abingdon: Routledge, 2020), 166–208.
21. NSW State Archives, Col Sec; 4/3476, 62/4222, Mollison & Black to Colonial Secretary, 26 August 1862.

present on those goldfields from the very beginning. That Zhongshan people were also on the Victorian goldfields in some numbers is likely, although the later dominance in Victoria of people from the Sze Yap (四邑) districts perhaps obscures this. At this early stage Zhongshan people were members of the Yeong Wo Benevolent Association (陽和會館) along with people from two counties that lie just across the Pearl River Delta, Dongguan (東莞) and Zengcheng (增城).[22] This was a link probably formed in Hong Kong, and this trio of counties can also be found in Hawaii and San Francisco. Later, however, a Sydney-based Zhongshan (or more specifically Long Du) organisation was founded separate from the other two, who remained linked and are joint owners of a Dixon Street property in Sydney's Haymarket Chinatown to this day.[23]

The people of Zhongshan were represented among these first arrivals on the goldfields along with people from several other Pearl River Delta counties. However, despite significant differences in dialect and language among these groups (greater than those between Scots and English in this period), these arrivals were perceived simply as 'Chinese' by white settlers and gold seekers from 'Europe' who themselves routinely distinguished their own dialect and more often religious divisions.[24] Yet the language, dialect, and district differences among these Pearl River Delta people, as well as the 'Amoy' indentured labourers, were of great and ongoing significance. For some one hundred years after these first gold seekers arrived, it was on the basis of district and dialect that much organisation, choice of location, whom to work or do business with, and even whom to marry took place among those generically labelled 'Chinese' in Australia.[25]

Motivations

The spread of villages and counties in Guangdong and the Pearl River Delta region of those who travelled was very unevenly distributed, and this feature provides a clue to the motivating and organisational factors of these movements. One such clue is a negative one since, as with the blanket label 'Chinese', many mistakenly attribute the large-scale movement of people from southern China to 'China' in

---

22. Williams, *Returning Home with Glory*, 116.
23. Williams, *Chinese Settlement in NSW*, 15–16.
24. The exception to this was when fighting occurred and such categories as 'Amoy', 'Canton', or 'Hong Kong' were used. See, for example, *Sydney Morning Herald*, 12 January 1857, 5.
25. See Mei-fen Kuo, *Making Chinese Australia* (Clayton, Victoria: Monash University Publishing, 2013), for a discussion of the gradual lessening of this distinction among the business elite in the early twentieth century, and the interview with Elizabeth Lee in Mavis Gock Yen, *South Flows the Pearl* (Sydney: Sydney University Press, 2022), 343–54, for its social significance well into the twentieth century among the Chinese Australian community. See also Williams, *Returning Home with Glory*, for the role of native place organisations in remittances, bones return, and employment.

general and to factors such as the Taiping rebellion.[26] The Taiping rebellion, despite its convenient dating from 1850 to 1864, did not directly impact upon Guangdong province but rather greatly devastated regions further north, whose peoples did not suddenly take up gold mining as a result. While Guangdong province was indirectly affected by a number of associated bandit uprisings, it was areas to the west and north of Guangzhou that were most affected, regions that also did not contribute to the movement to the white settler colonies.[27]

There is in fact no indication that the motivations of the Pearl River Delta gold seekers were radically different from those of gold seekers from Dublin, Berlin, or London. A general poverty, or at least the desire to gain more wealth, was undoubtedly a common factor, but there is no evidence of any more significant degree of poverty or famine in the Pearl River Delta during this period. The assumption otherwise is seemingly a carryover from the desire to distinguish the 'normal' (white) gold seekers from the 'exotic' and by implication 'improper' gold seekers from China, the viewpoint of those who saw Chinese goldminers as unfair competition in 'their' territory.[28]

In fact, the uneven distribution of villages and districts that participated in the gold rushes tells us that proximity to Hong Kong was a prime factor. This, combined with an established history of labour migration, including access to agents and merchants able to provide the initial capital for passage money and equipment, removes the need to imagine famines or rebellions that would make these gold seekers into 'coolies'. The correspondence of districts represented in California, Victoria, New South Wales, British Columbia, and Queensland (though not the proportions) would confirm the port of Hong Kong as the common factor.[29] None of this is remarkable given the history of Guangdong province, as the capital Guangzhou (Canton) had long been a major trading port with good river links to the west (Guangxi, 廣西) and sea links out from the Pearl River Delta along the coast to north and south. When the Qing were still able to resist the demands of European traders, the Portuguese took up residence in Macao, which was part of Zhongshan. Later the European trading warehouses were limited to a location just outside the Canton city walls. When the British set up on Hong Kong Island in 1841 and waged two Opium Wars from this base, their warships sailed to Canton past

---

26. Such assumptions are most common in general accounts presented by institutions; unfortunately, these superficial histories are often all many people see. For examples of such unfounded accounts, see Victorian Collections [https://victoriancollections.net.au/stories/many-roads-stories-of-the-chinese-on-the-goldfields], Sydney Living Museums [https://sydneylivingmuseums.com.au/stories/chinese-goldfields], and the State Library of Queensland [https://www.slq.qld.gov.au/blog/chinese-business-history-queensland-gold-rush-1851-1881].

27. For a detailed account of Guangdong province at the time of the Taiping Rebellion and the Second Opium War, see John Wong, *Deadly Dreams* (Cambridge: Cambridge University Press, 1998).

28. For an excellent account of this perspective, see Sophie Loy-Wilson, 'Coolie Alibis: Seizing Gold from Chinese Miners in New South Wales', *International Labor and Working Class History* 91 (2017): 28–45.

29. See Figure 1.1.

the northern coastline of Zhongshan to do so.[30] At the same time, among the many Chinese people who began to live and work in Hong Kong soon after its annexation by the British, people from Zhongshan were prominent.

It is no surprise, therefore, to find Zhongshan people represented among the first of those who began to travel via European ships around the Pacific. Yet even within Zhongshan the distribution of those who participated was not even, with the villages of the Long Du and Liang Du districts occupying the higher ridge east of the county capital Shekki (石岐, Shiqi) predominating. Shekki itself was also represented but by no means in proportion to its population, while outlying areas of Zhongshan such as Xiaolan (小欖) are hardly represented at all. This is partly due to the fact that, as among all the Pearl River Delta counties, distinctions of dialect, language, and village were significant. This is because, as with family, it was on the basis of these distinctions that people not only associated but also organised. Thus, how people sent remittances back to family, as well as how their bones were returned to the village, was based on associations and businesses run by people from those same villages or a district such as Long Du.[31] Further, the partnerships that founded such businesses were usually characterised by these same family-like relationships, which were often reinforced through marriages that turned 'family-like' into actual family bonds.[32]

Village Life

The Pearl River Delta was an area in which the majority of people lived in villages and pursued agricultural occupations.[33] While rice was the main crop, Guangdong province had long imported rice as much land, particularly in the fertile Pearl River Delta, was devoted to cash crops such as silk, sugar cane, and orchards.[34] Despite this, fields, fishponds, and orchards surrounded most villages and many were largely

---

30. First Opium War 1839–1842, Second Opium War 1856–1860. It is significant that the flow of gold seekers through Hong Kong to California and Victoria was apparently unaffected by the Second Opium War, which included the shelling of Canton and its brief occupation by British troops at the same time as thousands of villagers living just to the south of the fighting were freely travelling to the goldfields and back.
31. For details of bones return and remittances, see Williams, *Returning Home with Glory*.
32. For a case study of two prominent instances of this, see Wellington K. K. Chan, 'Personal Styles, Cultural Values and Management: The Sincere and Wing On Companies in Shanghai and Hong Kong', *The Business History Review* 70, no. 2 (1996): 141–66, https://doi.org/10.2307/3116879.
33. Much of the following was previously published in Williams, *Returning Home with Glory*.
34. For the history of Guangdong province's land use, see Robert Marks, *Tigers, Rice, Silk, and Silt: Environment and Economy in Late Imperial South China* (Cambridge: Cambridge University Press, 1998). For a description of such villages in South China, though not in the Pearl River Delta, see Chen Ta, *Emigrant Communities in South China: A Study of Overseas Migration and Its Influence on Standards of Living and Social Change* (New York: Secretariat, Institute of Pacific Relations, 1940), 65–73. For general accounts, see Hugh D. R. Baker, *Chinese Family and Kinship* (London: Macmillan Press, 1979). For an idea of the range of village types within China, see Ronald Knapp, ed., *Chinese Landscapes: The Village as Place* (Honolulu: University of Hawai'i Press, 1992).

self-sufficient as far as basic commodities were concerned.[35] Life in the villages could be harsh, and health hazards, bandit attacks, floods, and famines were often recorded in South China villages.[36] As mentioned earlier, these were all conditions that were general across southern China and there is no evidence of special circumstances in those villages or districts that provided the bulk of travellers overseas.

For most people, therefore, the greatest hazard was that life was lived close to the edge of poverty. Charitable organisations distributed food to the poor, not only during times of shortage but regularly.[37] While not perhaps exceptional in its degree, poverty in these villages often meant that many went hungry for days at a time, picking rice grains from the fields after the harvest and at times being driven to suicide by the hardship. Meals for some could regularly consist of 'one salted bean with each mouthful of rice'.[38] Families in desperate circumstances would sell their daughters, and this, for example, was one of the means by which some females arrived in the overseas destinations as servants or second wives.[39] Certainly such circumstances meant many were dependent to a greater or lesser degree upon monies remitted by those earning overseas.

Village life was in general close knit, with villages usually populated by people who shared a single family name or, at most, three or four such family names.[40] Relationships based on 'clan' or 'lineage' meant that members of the same 'clan' could expect to receive support, enter into business arrangements, and receive and make loans to others on the basis of this relationship.[41] Marriages were arranged by obtaining wives from nearby villages or the county capital or nearest market town, places that could be anything from a few hours' to a few days' walk away. Transport and communications were slow and, even as late as 1930 in an area as close to Hong

---

35. A survey of villages between 1922 and 1925 (not including Guangdong) estimated that 83.2 per cent of consumption was supplied from the farmland of a village and only 16.8 per cent was purchased from a market. Feng Ho-fa 馮和法, *Zhongguo nongcun jingji ziliao* 中國農村經濟資料 [Information on China's rural village economy] (Shanghai: Li Ming Publishers, 1933), 47. This was less likely to have been true of Long Du and Liang Du villages at that time but might indicate the position a generation or two earlier.

36. Chen Ta, *Emigrant Communities*, 175–80, analyses the prevalence of diseases in the villages of South China, though not the Pearl River Delta specifically. See Choi Chi-Cheng, 'Descent Group Unification and Segmentation in the Coastal Area of Southern China' (PhD diss., University of Tokyo, 1987), 142–43, on inter-family feuds as late as 1898–1899; Appendix 1, 490–92, provides a table of disasters, including floods, famines, and bandit attacks in Zhongshan county.

37. *Tung Wah News* 東華新報, 4 April 1900, 2; and Ya Da 亞達, 'Xiazexiang zhi jinxi' 下澤鄉之今昔 [Present and past of Xiaze Village], *Zhongshan yuekan* 中山月刊 [*Zhongshan Monthly News*] 2 (1946): 27.

38. Violet Mebig Chan Lew, 'A Sentimental Journey into the Past of the Chan and Jong Families', *Journal of the Hong Kong Branch of the Royal Asiatic Society* 28 (1988): 146.

39. Elizabeth Wong, 'Leaves from the Life History of a Chinese Immigrant', *Social Process in Hawaii*, 2 (May 1936): 39–40.

40. Baker, *Chinese Family and Kinship*, 65. Paul C. P. Siu, *The Chinese Laundryman: A Study in Social Isolation* (New York: New York University Press, 1987), 79, for example, defines 'clansman' as those who belong 'to the same village or the same native district'. For a detailed discussion of the difficulties of defining terms such as clan and lineage, see Allen Chun, 'The Lineage-Village Complex in Southeastern China: A Long Footnote in the Anthropology of Kinship', *Current Anthropology* 37, no. 3 (June 1996): 429–50.

41. See Lew, 'A Sentimental Journey', 94–184, for a detailed account over many generations of such a family and their interconnections.

Kong as Zhongshan, largely based on tracks and paths through the fields and boats on the waterways.

The majority of people in the Pearl River Delta spoke the Yue language (Cantonese), but dialect and language variations made members of the different counties and sub-districts not only easy to distinguish but sometimes mutually incomprehensible. Within, for example, Taishan (台山) county, language and dialect variations could be found between villages only a few kilometres apart, and Zhongshan is reported to have had up to six different dialect groups.[42] Other groups, such as the 'Hakka' (客家, pronounced in Cantonese) and people from Long Du, spoke non-Yue languages that were even more unintelligible to the majority of Cantonese speakers.[43]

Within this general picture there was great diversity both across the Pearl River Delta and within specific counties. Zhongshan county, as previously mentioned, was famous for its *shatian* (沙田) or 'sandy fields'.[44] These fertile fields had been gradually reclaimed from the Pearl River over many generations and this 'growth' of Zhongshan county land meant that its population, recorded in 1910 – the first reliable figures available – at over 800,000, was of diverse origins, with four main groups distinguished. These included the people of Shekki, the county capital, who were reported to be originally from Dongguan (東莞) county. The area around Xiaolan (小欖) city, at the northern edge of the county, was dominated by people who spoke the dialect of Shunde (順德), the county to the immediate north of Zhongshan. A third group, called the 'western village type', included the area of Long Du and Liang Du and was known for having many 'overseas Chinese' or *huaqiao* (華僑).[45] Finally, there were those around Doumen (斗門), whose people came mainly from neighbouring Xinhui (新會) county.[46] In addition to these broad geographical divisions, a small and scattered part of Zhongshan's population were Hakka.[47] Macao, at the

---

42. William John McCoy, 'Szeyap Data for a First Approximation of Proto-Cantonese: Survey of Szeyap Districts and Languages' (PhD diss., Cornell University, 1966), 39; and Choi, 'Descent Group Unification', 95, who mentions six Zhongshan dialects and, on p. 114, the Long Du dialect. See also Li, 'Long Du and Nam Long Dialects', 229.

43. See Leo J. Moser, *The Chinese Mosaic: The Peoples and Provinces of China* (Boulder, CO: Westview, 1985), 203–5 and 215, for a general discussion of Pearl River Delta dialects, the arrival of the Hakka in South China (208), their dialect enclaves (216), and the dialect enclave of Long Du (199); Edward J. M. Rhoads, *China's Republican Revolution: The Case of Kwangtung, 1895–1913* (Cambridge, MA: Harvard University Press, 1975), 12–14, discusses the tensions created by dialect differences; and Choi, 'Descent Group Unification', 90–91, discusses the importance of dialect in unifying groups.

44. For example, Feng Ho-fa, *Information on China's Rural Village Economy*, 926, refers to the richness of the *shatian* of Zhongshan.

45. Sometimes translated as 'sojourners'. See Ien Ang, Chapter 3 of this volume, for discussion of the political dimensions of this term. Local newspapers referred to such people as 'travellers' (旅).

46. See Figure 1.1.

47. He Dazhang 何大章, 'Zhongshan xian dili zhi xin renshi' 中山縣地理之新認識 [Zhongshan county new geographical perspective], *Guangdong Zhongshan huaqiao* 廣東中山華僑 [Guangdong Zhongshan Overseas Chinese] 12 (July 1949): 28–29.

southern tip of Zhongshan, under Portuguese administration for centuries, acted as a port of access to Hong Kong and in the 1930s had a population of around 12,000.

The northern plain around Xiaolan was the most fertile area and where the bulk of Zhongshan county's population lived. The central area of the county, which included Shekki and the Long Du and Liang Du districts, was hilly, relatively infertile, and according to one geographer of Zhongshan, it was from such hilly districts that the surplus population travelled overseas to earn money.[48] This distinction between the *huaqiao* of the hills and people of the more fertile *shatian* is confirmed by Bung Chong Lee, a Hawaii-based researcher.[49] According to Lee, the non-*huaqiao* villages or 'peasant villages', 'occupy the low land' and their 'villages are fairly well apart'; 'emigrant villages on the other hand are closely located to one another on the foot of hills and in the valleys. The villages are so closely located near each other that sometimes it is hard for a stranger to distinguish one from the other.'[50]

These reports date from the 1930s, and while there is less evidence from the earlier period, in the late nineteenth century there were sufficient numbers of people who had been overseas and returned that they were easily found, at least in Zhongshan. As a visitor to Zhongshan in 1884 reported:

> One long day's walk of many miles, enabled us to pass through village after village from which people have gone out to the Hawaiian Islands or other parts of the world. It was very strange every now and then to have a man look up from his work in the field, or run out from a shop to greet us in English or Hawaiian.[51]

Another observer reported a few years later that 'Shek Kéé' (石岐, Shekki) had 'many large towns and important centres of trade and influence' and was considered to be wealthy due to the earnings of its merchants abroad.[52]

These overseas connections undoubtedly included many with Australian links, links that were very evident in the late 1920s when the Australian-born Harry Gock Ming (郭桂芳) reported meeting numerous other Australians living in Shekki. Residing in the county capital was preferable to living in the villages at that time due to the threat of bandits who targeted returned travellers and their visiting

---

48. He Dazhang, 'Zhongshan County New Geographical Perspective', 28.

49. B. C. Lee was the Hawaiian-born son of a *huaqiao* of Buck Toy (北台) village in Liang Du (良都). He was a student and friend of the researcher Clarence Glick and wrote a number of papers on Chinese people in Hawaii, as well as assisting Glick in his field research.

50. University of Hawai'i, Glick Archive: notes of B. C. Lee, n.d. (circa 1930).

51. F. W. Damon, 'Rambles in China', *The Friend*, June 1884, 45. The Rev. Frank Damon was an Hawaiian missionary who worked with the *huaqiao* on the plantations and who made a trip to Zhongshan in 1884. Another missionary reporting on nearby Pearl River Delta villages wrote that in the 1870s, 'returned emigrants are as thick as blackberries, and every third man on the road makes free to accost the missionary as "John"'. Thomas G. Selby, *Chinamen at Home* (London: Hodder and Stoughton, 1900), 205.

52. James Dyer Ball, 'The Höng Shán or Macao Dialect', *The China Review* 22 (1896–1897): 503; and James Dyer Ball, *The Chinese at Home or the Man of Tong and his Land* (London: Tract Society 1912), 35.

Michael Williams

overseas-born families for kidnapping and ransom. Harry also reported that Long Du was more dangerous than Liang Du due to its bandits.[53]

Long Du (隆都) and Liang Du (良都)

Long Du makes up about 15 per cent of Zhongshan county's land area and at its northern end is only a few kilometres from the county capital of Shekki. Long Du begins on the opposite side of the river from Shekki and stretches as far as a day's walk to the south.[54] In 1910, the total population of Zhongshan was reported to be 163,315 households or 822,218 people. The population of Long Du was recorded as 27,992 households or around 140,000 people, which was 17 per cent of Zhongshan's population.[55] Long Du consisted of about eighty villages at this time, varying in size from Cheung Kok (象角, Xiangjiao) with 2,230 households (approximately 11,000 people) to Sun Ming Ting (申明亭, Shenmingting) with only 378 households (approximately 1,800 people).[56]

Long Du and Liang Du were known for having many travellers or *huaqiao*, but what proportion of the people of such districts and their villages actually went overseas? Proportions are difficult to estimate due to variations between areas and the fact that most calculations have only been done on a provincial or at best a county level. At the village level statistics are rare but those that exist provide sufficient information to give a rough figure. A village just across the river from Long Du, 'Háng Míe' (恒美, Hang Mei) in Liang Du, sent, according to Dyer Ball, writing in the 1890s, many 'to Hawaii and Australia', with one-third of the village said to be returned from Sydney.[57] Not long after this estimate was made, the large Long Du village of Chung Kok, with 2,300 households, compiled in 1913 a list of 220 of its members who were living overseas.[58] A generation later, in 1948, Chung Tau village (涌頭村, Chongtoucun) in Long Du, which in 1910 had 1,345 households, reported

---

53. See interviews with Harry Gock Ming (郭桂芳) and Leung Pui (梁杜培) in Yen, *South Flows the Pearl*, 161–63 and 224.

54. Long Du (隆都) was the official name of the district until the 1940s; it was also often referred to as Long Zhen (隆鎮). In the years after 1949 it was called No. 2 District (第二區) and its area is now divided into the two townships of Shaxi (沙溪) and Dachong (大涌). Throughout the villages today, however, the name Long Du is still recognised and used.

55. *Xiangshan xian xiangtu zhi* 香山縣鄉土志 [*Heung San County Local Gazetteer*] (Guangzhou: Zhongshan City Local History Compilation Committee [circa 1910] (1988), Vol. 1. While census figures at this time are suspect in China, comparisons with other data when possible seem to confirm the accuracy of these figures, in Long Du at least.

56. *Heung San County Local Gazetteer*, Vol. 1. Households rather than numbers of individuals are the usual figures given; however, where both are given, as for the total Zhongshan population, a ratio of 1:5 seems usual and this is used to estimate village populations by head. See *Zhongshan mingu ribao* 中山民國日報 [Zhongshan Republican Daily], 1930, Special Issue, 22 for a list of the eighty Long Du villages.

57. Dyer Ball, 'The Höng Shán or Macao Dialect', 505.

58. Chung Kok (象角) village hall, Zhongshan county, Guangzhou: donors tablets, 1913; Williams, *Returning Home with Glory*, 72.

Figure 1.2: Map of Long Du (隆都) and Liang Du (良都) villages

329 village members living in destinations around the Pacific.[59] These figures indicate that on average 20 to 30 per cent of the working male population of many villages went overseas in search of income.

But such averages do not mean that all villages would have sent similar proportions. There are also indications that villages varied greatly in their level of participation in 'travelling' even within Long Du or Liang Du and certainly throughout the rest of Zhongshan. The people of the town of Shekki, for example, did not usually travel themselves, according to a long-time Shekki resident, but ended up working for Long Du people who did.[60] Mrs Lim of Chew Kai village, Zhongshan, reported a very high proportion of travellers from her small village of a hundred families, claiming that only two families did not send members to overseas destinations.[61] B. C. Lee reported that as many as eighty-five people from Buck Toy village (北台村, Beitaicun), Liang Du, had left for Hawaii alone between 1920 and 1926.[62] According to Peng Qiqing (彭綺卿), the Long Du village of Ling Hou Heng (嶺後亨村) where she was born had many overseas connections (her own father had gone to Cairns, Queensland, and her two brothers to San Francisco), with nearly every family having a member who had been overseas at one time. The village of Hao Tu (豪吐村), however, only four kilometres away and where Peng Qiqing went to live after her marriage in the 1920s, was one with few overseas travellers and those few mainly 'young people' who went to Hong Kong.[63] Hong Kong was certainly a destination for many people from Zhongshan, with the 'Heong Shan' [香山Zhongshan] people there described at the end of the nineteenth century as 'compradores, boys, house and godown coolies, and agents for, or dealers in, Californian goods principally'.[64]

A *Huaqiao* Village

In addition to the variations in the proportion of villagers who travelled, the general diversity, even within the cluster of the eighty or so villages of Long Du, makes the development of an average picture of a village difficult. Even so, descriptions of villages are rare enough that they cannot be ignored. A 1947 account of Xiaze village (下澤村) as it was remembered just before the Japanese occupation gives a picture of a small, prosperous *huaqiao* village in Long Du. Xiaze is close to the main cluster of Long Du villages, immediately to the west of Shekki, and probably represents a village of the wealthier type in the late 1930s.[65] In 1939, according to this account looking back on its pre-war condition, Xiaze had 775 households

---

59. *Chongtou yuekan* 涌頭月刊 [Chung Tau Monthly], no. 2 (September 1948).
60. Interview, Zhao Yingxiong 趙應熊, Shekki, 8 December 2000.
61. Judy Yung, 'Angel Island oral history project, 1975–1990', Asian-American Studies Library, ARC 2000/62; Mrs Lim, interview 12 September 1976, 2–3. The village name in Chinese characters is unreported.
62. Glick Archive, File 2: notes of Bung Chong Lee, n.d. (circa 1935).
63. Peng Qiqing (彭綺卿), Shekki, 6 December 2000, Tape A, 30.
64. Dyer Ball, 'The Höng Shán or Macao Dialect', 502.
65. See Figure 1.2.

or 3,733 residents and a well-equipped school with over 330 pupils. There was a reading room with twenty-three regular subscribers, a women's society publication to educate the public, a 'National Skills Society' to promote traditional skills, and a 'People Learning School' to teach people to read and write. Transportation to Shekki and other towns was good and ferries carried goods to and from the county capital. There was a self-defence troop, and streetlights spaced at short distances were lit the whole night. The public granary often opened for those in need, orphans and widows received monthly benefits, a medical clinic gave out free medicines, and the streets were clean and waterways flowed smoothly.[66] While the account gives no indication, it is likely that most of the facilities of Xiaze were funded at least partly if not wholly by the earnings of those who travelled.

Another description, not necessarily of a less wealthy village but from someone brought up outside the village of origin (故鄉, *guxiang* in Mandarin), provides a contrasting view. For a teenager born in Hawaii and visiting her family's village of Buck Toy, Liang Du in the 1920s:

> life was almost unbearable. There was no place to go to, and the swarms of flies during the day and mosquitoes at night made me yearn for dear Honolulu.
>
> There is no transportation. The houses are very near together. Sanitation and sewage system are mere words. Illiteracy is the rule among the older people. Water must be drawn from wells or springs.
>
> How I survived it for nine months is still a mystery to me![67]

Qiaoxiang Identity

The focus on the '*qiaoxiang*' (僑鄉) – the migrant village or home district – as a basis for identities, as opposed to a broader China/Chinese focus, was usual for those who travelled, and it remained a strong focus for people's sense of identity until at least the 1920s and 1930s.[68] This level of identification with the *qiaoxiang*, as discussed earlier, determined much about patterns of behaviour and how people organised for movement and earning. However, it should be noted that the merchant elite that began to grow in the late nineteenth century were the first – for economic and political reasons – to begin to identify themselves in more broadly 'Chinese' terms. In the nineteenth century the term *Tang ren* (唐人, lit. people of Tang) was commonly used, increasingly with a non-Manchu emphasis, then later a general term for 'Chinese', *huaren* (華人, pronounced in Mandarin), or for those overseas, *huaqiao* (華僑, pronounced in Mandarin), was adopted. These new terms for identity were strengthened as the anti-Qing revolutionary movement coalesced around the Kuomintang (國民黨 lit. Nationalist Party), with a strong emphasis on the unity

---

66. Ya Da, 'Present and Past of Xiaze Village', 27.
67. Glick Archive, Box 2: Buck Toy Villager Families in Hawaii, n.d. [circa 1930], 9.
68. See Ien Ang, Chapter 3 of this volume, outlining the evolving sense of Chineseness.

of all 'Chinese' that very much included those overseas.[69] Despite this gradual shift in identification towards a more national, or at least civilisational/cultural, level, until the 1950s it was common, even for those born in Australia, to marry only people from the same district or county.[70] Even today this *qiaoxiang* identity plays a significant role in networking and support organisations in Australia and elsewhere, with older memberships of district- and county-level societies such as the Chung Shan Society of Australia (澳洲中山同鄉會) in Sydney continually supplemented with newer arrivals from the same districts.

Connections

For the bulk of those from the Pearl River Delta, therefore, the market gardeners, storekeepers, and others who made their living in Sydney, Australia, or elsewhere, the need to deal mainly with people of their same district remained central. Remittances and accompanying letters could be given to people of the same district returning home, as Bew Chip (劉妙捷), who lived most of his life at Hill End in central western New South Wales, did for many years.[71] Sometimes a store run by people of the same district would perform this service, linking up with similar businesses in Hong Kong and the district capital, such as Shekki in the case of Zhongshan.[72] From there specialist couriers could take the remittance letter to the family home in the village or a family member would pick up the letter at the nearest market town.[73]

All this activity was of course based on the continued existence of families in the villages of Zhongshan, in particular the women of those families. This is a point worth emphasising, as the focus in most Australian histories has been on men, since they made up the majority of those actually in Australia for most of the period. Some excellent research has endeavoured to bring to light the lesser-known history of the relatively few women who also came to Australia before the second half of the twentieth century, as well as the many more non-Chinese women who married Chinese men.[74] However, the emphasis on those in Australia, male or otherwise, means that the much greater numbers of women in the villages – wives, mothers,

---

69. See Kuo, *Making Chinese Australia*, for an account of this process by the merchant elite.
70. Interview with Elizabeth Lee in Yen, *South Flows the Pearl*, 353–54.
71. Juanita Kwok, 'The Life and Times of Bew Chip', in *Bew Chip's Register: A Chinese Australian Remittance Register from the Tambaroora and Hill End Goldfield*, trans. Ely Finch (Carlton, NSW: Hill End and Tambaroora Gathering Group, 2022), 1–31. For an excellent background history of the remittance network of the Chinese diaspora, see Gregor Benton and Hong Liu, *Dear China: Emigrant Letters and Remittances, 1820–1980* (Oakland: University of California Press, 2018).
72. Williams, *Returning Home with Glory*, 102, 118.
73. For an account of such a courier, see Li Huari 李華日, '*Qiao qing ji ku*' 僑情紀苦 [Account of *huaqiao* hardships], *Zhongshan qiaokan* 中山僑刊 [Zhongshan overseas magazine], 32 (April 1996): 29, and for couriers and the various ways remittances were delivered, see Benton and Liu, *Dear China*, 33–40.
74. Most recently, Kate Bagnall and Julia T. Martínez, eds., *Locating Chinese Women: Historical Mobility between China and Australia* (Hong Kong: University of Hong Kong Press, 2021). Despite the title the emphasis is almost entirely on women in Australia rather than China, with no accounts of the majority in the villages.

and daughters – have been relatively neglected along with their significance in maintaining the Zhongshan–Australia connections over many generations.[75]

Until well into the second half of the twentieth century most people continued to prefer the store-based remittance systems to using the services provided by the national banking systems. Why this was so can be understood from the level of service such a store could offer. In Sydney, the Kwong War Chong (廣和昌) store was a major remittance centre for Zhongshan people, though stores such as Wing On & Co. (永安公司) also facilitated remittances.[76] The Kwong War Chong charged a small commission on each remittance and consolidated all the monies into a single draft drawn on the English, Scottish & Australian Bank.[77] The draft was then sent to the Hong Kong branch, the Kwong War Fong (廣和豐), where it was converted into Hong Kong dollars and then into Chinese dollars to be sent to the Kwong War Cheong & Co. (廣和祥) branch in Shekki. The Shekki branch then distributed the money to the families, either by their collecting it or it being delivered to the village by the firm's clerks or by professional couriers.[78] Young Koon Nuen describes how his mother would regularly make the trip from their village into the district capital of Shekki. There she would pick up from a silver shop the letter and £2 that his father would send from Cairns, northern Queensland each month.[79] A receipt, which included a letter back to those at the destination, would be signed and returned to the store in Australia, where it was set up on a rack in the front window for people to collect.[80]

For those who became sick or needed other assistance while overseas, a district-based association such as the Long Du Society in Sydney would be contributed to according to means and its funds drawn upon according to need.[81] Such merchant-led *qiaoxiang*-centred associations in the frontier territories of Guangxi and what is now Vietnam, as well as later in Southeast Asia, date back to the Ming period of the fifteenth century, and similar ones were quickly set up in California and the Australian colonies. One of the first activities they performed upon being established was sending home the bones of those who died overseas, though assistance in sending the aged and sick back home was also a major role. Other activities included

---

75. For more on this aspect, see Michael Williams, 'Holding Up Half the Family', *Journal of Chinese Overseas* 17, no. 1 (2021): 179–95, https://doi.org/10.1163/17932548-12341438.
76. Interview, Victor Gow, Sydney, 30 October 1997 (9) and Norman Lee, Sydney, 25 September 1997 (2).
77. Perhaps from 1 to 5 per cent, according to Samuel L. Gracey, 'Chinese Letter Shops', *The Chautauquan* 21 (June 1895): 310.
78. See Lee Bung Chong, 'The Chinese Store as a Social Institution', *Social Process in Hawaii* 2 (May 1936): 35–38, for a similar account of Hawaiian stores.
79. Interview, Young Koon Nuen, Long Tou Wan (龍頭環), 20 May 2000 (5).
80. Interview, Norman Lee, Sydney, 25 September 1997 (2–4). The Tiy Loy & Co. (泰來有限公司) of the Gao Yao county (高要) people in Sussex St., Sydney still had (in 2015) such a letter rack.
81. For an example of a Long Du Society membership book, see *Chinese Australian History in 88 Objects*, No. 45, https://chinozhistory.org/index.php/45-long-du-society-members-book/.

assistance with immigration difficulties, providing bonds, and even funding court cases when necessary.[82]

These mechanisms supporting those in Australia were developed to ensure that support for the families in the village were maintained. However, support mechanisms linked to those overseas also developed to provide for the village itself and for community projects such as schools, hospitals, electric lights, and vaccinations. The soliciting of donations based on village and district ties reached overseas to their fellows, who were encouraged with rewards of recognition and prestige such as lists of names and amounts donated inscribed on plaques prominently set up on temples, clinics, and schools.[83] Magazines known as '*qiaokan*' (僑刊, pronounced in Mandarin) began to be published from the beginning of the twentieth century at the village and local district level to provide those overseas with information, to appeal for contributions to village projects, and to provide lists of donors.[84] Many of these mechanisms continue today, although the *qiaokan* are now government publications and the scope for private donations for schools is much less.[85]

Change and Evolution

To the extent that strong family and community as well as economic links were maintained between Australia and Zhongshan, changes in China and Zhongshan must also be considered as much as, if not more than, changes in Australia itself. Thus, the 1911 collapse of the government of the Qing and its replacement by a series of weak governments in the Republican period greatly impacted those in Australia and their links with Zhongshan. For those in Zhongshan this meant, among other things, a continuing if not increased dependence on the remittances from those overseas, an inability to establish much in the way of independent and viable enterprises in China outside the safe havens of Hong Kong and Shanghai, and an increased danger from bandits including kidnapping.

Despite these unstable conditions, people continued to send money from Australia for education and other community developments and also to send their children to be cared for and educated in the villages, Shekki, Hong Kong, and Shanghai. It was in the years after World War I that parts of Shekki became almost an 'Australian' district as Chinese Australians took up residence in the county capital, where bandit attacks were less likely and where it was also more comfortable than the outlying villages.[86] Bandits, it should be noted, very often simply meant poorer members of the village seeking money rather than outsiders as such.

---

82. See Williams, *Returning Home with Glory*, 118.
83. See Williams, *Returning Home with Glory*, 82, for an example of a clinic; and Chapter 7 of this volume for schools.
84. Williams, *Returning Home with Glory*, 106–7.
85. See Chapter 7 of this volume for schools.
86. For examples, see interviews with Harry Gock Ming (郭桂芳) and Leung Pui (梁社培) in Yen, *South Flows the Pearl*, 161–63 and 224.

At the same time as Shekki was considered safer than the villages, so too links with Hong Kong and Shanghai were particularly strong in the first half of the twentieth century for reasons of both safety and business. The income earned in these locations, like that earned in Australia, was often remitted to the villages or used to found schools or to build large homes, such as those of the Kwok (郭) and Ma (馬) families, both of Liang Du origin.[87] For people brought up in Australia, Hong Kong and Shanghai were attractive for reasons that included better jobs, education, and greater acceptance of their status as Chinese Australians, including those who were part Chinese and/or had better English than Chinese language skills.

Thus, by the eve of the Japanese invasions in the late 1930s, the links between Zhongshan and Australia were as strong as or stronger than ever and featured a complex of interactions based on many people living for periods of time in either location for parts of their lives. All this was in the context of the so-called 'White Australia policy' under which Australia sought to limit the entry of any 'non-white' person.[88] This context often saw both Australian and China-born people of Chinese heritage treated in much the same manner regardless of their supposed legal status. Additionally, the discrimination directed at 'non-white' people meant that the Zhongshan connection was often maintained through extra-legal means that included smuggling and false documents.[89] Overall, as a result of these restrictions, as more people returned to China on retirement than were able to replace them, the Australian Chinese community shrank in the period leading up to World War II but did not disappear entirely.[90]

Despite the White Australia policy and its restrictive laws and attitudes, it was events in China such as the Japanese invasion and the change in government after 1949 that had the most profound impact on the Zhongshan–Australia connections. The war period saw remittances cut off and people forced to remain in either Australia or the villages for many years. Many starved in the villages of Zhongshan, while those living in Shanghai and Hong Kong who did not flee to Australia in time were often interned.[91] The defeat of Japan saw many people attempt to restore things to their pre-war situation, though often those who had been in Shanghai or Hong Kong preferred to return to Australia when their Australian birth allowed. It was the new government of the People's Republic of China and its social and economic policies, however, that transformed the links more profoundly after 1949.

---

87. Williams, *Returning Home with Glory*, 79.

88. For a history of the White Australia policy, see Gwenda Tavan, *The Long, Slow Death of White Australia* (Melbourne: Scribe, 2005), and for a history of its administration including the impact on the Chinese Australian community and connections with China, see Michael Williams, *Australia's Dictation Test: The Test It Was a Crime to Fail* (Leiden: Brill, 2021).

89. For an analysis of the economic and family basis of smuggling in the White Australia policy period, see Michael Williams, 'Stopping Them Using Our Boats', *Australian Economic History Review* 61, no. 1 (2020): 64–79, https://doi.org/10.1111/aehr.12207.

90. The 'Chinese' population of NSW, for example, fell from around 10,000 in 1901 to some 3,000 by 1950. See Williams, *Returning Home with Glory*, 167 (Table 8.1).

91. Williams, *Returning Home with Glory*, 93–96.

Once again many people in the villages and those in Australia were cut off from each other as Zhongshan, along with the other remittance-dependent counties, was again plunged into a – this time much longer – period of poverty as remittances were, if not completely halted, severely reduced due to political and social considerations on both sides.[92]

Post-revolution

Despite the change of government in China and Cold War politics, the essentially family-based links between Zhongshan and Australia were never completely severed. A trickle of people continued to travel either way as some returned to the villages from Australia, while others moved from the villages to Macao and Hong Kong, and from there to Australia. Often people were able to use their Australian links to travel there as cafe workers or students, these two categories being most acceptable under the White Australia policy.[93] The infrastructure of schools, clinics, and grand homes in the villages deteriorated in this period of relative isolation until the 1970s, when China gradually opened again to the outside world and the remains of the diaspora began once again to donate funds to support schools and hospitals.[94] This was a relatively brief period, lasting only until the growing wealth of China, with the special economic zone of Shenzhen (深圳) nearby and that of Zhuhai (珠海) carved from Zhongshan itself, helped to transform the once remittance-dependent county into a wealth-generating one.

This growing economic wealth has brought rapid change, with new buildings swallowing many old villages and rice fields, and where agriculture continues new workers have often been brought in from other provinces to take up residence in the old villages. This last development perhaps more than any other has weakened the relationship with their villages of origin for those overseas and transformed the old links with Australia into those of heritage nostalgia.

Conclusion

This contextual overview of the role of Zhongshan in Chinese Australian history has many advantages, not least being that it helps broaden the perspective away from a narrow nation-state one. It is common for the history of the Chinese in Australia to be seen purely in terms of their actions and reactions in Australia. Yet

---

92. See Ien Ang and Alexandra Wong, Chapter 8 of this volume, for further discussion of this period. See also Andrew Kwong, *One Bright Moon: A Memoir of Famine and Freedom* (Sydney: HarperCollins, 2020) for a first-hand account of the early post-PRC period in Shekki.
93. See Kwong, *One Bright Moon: A Memoir of Famine and Freedom* (Sydney: HarperCollins, 2020) for a typical example of a student entry at this time; and Williams, *Australia's Dictation Test*, for details of White Australia policies and the evolving categories and exemptions in the post-war period.
94. See Chapter 7 of this volume.

as this overview makes clear, such an approach neglects much that is relevant for a community that has been closely linked over many generations with families and villages in southern China. Two examples – in addition to the main aim here of providing a context for the heritage corridor itself – are the sojourner/settler debate and perceptions of a lack of agency. The first, framed by a European settler viewpoint, asks whether Chinese people in Australia came as sojourners intending to return or as settlers?[95] Consideration of the movements of generations of people, which included Australian-born people raising children in China and people of Australian birth returning to Australia after many years, reveals the narrowness of this binary perspective. Similarly, much of Chinese Australian history is couched in terms of racism and discrimination, which regularly positions Chinese people as victims, or at best as 'resistors'. Again, the building of homes and village infrastructure alone, not to mention the complex system of organisation for maintaining the movement of people and monies between Australia, the villages, and elsewhere, requires greater consideration of the agency of Chinese people.

This chapter has introduced the Pearl River Delta county of Zhongshan in terms of its geographical and historical context. Geographically both the diversity within the county as well as its links with neighbouring regions such as Guangxi, Vietnam, and the Nanyang, and more recently Hong Kong and the Asia-Pacific, are all seen to be of significance. Historically the long history of the region as an exporter of labour dating back to at least the fifteenth century and modified by European colonialism and the establishment of Hong Kong was also examined. The Australian gold rushes, which loom large in popular histories, can be seen as only one factor among a range of others shaping Chinese Australian history. More specifically, the conditions of village life as transformed by the connections with Australia and elsewhere over time were seen along with the role of identification by village and dialect in the organisation and maintenance of these connections over generations. Finally, the importance of considering changes within both China and Australia in the evolution of these connections helps provide the context for understanding the heritage corridor that is the subject of this book and the chapters that follow.

Moreover, it should not be forgotten that the Zhongshan–Australia heritage corridor was only one of numerous interconnecting corridors that included Hong Kong, Shanghai, and many locations in Southeast Asia and around what some have called the Cantonese Pacific.[96] Nevertheless, the central place of the home village in the life of the overseas Chinese remained at the core of these corridors for many generations and only gradually evolved under the stress of such major events as a world war and a political revolution. It is this centrality of the home village in

---

95. For a fuller discussion of the sojourner debate, see Williams, *Returning Home with Glory*, 21–24; and for the lack of agency, see Karen Schamberger, 'Identity, Belonging and Cultural Diversity in Australian Museums' (PhD thesis, Deakin University, 2016).
96. Henry Yu, 'The Cantonese Pacific in the Making of Nations', in *The Relevance of Regions in a Globalized World*, ed. Galia Press-Barnathan, Ruth Fine, and Arie M. Kacowicz (Abingdon: Routledge, 2018), 123–36.

the lives of people that provides essential background for the other chapters in this book.

Bibliography

Bagnall, Kate, and Julia T. Martínez, eds. *Locating Chinese Women: Historical Mobility between China and Australia*. Hong Kong: University of Hong Kong Press, 2021.

Baker, Hugh D. R. *Chinese Family and Kinship*. London: Macmillan Press, 1979.

Benton, Gregor, and Hong Liu. *Dear China: Emigrant Letters and Remittances, 1820–1980*. Oakland: University of California Press, 2018.

Chan, Wellington K. K. 'Personal Styles, Cultural Values and Management: The Sincere and Wing On Companies in Shanghai and Hong Kong'. *The Business History Review* 40, no. 2 (1996): 141–66. https://doi.org/10.2307/3116879.

Chen, Ta. *Emigrant Communities in South China: A Study of Overseas Migration and Its Influence on Standards of Living and Social Change*. New York: Secretariat, Institute of Pacific Relations, 1940.

Choi, Chi-Cheng. 'Descent Group Unification and Segmentation in the Coastal Area of Southern China'. PhD diss., University of Tokyo, 1987.

Chongtou yuekan 涌頭月刊 [Chung Tou Monthly], 2 (September 1948).

Chun, Allen. 'The Lineage-Village Complex in Southeastern China: A Long Footnote in the Anthropology of Kinship'. *Current Anthropology* 37, no. 3 (June 1996): 429–50.

Chung Kok (象角) village hall, Zhongshan County, Guangzhou: donors tablets, 1913.

Damon, F. W. 'Rambles in China'. *The Friend* (June 1884), 41–45.

Darnell, Maxine. 'The Chinese Labour Trade to New South Wales, 1783–1853'. PhD thesis, University of New England, 1997.

Dyer Ball, James. 'The Höng Shán or Macao Dialect'. *The China Review* 22 (1896–1897): 501–31.

Dyer Ball, James. *The Chinese at Home or the Man of Tong and His Land*. London: Tract Society, 1912.

Emmer, P. C., ed. *Colonialism and Migration: Indentured Labour before and after Slavery*. Dordrecht: Martinus Nijhoff, 1986.

Farrell, Frank. 'Who Discovered Australia?' In *Themes in Australian History: Questions, Issues and Interpretation in an Evolving Historiography*, 1–21. Kensington: UNSW Press, 1990.

Feng, Ho-fa 馮和法. *Zhongguo nongcun jingji ziliao* 中國農村經濟資料 [Information on China's rural village economy]. Shanghai: Li Ming Publishers, 1933.

Glick Archive, File 2: notes of Bung Chong Lee, n.d. (circa 1935).

Gracey, Samuel L. 'Chinese Letter Shops'. *The Chautaquan* 21 (June 1895): 309–12.

He, Dazhang 何大章. 'Zhongshan xian dili zhi xin renshi' 中山縣地理之新認識 [Zhongshan County new geographical perspective]. *Guangdong Zhongshan huaqiao* 廣東中山華僑 [Guangdong Zhongshan Overseas overseas Chinese] 12 (July 1949): 28–29.

Knapp, Ronald, ed. *Chinese Landscapes: The Village as Place*. Honolulu: University of Hawai'i Press, 1992.

Kuo, Mei-fen. *Making Chinese Australia*. Clayton, Victoria: Monash University Publishing, 2013.

Kwok, Juanita. 'The Life and Times of Bew Chip'. In *Bew Chip's Register: A Chinese Australian Remittance Register from the Tambaroora and Hill End Goldfield*, translated by Ely Finch, 1–31. Carlton, NSW: Hill End and Tambaroora Gathering Group, 2022.

Kwong, Andrew. *One Bright Moon: A Memoir of Famine and Freedom*. Sydney: HarperCollins, 2020.

Lee, Bung Chong. 'The Chinese Store as a Social Institution'. *Social Process in Hawaii* 2 (May 1936): 35–38.

Lew, Violet Mebig Chan. 'A Sentimental Journey into the Past of the Chan and Jong Families'. *Journal of the Hong Kong Branch of the Royal Asiatic Society* 28 (1988): 94–184.

Li, Huari 李華日. 'Qiao qing ji ku' 僑情紀苦 [Account of *huaqiao* hardships]. *Zhongshan qiaokan* 中山僑刊 [Zhongshan overseas magazine] 32 (April 1996): 29.

Li, Zhaoyong 李兆永. 'Longduhua, Nanlongcunhua yuan shi Fuzhouhua' 隆都話，南朗村話原是福州話 [Long Du and Nam Long dialects origins in Fujian dialect]. *Zhongshan wenshi* 中山文史 [*Zhongshan Cultural History*] 31 (1994): 229–30.

Loy-Wilson, Sophie. 'Coolie Alibis: Seizing Gold from Chinese Miners in New South Wales'. *International Labor and Working Class History* 91 (2017): 28–45.

Marks, Robert. *Tigers, Rice, Silk, and Silt: Environment and Economy in Late Imperial South China*. Cambridge: Cambridge University Press, 1998.

McCoy, William John. 'Szeyap Data for a First Approximation of Proto-Cantonese: Survey of Szeyap Districts and Languages'. PhD diss., Cornell University, 1966.

Miles, Steven B. *Upriver Journeys: Diaspora and Empire in Southern China, 1570–1850*. Harvard-Yenching Institute Monograph Series 106, Harvard University Asia Center, 2017.

Moser, Leo J. *The Chinese Mosaic: The Peoples and Provinces of China*. Boulder, CO: Westview Press, 1985.

Rhoads, Edward J. M. *China's Republican Revolution: The Case of Kwangtung, 1895–1913*. Cambridge, MA: Harvard University Press, 1975.

Robert, Willem. *The Dutch Explorations of 1605–1756, of the North and Northwest Coast of Australia*. Amsterdam: Philo Press, 1973.

Schamberger, Karen. 'Identity, Belonging and Cultural Diversity in Australian Museums'. PhD thesis, Deakin University, 2016.

Schamberger, Karen. 'Whose Stories Are We Telling? Chinese Australian History in New South Wales and Victorian Museums'. *Australian Historical Studies* 52, no. 4 (2021): 567–90. https://doi.org/10.1080/1031461X.2021.1926521.

Selby, Thomas G. *Chinamen at Home*. London: Hodder and Stoughton, 1900.

Siu, Helen F. *Agents and Victims in South China: Accomplices in Rural Revolution*. New Haven, CT: Yale University Press, 1989.

Siu, Paul C. P. *The Chinese Laundryman: A Study in Social Isolation*. New York: New York University Press, 1987.

Tavan, Gwenda. *The Long, Slow Death of White Australia*. Melbourne: Scribe, 2005.

Wang, Gungwu. *Short History of the Nanyang*. Singapore: Eastern Universities Press, 1959.

Wang, Sing-wu. *The Organisation of Chinese Emigration 1848–1888: With Special Reference to Chinese Emigration to Australia*. San Francisco: Chinese Materials Centre, 1978.

Williams, Michael. *Chinese Settlement in NSW: A Thematic History*. Sydney: Heritage Office of NSW, 1999.

Williams, Michael. *Returning Home with Glory: Chinese Villagers around the Pacific, 1849 to 1949*. Hong Kong: Hong Kong University Press, 2018.

Williams, Michael. 'Smoking Opium, Puffing Cigars, and Drinking Gingerbeer: Chinese Opera in Australia'. In *Opera, Emotion, and the Antipodes*, edited by Jane W. Davidson, Michael Halliwell, and Stephanie Rocke, 166–208. Abingdon: Routledge, 2020.

Williams, Michael. 'Sojourners & Birds of Passage: Chinese and Italian Migrants in Australia and the United States in Comparative Perspective, 1871–1914'. *Journal of the European Association for Studies on Australia* 11, no. 2 (2020): 2–16.

Williams, Michael. 'Stopping Them Using Our Boats'. *Australian Economic History Review* 61, no. 1 (2020): 64–79. https://doi.org/10.1111/aehr.12207.

Williams, Michael. *Australia's Dictation Test: The Test It Was a Crime to Fail*. Leiden: Brill, 2021.

Williams, Michael. 'Holding Up Half the Family'. *Journal of Chinese Overseas* 17 no. 1 (2021): 179–95. https://doi.org/10.1163/17932548-12341438.

Wong, Elizabeth. 'Leaves from the Life History of a Chinese Immigrant'. *Social Process in Hawaii* 2 (May 1936): 39–42.

Wong, John. *Deadly Dreams*. Cambridge: Cambridge University Press, 1998.

Xiangshan xian xiangtu zhi 香山縣鄉土志 [Heung San County Local Gazetteer]. Guangzhou: Zhongshan City Local History Compilation Committee [circa 1910] (1988), Vol. 1.

Ya Da 亞達. 'Xiazexiang zhi jinxi' 下澤鄉之今昔 [Present and past of Xiaze village]. *Zhongshan yuekan* 中山月刊 [*Zhongshan Monthly News*] 2 (1946): 27.

Yen, Mavis Gock. *South Flows the Pearl: Chinese Australian Voices*, edited by Siaoman Yen and Richard Horsburgh. Sydney: Sydney University Press, 2022.

Yu, Henry. 'The Cantonese Pacific in the Making of Nations'. In *The Relevance of Regions in a Globalized World*, edited by Galia Press-Barnathan, Ruth Fine, and Arie M. Kacowicz, 123–36. Abingdon: Routledge, 2018.

Yung, Judy. 'Angel Island Oral History Project, 1975–1990'. Asian-American Studies Library, ARC 2000/62; Mrs. Lim, interview 12 September 1976, 2–3.

Interviews

Victor Gow, Sydney, 30 October 1997.
Norman Lee, Sydney, 25 September 1997.
Peng Qiqing 彭綺卿, Shekki, 6 December 2000.
Young Koon Nuen, Long Tou Wan, 20 May 2000.
Zhao Yingxiong 趙應熊, Shekki, 8 December 2000.

2

A Heritage of Lifelines in the Migration Corridor

Denis Byrne

A key theme taken up by the contributors to this volume is the mobility that continued to characterise the lives of Chinese migrants even after their arrival in Australia. Many of them pursued peripatetic lives, moving, for example, between goldfields and between different country towns and cities, as well as making return visits to their home villages in the Pearl River Delta, via Hong Kong, on an occasional and in some cases regular basis.[1] The mobility of many Chinese migrants in Australia in the period between the 1840s and 1940s is well documented in major academic works, as is the circulatory traffic that took place along the China–Australia migration corridor in this same period.[2] An enormous volume of work has also been done by descendants of Chinese migrants in tracing the trajectories of their forebears in Australia and discovering their origin places in China.[3] The mobility of Chinese migrants and the transnational extent of their lifelines poses a challenge to conventional heritage practice – a challenge this chapter explores from a range of perspectives.

---

1. See Michael Williams, Chapter 1 of this volume.
2. See, for example, Kate Bagnall and Julia T. Martinez, eds., *Locating Chinese Women: Historical Mobility between China and Australia* (Hong Kong: Hong Kong University Press, 2021); John Fitzgerald, *Big White Lie: Chinese Australians in White Australia* (Sydney: UNSW Press, 2007); David Walker and Agnieszka Sobocinska, eds., *Australia's Asia: From Yellow Peril to Asian Century* (Perth: University of Western Australia Press, 2012); Michael Williams, *Returning Home with Glory: Chinese Villagers around the Pacific, 1849 to 1949* (Hong Kong: Hong Kong University Press, 2018).
3. Sophie Couchman and Kate Bagnall, 'Memory and Meaning in the Search for Australian-Chinese Families', in *Remembering Migration: Oral Histories and Heritage in Australia*, ed. Kate Darian-Smith and Paula Hamilton (London: Palgrave Macmillan, 2019), 331–46; see also Bagnall's website, *The Tiger's Mouth* (http://chineseaustralia.org/publications/), in which she describes accompanying Chinese Australians on visits to emigrant regions of the Pearl River Delta to visit their ancestral villages.

A Mobilities Ontology

This chapter offers a critique of the way that, with its focus on old buildings and other 'sites', heritage practice has been unable or unwilling to adequately capture the mobility of Chinese migrant lives. Indeed, the heritage record of Chinese migration in Australia creates a skewed impression of migrant lives post-arrival as not merely contained by Australia's borders but as anchored in and contained by particular places, such as the Chinatowns of Sydney and Melbourne. It largely ignores the circulatory flows between Australia and China and fails to acknowledge the dynamic connectivity between the built environment of Chinese migration in Australia and that of the emigrant villages of southern China. In this respect, heritage practice follows the social sciences in general, which, as Sheller and Urry have remarked, have historically been 'a-mobile', their approach to human existence being markedly sedentarist, fostering the impression that stability is 'normal' and mobility and instability are 'abnormal'.[4]

Though the historical circumstances obviously differ, the mobile lives of the early wave of Chinese migrants to Australia in many ways mirror the lives of contemporary Chinese migrants in Australia, such as those recently studied by Rosie Roberts.[5] Roberts refers to them as 'mobile settlers' who view Australia as a site 'within a range of transnational connections, recognising contemporary mobility as a complex system of interactions rather than one-way permanent relocation'.[6] Michael Williams's research on the intentions and movement patterns of emigrants from Zhongshan county in the 1840s–1940s period suggests they regarded Australia similarly.[7] The flows of people, ideas, and money between Australia and China that this phase of Chinese migration precipitated had the effect of greatly enhancing Australia's connectivity, not just with China, and migrant-sending regions of southeast China in particular, but with the Chinese diaspora in Southeast Asia, California, and elsewhere. In a symmetrical fashion, the effect on China of that century of transnational migration to multiple destinations in the Pacific, the Americas, and Europe was also significant. In Shelley Chan's words, '[i]t pulled China's center of gravity outward'; among other things, it brought China into conversation with the various developments that constituted modernity in the Global North and thus helped to 'create modern China'.[8] It should also be mentioned that circulatory flows along the China–Australia migration corridor included those white Australians who travelled

---

4. Mimi Sheller and John Urry, 'The New Mobility Paradigm', *Environment and Planning A* 38, no. 2 (2006): 208, https://doi.org/10.1068/a37268.
5. Rosie Roberts, *Ongoing Mobility Trajectories: Lived Experiences of Global Migration* (Singapore: Springer, 2019), 6.
6. Roberts, *Ongoing Mobility*, 4.
7. Williams, *Returning Home with Glory*, 41–42. See also Williams in Chapter 1 of this volume.
8. Shelley Chan, *Diaspora's Homeland: Modern China in the Age of Global Migration* (Durham, NC: Duke University Press, 2018), 3.

to China in the 1920s and influenced the nationalist movement there,[9] as well as those who went to Chinese cities such as Shanghai during the Depression in the 1930s in search of work.[10]

Focusing on Chinese migration to Australia in the period prior to the 1940s, this chapter looks below the macro effects of migration on the nation-state to the level of individual migrant trajectories. It is especially interested in the material heritage of Chinese migrant lives, recognising that the factor of mobility in these lives meant this material heritage is often transnationally dispersed. For example, the fact that a migrant from Zhongshan may have been living and working in Sydney in the 1920s does not mean the material evidence of his life in those years was confined to Sydney. In Chapter 6 of this volume it is shown that such men often put most of their earnings into building houses that were located not in Australia but in their home village in China. Many also contributed money to building schools and restoring temples and ancestral halls in their home villages.[11] The physical labour involved in constructing or renovating these buildings in the home village has been secondary, in a sense, to the labour expended by those living abroad, since it is this latter labour which, converted into remittance funds, paid for the construction or renovation work. To this extent, remittances are a crystallisation of the sender's labour.[12] The sender's productivity abroad translated into productivity at 'home', and the products in question served as placeholders that lent migrants an 'absent presence' in their home villages. It is in this sense that throughout the present book we put forward the concept of a 'heritage corridor' spanning and linking Australia and China.[13]

Chinese Migrant Invisibility in the Heritage Record

Although Chinese migrants lived lives characterised by mobility, in Australia's official heritage record these lives are represented by 'sites' that are fixed and static. In New South Wales they include old shops, temples, gold mining camps, and market gardens, as well as buildings such as the Chinese Masonic hall (澳洲洪門致公總堂) and the Kuomintang building (中國國民黨部大樓) in Sydney.[14] There is

---

9. Hannah Forsyth and Sophie Loy-Wilson, 'Seeking a New Materialism in Australian History', *Australian Historical Studies* 48, no. 2 (2017): 174, https://doi.org/10.1080/1031461X.2017.1298635.

10. Sophie Loy-Wilson, *Australian in Shanghai: Race, Rights and Nation in Treat Port China* (London: Routledge, 2017).

11. For diaspora involvement in school construction, see Chapter 7 of this volume; for their involvement in ancestral hall restoration, see Chapter 9 of this volume.

12. David P. Sandall, 'Where Mourning Takes Them: Migrants, Borders, and an Alternative Reality', *Ethos* 38, no. 2 (2010): 194.

13. See also Denis Byrne, 'Heritage Corridors: Transnational Flows and the Built Environment of Migration', *Journal of Ethnic and Migration Studies* 42, no. 14 (2016): 2360–78.

14. For a survey of the kinds of places associated with Chinese migrants in New South Wales, see Michael Williams, 'Chinese Settlement in New South Wales: A Thematic History', NSW Heritage Office, September 1999, https://www.heritage.nsw.gov.au/assets/Uploads/a-z-publications/a-c/chinesehistory.pdf.

nothing very surprising in the fact that mobile lives end up represented by heritage objects that are anything but mobile. For example, the 'objects' that moved Chinese migrants across the sea and through the landscape, including the steamships plying the Hong Kong–Australia sea route, and the trains and horse-drawn carts and coaches that carried them between goldfields and country towns, either have not survived into the present or their significance to Chinese migrant lives has been forgotten. The routes survive only as lines on maps or as memory traces. Moreover, the occupations pursued by many Chinese migrants in Australia in the pre-1940s period were transitory in nature: the gold-mining camp lasted only as long as the gold, employment in bush-clearing gangs was ephemeral by definition, and the lease on a market garden often lasted only until the local council resumed the land for other purposes. The dwellings associated with these forms of employment were mostly tents and huts, which were equally ephemeral. And while it has sometimes been possible to find archaeological traces of them – Lindsay Smith, for example, discusses the distinctive floor plans of huts occupied by Chinese gold miners in the 1860s at Kiandra, New South Wales, which were revealed in his excavations – most have left no readily visible traces in the landscape, at least not the kind of highly visible traces that might come to be recognised as heritage sites.[15]

Then there are the places inhabited by Chinese migrants on a more sedentary basis. These included houses in the cities and country towns where they dwelt and the shops and restaurants many operated or worked in, sometimes for long periods of time. Many such houses and business premises were rented rather than owned, which meant there was limited scope for them to renovate or expand the buildings to fit their own needs and desires. This in turn means there is less chance the buildings would be remembered in the broader community for their history of occupation by Chinese Australians. To the extent that the buildings were *marked* by this occupation it was not the kind of marking that would usually endure long after occupation ended. A Chinese shop or restaurant that catered mainly to a Chinese clientele, for example, may have been redolent with colourful signage in Chinese characters, clearly marking it to white Australians as well as to fellow Chinese *as Chinese*, but within days of the expiry of the lease all this might be gone, leaving the building to revert back to its former identity. The transience of such markings means there is little chance the buildings would be commemorated as sites of Chinese migrant heritage.

In general, it can be said that heritage favours stasis, which is to say that places associated with people who are settled in one location are more likely to be regarded retrospectively as heritage than places associated with mobile lifestyles. There is a correlation between settled status and the size or bulk of buildings: those who have settled in a single location are more likely to erect substantial buildings than those

---

15. Lindsay Smith, 'Identifying Chinese Ethnicity through Material Culture: Archaeological Excavations at Kiandra, NSW', *Australasian Historical Archaeology* 21 (2003): 18–29.

who are more mobile. The Englishman John MacArthur, for example, was granted 200 acres of land at Parramatta, Sydney, in the 1790s and built a homestead in the Georgian style there in 1793, a dwelling that over the following twenty years was expanded into a substantial house, known as Elizabeth Farm, that has now become a museum and is regarded as one of Australia's most important colonial heritage sites.[16] The present heritage status of the house derives partly from it having been constructed solidly enough – it was built to be permanent – that it would survive decades of neglect until it was restored in the 1970s. Those with greatest power in society have the most potential to create buildings that are large, substantial, and long-lasting. Broadly speaking, the colonial system endowed white settlers with greater power to alter the landscape than either indigenous Australians, once they had displaced them, or non-European migrant sojourners or settlers.[17] One notices, for example, that although it is known that the MacArthurs employed Chinese cooks at Elizabeth Farm, no material trace of them remains there.

The fact that Australia's official heritage inventories disproportionately favour buildings constructed by and associated with white Australians rather than non-European migrants such as the Chinese also reflects the historical reality that the majority of white migrants arrived with the intention to settle and build in Australia and that they were assisted in this by government policies, at least in the colonial era. Chinese migrants, by contrast, faced widespread hostility from white Australians and after 1901 were discouraged from settling by anti-Chinese immigration laws and laws that prevented them becoming Australian citizens. Further to that, they were engaged in what Williams describes as a 'huaqiao lifestyle' (華僑生活模式) in which male members of households travelled overseas to earn money to support the family back in the village, most of them, initially at least, not aiming to settle permanently in their destination countries.[18] Their incentive to add to the built environment of Australia was thus presumably weaker than that of white settlers. Many, however, did end up staying and settling, even if this had not been their original intention, and often they did leave their mark on the built environment of Australia.

A key factor reflected in the poor visibility of Chinese migrants in Australia was that both those who eventually returned to China and those who stayed tended to adopt the architecture of the white majority rather than construct buildings or modify existing buildings in the style of their parent culture, as, for example, Chinese migrants in Southeast Asia often did.[19] This speaks partly to a pragmatic

---

16. Elizabeth Farm museum: https://sydneylivingmuseums.com.au/elizabeth-farm.
17. For a discussion of how this power dynamic affected Aboriginal people in New South Wales, see Denis Byrne, 'Nervous Landscapes: Race and Space in Australia', *Journal of Social Archaeology* 3, no. 2 (2013): 169–93, https://doi.org/10.1177/1469605303003002003.
18. Williams, *Returning Home with Glory*, 74.
19. On Chinese architecture in Southeast Asia, see, for example, David G. Kohl, *Offshore Chinese Architecture: Insights on Five Centuries of Overseas Chinese Building Practices* (Portland, OR: One Spirit, 2018). Post-war European migrants in Australia frequently did build or modify existing houses in their 'own' style but very few

preference to utilise existing building stock but also, I suggest, to an unwillingness to assert their own cultural identity in the built environment of what was very much a 'white Australia'. While this is likely to have applied to other non-white migrants as well, it may have been particularly true of Chinese migrants, who in this period were exposed, albeit unevenly, to anti-Chinese sentiment and outright racist hostility by sections of the white population and media. To risk a somewhat simplistic comparison, one notices that John MacArthur in the 1790s did not hesitate to build a house in Parramatta 'in his own image', which is to say a house whose architecture asserted his identity as an English colonial, whereas the commercially successful Chinese migrant Quong Tart (梅光達, 1850–1903), in 1890 displayed his wealth by commissioning a Victorian-style villa in the Sydney suburb of Ashfield, a building whose architecture was devoid of any Chinese design or decorative elements.[20]

Returning to my point about the heritage record favouring settlement over mobility, it is worth considering briefly how the nature of heritage practice in a sense conspires to render the presence of Chinese migrants invisible in the built environment. There is in Australia and the Western world in general a dominant strain of heritage practice that privileges the original fabric of old buildings over later accretions and modifications. This is seen in restoration projects that aim to 'restore' buildings to a semblance of their material state at the time they were built. In the course of such projects, the material traces of the Chinese occupation of buildings originally constructed by Anglo-Australians in styles favoured by them will likely be erased.

The whole notion of heritage 'restoration' indulges in the myth that it is possible to take a building back in time to its original state, a myth sustained in conventional heritage practice by erasing all trace of the changes a building accumulates through its history of occupation and use. And yet the end product of this can, of course, only ever be some semblance or simulacrum of the original, since even the act of restoration itself inevitably adds to the original building fabric – for example by the application of chemical stabilising agents, the insertion of 'damp courses' in walls, or the repointing of brick or stone walls with new mortar. Restoration is thus always additive as much as it is subtractive (of accretions) and is best thought of as a building practice in its own right.[21] A further reason a building can never be restored to its original condition is that the events of its post-construction life will almost always leave marks on its physical fabric that with all the will in the world cannot be erased. These 'marks' include nail and screw holes in walls and use-wear on

---

such houses have found their way onto official heritage lists; see, for example, Mirjana Lozanovska, *Migrant Housing: Architecture, Dwelling, Migration* (London: Routledge, 2019).

20. For Quong Tart's Ashfield house, see Robert Travers, *Australian Mandarin: The Life and Times of Quong Tart* (Sydney: Kangaroo Press, 1981), 146–47.

21. Denis Byrne, 'Divinely Significant: Towards a Postsecular Approach to the Materiality of Popular Religion in Asia', *International Journal of Heritage Studies* 26, no. 9 (2020): 867, https://doi.org/10.1080/13527258.2019.1 590447.

floorboards and stair surfaces – scars that can only be erased by grinding or planing back the surfaces of walls and floors, leading to a physical diminishment of the original and, hence, to a changed building.

Attempts to restore buildings in this way do, however, testify to an assumption in heritage practice that a building always retains its original identity. Indeed, in most cases where old buildings are listed in heritage inventories, it is on the basis of their original architectural identity. An 1880s terrace house in Surry Hills, for example, is much more likely to be listed and conserved as a 'late-Victorian terrace house' than on the basis of it having been occupied for perhaps half its life by Chinese Australians. Against the grain of conventional heritage practice, one could well argue that such a house is as much an item of Chinese migrant heritage as it is an item of Victorian architectural heritage, or rather that it is a hybrid of both. Implicit in the 'late-Victorian terrace house' heritage classification is a racial identifier – 'Victorian' is equated with people of white Australian heritage. Who or what could be more white, after all, than Queen Victoria? By privileging the architectural character of buildings over their social history, they tend often to be misrecognised as white, or, to put it slightly differently, no matter how much of the social history of a building may have been associated with and intimately entwined with the lives of non-European Australians, in the context of heritage it will *default* to being white.

In summary, migrants from China have had a major presence in Australia since the 1840s, but as non-white mobile subjects in a white settler colony their material presence in the landscape has tended to be subtle rather than monumental. Compounding that, their legacy has been rendered marginal by a heritage system skewed towards settlement over mobility and a heritage classificatory system that privileges architectural character over the social character of buildings. What is needed is a practice of heritage that can rise to the occasion of what migration actually entails and produces.

Ingold's Meshwork and the Landscape of Chinese Migration

In order to better capture the fluidity of Chinese migrant lives and the material dimension of those lives, I draw here on Tim Ingold's meshwork concept.[22] Ingold proposes that we think of human lives as lived along 'lines of becoming' which, like trails, are formed by the histories and trajectories of individual lives. The line or trajectory of an individual human life interweaves and entangles with other such lines to form what Ingold calls a meshwork. He sees the lines and the points at which they meet as representing stories (or storylines) that intertwine.

---

22. Tm Ingold, *Lines: A Brief History* (London: Routledge, 2007); Tim Ingold, *Being Alive: Essays on Movement, Knowledge and Description* (New York: Routledge, 2011); Tim Ingold, 'On Human Correspondence', *Journal of the Royal Anthropological Institute* 23, no. 1 (2017): 9–27, https://doi.org/10.1111/1467-9655.12541.

> The storied world is a world of movement and becoming, in which anything, caught at a particular place and moment, enfolds within its constitution the history of relations that have brought it there. We can only tell the nature of things by attending to their relations, by telling their stories. For the things of the world are their stories, identified by their paths of movement in an unfolding field of relations. Things occur where things meet, occurrences intertwine, as each becomes bound up in the other's story.[23]

In simple terms, any individual life, or 'lifeline', can be thought of as a combination of *lines* inscribed by their movements through space and *knots*, those points at which the lines converge and overlap with those of other people. One of the virtues of the meshwork concept for thinking about Chinese migrant lives in the China–Australia migration corridor is the equal importance it gives to lines and knots. Buildings represent an obvious form of knot – we enter them, meet and socialise with others in them, eat and sleep in them, transact business in them – but these activities are connected with activities we perform elsewhere. Our lives are not contained by buildings; they flow through them. As Ingold puts it, lives unfold 'not inside places but through, to and from them, from and to places elsewhere'.[24] Heritage practice, however, tends to reduce the human past to various kinds of buildings and places (knots in the meshwork) and to deal with them as individual entities with carefully defined boundaries, for example, the actual walls of a building or the boundaries of the parcel of land it sits on. In other words, it treats a building as a closed circle, as against the meshwork's conception of it as an open circle.

As an example of a knot in the meshwork formed by Chinese migrant lifelines in Sydney, we might consider the case of the Kwong War Chong (廣和昌), a building situated in Dixon Street in Sydney's Haymarket (孖結/禧市).[25] Constructed in 1910 by Phillip Lee Chun (李臨春, 1865–1935) using one of the popular styles for commercial architecture in Australia at the time, the ground floor was a general store whose merchandise included food and other goods imported from China but whose business also included acting as a remittance agency for Chinese migrants in Sydney and surrounding rural areas who wished to send money back to their relatives in China. Lee Chun had migrated from Long Du district (隆都) in Zhongshan county in 1875 and most of his remittance clients also hailed from there. The Kwong War Chong served as a social hub for Long Du people, who held meetings on the building's second floor, and it hosted Sunday lunches for Chinese market gardeners, who were able to stay overnight there in dormitory accommodation on the first floor. From this account one can appreciate how the building in Dixon Street can be defined as much in terms of the lifelines that converged in and moved through the building as it can in terms of its architectural character. Rather than thinking of the

---

23. Ingold, *Being Alive*, 159–61.
24. Ingold, *Being Alive*, 148.
25. See Ang and Wong, Chapter 8 of this volume.

building as a central point with lines radiating out from it – for example to Chinese market gardens in Sydney's suburbs and further afield – it should be understood as one among the multitude of 'knots' making up a certain meshwork, included among them the market gardens themselves, the Haymarket produce markets where the market gardeners sold their fruit and vegetables, and the various places/knots where other clients of and visitors to the Kwong War Chong spent time before and after they were there.

The meshwork of Chinese migrant lives in Australia consists not only of the lines and knots representing the complex trajectories of Chinese migrant lives but also the flow of objects and substances associated with those lives, including money, food, horses and trucks, cooking and eating utensils, clothes, books, letters, religious objects, and woodworking and gardening tools. One can imagine, for instance, imported foods such as preserved ginger in ceramic jars flowing into and out of the Kwong War Chong general store. The movement of such objects inscribes lines that do not end at the knot represented by the Dixon Street building; they simply pause there before moving on. As Ingold puts it, 'every line overtakes the knot in which it is tied'.[26] Multiple lines entangle in and at the building, in the way that individual lines of rope or string embrace and circle each other to form a knot before disentangling and moving on. While the individual lines, and the life trajectories of people or objects that formed them, retain their integrity in the meshwork, they are also defined by their relations with other lifelines.

Also flowing through the Kwong War Chong were the banknotes and small amounts of gold brought there by Long Du migrants to be converted into remittance payments that were generally accompanied on their journey back to the home village by letters from the sender.[27] The flow of 'remittance-bearing letters' or *qiaopi* (僑批) inscribed their own lines in a meshwork that was transnational in its extent, and they passed through a series of knots which included the Kwong War Chong & Co.'s offices (or agents' offices) in Hong Kong and Shekki (石岐), Zhongshan's county town, until they came to rest in the hands of the recipient in the migrant's home village. There the remittances often 'congealed' in the form of the new houses they paid for, in that way projecting the sender's agency out across the Zhongshan–Australia migration corridor.[28] This kind of agency is not to be understood to be separate from the imaginative and emotional dimension of a migrant's existence – a new house in the home village might, for example, have originated in the dreams of a market gardener in the suburban landscape of Sydney: waking dreams he entertained as he watered the rows of vegetables which would help finance the house, or dreams which occupied his sleep as he lay in his hut at night. These are dreams – the 'work' of imagination – which project certain futures out through the meshwork.

---

26. Tim Ingold, *Making: Anthropology, Archaeology, Art and Architecture* (London: Routledge, 2013), 132.
27. Williams, *Returning Home with Glory*, 101; Gregor Benton, Hong Liu, and Huimei Zhang, *The Qiaopi Trade and Transnational Networks in the Chinese Diaspora* (London: Routledge, 2021).
28. See Denis Byrne, Chapter 6 of this volume.

The notion of a building such as the Kwong War Chong as being an open rather than a closed circle helps to counter the way buildings are conceptualised in the discourse and practice of heritage, a conceptualisation that has contributed to the low visibility of Chinese migrants in the official heritage record. The meshwork concept is open to the mobility of migrant lives and is amenable to the reality that people's lives are lived as much *between* buildings as in them. It helps weaken the grip of the 'site' as the default unit of analysis in heritage work. Though it still holds sway in the heritage field, the hegemony of the 'site' was critiqued and undermined in the field of archaeology in the 1970s and 1980s by those who saw that the drawing of artificial boundaries around archaeological remains, particularly in the context of archaeological field surveys, came at the cost of severing the connections between the corpus of artefacts found within such boundaries and the artefacts distributed around it. The critique of the site concept at that time saw terms such as 'siteless survey' and 'nonsite archaeology' enter the archaeological lexicon.[29] It marked a shift from a site-centred approach to the human past to a practice of 'landscape archaeology'.[30]

The meshwork representing the Chinese migration experience in Australia between the 1840s and 1940s is not to be seen as an *overlay* inscribed onto Australia's existing natural (non-human) and human landscape but rather as a pattern *meshed into* it. One is mindful, for example, that a large proportion of the Chinese who came to Australia made their living in the course of direct and intimate engagement with the country's physical environment, in activities that included gold mining, bush clearing, shepherding, sugar cane growing, market gardening, and commercial fishing. These variously entailed detailed knowledge of the country's geology, weather patterns, soil properties, and marine environments. As Paul Gilbert has observed of migrants arriving in a new environment, despite their cultural difference to the majority population there they share the same basic human biological and intellectual capacities to become familiar with it.[31]

At the same time, activities such as general store retailing in country towns and the hawking door-to-door of market garden produce brought Chinese migrants into direct everyday contact with white Australians and required knowledge of white society's social conventions. Far from remaining aloof from the cultural

---

29. For 'siteless survey', see Robert C. Dunnell and William S. Dancey, 'The Siteless Survey: A Regional Scale Data Collection Strategy', *Advances in Archaeological Method and Theory* 6 (1983): 267–87. For 'nonsite archaeology', see David H. Thomas, 'Nonsite Sampling in Archaeology: Up the Creek Without a Site?', in *Sampling in Archaeology*, ed. W. J. Meuller (Tucson: University of Arizona Press, 1975), 61–81.

30. For a history of landscape archaeology, see Bruno David and Julian Thomas, 'Landscape Archaeology: Introduction', in *Handbook of Landscape Archaeology*, ed. Bruno David and Julian Thomas (London: Routledge, 2008), 27–43.

31. Paul Gilbert, 'Ancient Places, New Arrivals and the Ethics of Residence', in *Cultural Heritage, Ethics and Contemporary Migrations*, ed. Cornelius Holtorf, Andreas Pantazatos, and Geoffrey Scarre (London: Routledge, 2019), 31–32.

and technological environment they found themselves in, many Chinese migrants actively immersed themselves in it. They were, according to John Fitzgerald,

> among the first Australians to embrace modern technologies and take up modishly modern lifestyles. In the 1890s they rode the latest bicycles, in the 1900s they wore sober business suits and flounced dresses, in the 1910s they picnicked by the seaside, in the 1920s they ran radio repair shops and in wartime they flew Australian flags. Chinese Australians probably travelled more frequently than whites and they discovered in their travels that Australia was one of the very few countries where all of the technological and ethical promises of modernity were on offer.[32]

Many Chinese migrants in Australia, in what Shirley Lim describes as an enactment of 'cultural citizenship', played tennis, attended debutante balls, and had their photos taken in front of the late-model cars and trucks they owned.[33]

The 'landscape' of Chinese migration was also, importantly, a seascape. Chinese migrants spent significant periods of time on the sea route between Hong Kong and Australia, at first on sailing ships and from the late nineteenth century on steamships. Rarely were these trips one-way; migrants either returned to China after a stay in Australia or settled there but made visits back to the homeland, sometimes on a frequent basis. An indication of the extent of return travel is given by Michael Williams's calculation that although nearly 22,000 Chinese arrived in New South Wales from China between 1881 and 1891, the Chinese population there over this period increased by fewer than 3,000, to a total of 13,157.[34] In respect to the seascape of Chinese migration, it is also worth noting that the increasingly large ships that plied the Hong Kong–Australia sea route were connected at either end of the route to local networks of water travel. In the waterworld of the Pearl River Delta, junks ferried returning migrants from the port of Hong Kong to Zhongshan county and sampans then took them up rivers and the maze of creeks to their ancestral villages. At the Australian end of the migration corridor, Chinese migrants were frequent passengers on the coastal shipping that linked the country's ports and coastal towns. In some places, including northern Queensland, they also built boats of their own: junks and sampans they used for river transport and ocean-going junks for the trade they engaged in between the far-north Queensland coast and New Guinea.[35] None of these craft are known to have survived and even the memory of them barely persists.

---

32. Fitzgerald, *Big White Lie*, 29.
33. Shirley Jennifer Lim, 'Glamorising Racial Modernity', in *Australia's Asia: From Yellow Peril to Asian Century*, ed. David Walker and Agnieszka Sobocinska (Perth: University of Western Australia Publishing, 2012), 162.
34. Williams, *Returning Home with Glory*, 44.
35. Stephen Gapps, 'Made in Australia: Chinese Junks and Sampans in North Queensland 1880s–1910', *Signals* 118 (March 2017): 30–33; see also Stephen Gapps, 'Chinese-Australian Junks and Sampans', http://www.sea.museum/2014/02/27/australian-chinese-junks-and-sampans.

A Closer Look at the Chinese Migrant Meshwork

In the following pages I will bring into closer focus the lifelines of two individual Chinese migrants, Stanley Hunt (birth name 陳沛德 Chan Pui-Tak), who arrived in Australia in 1939, and Jang Tim (鄭添), who arrived fifty years earlier, in 1898. The information on Stanley Hunt's migration experience and subsequent life comes from an interview conducted with him in Sydney in 2017 and from his autobiography, *From Shekki to Sydney*, published in 2009.[36] In the case of Jang Tim, who died in Queensland in 1952 and was buried in an unmarked grave, it has been possible to give an account of his life only because his Zhongshan-based granddaughter, Zheng Si-Hang (鄭思航), set out to discover the location of his grave and, by travelling to Australia in 2008 and 2015, sought to piece together something of his life there.

Stanley Hunt

Stanley Hunt was born in Zhongshan in 1927 and migrated to Australia in 1939 with his mother and two younger siblings, fleeing the Japanese who had invaded Guangdong the year before. In Australia they joined Stanley's father who had been there for some years, and who at the time of their arrival was operating a general store at Warialda, a small town in northern New South Wales, population 1,025.

Stanley adapted well to life in Warialda. He barely knew the English alphabet when he first arrived, but he learnt English quickly with the help of one of the nuns from the Warialda Catholic school who tutored him after school hours. Apart from running a store, Stanley's family also bought a market garden in Warialda from an old Chinese man who had become ill. Stanley was sixteen years old at that time. He delivered groceries around Warialda on a bicycle and drove the family's horse and cart around the neighbouring country towns selling vegetables from the market garden. From his book, *Shekki to Sydney*, one gets the impression of someone who, although still young, had already experienced life in bustling Shekki (石岐, Shiqi, the county town of Zhongshan county) and briefly in Hong Kong and was now open to what the Northern Tablelands of New South Wales had to offer.

Using the meshwork metaphor, his life in and around Warialda inscribed quite an extensive pattern of lines woven around a few key 'knots', which included the family's shop, adjacent house, and the market garden. It is important to notice that these lines embody a significant element of repetition. We can assume, for example, that his grocery deliveries took the form of bicycle runs along much the same pattern of streets and country roads day after day or week after week. While it may seem to us that it is through acts of exploration that a new place – a new country, city, or neighbourhood – becomes known to us, it is through repetition that places become familiar at a corporeal level. And oddly, while the repetitive retracing of our steps

---

36. Stanley Hunt, *From Shekki to Sydney* (Sydney: Wild Peony, 2009).

along customary paths makes places familiar to us in a cerebral and embodied way, it can also make them disappear through familiarity.[37] Which is to say we become so close to certain places and routes that we can, so to speak, no longer see them. Yet it is also via repetition and embodied memory that we become attached to certain objects, places, and lines of movement. The familiar staircase to an apartment may become invisible through repeated use but our body 'knows' it in intimate detail; it knows all the moves – our feet are aware of the precise rise of the stairs, and

Figure 2.1: Stanley Hunt (陳沛德) (left) and his brother Desmond (right) standing on the running board of Stanley's truck, Sydney, 1950s. Photo courtesy of Mabel Lee.

---

37. Ahmed writes that 'the labor of . . . repetition disappears through labor: if we work hard at something, then it seems "effortless"'. Sara Ahmed, 'Orientations: Toward a Queer Phenomenology', *GLQ: A Journal of Lesbian and Gay Studies* 12, no. 4 (2006): 553.

our hand finds the balustrade, knowing it is there, without us having to look.[38] It is, I would argue, via repetitive behaviour in such mundane settings as this that a migrant becomes attached to the landscape of their destination country. It is thus that they come to have a history with it and it comes to have a history with them.

By 1945 Stanley had six siblings and it was then that his parents decided to move from Warialda to Sydney. Once there they bought a fruit and vegetable shop in Merrylands in the city's western suburbs and the family of nine moved into the three-bedroom flat above the shop. The business did so well that after a year they acquired another such shop, in the nearby suburb of Auburn, which was given over to Stanley to run. He quickly built the business up to the point that he was employing twenty-eight people, Chinese and Anglo-Australian, to help run it. He married Valmai Tuck-Lee in 1948 and together they had four children. A new meshwork of lines and knots developed around Stanley's life in Sydney. There is a black-and-white photograph of him and his brother standing on the running board of a 1950s truck piled high with crates of vegetables they have brought back from the produce markets in the Haymarket for their shops in Merrylands and Auburn (Figure 2.1).[39] The image is a pointer to the fact that Stanley's life at this time involved routine travel along a thirty-kilometre 'line' between the suburbs of western Sydney and the Haymarket.

Stanley Hunt's first visit back to Zhongshan since leaving there in 1939 did not take place until 1979, immediately after the 1978 'opening' of China that followed on from Mao's death in 1976. On this occasion, Stanley and Valmai were on a group tour and were unable to visit his ancestral village, Mashan (馬山), situated on the eastern edge of the delta of the Tan River (譚江), to the southwest of Zhongshan (in present-day Doumen district (斗門區) of Zhuhai), but he did so on a trip he made the following year with Valmai and his father. He recalls that while strolling around the edge of the village he came upon a boy tending pigs and ducks and he asked him why he was not at school. 'I said to him, "How come? Chairman Mao said no child will go without school." He said, "We don't have any classroom." So I decided to build a school for them.'[40] The two-storey classroom block of the new school opened in 1983 and was named the Sung-Sun Hall of Learning (崇信教學樓) after Stanley's father (Figure 2.2). From 1979 almost until his death in July 2019, Stanley visited Mashan every year, overseeing a series of additions to the school that he and his siblings funded: a school library that was opened in 1985, named after their mother, and later a sealed running track and a residential block for teachers.

Mashan School has since been absorbed into China's public school system, but the contribution of Stanley and his family is commemorated on a plaque in one of the 1980s buildings and their philanthropy continues to be applauded by

---

38. Denis Byrne, 'Love and Loss in the 1960s', *International Journal of Heritage Studies* 19, no. 6 (2013): 602, https://doi.org/10.1080/13527258.2012.686446.

39. See https://www.heritagecorridor.org.au/people/stanley-hunt.

40. Interview with Stanley Hunt, October 2017, Sydney.

Figure 2.2: The 1983 classroom block at Mashan school (馬山小學), built by Stanley Hunt (陳沛德). This 2017 photograph shows the exterior as renovated in the 2000s. Photo by Denis Byrne 2017.

Figure 2.3: A detail of the ceramic tile map at Mashan school showing sea routes taken by Chinese migrants. The map is visible in Figure 2.2 behind the three flagpoles on the left. Photo by Denis Byrne 2017.

the teachers and students. A paperbark tree planted in front of the 1983 classroom block, pointed out to us during a visit to the school in late 2017, commemorates the school's connection to Australia.[41] Overlooking the running track there is a large ceramic-tile mural depicting a map of the world upon which numerous dashed lines originating in southern China represent the routes taken by Chinese migrants across the oceans to ports in Southeast Asia, Australia, and the Americas (Figure 2.3).[42] The long, curved line on the map that, swerving around the Philippines and then New Guinea, reaches from the Pearl River Delta down to the port of Sydney represents a key trajectory in Stanley Hunt's own lifeline, one first inscribed by his 1939 voyage to Sydney and then, after a forty-year hiatus, retraced annually until the time of his death. The line also speaks to the way the migrant heritage of Australia is woven into that of China.[43] The school buildings erected by Stanley in Mashan in the 1980s are elements of southern China's educational heritage, but this is a heritage that 'belongs' equally to Australia. More accurately, and to avoid the nationalism that flavours so much of heritage discourse, the buildings occupy the space of a transnational meshwork that, courtesy of a history of migration, incorporates both countries.

Ingold points out that lines in the meshwork have a genealogical dimension – they extend through time and are given substance, for example, by the filial ties that bind parents and their children.[44] We are reminded here that the meshwork is three-dimensional, something that makes it especially useful for conceptualising the heritage of migration. Stanley Hunt, in naming the classroom block of the Mashan School for his father and the adjacent library for his mother, was ensuring that the school would have this temporal dimension. His vision was, however, very much future oriented. His first visit to his ancestral village triggered a futuring project rather than a restoration one. He showed no interest in restoring his small ancestral house in Mashan village, which had fallen into ruin, its interior colonised by weeds after the roof fell in. Instead, he built a new house for his father's sister who had remained in the village and then directed his money and energy to the education of Mashan's new generation.

After the 1980s Stanley continued to fund maintenance work, renovations, and new equipment for Mashan School, but despite his efforts to keep it up to date, his 1983 classroom block was demolished in 2020 after it was found not to comply with new national standards for earthquake resistance. It was replaced by a larger classroom block paid for by the government, but his 1985 library building remains. It is characteristic of meshworks that they reconfigure over time; lines end when people

---

41. Ien Ang, Denis Byrne, Christopher Cheng, Michael Williams, and Alexandra Wong visited the school during fieldwork in the Zhongshan area in December 2017.
42. Similar maps are present at some of the village schools in Zhongshan that were founded or supported by diaspora funding, including the 1920s school in Caobian village (see Cheng and Mar, Chapter 7 of this volume).
43. Byrne, 'Heritage Corridors'.
44. Ingold, 'On Human Correspondence', 13–14, 22.

die and gaps appear where buildings are demolished or disintegrate. The fate of Stanley's classroom block is representative of what has happened to many thousands of buildings that were erected in China in the Reform Era (beginning 1978), only to be abandoned and demolished a few decades later, having been deemed obsolete, dangerous, or simply unfashionable. This has led to the lifespan of buildings in China measuring only thirty-five years on average and commonly only twenty years, well under half the building turnover rate of the United States and Europe.[45] When interviewed in 2017, Stanley, however, gave no indication of being dismayed by the ephemerality of his classroom block. Loss, in this respect, can be a diminishment but can equally be 'generative and emancipatory'.[46] The classroom block will be replaced by a building better aligned to contemporary needs, but Stanley's legacy, I suggest, never resided in the school as a material thing. Rather it lies in the learning acquired by the schools' students and how that learning has rippled through their future and the future of Mashan.[47]

Zheng Si-Hang and Jang Tim

Returning to the temporal dimension of migration heritage, viewed as a meshwork, the threads giving depth to the meshwork include those woven by descendant generations of migrants who visit their ancestral country in the context of what has been termed 'roots tourism'.[48] These threads are sutured, in a sense, to the transnational lines of movement of forebears. A counterpart of roots tourism, though it probably occurs on a much smaller scale, are the journeys that Chinese citizens undertake to the countries their forebears migrated to, hoping to find out something of their lives there and visit places they had frequented. To illustrate this phenomenon I turn now to the case of Zheng Si-Hang (鄭思航) and her quest to discover the location of the grave of her paternal grandfather, Jang Tim (鄭添), who had migrated to Queensland in 1898.

Jang Tim's destination had been Cooktown in tropical north Queensland but upon his arrival he found the gold rush that had begun there in 1873 was already over. He chose to move south to Gordonvale, a small town about 28 kilometres south of Cairns, still in far-north Queensland, where he took up market gardening, growing potatoes, beans, lettuce, and other vegetables. He lived in a shed-like structure in the garden and sold his produce around the streets of Gordonvale from his

---

45. 'How Will a Slowing China Cope with Rapidly Aging Buildings', *China Economic Review*, 28 June 2013, https://chinaeconomicreview.com/unstable-foundations-part-2/.
46. Caitlin DeSilvey and Rodney Harrison, 'Anticipating Loss: Rethinking Endangerment in Heritage Futures', *Journal of Critical Heritage Studies* 26, no. 1 (2020): 3, https://doi.org/10.1080/13527258.2019.1644530.
47. For a discussion of the fate of diaspora-funded schools in China, see Christopher Cheng, 'Beacons of Modern Learning: Diaspora-Funded Schools in the China–Australia Corridor', *Asian and Pacific Migration Journal* 29, no. 2 (2020): 139–62, https://doi.org/10.1177/0117196820930309.
48. See Alexandra Wong, Chapter 4 of this volume. See also Naho Maruyama and Amanda Stronza, 'Roots Tourism of Chinese Americans', *Ethnology* 49, no. 1 (2010): 23–44.

horse and dray.[49] Eventually he made enough money to own a greengrocer shop in town but he lost it during the 1930s Depression, after which he lived on his market garden. On a visit home to Zhongshan in 1911 when he was thirty years old, Jang Tim married a woman from the Low clan (劉信英) and the following year their first daughter was born. He fathered a child on each of his following visits to Zhongshan: his second daughter, born in 1926, and his son, born in 1928. He made his final visit home in 1932. On that occasion he had wanted his only son to accompany him back to Australia, but the boy had not wanted to leave his mother. He continued sending money back to Zhongshan from Queensland, remitting a large sum in 1951 which his son collected in Hong Kong.[50] Jang Tim died on 25 May 1952 at Cairns Base Hospital at the age of seventy-one, after a long period of illness, and was buried in a Cairns cemetery in an unmarked grave. It had been twenty years since he had last seen his family in Pong Tau village (龐頭村), reminding us how tenuous the lines connecting Chinese migrants with their homeland could be in that era.

In 2008, Zheng Si-Hang set off for Australia with her husband in the hope of fulfilling her father's wish that Jang Tim's grave be located. They failed to find any trace of Jang Tim on that visit but returned in 2015 when, with the aid of members of the local Chinese community in Cairns, they found the site of his market garden and the location of the building that housed his former grocery shop. With the help of the Chinese community members, they also located his unmarked grave, installed a temporary plastic plaque on it containing a hand-carved epitaph in Chinese characters, and offered incense and prayers to Jang Tim's spirit. In 2022, Chinese community members made offerings to Jang Tim's spirit at the grave as part of a Ching Ming event they held at the cemetery.[51]

For Zheng Si-Hang, it was not enough to know her grandfather had a life in Australia; she wanted to visit the actual landscape of his life there and to find his final resting place. Like thousands of migrant descendants globally, she was engaged in the kind of heritage-making project in which 'being there' is crucial. What makes her journey different to those of most migrant descendants is that it moved in the opposite direction to theirs; it is a journey *out* along the migration corridor rather than a journey back to the ancestral land.

When interviewed in December 2017 at the house her grandfather had built in Pong Tau village, Zheng Si-Hang spoke with emotion of the sacrifices her grandfather had made for his family and how sad it made her feel that he had died alone so far from home. Ingold stresses that the lines formed in a meshwork by the movements of people within it are not be be abstracted as mere lines on a map. The lines are constituted by living, breathing people; to Ingold, 'the lines *are* living

---

49. Lai Chu Chan, 'Jang Tim: Father, Grandfather, Greengrocer' (unpublished paper, Cairns and District Chinese Association Inc, 2015), 16.
50. Chan, 'Jang Tim', 16.
51. Personal communication from Christopher Cheng.

people'.[52] The lines formed by kinship are, he says, 'lines of affect or sentiment'.[53] At one point during our interview with Zheng Si-Hang she showed us a carton of jumbled-together woodworking tools which her grandfather had brought back from Australia and which he may have used to work on the house in Pong Tau. They included two wood planes manufactured by Tertius Keen and Co. of Glascow, an Australian-made Eureka brand cold chisel, wooden-handled files, and a bit-braced hand drill (Figure 2.4).[54] The metal components of the tools were covered with a thin patina of rust but were otherwise quite serviceable. The way Zheng Si-Hang spoke about these objects and her care for them indicated that for her they were more than inert compositions of wood and steel. They were, in Sara Ahmed's terms, objects that had become 'sticky' with affect.[55] According to Ahmed, what an object 'picks up on its surface "shows" where it has travelled and what it has come into contact with'.[56] Jang Tim had held and worked with these tools and it seemed that for Si-Hang they were still imbued with his presence. They had, I suggest, the kind of capacity to trigger an immediate and preconscious response in Zheng Si-Hang

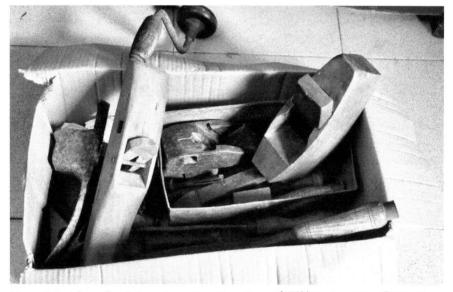

Figure 2.4: A box of tools brought to Pong Tau village (寵頭村) by Jang Tim (鄭添). Photo by Denis Byrne 2018.

---

52. Ingold, 'On Human Correspondence', 22.
53. Ingold, 'On Human Correspondence', 22.
54. On his visits home, Jang Tim had carried with him camphorwood chests packed with objects that included Akubra brand hats (commonly worn by Australian farmers), oil lamps, and tools; see Chan, 'Jang Tim', 16.
55. Sara Ahmed, 'Happy Objects', in *The Affect Reader*, ed. Melissa Gregg and Gregory J. Seigworth (Durham, NC: Duke University Press, 2010), 35.
56. Sara Ahmed, *Queer Phenomenology: Orientations, Objects, Others* (Durham, NC: Duke University Press, 2006), 40.

that scholars of affect have theorised.[57] We can only suppose that migrant worlds are teeming with things laden with such capacities. This is something heritage practitioners and heritage scholars, in particular, need to be mindful of in the interests of endeavouring to be true to the lives of past others. The alternative is that things become hollowed-out vestiges.

Concluding Thoughts

This chapter has sought to close the distance between the surviving material traces of Chinese migrant lives in the China–Australia migration corridor and the animated reality of those lives. This 'closure' is also implicitly an objective of the journeys that migrant descendants such as Zheng Si-Hang embark on to discover traces of their ancestors. There is a sense that in doing so they are countering the failure of official heritage practices to afford the kind of visibility to migrant heritage sites that they have given, in the case of Australia, to the material remains left by white settlers. The low visibility of much of the Chinese migrant experience in Australia is due partly, I have argued, to the degree of mobility in the lives of many or most of these migrants, but this is not enough to explain the scarcity of the remains of Chinese migration in Australia's official heritage inventories. While it is, for example, true that no trace survives of the hut that Zheng Si-Hang's grandfather erected on his market garden outside the town of Gordonvale, Queensland, except perhaps at an archaeological level, the shop he owned in the town during his prosperous years still stands. The problem is that his association with the shop went unremarked until, responding to a request from Si-Hang to find traces of her grandfather, a group of Zhongshan descendants from Cairns were shown an early cadastral map at the Gordonvale Settlers' Museum which indicated the shop's location. By tracking down the location of Jang Tim's unmarked grave, and marking it with a temporary plastic plaque, Si-Hang and her husband thus lifted it, too, from the realm of the invisible and 'underground' into the light of day, lending it presence in the contemporary landscape.

This is not to maintain that all sites of Chinese migrant heritage should be marked and preserved or that this is what all migrant descendants necessarily desire. It is worth mentioning that the house Jang Tim built for his family in Pong Tau village was not preserved by his descendants, at least not in the conventional sense. It was literally encased within a new house built in the 1980s or 1990s with the money the family earned as small-scale entrepreneurs at a time when Mao's successor, Deng Xiaoping, is reputed to have pronounced that 'to get rich is glorious'.[58] The new and larger house with its ferro-concrete balcony and its surfacing of

---

57. Melissa Gregg and Gregory J. Seigworth, eds., *The Affect Reader* (Durham, NC: Duke University Press, 2010).
58. While there is dispute over whether Deng ever actually said this, there is no question that his Reform Era policies, beginning in 1978, favoured individuals and collectives initiating capitalist-style enterprises.

colourful mosaic tiles – the fashion of the times – is as much a material statement of the success of Jang Tim's descendants as the remittance houses of the early twentieth century in the same village were statements of the new wealth and aspirant social status of migrant families of that era. Zheng Si-Hang made it clear that she regarded her grandfather's legacy as residing in the relative affluence of his descendants, much as Stanley Hunt saw his legacy not in terms of the school he built but in the generation of children the school gave an education to.

Some migrant descendants do express a desire for the heritage of their migrant forebears to be preserved, and we should also consider the value of this heritage to a country such as Australia as a whole. Australia's official heritage record offers a lamentably poor representation of the country's history of migration and this amounts to more than an unfortunate lapse; it supports a warped version of the nation's narrative.

Bibliography

Ahmed, Sara. 'Orientations: Toward a Queer Phenomenology'. *GLQ: A Journal of Lesbian and Gay Studies* 12, no. 4 (2006): 543–74.

Ahmed, Sara. *Queer Phenomenology: Orientations, Objects, Others*. Durham, NC: Duke University Press, 2006.

Ahmed, Sara. 'Happy Objects'. In *The Affect Reader*, edited by Melissa Gregg and Gregory J. Seigworth, 29–51. Durham, NC: Duke University Press, 2010.

Bagnall, Kate, and Julia T. Martinez, eds. *Locating Chinese Women: Historical Mobility between China and Australia*. Hong Kong: Hong Kong University Press, 2021.

Benton, Gregor, Hong Liu, and Huimei Zhang. *The Qiaopi Trade and Transnational Networks in the Chinese Diaspora*. London: Routledge, 2021.

Byrne, Denis. 'Nervous Landscapes: Race and Space in Australia'. *Journal of Social Archaeology* 3, no. 2 (2003): 169–93. https://doi.org/10.1177/1469605303003002003.

Byrne, Denis. 'Love and Loss in the 1960s'. *International Journal of Heritage Studies* 19, no. 6 (2013): 596–609. https://doi.org/10.1080/13527258.2012.686446.

Byrne, Denis. 'Heritage Corridors: Transnational Flows and the Built Environment of Migration'. *Journal of Ethnic and Migration Studies* 42, no. 14 (2016): 2360–78.

Byrne, Denis. 'Divinely Significant: Towards a Postsecular Approach to the Materiality of Popular Religion in Asia'. *International Journal of Heritage Studies* 26, no. 9 (2020): 857–73. https://doi.org/10.1080/13527258.2019.1590447.

Chan, Lai Chu. 'Jang Tim: Father, Grandfather, Greengrocer'. Unpublished paper, Cairns and District Chinese Association Inc., 2015.

Chan, Shelley. *Diaspora's Homeland: Modern China in the Age of Global Migration*. Durham, NC: Duke University Press, 2018.

Cheng, Christopher. 'Beacons of Modern Learning: Diaspora-Funded Schools in the China–Australia Corridor'. *Asian and Pacific Migration Journal* 29, no. 2 (2020): 139–62. https://doi.org/10.1177/0117196820930309.

Couchman, Sophie, and Kate Bagnall. 'Memory and Meaning in the Search for Australian-Chinese Families'. In *Remembering Migration: Oral Histories and Heritage in Australia*, edited by Kate Darian-Smith and Paula Hamilton, 331–46. London: Palgrave Macmillan, 2019.

David, Bruno, and Julian Thomas. 'Landscape Archaeology: Introduction'. In *Handbook of Landscape Archaeology*, edited by Bruno David and Julian Thomas, 27–43. London: Routledge, 2008.

DeSilvey, Caitlin, and Rodney Harrison. 'Anticipating Loss: Rethinking Endangerment in Heritage Futures'. *Journal of Critical Heritage Studies* 26, no. 1 (2020): 1–7. https://doi.org/10.1080/13527258.2019.1644530.

Dunnell, Robert C., and William S. Dancey. 'The Siteless Survey: A Regional Scale Data Collection Strategy'. *Advances in Archaeological Method and Theory* 6 (1983): 267–87.

Fitzgerald, John. *Big White Lie: Chinese Australians in White Australia*. Sydney: UNSW Press, 2007.

Forsyth, Hannah, and Sophie Loy-Wilson. 'Seeking a New Materialism in Australian History'. *Australian Historical Studies* 48, no. 2 (2017): 169–88. https://doi.org/10.1080/1031461X.2017.1298635.

Gapps, Stephen. 'Made in Australia: Chinese Junks and Sampans in North Queensland 1880s–1910'. *Signals* 118 (March 2017): 30–33.

Gilbert, Paul. 'Ancient Places, New Arrivals and the Ethics of Residence'. In *Cultural Heritage, Ethics and Contemporary Migrations*, edited by Cornelius Holtorf, Andreas Pantazatos, and Geoffrey Scarre, 27–38. London: Routledge, 2019.

Gregg, Melissa, and Gregory J. Seigworth, eds. *The Affect Reader*. Durham, NC: Duke University Press, 2010.

Hunt, Stanley. *From Shekki to Sydney*. Sydney: Wild Peony, 2009.

Ingold, Tim. *Lines: A Brief History*. London: Routledge, 2007.

Ingold, Tim. *Being Alive: Essays on Movement, Knowledge and Description*. New York: Routledge, 2011.

Ingold, Tim. *Making: Anthropology, Archaeology, Art and Architecture*. London: Routledge, 2013.

Ingold, Tim. 'On Human Correspondence'. *Journal of the Royal Anthropological Institute* 23, no. 1 (2017): 9–27. https://doi.org/10.1111/1467-9655.12541.

Kohl, David G. *Offshore Chinese Architecture: Insights on Five Centuries of Overseas Chinese Building Practices*. Portland, OR: One Spirit, 2018.

Lim, Shirley Jennifer. 'Glamorising Racial Modernity'. In *Australia's Asia: From Yellow Peril to Asian Century*, edited by David Walker and Agnieszka Sobocinska, 145–69. Perth: University of Western Australia Publishing, 2012.

Loy-Wilson, Sophie. *Australian in Shanghai: Race, Rights and Nation in Treat Port China*. London: Routledge, 2017.

Lozanovska, Mirjana. *Migrant Housing: Architecture, Dwelling, Migration*. London: Routledge, 2019.

Maruyama, Naho, and Amanda Stronza. 'Roots Tourism of Chinese Americans'. *Ethnology* 49, no. 1 (2010): 23–44.

Roberts, Rosie. *Ongoing Mobility Trajectories: Lived Experiences of Global Migration*. Singapore: Springer, 2019.

Sandall, David P. 'Where Mourning Takes Them: Migrants, Borders, and an Alternative Reality'. *Ethos* 38, no. 2 (2010): 179–204.

Sheller, Mimi, and John Urry. 'The New Mobility Paradigm'. *Environment and Planning A* 38, no. 2 (2006): 207–26. https://doi.org/10.1068/a37268.

Smith, Lindsay. 'Identifying Chinese Ethnicity through Material Culture: Archaeological Excavations at Kiandra, NSW'. *Australasian Historical Archaeology* 21 (2003): 18–29.

Thomas, David H. 'Nonsite Sampling in Archaeology: Up the Creek without a Site?' In *Sampling in Archaeology*, edited by W. J. Meuller, 61–81. Tucson: University of Arizona Press, 1975.

Travers, Robert. *Australian Mandarin: The Life and Times of Quong Tart*. Sydney: Kangaroo Press, 1981.

Walker, David, and Agnieszka Sobocinska, eds. *Australia's Asia: From Yellow Peril to Asian Century*. Perth: University of Western Australia Press, 2012.

Williams, Michael. 'Chinese Settlement in New South Wales: A Thematic History'. NSW Heritage Office, September 1999. https://www.heritage.nsw.gov.au/assets/Uploads/a-z-publications/a-c/chinesehistory.pdf.

Williams, Michael. *Returning Home with Glory: Chinese Villagers Around the Pacific, 1849 to 1949*. Hong Kong: Hong Kong University Press, 2018.

3

(Un)making Transnational Identities

Migration and Chineseness

Ien Ang

This chapter puts the China–Australia heritage corridor in the broader context of understandings of the Chinese diaspora and the diasporic identities of Australian Chinese migrants and their descendants. Migration is inexorably a disruptive experience that generates split connections between home and host countries. Most migrants are faced with the life-long challenge of figuring out where they belong and who they are as a consequence of their experience of displacement. For generations of Chinese migrants in Australia, this experience of displacement was exacerbated by the pervasive racial discrimination they faced in the country, marginalising them from dominant white society and problematising their sense of belonging and identity as 'Australian' (澳洲人). At the same time, whenever they returned to China – which, as discussed throughout this book, until the Second World War was a regular undertaking for many migrants – their sense of place in their home villages would have been deeply altered by their experience overseas, dislocating their given sense of being a 'Chinese' person. As a result, migrants tend to have unsettled identities, fully belonging in neither country and disposed to embracing multiple attachments beyond fixed national boundaries. Descendants of migrants, who tend to be much more settled in the new country, nevertheless inherit a sensitivity to such flexible identifications spurred by the memory of their ancestors' experience of transnational migration. Our interviews with Zhongshan migrants and their descendants testify to this lived transnationalism, which is expressed in a desire to rediscover and reconnect with the family's Chinese past, including physical return visits to the ancestral village.

Transnational mobility, then, is central to the experience of migrants and, hence, to their transgressive, boundary-blurring, hybrid sense of identity.[1] But, as I will highlight in this chapter, this fluid hybridity is delimited by the imposition of essentialising understandings of 'Chineseness', both by white society and

---

1. For the concept of hybridity, see Ien Ang, 'Together-in-Difference: Beyond Diaspora, Into Hybridity', *Asian Studies Review* 27, no. 2 (2003): 141–54, https://doi.org/10.1080/10357820308713372.

through China-based efforts to rally dispersed diaspora populations under the wing of the national homeland. Thus, the Chinese state has exhibited a long history of projects to call upon Chinese diasporic subjects – generally called the 'overseas Chinese'[2] – to serve the motherland by imposing a reified, nation-centric meaning of 'Chineseness'.

It is clear, however, that what is loosely called the 'Chinese diaspora' is by no means a homogeneous entity. On the contrary, diasporic Chinese are a very heterogeneous, widely dispersed group of people, differentiated by very different histories of migration, generational differences, countries of destination, and so on. What this book calls the China–Australia heritage corridor has taken shape mainly through the transnational connections sustained by Chinese migrants to Australia in the first half of the twentieth century. As this chapter will show, following China's opening up in 1978 under Deng Xiaoping, the People's Republic of China (PRC) made concerted efforts to re-engage with these older migrant generations, as well as their descendants, and to repair the virtual disconnect between diaspora and homeland that took place between 1949 and 1978, the first three decades of the PRC. These were turbulent years, when the newly established Communist nation-state was effectively isolated from the West in the context of the Cold War and when society was massively disrupted by Mao Zedong's fervent political radicalism, with major implications not only for the Chinese overseas, including those in Australia, but also for their families in China. As I will discuss below, these difficult historical experiences have deeply impacted our informants' sense of identity and particularly their complex relationship with 'Chineseness'.

As several chapters of this book will show, since 1978 migrants and their descendants have been able to return to their ancestral villages in China, and many have shown an appetite to do so. In this sense, these people have exhibited a desire to rediscover their Chinese heritage. However, it is important not to conflate this embrace of ethnic Chineseness with political support for the PRC, or with a wholesale identification of China as the motherland. Drawing on interviews with four of our informants, this chapter will illuminate how Zhongshan migrants and their descendants in Australia show a wide range of experiences and identifications in relation to China, which by no means align with reductionist understandings of diaspora as a return to 'roots'.[3] Moreover, even though most of them now call

---

2. The term 'overseas Chinese', while commonly used, is contested, as it is associated with a Sinocentric understanding of Chinese migrants' identities, related to the Chinese term (pronounced in Mandarin) *huaqiao* 華僑 (see note 10). Some authors therefore prefer to use the term 'Chinese overseas', 'ethnic Chinese', or 'diasporic Chinese' to refer to people of Chinese descent who live outside China and are not citizens of China (華人, *huaren* in Mandarin). In this chapter, I will use these terms interchangeably. See, for example, Tan Chee-Beng, *Chinese Overseas: Comparative Cultural Issues* (Hong Kong: Hong Kong University Press, 2004), 1–2.

3. For scholarly critiques of the notion of diaspora as a return to 'roots', see Paul Gilroy, *The Black Atlantic: Modernity and Double Consciousness* (London: Verso, 1993); James Clifford, *Routes: Travel and Translation in the Late Twentieth Century* (Cambridge, MA: Harvard University Press, 1997); Ien Ang, *On Not Speaking Chinese: Living Between Asia and the West* (London: Routledge, 2001).

Australia 'home', they also – by virtue of their Chinese heritage – retain a minoritarian sense of 'Australianness', living in a country where Chineseness has long been, and in many ways continues to be, associated with otherness. As illustrated by the life trajectories of our four interviewees, being Chinese in Australia comprises evolving identities whose formations are shaped by a complex entanglement of personal and familial circumstances with grander historical developments in China, Australia, and globally.[4] The chapter will conclude with some thoughts on the implications of these identity issues for our conception of transnational heritage in relation to the cross-border dynamic between China and Australia.

Before the Communists: Becoming 'Chinese' in White Australia

The transnational zone of flows and linkages which we have called the China–Australia migration corridor has generated a dynamic legacy built up by Chinese migrants who, upon coming to Australia, continued to maintain diasporic connections with their homeland – through letters and remittances as well as regular physical returns – to support their families left behind in their ancestral villages and hometowns. In the first hundred years since the mid-nineteenth century, there were mostly in the Pearl River Delta, particularly Zhongshan county. Michael Williams insists on the importance of not relying too heavily on nation-state concepts to understand what mattered most for these migrants: the family, the home villages, the *qiaoxiang* (僑鄉, pronounced in Mandarin).[5] This localism is underscored by the myriad, often mutually exclusive dialects spoken in different Pearl River Delta villages, which led to the creation of multiple native-place associations (同鄉會, *tongxiang hui* in Mandarin) among early Chinese migrants in Australia at the end of the nineteenth century, as was the case in other destination sites where Chinese migrants set down, such as in Southeast Asia and North America.[6] In other words, their principal identifications and affections were familial and local rather than national. As Philip Kuhn has noted, among these early migrants, community belonging based on dialect, kinship and native place took precedence over the emergence of a national or pan-ethnic 'Chinese' identity.[7]

---

4. All interviewees featured in this chapter are men. This does not mean that women's stories are not relevant, but simply that the stories of these four men most vividly represent the narrative argument developed in this chapter. For an account on the difficulty of making visible women's lives in the history of Chinese migration, see, for example, Kate Bagnall, 'Chinese Women in Colonial New South Wales: From Absence to Presence', *Australian Journal of Biography and History* 3 (2020): 3–20, http://doi.org/10.22459/AJBH.2020.
5. Michael Williams, *Returning Home with Glory: Chinese Villagers around the Pacific, 1849 to 1949* (Hong Kong: Hong Kong University Press, 2018), 2.
6. Mei-fen Kuo, *Making Chinese Australia: Urban Elites, Newspapers and the Formation of Chinese-Australian Identity, 1892–1912* (Clayton, Victoria: Monash University Publishing, 2013), 18.
7. Philip A. Kuhn, *Chinese among Others: Emigration in Modern Times* (Lanham, MD: Rowman and Littlefield Publishers, 2008), 171.

Nevertheless, the overlay of a national dimension of identification was unavoidable, especially in a time when the global order was increasingly structured by the governing powers and the sovereignty claims of nation-states. To be sure, appeals to dispersed Chinese overseas to unite and rally for the motherland were made with ardour in the first half of the twentieth century by the Chinese state. This was a period when the singular term *huaqiao* (華僑, meaning Chinese sojourner) was applied to all Chinese overseas, a highly political and emotive term that signifies the unity of overseas Chinese as one community and their unbroken ties with the Chinese homeland.[8] The term emerged in the 1890s, in the latter years of the Qing empire, but became a particularly powerful concept to recruit the diaspora for the Republican cause after the revolution of 1911, as China struggled to become a modern nation-state. For successive Chinese governments, *huaqiao* was a convenient catch-all label to encompass the large but dispersed emigrant populations worldwide, regardless of their geographical origins in China, their linguistic affiliations, or their locations of settlement abroad, emphasising their shared Chineseness and, in the process, interpellating them as Chinese national subjects and irrevocable members of the Chinese nation, even if they had long lived overseas and had creolised into local cultures, as in Southeast Asia. The central rationale for the Chinese state to call upon Chinese overseas was based on monetary grounds, namely, the financial contributions they could make to the state-building projects of a weakened China.[9] And indeed, China's early modernisation was substantially financed by overseas Chinese capital investments, as overseas Chinese around the world accepted their identification as *huaqiao* – an identity that gave them a sense of belonging in an uncertain world where they were often marginalised – and responded to the calls from the homeland. From the late Qing through the Republican era, China's national economy benefited greatly from contributions and remittances sent by overseas Chinese, who were encouraged to demonstrate their loyalty to the Chinese nation through their generosity.[10]

---

8. For the historical background of the term, see Wang Gungwu, 'A Note on the Origins of Hua-ch'iao', in *Community and Nation: Essays on Southeast Asia and the Chinese* (Singapore: Heinemann Educational Books, 1981), 118–27. The political connotations of the term *huaqiao* are controversial because it implies the legal incorporation of all overseas Chinese by the Chinese state through the idea of *ius sanguinis* (blood-based citizenship), which was particularly problematic for post-colonial Southeast Asian nation-states, which have very sizeable Chinese minorities within their borders. As a consequence, the PRC abandoned the principles of *ius sanguinis* in the 1950s and limited the use of *huaqiao* only to those Chinese overseas who have retained Chinese nationality. However, in recent times there has been a resurgence in the application of *huaqiao* to an undifferentiated, global Chinese diaspora. See, for example, Shao Dan, 'Chinese by Definition: Nationality Law, Jus Sanguinis, and State Succession, 1909–1980', *Twentieth Century China* 35, no. 1 (2009): 4–28, https://doi.org/10.1353/tcc.0.0019.
9. Soon Keong Ong, '"Chinese, but Not Quite": *Huaqiao* and the Marginalization of the Overseas Chinese', *Journal of Chinese Overseas* 9, no. 1 (2013): 1–32, https://doi.org/10.1163/17932548-12341247.
10. Ong, '"Chinese, but Not Quite"', 9.

In Australia too, Chinese migrants and residents were drawn to the idea of *huaqiao*, implying that they were part of a 'single body of overseas Chinese'[11] and, as such, belonged to a transnational Chinese diaspora that brought overseas Chinese around the world together with the homeland. As Mei-fen Kuo has argued, mobilising in the name of the *huaqiao* diaspora made sense for Chinese in early twentieth-century Australia because 'it offered an avenue for redress of local political grievances that were now seen as embedded in trans-Pacific racism'.[12] In other words, it was not only the Sinocentric appeals of the homeland, but also the injustices of the White Australia policy and associated forms of anti-Chinese discrimination – mirrored in exclusionary racisms suffered by Chinese elsewhere in diasporic sites around the Pacific – that contributed to an increased sense of shared Chineseness among Chinese in Australia. In the Australian context, then, *huaqiao* (self)-identification was the result of a push and pull between two nationalisms: the patriotic rallying call of Chinese nationalism, on the one hand, and exclusion from white Australian nationalism, on the other. In this regard, Chinese Australian identity in the period of the White Australia policy was more than merely a refinement of native kinship practices and inherited identities.[13] Marginalised in Australia, many Chinese migrants and residents became politically active around the revolution of 1911 and mobilised themselves in support of Sun Yat-sen's Chinese Nationalist Party, or the Kuomintang (KMT).[14] Thus, they were diasporic subjects who became patriotic agents of what Benedict Anderson has called long-distance nationalism.[15]

For example, Gordon Mar's father, Mar Leong Wah (馬亮華), who came to be known as Harry Mar in Australia, was born in 1902 in Sha Chong village (沙涌村) in Zhongshan and migrated to Australia in 1921. He became a leader of the Australian headquarters of the Kuomintang (國民黨, lit. Nationalist Party) in Sydney in the 1930s and remained loyal to the party until his death in 1981. As Gordon describes:

> Yes, he was in the KMT since very early, as a young man . . . Naturally, [in Australia] you're not a citizen; you're excluded from citizenship. So where is your allegiance? Your allegiance is to your home country, and the allegiance of him and his peers

---

11. Wang Gungwu, 'A Single Chinese Diaspora? Some Historical Reflections', in *Imagining the Chinese Diaspora: Two Australian Perspectives*, by Wang Gungwu and Annette Shun-wah (Canberra: Centre for the Study of the Chinese Southern Diaspora, 1999), 2.

12. Kuo, *Making Chinese Australia*, 280.

13. Kuo, *Making Chinese Australia*, 216–21.

14. On the evolution of the KMT in Australia, see Mei-fen Kuo and Judith Brett, *Unlocking the History of the Australian Kuo Min Tang, 1911–2013* (Kew, Victoria: Australian Scholarly Publishing, 2013); John Fitzgerald, *Big White Lie: Chinese Australians in White Australia* (Sydney: UNSW Press, 2007), Chapter 6.

15. Benedict Anderson, *The Spectre of Comparison: Nationalism, Southeast Asia, and the World* (London: Verso, 1998), 58–74. See also Prasenjit Duara, 'Nationalists among Transnationals: Overseas Chinese and the Idea of China, 1900–1911', in *Ungrounded Empires: The Cultural Politics of Modern Chinese Transnationalism*, ed. Aihwa Ong and Donald Nonini (New York: Routledge, 1997), 39–60.

was to China; and to China, it was only the nationalist party. There were no communists yet.[16]

The Kuomintang came to power in mainland China in 1928 when Chiang Kai-shek managed to end the reign of the warlords and unified the country as the Republic of China. Chiang's Nationalist government depended heavily on *huaqiao* investments and donations to revive the country's economy. Financial support from overseas Chinese became particularly intense when China was attacked by Japan, culminating in a full-scale invasion in 1937, which generated a deep national crisis that continued into the period of the Pacific War. The Nationalist government was also well aware of the importance of overseas Chinese remittances to their families for the country's economy.[17] It can be argued, then, that during this period there was a relatively harmonious bond between diaspora and nation, cemented by a joint Nationalist commitment to the fate of the motherland.

However, after fighting a ferocious civil war (1946–1949) against the Communist forces of Mao Zedong, the Nationalists eventually lost, forcing Chiang Kai-shek's Nationalist Party to retreat to Taiwan after their defeat. This momentous historical event shocked many overseas Chinese and disrupted their relationship to the homeland. Harry Mar, for example, was shattered when he heard 'the devastating news that the Communists had taken over, and he couldn't accept that', according to his son Gordon. The last time Harry went back to China was in 1937, when his father passed away. After that, he never returned to his home village, although he did go to Taiwan.

Others of Harry's generation experienced a similar rupture with the homeland as a consequence of the turbulent historical developments there. For example, George Wing Kee's father was born in 1905 in Darwin but spent most of his youth in his ancestral hometown of Shaxi (沙溪) in Zhongshan, returning to Australia when he was eighteen years old.[18] He returned to China to marry George's mother in 1933 and took her back to Australia a year later, where they first had a small shop in Queensland but eventually settled in Sydney after the Second World War. George, the couple's eldest son and now in his eighties, says about his father:

> My father never ever went back. My mother did, but my father, he only went back when he was young. After they married, he never went back. He was very . . . disappointed at the way of the country. Because he was born in 1905 and of course they went through the first World War, and then the changeover from Chiang

---

16. Gordon Mar (馬國棟), interview with Ien Ang and Alexandra Wong, 21 September 2018. All unreferenced quotes attributed to Gordon Mar in this chapter are taken from this interview.
17. Ong, "'Chinese, but Not Quite'", 8–9.
18. George Wing Kee's name should actually have been George Wong. His official surname, Wing Kee, is a legacy of Australians' ignorance about the structure of Chinese names. When his grandfather, Wong Wing Kee, first came to Australia in the late nineteenth century, George told us, 'the Australian people weren't aware that Chinese surnames came first, so they called my grandfather Wing Kee on his passport, so forever we had to be Wing Kee. We lost our clan name (黃 Wong)'.

Kai-shek to Communism. He was there, he witnessed the change in 1929, where the Nationalist government came in and promised the people democracy, but instead there was a lot of starvation, poverty. It wasn't what they expected. Because when the Communist Party of Mao Zedong came, he promised that everybody would be equal, there would be no capitalism, property owners would have to get rid of their property. And so there was a purge. They killed the educated people, burnt all the books, and my father was very disappointed with the way China was, and he said he'd never go back.[19]

The emergence of the People's Republic of China (PRC) in 1949 had a profound impact on the relationship between Chinese overseas and the ancestral homeland. People such as Harry Mar and George Wing Kee's father, who were young adults in the 1930s, witnessed the rise and fall of republicanism in China and the dissolution of the promise of a modern, liberal democratic China. They would also have heard about the harassment and abuse that their families in their home villages had to suffer during the radical transition to Communist rule after 1949, as will be discussed in the next section. As a result, a significant number of them, in particular passionate Kuomintang supporters such as Harry Mar, to all intents and purposes chose to repudiate their homeland. In this regard, they can be considered self-imposed exiles, severed from their native country and forced to live out their days in Australia, a country in which, at that time, they were treated as second-class citizens. Their Australian-born children, represented here by Gordon Mar and George Wing Kee, grew up and became adults in the 1940s and 1950s, when the White Australia policy was still firmly in place. This would have strongly affected their sense of Chineseness as a distinctly beleaguered identity, but also, we can surmise, as an inheritance that they wished to cherish. Firmly rooted in Australia, they did not have personal knowledge of China at all: their diasporic Chineseness was thus a relatively detached one. But as we will see, while their parents chose never to return to the ancestral village in Zhongshan, they themselves did – many years later. Thus, this generation plays a particularly important role as agents in nurturing the legacy of the China–Australia migration corridor.

The Mao Years: State Control and Severed Links

Regime change in 1949 brought radical transformation in mainland China, with serious implications for overseas Chinese migrants and their families back in the home villages. Soon after coming to power, the new Communist government banned emigration and imposed strict entry/exit controls on the movement of people and capital.[20] This brought an end to the relatively fluid cross-border flows of people,

---

19. George Wing Kee (黃祖發), interview with Ien Ang and Alexandra Wong, 10 October 2018. All subsequent unreferenced quotes attributed to George Wing Kee in this chapter are taken from this interview.
20. Glen Peterson, *Overseas Chinese in the People's Republic of China* (Abingdon: Routledge, 2012), 27.

money, and goods that previously had linked the home villages with transnational emigrant networks, including in Australia. But the PRC could not ignore the fact that the *huaqiao* legacy was one of the most salient features of the economic, social, and political landscape of South China, not least Guangdong province (廣東). It was also, as Glen Peterson has observed, one of the most complex and intractable issues that the Chinese Communist Party (CCP) had to deal with. There was great ideological uncertainty and controversy over what the *huaqiao* represented to socialist China, leading to conflicting and contradictory approaches towards Chinese overseas after 1949.[21] As Peterson puts it, 'the PRC regarded overseas Chinese with a deep sense of ambiguity, attracted by their economic wealth but deeply suspicious of their political loyalty'.[22]

By 1949, as many as one in five residents in Guangdong belonged to a transnational family, where women, children, elderly parents, and other relatives called *qiaojuan* (僑眷, meaning dependants of overseas Chinese, pronounced in Mandarin) relied on remittances sent home by *huaqiao* men as an important source of household income.[23] Remittances were therefore a very important part of the socio-economic landscape of many parts of rural South China, especially the *qiaoxiang*, where decades of money flows from foreign lands had made these areas relatively well-off and provided higher living standards for these families. For the PRC, remittances from overseas Chinese were also a critical resource for foreign exchange, which was in short supply due to the international embargo imposed by the United States on trade with China.[24] As Peterson remarks, 'if there was a single aspect of the *Huaqiao* legacy that the CCP was determined to preserve after coming to power in 1949, it was the role of family remittances'.[25] But remittances dropped significantly in the 1950s, as many overseas Chinese men failed to send money home.[26] Long-distance relationships between men overseas and their kin at home had become strained and difficult to sustain after years of war, and when the Communists finally triumphed many migrants had had little or no contact with their relatives in China for well over a decade. To remedy the situation, the PRC government embarked on a massive, state-supervised overseas Chinese letter-writing campaign which aimed not only to reunite families, but also to encourage the resumption of remittance inflows.[27] Family members in China were encouraged to write directly to their husbands and relatives abroad, assisted by local authorities who helped determine the whereabouts of missing or lost relatives and provided

---

21. For a detailed overview, see Stephen Fitzgerald, *China and the Overseas Chinese: A Study of Peking's Changing Policy 1949–1970* (London: Cambridge University Press, 1972).
22. Peterson, *Overseas Chinese*, 22.
23. Shelly Chan, *Diaspora's Homeland: Modern China in the Age of Global Migration* (Durham, NC: Duke University Press, 2018), 107.
24. Peterson, *Overseas Chinese*, 32.
25. Peterson, *Overseas Chinese*, 66.
26. Fitzgerald, *China and the Overseas Chinese*, 56.
27. Peterson, *Overseas Chinese*, 31–36.

official scribes literate in both Chinese and foreign languages to help write the letters, in which family members were typically asked to paint a positive image of the new China and, especially, to stress the need for remittances. In the campaign, as Shelly Chan has argued, the women who stayed behind were cast as intermediaries between diaspora and nation, serving as actors to enhance *huaqiao* integration with the aims and goals of socialism.[28]

By 1957, as many as 500,000 letters had been sent to overseas relatives from families in Guangdong alone, resulting in the reunion of thousands of transnational families each year.[29] Despite these efforts, however, remittances continued to decline over the decade. Between June and September 1951 alone, remittances to Guangdong fell more than 30 per cent.[30] This downward trend was not only a consequence of international restrictions on the transfer of funds to Communist China (the United States banned remittances by Chinese American migrants to their families in the PRC in 1950);[31] it was also the effect of severe disenchantment among both Chinese overseas and their families back home with the new political circumstances they found themselves in, which placed them under strict state control and caused a major deterioration of their social status. To begin with, although the government decreed that *qiaojuan* families were allowed to receive and dispose of remittances as they wished, without official interference, the state 'encouraged' them to invest the incoming funds in local production, social welfare, and various public undertakings to the benefit of socialist construction.[32] Such mixed messages gave local cadres ample reason to commandeer *qiaojuan* into allocating family remittances to public and collective uses. The PRC government sought to bring the remittance trade under state control by placing private remittance shops (*jinshanzhuang* 金山莊 Romanised in Mandarin, lit. 'Gold Mountain firms'), which had flourished since the late nineteenth century, under government supervision, but reports in the overseas Chinese press about the political pressure suffered by their families at home discouraged many Chinese overseas from sending money through official channels. Instead, many preferred to use Hong Kong–based informal couriers (popularly known as 水客 *shuike* in Mandarin) to get their hard-earned remittances to their loved ones.[33]

The fears of overseas Chinese for the safety and welfare of their family members in China were also particularly heightened by another Communist state initiative, land reform. Almost immediately after assuming power, the PRC embarked on an ambitious land reform programme, aimed to dismantle traditional power structures

---

28. Chan, *Diaspora's Homeland*, 141–42.
29. Peterson, *Overseas Chinese*, 31.
30. Peterson, *Overseas Chinese*, 33.
31. Peterson, *Overseas Chinese*, 68.
32. Peterson, *Overseas Chinese*, 73.
33. Peterson, *Overseas Chinese*, 70–71.

and modernise the agrarian system.[34] These policies seriously impacted overseas Chinese transnational families, who had invested heavily in the accumulation of land and real estate until 1949. As discussed in detail in Chapter 7 of this volume, the building of an ancestral house in the home village was a symbol of migrant success for the family. Investment in land and houses was also seen as a way of providing income for stay-at-home wives and family members and guaranteeing a place for migrants to return to in their old age.[35] Government land survey teams estimated that in Guangdong province, overseas Chinese owned up to one-fifth of all land, although in the greater Pearl River Delta region of the province overseas Chinese were found to dominate the socio-economic landscape and control much of the agricultural land. Nevertheless, while there were certainly fabulously wealthy overseas Chinese who owned large tracts of land and real estate, the vast majority of transnational families owned properties that were only modestly larger than the average-sized holding for the population at large.[36] This fact alone, however, made *qiaojuan* the target for social and economic levelling. The land reform policy stipulated that agricultural land and other rural property were to be expropriated and redistributed on the basis of officially assigned class designations: 'landlord' (地主), 'rich peasant' (富農), 'middle peasant' (中農), 'poor peasant'(貧農), and 'landless agricultural labourer' (雇農). In this exercise, many overseas Chinese families were – often wrongly – assigned the status of 'landlord' and therefore subject to expropriation. In this way, the CCP drove a wedge into the rural economy by pitting *huaqiao* against peasants in a ferocious class struggle.[37] Overseas Chinese families were accused of having 'bourgeois' lifestyles, visibly represented by their grand 'foreign-style' (洋樓, *yanglou* in Mandarin) houses. By 1953, it was reported that up to 90 per cent of all houses owned by overseas Chinese families in Guangdong had been confiscated and generally redistributed to poorer villagers or repurposed for government uses.[38] It is not surprising that this caused fear and resentment among many overseas Chinese, resulting in a further drop in remittances. In 1954, in a bid to restore the confidence of overseas Chinese within and outside China and to spur remittances and investment, the central PRC government decreed that overseas Chinese–owned houses expropriated during land reform were to be returned to their original owners. This 'preferential treatment' (優待, *youdai* in Mandarin) was pursued because the government recognised that there was a direct relationship between their treatment of overseas Chinese and the latter's response.[39] It was a

---

34. See Brian DeMare, *Land Wars: The Story of China's Agrarian Revolution* (Stanford, CA: Stanford University Press, 2019).
35. Peterson, *Overseas Chinese*, 43.
36. Peterson, *Overseas Chinese*, 44.
37. Chan, *Diaspora's Homeland*, 112.
38. Peterson, *Overseas Chinese*, 52, 61.
39. Fitzgerald, *China and the Overseas Chinese*, 53; Shen Huifen, '*Qiaojuan* Politics: Government Policies toward the Left-Behind Family Members of Chinese Overseas 1880s–1990s', *Journal of Chinese Overseas* 6, no. 1 (2010): 43–79, https://doi.org/10.1163/179325410X491464.

politically sensitive move, however, as it was seen as a betrayal of collectivist socialist principles. Moreover, the decree exacerbated social discontent as it required local peasant families who had occupied the houses to either vacate them or pay rent to the overseas Chinese owners, entrenching the class privilege of the latter. Thus, as Peterson remarks, the issue of property restitution, first raised in 1954, was destined to drag on for decades and was not fully resolved until well into the 1990s. In fact, the problem was repeated over and over again. During the Great Leap Forward (1958–1960), overseas Chinese–owned houses were treated as 'excess' property and occupied by local communes. During the Cultural Revolution (1966–1976), confiscation of overseas Chinese properties intensified as their owners were condemned as 'capitalists' (資本家) and 'counter-revolutionaries' (反革命分子).[40] In fact, the Cultural Revolution marked a climax of anti-*huaqiao* politics in the PRC. *Qiaojuan* were not only denounced as 'enemies of the people' and as 'foreign spies' but also suffered violent abuse and physical attack, especially in the early stages of the Cultural Revolution.[41] By 1971, regulations under which returned overseas Chinese were allowed to leave China were eased. Not long after, *qiaojuan* with family members in Hong Kong and Macao or overseas were also allowed to leave on grounds of family reunification.[42]

This brief historical overview of the heavy-handed way in which the PRC intervened in the lives and livelihoods of transnational families during the Mao years illuminates the harrowing experience of dispossession and maltreatment that many transnational families had to endure. Some of our informants who lived in the home village as part of a *qiaojuan* household during this time still have vivid memories of this ordeal. Douglas Lam was born in 1947 and lived in his ancestral village of Antang (安堂村, On Tong in Cantonese) in Dachong town (大涌鎮), Zhongshan in the early 1950s with his grandmother, mother, and aunts. Douglas's grandfather had sojourned to Vancouver in 1914, where he worked in a sawmill. He regularly returned to Antang, where he eventually fathered seven children. As with so many *huaqiao*, he also built a house and bought land for his family. When the Communists came to power in 1949, however, he was classified as a 'landlord' (地主, *dizhu* in Mandarin) while he was away in Canada, with horrible consequences for the family. Douglas remembers the traumatic experience from the point of view of a young child:

> School was quite turbulent because we were the landowner class. We were the people's enemy. So at times I wasn't allowed to go to school. Even when I was at school I was not given a Mao's red scarf. That was very traumatic, you know, as a

---

40. Peterson, *Overseas Chinese*, 60–63.
41. Peterson, *Overseas Chinese*, 162.
42. Peterson, *Overseas Chinese*, 163; Wu Xiao An, 'China's Evolving Policy towards the Chinese Diaspora in Southeast Asia (1949–2018)', *Trends in Southeast Asia*, no. 14 (Singapore: ISEAS, 2019), 12.

little boy. Everybody had a red one and I didn't. And I wasn't given one because I was the son of a landlord. So I was a pariah and an outcast.[43]

Even worse, Douglas's father, the only adult male in the household who was not overseas at that time, was shot and killed in front of the family when Douglas was three years old. His grandmother was humiliated and denounced in public and made to kneel on broken glass in the midday sun during so-called struggle sessions (批鬥, *pidou* in Mandarin). His mother was forced to live in a pigsty. These painful incidences drove the family to plot their exit. In 1956 Douglas fled to Hong Kong with his grandmother and aunt (his father's youngest sister) on the pretext that his grandmother required medical treatment.[44] However, his mother stayed behind in the village. Douglas described the rationale:

> We left my mother in China because if four of you left the village together it's not very convincing. So we had a two-way visa to go to Hong Kong, but once you cross the big seas you are not going to go back.

After a few years in Hong Kong, Douglas's uncle, who had migrated to Sydney, managed to get permission for Douglas to come to study in Australia in 1961. From Sydney he wrote to his mother in China and his grandfather in Vancouver. His mother was very courageous, says Douglas, letting her only son go:

> My mother was quite emphatic: 'If I didn't let my son go he might not live to see his 21st.' Because [there was] so much political turmoil, then there was the Cultural Revolution, we were in the thick of the mix. I would be picked on.

In 1973, Douglas went back to his ancestral village to visit his mother for the first time. As an overseas Chinese, he was allowed to bring presents for his family – 'bicycle, sewing machine, electric fan, radio, clock, food, clothing, a bolt of fabric, everything, like the men who made good returning home' – purchased in Hong Kong and sent off to the village by a Chinese travel service. 'That was a very proud day for my mother because she had suffered so much, and her son is coming home somebody', Douglas says. By this time, the PRC's collectivised planned economy was already showing signs of unravelling due to myriad dispersed acts of resistance.[45] After 1970 goods and remittances had once again started to pour across the border and by 1974, the amount of money reaching villagers from overseas was twice as high as in 1965. As Frank Dikötter has noted, 'families with overseas connections had been the first to suffer the onslaught of the Cultural Revolution, and now they

---

43. Interview with Douglas Lam (林源) by Ien Ang, Denis Byrne, and Alexandra Wong, 1 November 2017. All unreferenced quotes attributed to Douglas Lam in the rest of the chapter are taken from this interview.
44. *Qiaojuan* families often used such pretexts to get out of mainland China and go to Hong Kong or Macao during this time. Shen, '*Qiaojuan* Politics', 61.
45. Frank Dikötter, 'The Silent Revolution: Decollectivization from Below during the Cultural Revolution', *The China Quarterly* 227 (September 2016): 796–811, https://doi.org/10.1017/S0305741016000746.

were the first to emerge from uniform poverty'.[46] But at the tail end of the Cultural Revolution, it was not possible to feel relaxed in China, certainly not as a visiting overseas Chinese. Douglas declares that he loathes Mao: 'His policies were really brutal.' His grandfather, who remained in Vancouver but spent his dying days being cared for by his family in Hong Kong, was also full of disdain for the Communists, not least because of the execution of his son (Douglas's father). Nevertheless, a younger daughter and son ran away from the family and joined Mao's revolutionary forces, caught up, Douglas says, in the romantic idea of building a new China. The Communist revolution has thus torn the Lam family apart, both spatially and ideologically.

Douglas's experiences resonate with those of another of our informants, Kam Louie, who was born in 1949 in Dutou village (渡頭村), Zhongshan, also into a typical transnational family. His paternal grandfather, born in 1885, went to Australia in the early twentieth century and worked as a market gardener in Sydney. He returned to the home village regularly to be with his family, father children, and buy land and build houses. Kam's father, born in 1918, also went to Australia shortly after Kam was born, leaving Kam, his mother, older sisters, grandmother, and other relatives behind in the village. By that time, the Communists had come to power and they soon introduced land reforms. Kam still remembers the fear that featured in that turbulent period:

> After 1949 we were classified as 'landlords'. And there were many struggle meetings. I still remember those days because although I was only four or five years old, I was the oldest male in the family . . . So there wasn't a male in the family to attend the struggle meetings. There was a lot of fear associated with those meetings.[47]

A few years later the government relaxed the treatment of overseas Chinese somewhat, but part of the family home was confiscated and given to a poor peasant. The family lived in the other part of the house. When Kam was about eight years old, he left for Hong Kong with his mother, eldest sister, and younger brother, officially to join his overseas grandfather, and when he was ten, in 1959, he and his sister journeyed on a passenger ship to Sydney where he joined his father, followed some time later by his mother. The parents were finally reunited after a separation of more than ten years, although Kam's grandmother, second eldest sister, and some other relatives had stayed behind in the village. Kam's father sent remittances throughout the Mao years, using informal (but reliable) couriers. The family exchanged letters regularly. Kam says that after he began to write, he corresponded often with the sister who stayed in China to look after their grandmother. 'We wrote to each other regularly. Our writing skills [in Chinese] were very limited, but we managed to

---

46. Dikötter, 'Silent Revolution', 804.
47. Interview with Kam Louie (雷金慶) by Ien Ang, Denis Byrne, and Alexandra Wong, 12 December 2018. Further quotes attributed to Kam Louie in this chapter are taken from this interview.

88 (Un)making Transnational Identities

express complex information and feelings reasonably, I think.'[48] About his grandmother, he says:

> My grandmother was an incredibly smart and astute woman. I guess she had to be, being a woman running a big household of eight people when all the adult men (her husband and children) were in Australia or America. She did not know when she said goodbye to them before 1950 that she would never see them again. She managed the periods through the Republican chaos, the Sino-Japanese war, the Communist revolution and the Cultural Revolution with all of us doing reasonably well. Yet she was illiterate. My parents wrote to her but she, like many others similar left-behind women, had to get someone else to read the letters and write replies on her behalf.[49]

When his grandmother was dying in 1973, Kam was sent back to the village by the family. It was still the Cultural Revolution then, but interestingly Kam enjoyed being back and has returned many times since then. In fact, by that time Kam was a philosophy student at Sydney University and was highly influenced by Mao and Marxism. As he says: 'The Cultural Revolution was a real godsend for me because its ideology of being radically Marxist and yet Chinese allowed me to play with the two seemingly incompatible doctrines – communism and nationalism – as a means to understand China. So I really wanted to go back, and I did get a much better understanding of the many changes that occurred.'

In sum, the Mao years were a traumatic time for diasporic Chinese families, as the spatial separation between those who had remained in the home village and those who had gone away became more definitive and permanent. Men such as Douglas Lam and Kam Louie, who were very young in the 1950s and potentially in most danger as political targets of the revolutionary forces, were sent to safety abroad by their families; due to pre-existing family connections, both Douglas and Kam ended up in Sydney. But they both remained strongly committed to their transnationally dispersed families, returning to China even before the Cultural Revolution had ended to visit those who had been left behind. As we will see, this affective transnationality has remained a defining aspect of their sense of identity to this day.

Becoming Australian (with Chinese Characteristics)

For other diasporic Chinese families in Australia, the Mao years resulted in increasingly broken connections with the homeland. The establishment of the People's Republic of China intensified the Cold War between the West and the Communist world, aggravating the situation for Chinese living in Australia. In the United

---

48. Kam Louie, email correspondence, 24 May 2021.
49. Kam Louie, email correspondence, 24 May 2021.

States, state repression of Chinese migrants suspected of supporting the new China occurred on a massive scale, whereas in Australia, where by 1949 only a few thousand Chinese lived, mostly in the Sydney and Melbourne Chinatowns or in isolated country towns, state surveillance was carried out on specific individuals and organisations.[50] Few Chinese in Australia, mostly labourers and seamen, supported Communism, and during the Cold War it was almost impossible to be Chinese and Communist due to the threat of deportation and denial of residency. In Sydney's Chinatown, the merchant class, who mostly supported the Kuomintang, strengthened its dominance within the Chinese community. Most Chinese chose to endure the Cold War in silence. As Drew Cottle and Angela Keys note: 'As the prospect of Chinese returning to China to visit relatives or assist family members migrating to Australia became impossible during the early years of the Cold War, the majority of Chinese in Sydney's Chinatown abandoned any radical political activity.'[51] Instead, they concentrated on building their lives in Australia. In other words, if the White Australia policy and the Nationalist call from the motherland before 1949 enhanced their sense of patriotic Chineseness, the coming to power of the CCP and the Cold War compelled them to move more strongly towards Australianness. This was certainly the case for the families of both Gordon Mar and George Wing Kee.

Gordon's father Harry (Mar Leong Wah) managed the family's banana business, Wing Sang & Co. (永生果欄), in Sydney's Chinatown until his retirement in the late 1970s, and all his six children received an Australian education. As Gordon says: 'We were raised as Aussies.' He became a chartered accountant and managed Wing Sang until he sold it to Italian buyers in 1984. Commenting on the ending of nearly a hundred years of Wing Sang, Gordon emphasised the company's importance for the family's livelihood in a new country:

> It served its purpose. The purpose of the company was to bring our family to Australia, to find work, and that's what it did. Eventually we decided the banana business was not for us, because the next generation is professional. We had no interest in selling bananas.

Gordon stresses his Australianness: 'I'm proud to be known as an Australian, and have Australian attitudes.' He even did his military service for Australia. He speaks with pride and respect about the generations that came before him, the Chinese men who took the dive and made the migration journey to Australia:

> My father and grandfather and forebears, they had nothing except their hands, and hard work. So they worked harder than the white man, and sold goods cheaper than the white man, in order to get ahead. What they did have was enterprise, initiative. They had the courage to start businesses, big businesses.

---

50. Drew Cottle and Angela Keys, 'Red-Hunting in Sydney's Chinatown', *Journal of Australian Studies* 31, no. 91 (2007): 25–31, https://doi.org/10.1080/14443050709388125.
51. Cottle and Keys, 'Red-Hunting', 30.

Gordon is grateful for his forebears' leap into the unknown by making the migration journey, which made it possible for the family to embark on a new life in Australia. Many decades later, this leap of faith has evidently paid off, as Gordon stresses. This was not only because of the hard work of the generations that came before him, but also because the political circumstances in Australia had much improved, as the White Australia policy was slowly but surely dismantled and the idea of multiculturalism began to gain traction in the 1970s.[52] Chinese in Australia were no longer marginalised, second-class citizens but were recognised, officially at least, as legitimate members of the diverse Australian nation. The successful rise to comfortable, middle-class status would have given people such as Gordon reason to embrace the family's Australian destiny. But the memory of the past has not disappeared. Asked how he would describe his identity, he calls himself 'Chinese Australian' or 'Australian with Chinese heritage'. 'We really have been successful in being assimilated as Australians', he says, 'but I believe you should never forget that you do have this Chinese heritage.' At the same time, however, his cultural sense of Chineseness is tenuous. For example, his parents never really explained the background of Chinese customs.

> What are mooncakes (月餅)? What's the story of mooncakes and how did they originate, and why do they make mooncakes at a certain time? Then there's *joong* 粽 [Cantonese word for sticky rice dumpling]. In a certain season you have *joong*. You know, the rice wrapped in the leaves? That's another festival. I don't know what festival it is. We just eat it, and accept that it's part of our culture. But we didn't really understand it.

Gordon does not speak Chinese, although he and his siblings did speak in dialect with his parents, uncles and aunts, and relatives. Once this older generation was gone, however, 'English is really our language'. Gordon lived and worked in Canada for ten years before returning to Sydney, and his wife is a Chinese Canadian. In fact, all his male siblings married Chinese women, 'of which', Gordon says with a laugh, 'my mother was very proud'. Despite being resolutely settled in Australia and embracing Australianness, then, a strong hybrid Chineseness is laced through Gordon's sense of identity.

George Wing Kee's family, meanwhile, also went through a thoroughly Australianising experience before and after the Second World War, when white Australia and its prejudices were still hegemonic. Upon arriving in Australia in the late 1930s, his parents settled in the small country town of Maryborough in South Queensland, where they ran a small mixed business shop that was given to them

---

52. On the demise of the White Australia policy and the rise of multiculturalism in Australia, see Jon Stratton and Ien Ang, 'Multicultural Imagined Communities: Cultural Difference and National Identity in the USA and Australia', in *Multicultural States: Rethinking Difference and Identity*, ed. David Bennett (London: Routledge, 1999), 135–62; Mark Lopez, *The Origins of Multiculturalism in Australian Politics 1945-1975* (Carlton South, Victoria: Melbourne University Press, 2000); Gwenda Tavan, *The Long Slow Death of White Australia* (Melbourne: Scribe, 2005).

by an uncle when he decided to go back to China himself. 'It was a very hard time as my mum couldn't speak English and there was no way of learning to speak at that time', George says. He was born in Maryborough in 1934, followed by more children. The family stayed in the little township until 1942, when they moved to Brisbane to seek better opportunities. It was wartime. His father started a little café near the American military base, where they learned to make steaks and chicken, which were very popular with the American troops. 'We used to wait on the tables and they'd give you money, tips, dollars, chewing gum, bars of chocolate', George recalls. But Brisbane people didn't come to Chinese shops at that time, 'so when the war ended, 1945, our business ended, because we found that when the troops moved away, there were no customers'. His father then decided to move to Sydney, where there were more Chinese people and doing business was more viable. The first business his father set up in Sydney was selling roasted peanuts in hotels – 'myself and my two younger brothers used to go around the hotels with a bag to sell peanuts every afternoon after school' – but eventually the family occupied a shop with a residence upstairs, on Elizabeth Street, Zetland in South Sydney. The shop sold everything from sandwiches to toilet seats to Christmas giftware. There were not many Chinese in the neighbourhood but the young George went to the market in Chinatown with his father every day to buy vegetables. George later took over the business, which he closed after fifty-two years in 2002, when he retired. Since his retirement George has become active in Sydney's Chinatown, where his son, Peter Wong, has a real estate agency.

Although he has become, to all intents and purposes, 'Australian', George maintains a strong sense of Chinese identity, which was augmented by his marriage. As the eldest son in the family, he was required 'to marry within our culture'. He ended up marrying a woman who also has origins in Zhongshan, having been born in Heng Mei village (恆美村), close to Shaxi (沙溪), George's ancestral home. Unlike George, who knew little about China at that time, his wife had personal experience of the Mao years, having arrived in the 1960s. She came to Australia as an eighteen-year-old to escape a China that was being terrorised by the Red Guards in the early days of the Cultural Revolution. Still, in a similar move to Douglas Lam and Kam Louie described earlier, she went back to Zhongshan on her own in 1972 to visit her relatives. In 1975, the couple went together, George's first-ever visit to China. George's venture to the ancestral homeland, then, was encouraged by his wife's more tangible family connections there; his own close relatives had long moved out to Australia or America.

China Opens Up: Resuming Diasporic Links

After Mao's death in 1976, there was a radical shift in overseas Chinese policy in the PRC under Deng Xiaoping. Deng declared that the era of class struggle was over and that the nation's focus should now be on economic modernisation, to be achieved by joining the capitalist world economy. For this grand project, the role of Chinese overseas, especially those in Hong Kong, Taiwan, and Southeast Asia, as a source of investments and capital was crucial. As Peterson remarks, 'while Deng and his reform allies may have been innovators in the context of recent PRC history, seen from a longer perspective they were reverting to a strategy that was consistent with that of every Chinese national government since the late nineteenth century: wooing the wealth and business acumen of Chinese overseas for China's modernization'.[53]

Seeking to remedy the alienation of Chinese overseas from China due to the excesses of the preceding three decades, the PRC sought to regain their trust and confidence by rehabilitating their dependants in China (僑眷 *qiaojuan* in Mandarin) and overseas Chinese returnees (歸僑 *guiqiao* in Mandarin). A directive was put in place in 1984 to restore legal ownership of houses and other real estate that had been confiscated or expropriated since 1949. Significantly, the directive applied not only to overseas Chinese–owned residential properties but also to ancestral halls, family temples, association halls, lineage schools, and other privately owned buildings.[54] Houses and property were regarded as essential symbols of national attachment to China for the Chinese overseas. Returning them to their owners was thus seen as essential for the restoration of the CCP's reputation among the Chinese overseas. It was also a means of encouraging the re-engagement of the Chinese overseas with their ancestral villages.[55] These initiatives were accompanied by a new state discourse glorifying the enduring ties of the overseas Chinese to their *qiaoxiang* (僑鄉), which were constructed, in Mette Thunø's words, as 'geographical areas of emotional attachment'.[56] The *qiaoxiang* were enlisted as conduits to induce Chinese overseas to return to their ancestral villages and to identify with China, stimulating – it was hoped – patriotism, donations, and investments.[57] Official roots-searching programmes were initiated, aimed at bringing Chinese overseas back to China.[58] Local authorities were instructed to welcome visiting diasporic Chinese in their search for their roots by facilitating visits, assisting in the search for their old family homes, ancestral graves, or ancestral halls, and reuniting them with relatives. This state-sponsored elevation of *qiaoxiang* as recognised sites of overseas Chinese belonging to China was designed to strengthen diasporic ties and national

---

53. Peterson, *Overseas Chinese*, 172.
54. Peterson, *Overseas Chinese*, 173.
55. Mette Thunø, 'Reaching Out and Incorporating Chinese Overseas: The Transterritorial Scope of the PRC by the End of the 20th Century', *The China Quarterly* 168 (December 2001): 915.
56. Thunø, 'Reaching Out', 918.
57. For discussion of the instrumentalisation of '*qiaoxiang* ties' in order to attract foreign investment in China's capitalist modernisation, see Leo Douw, Cen Huang, and Michael Godley, eds., *Qiaoxiang Ties: Interdisciplinary Approaches to 'Cultural Capitalism' in South China* (Abingdon: Routledge, 2010).
58. See Andrea Louie, *Chineseness across Borders: Renegotiating Chinese Identities in China and the United States* (Durham, NC: Duke University Press, 2004).

identification based on the assumption of a shared Chineseness. In this regard, as Yow Cheun Hoe puts it, the *qiaoxiang* is posited as 'an enlarged version of home and a reflection of a nation'.[59]

This renewed call from the motherland certainly did not remain unanswered. Beginning in the 1980s, many diasporic Chinese from around the world, especially from Hong Kong and Macao, Southeast Asia, and North America but also Australia, responded to the opening up of China by making return visits to their *qiaoxiang*, which became sites of pilgrimage for descendants in search of their ancestral origins. With them came a significant amount of donations and investments, not least in social and cultural benefits such as schools,[60] but, particularly, the rebuilding of temples and lineage halls and other ways of reviving 'traditional' Chinese culture and society.[61] Such 'traditions' and their associated ritual practices were generally suppressed during the Cultural Revolution and, as Thunø remarks, condemned as 'superstitious' (迷信) or 'feudal' (封建) in other parts of China, but they were sanctioned in the *qiaoxiang* as a way of protecting the interests of the overseas Chinese and their families.[62]

However, this reintroduction of tradition is not a universal development; much depends on where the returning diaspora comes from. For example, in Anxi, Fujian, cultural knowledge of pre-Communist-era practices was brought back by diasporic Singaporean Chinese to their ancestral villages because such practices were still active in Singapore, which has a large overseas Chinese community, leading to a 'reinvention of tradition' in Anxi and a revitalisation of the lineage structure.[63] In the Western societies of North America, Europe, and Australasia, by contrast, most Chinese, especially those of third, fourth, or even fifth generations, have very little knowledge of their ancestral villages and lineages. When they make visits to the villages of their ancestors, therefore, they tend to do so as foreigners interacting with people, places, and modes of Chineseness they do not really know. As Andrea Louie argues in her discussion of returning Chinese Americans, 'rather than producing firmly rooted and unambiguous Chinese identities, these transnational interactions more often result in encounters with unfamiliar ways of being Chinese'.[64] Moreover, as time has passed and Zhongshan – and China more generally – has undergone rapid change, diasporic links have weakened, punctuated by the unhappy fate of many ancestral houses that bind diasporic Chinese materially to their villages. In general, these houses are now abandoned, run-down, or disowned, as the stories of our four informants testify.

---

59. Yow Cheun Hoe, *Guangdong and Chinese Diaspora* (Abingdon: Routledge, 2013), 142.
60. See Cheng and Mar's contribution to this volume (Chapter 7).
61. Peterson, *Overseas Chinese*, 176.
62. Thunø, 'Reaching Out', 924–25.
63. Khun Eng Kuah, *Rebuilding the Ancestral Village: Singaporeans in China* (Aldershot: Ashgate, 2000), 23.
64. Louie, *Chineseness across Borders*, 8.

Gordon Mar made a visit to his ancestral village of Sha Chong (沙涌村) with his mother and two of his brothers in 1997. His mother was diagnosed with a terminal disease and her final wish was to travel to the village. As Gordon explained, 'she felt it was her duty to bring her sons back to the village to be acknowledged'. He continued: 'The most important thing was to visit the cemetery. It was at the old cemetery which had been restored. Each of us had to stand in front [of the tomb] and be announced and give three bows to the ancestors.' However, for Gordon the visit to Sha Chong was not the beginning of a longer-term reconnection with the ancestral home, but a one-off visit that closed the book on the lineage, marking the end of a tradition. Indeed, the visit only seems to have reinforced his Australianness, rather than his Chineseness:

> Find[ing] your roots . . . emotionally benefits you. To know that this is where our roots are; this is where we first originated from. There is a village there, and you look at the village and think: 'Thank god I wasn't born here.' There's no attachment to the place. It was interesting to go and see, but not a place that I'd want to be, or I'd want to stay. But we did our duty to our mother, and that was her desire, to take us there.

The Mar family's ancestral house in Sha Chong, a grand three-storey mansion built by Gordon's grandfather, was confiscated during the land reform period, as were so many overseas Chinese–owned houses (see Figure 3.1). According to Gordon, 'the building was used as a prison during the time of the Red Guards, and then at one time it was used as a storeroom for farming products'. After the Cultural Revolution the Chinese government gave the property back to the family in the late 1970s, but Gordon and his siblings have no interest in it. Distrust of the government is part of this, as Gordon explains:

> We thought, 'Why don't we claim the house back?' For what? You don't know what the authorities will charge you with. Back payments for all sorts of repairs, and rates, you name it. Besides, we did not want to emphasize the fact that it was at one time owned by my father who was part of the KMT. Let's keep quiet. We don't need the house. We don't need the money.

From the 1980s to the 2000s the house was rented out as a dormitory for female factory workers in the village. More recently, the house was given a heritage listing by the government. It is looked after by an uncle in the village and has been leased to an artist to be used as an art gallery. The government asked the family whether they would like to donate the house back to the government, which the family was fine with, although Gordon does not know whether that has actually happened. When the family visited in 1997, it was clear that his father's old village no longer existed. As Gordon says, 'we didn't know what to expect when we went to the village; we thought all these relatives would want us to give them presents. Instead, the relatives turned up with big cars to chauffeur us to the hotel.' This sense of disconnect has

Figure 3.1: Gordon Mar's grand ancestral house in neoclassical style, Sha Chong village (沙涌村). Photo by Denis Byrne.

only increased since the visit: 'We wouldn't have any contact with anybody there now.'

A decision to let go of the ancestral house was also made by George Wing Kee. As noted earlier, he went to Zhongshan for the first time in 1975 in the footsteps of his wife, who was a much more recent immigrant and still had a close connection with her relatives in her home village. But this was not the case for George. Some years later he tracked down his own ancestral home village of Long Ju Huan (龍聚環村) in Shaxi town, which was occupied by some ageing distant cousins. But, he says, he never contacted them to avoid getting into a complicated remittance tangle.

> Several years earlier they had written a letter to us, saying that the home needed a lot of money to renovate. Something in the order of $30,000. Our friends said to us, 'Don't respond to it, because once you respond, they'll keep asking you for money all the time. Let them live in the house; let it go, don't chase it.' So that's what we did.

This suggests that the legacy of the letter-writing campaign of the 1950s still had purchase in the 1990s, reproducing historical expectations of those remaining in the village with regard to remittances – the lifeblood of families in the *qiaoxiang* for many decades. It was a familial duty, however, that George no longer felt obliged to abide by. There was thus a definitive break in the (extended) family, entirely disconnecting those who ended up in Australia from those who remained in China.

Nevertheless, over the years George and his wife have made more than twenty return trips to Zhongshan, during which they have witnessed dramatic change in the city and the country as China's economy opened up after 1978. In the beginning they tended to stay with his wife's relatives, where, according to George, facilities were still very basic, but in later years, which saw a building boom in Zhongshan including of luxury hotels, they opted to stay at the Crowne Plaza. The key reason for them to keep returning has to do with his wife's deep sense of belonging to China. As George says: 'Every time she lands in China, she's a bird. Because it's her country. Everything she reads is in Chinese. I'm lost, because I can't read Chinese.' For George personally, going to China has also been very meaningful for his sense of identity: 'I'd been in Australia and been Chinese; I wanted to find out what it was like to be Chinese in China.' For George, then, going to China meant reconnecting with his Chinese heritage. 'Since going back to China,' he says, 'I've begun to realise what it means to be Chinese.' And Chineseness, for him, refers to cultural traditions such as going to the temple and to the cemetery to pay one's respect to the ancestors. 'A lot of the modern people don't do these things [but] there's a lot of meaning, because it's honouring and keeping alive your heritage,' he says. It is a heritage, however, that is gradually being cast out in a rapidly modernising China, which George regrets.

> That's why when I go back to China, I look for the parts where nothing is modern. We go to a little village and a little restaurant there under a tent, and they've got one stove, and the mother and the husband are there making 'wonton' (雲吞, pronounced in Cantonese). The proper pork, done in proper pastry, and the soup is not packaged soup. They boil the pork bones, and it's such a different taste.

George's romantic affection for Chinese culture has little to do with today's 'modern', prosperous China. 'For all that', he says, 'even though China is now becoming a world power, it is still backwards in many things.'

For Douglas Lam and Kam Louie, returning to the ancestral village was a more tangible affair, given that they had lived in their respective family homes when they were very young and still had close family members living there decades after they migrated to Australia in the early 1960s. Since the early 1970s, when entering and visiting China was made easier for overseas Chinese, they had returned to the village regularly to visit their relatives (and to bring much-needed gifts). By the 2010s, however, their connection to the village became more and more tenuous as the houses had begun to fall down and Zhongshan underwent rapid modernisation.

Douglas's ancestral house in Antang village, built in the early twentieth century with money sent back to Zhongshan by his grandfather, is now under his name – 'my mother made sure of it'. Douglas says the house is still there but is in a very poor condition now. 'It was the biggest house in the neighbourhood with two stories. We had an attic and a roof top balcony. It was a big building [by the standards then], a gold mountain house.' His mother lived in the house until she died in her nineties in 2006. After his mother's passing Douglas let a family of distant relatives live in the house rent-free, but they have since moved out to buy a unit in a high-rise building,

Figure 3.2: Kam Louie's family home in Dutou village (渡頭村) in 2018. Photo courtesy of Kam Louie.

a clear sign of the modernisation of Zhongshan. It is uncertain what will happen to the house in the future. He would like to do major remedial work and rebuild the house, but he would need to raise the funds to do so. He donated a modest amount for the renovation of the village hall, but says that the village is now unrecognisable due to recent demographic changes. There are now more outsiders, internal migrants from other parts of China, than true local villagers, he says, some of whom left the village some decades ago. The newcomers 'don't speak our dialect, they don't even understand mainstream Cantonese'.

Kam Louie has had similar experiences with his family home in Dutou village (see Figure 3.2). It was built by Kam's grandfather, a two-storey *huaqiao* house (僑房, *kiu fong* in Cantonese) with colourful ornate paintings and gilding on the façade of the house. The gilding was scraped off by his grandmother and sister on the eve of the Cultural Revolution to avoid attacks by the Red Guards, so that the house's exterior now looks barren. A very distant uncle of Kam's lived in the house until some fifteen years ago when he died, but since then the house, now very dilapidated, has been vacant. It is locked up and Kam does not even have the keys for it. As Kam says, the last time he went (in 2018), 'it was literally falling down, so you could kick the door and it would probably open'. Kam says he would like to get rid of the house, perhaps to donate it, but he finds the complicated bureaucratic process he would have to go through daunting.

Like our other informants, Kam stresses that Zhongshan has undergone rapid change and that the old village life no longer exists. Many old villagers have moved to a new part of the town. 'They are getting away from the tradition of villages, they want to be modern and live in Western-style houses with lots of room and big windows.' The Zhongshan (Shekki) dialect (石岐話) is also no longer much in use. 'You get into a taxi, you go to the shops, they always speak Cantonese rather than Zhongshan. The younger people all speak Cantonese and Mandarin now.' Such observations speak to the intense pace of the change that has taken place in China since the 1980s. As Kam says, 'it's nice to come back to Australia where change is not so drastic. Not so swinging from one extreme to the other.'

The Precarity of Transnational Identities

Each of our four informants, all settled in Sydney, in their own way have life trajectories that are a testimony to the transnationality of their identities, bridging and joining Australia and China – or more specifically, Sydney and Zhongshan – through their diasporic links to the homeland, by physically returning to it or symbolically connecting with it. They inhabit transnational identities marked by an in-betweenness that transcends fixed and closed ideas of the national, both problematising and dynamising Australianness and Chineseness. In this way, they personify the living energy that animates the China–Australia heritage corridor. This transnational heritage is embodied not only in the material legacy left behind by returned migrants in their ancestral villages – particularly in the form of the homes they built for their families – but also in the social and cultural meanings that their descendants in Australia continue to invest in the memory of this migration history, a history that has bound China and Australia irrevocably together.

Even Gordon Mar, who is the most emphatic in his claim of Australianness and has expressed no sense of attachment to his ancestral home, is steadfast in the affirmation of his Chinese identity. Since his retirement he has enacted this commitment to Chineseness by making a hobby of giving talks about China and the Chinese at Rotary Clubs and the University of the Third Age around Sydney, featuring topics such as anti-Chinese racism, the impact of the Opium Wars, and the forgotten role of Chinese labourers in the First World War.[65] His motivation is to enhance intercultural understanding, to impress on Australians that the Chinese have been in Australia since the 1840s and that their contribution to this country should not be overlooked: 'I've done about 230 talks. It's a good way of getting to an audience. Over the years, I have spoken to thousands of people with this message

---

65. John Fitzgerald (*Big White Lie*, 250) notes that 50,000 Chinese labourers were contracted to build trenches in France in 1917 and an additional 100,000 in 1918.

that you should get to know the Chinese in your community, just to create greater understanding of who we are, and our background, and our culture.' For Gordon, the meaning of his Chineseness is significant particularly in the context of Australia: it is a diasporic Chineseness that is not associated with a lived, physical or material connection with the ancestral home village but is enduringly indebted to the migrant enterprise of previous generations who first journeyed to Australia.

For George Wing Kee too, whose life trajectory was similar to Gordon's in that he also grew up in a hostile white Australia in a tight-knit Chinese Australian family, Chineseness has been a central motif in his life. In his later years, he became a prominent local Chinese Australian community leader, with a strong commitment to the heritage of Sydney's Chinatown. Since Australia adopted multiculturalism in the 1980s, Chinatown – the area where many migrants from Zhongshan converged in the early days – has become a popular tourist destination, which has given the area a new lease of life.[66] George helped set up the Haymarket Chamber of Commerce to support the business community in the Chinatown area, and he has led regular walking tours around Chinatown, sharing his in-depth knowledge of Chinatown's history, architecture, and people. In his own way, George contributes to the maintenance of the China–Australia heritage corridor by bringing to life, for today's audiences, a migration history that has deeply shaped Australia's past and present and its relationship to China. He regularly returns to Zhongshan with his wife, who was born there, a transnational back-and-forth that gives him an opportunity to experience his diasporic Chineseness in a visceral way.

Kam Louie, meanwhile, has also lived a life in the hybrid in-between zone that connects Australia and China. Kam's story demonstrates how the political fallout of the Communist revolution did not inevitably turn overseas Chinese away from China, even though his family suffered greatly from the violence of the Mao years. He even studied in Hong Kong for two years and worked as an English teacher at Nanjing University for another two years in the 1970s, just after the death of Mao. More recently, he spent almost ten years as Dean of Arts at the University of Hong Kong, until his retirement in 2014. As a scholar, Kam has dedicated his work to Chinese philosophical and cultural history, and he is married to a New Zealander who is also a China scholar. As he said in an interview, 'throughout my life, I have been trying to explain "China" to Westerners and explain the "West" to Chinese people.'[67] Kam thus occupies a pivotal diasporic identity which uniquely fuses a personal and an intellectual dimension in Australia's connection with China. As such, he also insists on a nuanced assessment of the complex history of the People's Republic of China.

---

66. Kay Anderson, Ien Ang, Andrea Del Bono, Donald McNeill, and Alexandra Wong, *Chinatown Unbound: Trans-Asian Urbanism in the Age of China* (London: Rowman and Littlefield, 2019).
67. Kam Louie, interview with Ruolan Yi, 26 March 2015, http://www.china-studies.taipei/comm2/interview/australia/interviewAU03.pdf.

Like Douglas Lam, Kam personally witnessed the brutal shaming of overseas Chinese families at the hands of the Communists as a young child. But while Kam does not bear a grudge against Communist China despite some of the horrible things that happened, because he thinks many in the government genuinely wanted to do good, Douglas remains resentful. Yet he has never forsaken his loyalty to family and his attachment to the ancestral village. Of our four informants, he has been the most hands-on in keeping the diasporic link with Zhongshan alive, having returned there about once a year (until the COVID-19 pandemic). In recent years he has developed an interest in genealogy research and has helped a number of diasporic Chinese families find their ancestral villages and family linkages in Zhongshan. For example, he acted as a guide and translator to help Glenn and Phillip Mar and their uncle, Jimmy, to find their ancestral home and ancestors' grave in Sha Chong village.[68] Douglas thinks that many families now want to know about their ancestors because of what he calls an 'emancipation of mind'. 'They are no longer ashamed of their ancestors who worked at a laundry or was a chop suey house owner and all that. They now appreciate that their ancestors worked day and night, and only have one day off for Chinese New Year. They had a very, very hard life, and they have come to appreciate that.' Douglas, then, is playing a very active instrumental role in reviving the heritage corridor that binds the *qiaoxiang* of Zhongshan with the descendants of those who, generations ago, left to seek their fortunes overseas.

Nevertheless, as passionate and committed as Douglas is in sustaining this connection to the past and to the home village, he is one of a diminishing cohort. He thinks no one else in his family – neither his cousins nor his children – cares about it: 'they don't have the same degree of attachment that I have to the old place'. Kam Louie also says he is the only one of his family who has returned regularly to the village; none of his brothers and sisters have done so, let alone his children, although the latter have followed their father's example and studied Chinese at university. His son even gained a master's degree at Peking University, where Kam also studied as a postgraduate student. Gordon Mar similarly says that there is no interest from the next generations in the family's history. 'They'd be curious to know, yes, we used to sell bananas, and we got this and that, but they don't really have any interest in our connections.' It would seem then that the transnational connection to the ancestral village has faded greatly among Australian descendants of the *huaqiao* generation, who tend to be firmly integrated in the society in which they were born and who, as Peterson observes, 'have only meagre and largely sentimental links to their ancestral homeland'.[69] If they do identify with Chineseness, it is associated more with its meaning as an ethnic identity in a multicultural Australia than with its transnational diasporic dimension.

---

68. See Chapter 5 of this volume.
69. Peterson, *Overseas Chinese*, 177.

But there is a more important reason why our informants may represent the last generation to sustain, each in their own way, the transnational connections of Sydney's Zhongshan diaspora with their home villages. This is because the rapid modernisation and economic growth that has swept across China in the past few decades has turned the *qiaoxiang* into very different places, as our informants themselves have already experienced first-hand. These villages have, to a large extent, de-traditionalised. They have become more prosperous and have seen an influx of migrants from other parts of China. If there are still family members left in these villages, most of them would no longer rely on remittances from their overseas kin.[70] Moreover, the PRC government no longer makes the quest for donations and investments through transnational families in the *qiaoxiang* a priority, as it has become clear that their importance for China's economic growth is increasingly insignificant. By the early twenty-first century, remittances made up only 0.7 per cent of GDP and played a minimal role in China's development.[71] As a consequence, the old *qiaoxiang* are increasingly irrelevant for the prosperity of the Chinese nation as a whole. Their histories as the migrant-sending native places of sojourners may still be remembered, but their lucrative transnational past has little bearing on their economic and social fortunes today. As Yow Cheun Hoe has shown, these old *qiaoxiang* areas can no longer rely on appeals to familial ties, primordial sentiment, and patriotism to attract investments, as diasporic Chinese have drifted away from their ancestral home villages. Instead, overseas Chinese investments in China are now overwhelmingly motivated by business calculations rather than ancestral roots.[72]

This does not mean that the PRC is no longer interested in appealing to its diaspora for national benefit or no longer sees the diaspora as an asset – on the contrary. But the main focus of the PRC's diaspora policy in recent times has been on the so-called new migrants (新移民, *xin yinmin* in Mandarin), who have spread across the world since China's opening up in 1978 and who hail from the rapidly expanding urban middle class, originating from all parts of China.[73] These are the first-ever emigrants from China who have grown up in and experienced the economic rise of the People's Republic and who may be more disposed to long-distance nationalism today. It is this new diaspora that the PRC government now reaches out to with patriotic calls to 'serve the nation' (為國家服務, *wei guojia fuwu* in Mandarin) and loyalty to the 'motherland'.[74] What is most important for the PRC leadership today,

---

70. Yow, *Guangdong and Chinese Diaspora*, 145.
71. Mette Thunø, 'China's New Global Position: Changing Policies towards the Chinese Diaspora in the Twenty-First Century', in *China's Rise and the Chinese Overseas*, ed. Bernard Wong and Chee-Beng Tan (Abingdon: Routledge, 2018), 187.
72. Yow, *Guangdong and Chinese Diaspora*, 149.
73. Peterson, *Overseas Chinese*, 176.
74. See, for example, Thunø, 'Reaching Out'. See also Pal Nyiri, 'Expatriating Is Patriotic? The Discourse on New Migrants in the People's Republic of China and Identity Construction among Recent Migrants from the PRC', *Journal of Ethnic and Migration Studies* 27, no. 4 (2001): 635–53, https://doi.org/10.1080/13691830120090421; Hong Liu, 'New Migrants and the Revival of Overseas Chinese Nationalism', *Journal of Contemporary China* 14, no. 43 (2005): 291–316, https://doi.org/10.1080/10670560500065611.

however, is no longer the inflow of overseas funds but that of knowledge and talent, and for diasporic Chinese to act as 'public diplomats' on behalf of China's foreign affairs.[75] One of the intentions of President Xi Jinping's highly publicised idea of the China Dream, for example, is to encourage diasporic Chinese communities across the globe, whether foreign or Chinese nationals, to engage and assist in the national rejuvenation of the Mainland.[76] Imagined here is a global Chinese community that is presumably united in its patriotic allegiance to China.

However, such Sinocentric attempts to bind ethnic Chinese abroad together and mobilise their attachment to the ancestral homeland through essentialised appeals to a primordial 'Chineseness' are unlikely to attract members of the old diaspora, those earlier generations of Chinese overseas who migrated many decades ago, such as those featured in this chapter. In other words, the representation of diasporic Chinese as a singular China-oriented patriotic subject, as rendered in the PRC's dominant state discourse, flies in the face of the heterogeneous, hybridised, and fundamentally dis-placed identities of diasporic subjects, as the examples presented in this chapter have shown. The complex and often violent histories which have affected the transnational lives of such subjects and their families – exclusions, wars, revolutions, expropriations, assimilations – intensify the ways in which their identities 'hover in a movement between "home and away," attachment and detachment, identification and disidentification',[77] which are ultimately agnostic or resistant to the homogenising and nationalising pull of Xi's Chinese Dream. When Douglas Lam returns to Zhongshan to search for the ancestral homes and genealogies of diaspora descendants eager to find their 'roots', he does so not out of patriotism or national pride. Nor does he seek the assistance of the Overseas Chinese Affairs Bureau: he enters China on a tourist visa and roams the villages himself using his local grassroots connections, bypassing the official channels of the state. 'I'm just having fun. I eat and drink my way from village to village.' His attachment is highly localised and personal, associated with the villages of Zhongshan, not with the nation as a whole and certainly not with the political entity of the PRC.

The descendants themselves, meanwhile, are also unlikely to accede to the nationalist narrative of the Chinese state. In this regard, as Andrea Louie remarks, it is a fallacy to equate Chinese heredity with patriotism for the motherland.[78] Just like the American-born Chinese Americans studied by Louie, descendants of Zhongshan migrants in Australia may acknowledge their Chinese heritage but tend to embrace a modern and hybrid 'Chinese Australian' identity 'that stands

---

75. Thunø, 'China's New Global Position'.

76. James Jiann Hua To, *Qiaowu: Extra-Territorial Policies for the Overseas Chinese* (Leiden: Brill, 2014); Hong Liu and Els van Dongen, 'China's Diaspora Policies as a New Mode of Transnational Governance', *Journal of Contemporary China* 25, no. 102 (2016): 805–21, https://doi.org/10.1080/10670564.2016.1184894; Wu, 'China's Evolving Policy'.

77. Ien Ang, 'Unsettling the National: Heritage and Diaspora', in *Heritage, Memory and Identity*, ed. Helmut Anheier and Yudhisthir Raj Isar (London: SAGE, 2011), 86.

78. Louie, *Chineseness across Borders*, 27.

on its own in relation to mainland China', which is no longer 'the symbolic center of Chinese identities abroad'.[79] At the same time, their inherited symbolic link to China articulates how the conception of Australianness can never be thought of in isolation from the transnational formation of diasporic identities among the country's multicultural populations, including the Chinese. Both Chineseness and Australianness are therefore fundamentally unsettled and transnationalised from below. This is the enduring legacy of the China–Australia heritage corridor.

Bibliography

Anderson, Benedict. *The Spectre of Comparison: Nationalism, Southeast Asia, and the World*. London: Verso, 1998.

Anderson, Kay, Ien Ang, Andrea Del Bono, Donald McNeill, and Alexandra Wong. *Chinatown Unbound: Trans-Asian Urbanism in the Age of China*. London: Rowman and Littlefield, 2019.

Ang, Ien. *On Not Speaking Chinese: Living Between Asia and the West*. London: Routledge, 2001.

Ang, Ien. 'Together-in-Difference: Beyond Diaspora, into Hybridity'. *Asian Studies Review* 27, no. 2 (2003): 141–54. https://doi.org/10.1080/10357820308713372.

Ang, Ien. 'Unsettling the National: Heritage and Diaspora'. In *Heritage, Memory and Identity*, edited by Helmut Anheier and Yudhisthir Raj Isar, 82–94. London: SAGE, 2011.

Bagnall, Kate. 'Chinese Women in Colonial New South Wales: From Absence to Presence'. *Australian Journal of Biography and History* 3 (2020): 3–20. http://doi.org/10.22459/AJBH.2020.

Chan, Shelly. *Diaspora's Homeland: Modern China in the Age of Global Migration*. Durham, NC: Duke University Press, 2018.

Clifford, James. *Routes: Travel and Translation in the Late Twentieth Century*. Cambridge, MA: Harvard University Press, 1997.

Cottle, Drew, and Angela Keys. 'Red-Hunting in Sydney's Chinatown'. *Journal of Australian Studies* 31, no. 91 (2007): 25–31. https://doi.org/10.1080/14443050709388125.

DeMare, Brian. *Land Wars: The Story of China's Agrarian Revolution*. Stanford, CA: Stanford University Press, 2019.

Dikötter, Frank. 'The Silent Revolution: Decollectivization from Below during the Cultural Revolution'. *The China Quarterly* 227 (September 2016): 796–811. https://doi.org/10.1017/S0305741016000746.

Douw, Leo, Cen Huang, and Michael Godley, eds. *Qiaoxiang Ties: Interdisciplinary Approaches to 'Cultural Capitalism' in South China*. Abingdon: Routledge, 2010.

Duara, Prasenjit. 'Nationalists among Transnationals: Overseas Chinese and the Idea of China, 1900–1911'. In *Ungrounded Empires: The Cultural Politics of Modern Chinese Transnationalism*, edited by Aihwa Ong and Donald Nonini, 39–60. New York: Routledge, 1997.

---

79. Louie, *Chineseness across Borders*, 190.

Fitzgerald, John. *Big White Lie: Chinese Australians in White Australia*. Sydney: UNSW Press, 2007.

Fitzgerald, Stephen. *China and the Overseas Chinese: A Study of Peking's Changing Policy 1949–1970*. London: Cambridge University Press, 1972.

Gilroy, Paul. *The Black Atlantic: Modernity and Double Consciousness*. London: Verso, 1993.

Kuah, Khun Eng. *Rebuilding the Ancestral Village: Singaporeans in China*. Aldershot: Ashgate, 2000.

Kuhn, Philip A. *Chinese among Others: Emigration in Modern Times*. Lanham, MD: Rowman and Littlefield, 2008.

Kuo, Mei-fen. *Making Chinese Australia: Urban Elites, Newspapers and the Formation of Chinese-Australian Identity, 1892–1912*. Clayton, Victoria: Monash University Publishing, 2013.

Kuo, Mei-fen, and Judith Brett. *Unlocking the History of the Australian Kuo Min Tang, 1911–2013*. Kew, Victoria: Australian Scholarly Publishing, 2013.

Liu, Hong. 'New Migrants and the Revival of Overseas Chinese Nationalism'. *Journal of Contemporary China* 14, no. 43 (2005): 291–316. https://doi.org/10.1080/106705605 00065611.

Liu, Hong, and Els van Dongen. 'China's Diaspora Policies as a New Mode of Transnational Governance'. *Journal of Contemporary China* 25, no. 102 (2016): 805–21. https://doi.org /10.1080/10670564.2016.1184894.

Lopez, Mark. *The Origins of Multiculturalism in Australian Politics 1945–1975*. Carlton South, Victoria: Melbourne University Press, 2000.

Louie, Andrea. *Chineseness across Borders: Renegotiating Chinese Identities in China and the United States*. Durham, NC: Duke University Press, 2004.

Nyiri, Pal. 'Expatriating Is Patriotic? The Discourse on New Migrants in the People's Republic of China and Identity Construction among Recent Migrants from the PRC'. *Journal of Ethnic and Migration Studies* 27, no. 4 (2001): 635–53. https://doi.org/ 10.1080/13691830120090421.

Ong, Soon Keong. '"Chinese, but Not Quite": *Huaqiao* and the Marginalization of the Overseas Chinese'. *Journal of Chinese Overseas* 9, no. 1 (2013): 1–32. https://doi. org/10.1163/17932548-12341247.

Peterson, Glen. *Overseas Chinese in the People's Republic of China*. Abingdon: Routledge, 2012.

Shao, Dan. 'Chinese by Definition: Nationality Law, Jus Sanguinis, and State Succession, 1909–1980'. *Twentieth-Century China* 35, no. 1 (2009): 4–28. https://doi.org/10.1353/ tcc.0.0019.

Shen, Huifen. '*Qiaojuan* Politics: Government Policies toward the Left-Behind Family Members of Chinese Overseas 1880s–1990s'. *Journal of Chinese Overseas* 6, no. 1 (2010): 43–79. https://doi.org/10.1163/179325410X491464.

Stratton, Jon, and Ien Ang. 'Multicultural Imagined Communities: Cultural Difference and National Identity in the USA and Australia'. In *Multicultural States: Rethinking Difference and Identity*, edited by David Bennett, 135–62. London: Routledge, 1999.

Tan Chee-Beng. *Chinese Overseas: Comparative Cultural Issues*. Hong Kong: Hong Kong University Press, 2004.

Tavan, Gwenda. *The Long Slow Death of White Australia*. Melbourne: Scribe, 2005.

Thunø, Mette. 'Reaching Out and Incorporating Chinese Overseas: The Transterritorial Scope of the PRC by the End of the 20th Century'. *The China Quarterly* 168 (December 2001): 910–29. https://doi.org/10.1017/S0009443901000535.

Thunø, Mette. 'China's New Global Position: Changing Policies towards the Chinese Diaspora in the Twenty-First Century'. In *China's Rise and the Chinese Overseas*, edited by Bernard Wong and Chee-Beng Tan, 184–208. Abingdon: Routledge, 2018.

To, James Jiann Hua. *Qiaowu: Extra-Territorial Policies for the Overseas Chinese*. Leiden: Brill, 2014.

Wang, Gungwu. 'A Note on the Origins of Hua-ch'iao'. In *Community and Nation: Essays on Southeast Asia and the Chinese*, 18–27. Singapore: Heinemann Educational Books, 1981.

Wang, Gungwu. 'A Single Chinese Diaspora? Some Historical Reflections'. In *Imagining the Chinese Diaspora: Two Australian Perspectives*, by Wang Gungwu and Annette Shun-wah, 1–17. Canberra: Centre for the Study of the Chinese Southern Diaspora, 1999.

Williams, Michael. *Returning Home with Glory: Chinese Villagers around the Pacific, 1849 to 1949*. Hong Kong: Hong Kong University Press, 2018.

Wu Xiao An. 'China's Evolving Policy towards the Chinese Diaspora in Southeast Asia (1949–2018)'. *Trends in Southeast Asia*, no. 14, Singapore: ISEAS, 2019.

Yow, Cheun Hoe. *Guangdong and Chinese Diaspora*. Abingdon: Routledge, 2013.

4
Diaspora Tourism and Homeland Travel

Alexandra Wong

Introduction

In this chapter, we turn our focus to how descendants of Australian Chinese migrants maintain transnational connections with their ancestral villages in Zhongshan through diaspora tourism. It is hard to define what constitutes 'diaspora tourism', as it goes by many names, including heritage tourism, legacy tourism, ancestry tourism, genealogy tourism, roots tourism, and visiting friends and relatives tourism, to name a few.[1] Diaspora tourism also occurs on different scales and levels of formality, ranging from grassroots initiatives such as trips taken by individuals, families, or small historical groups,[2] to nationally organised events such as Homecoming Scotland[3] and Homecoming Ireland,[4] which feature large-scale, year-long festivals, usually organised by national tourist agencies to attract diasporas worldwide to visit their 'home' countries. Regardless of its scale, diaspora tourism can be broadly defined as 'the travel of people in diaspora to their ancestral homelands in search of their roots or to feel connected to their personal heritage'.[5]

Diaspora tourism has become popular among Chinese Australians in recent years. Following the broadcast of the popular reality TV show *Who Do You Think You Are?* featuring celebrities searching for their family history since the late 2000s,

---

1. Yongguang Zou, Fang Meng, and Qianghong Li, 'Chinese Diaspora Tourists' Emotional Experiences and Ancestral Hometown Attachment', *Tourism Management Perspectives* 37 (2021): 100768, https://doi.org/10.1016/j.tmp.2020.100768.
2. Sophie Couchman and Kate Bagnall, 'Memory and Meaning in the Search for Chinese Australian Families', in *Remembering Migration: Oral Histories and Heritage in Australia*, ed. Kate Darian-Smith and Paula Hamilton (Cham: Palgrave Macmillan, 2019), 339.
3. VisitScotland, 'Scotland's Themed Years', accessed 8 September 2021, https://www.visitscotland.com/about/themed-years/.
4. Ronan McGreevy, 'Plans for Global Irish Homecoming', accessed 8 September 2021, https://www.irishtimes.com/news/plans-for-global-irish-homecoming-1.884890.
5. Wei-Jue Huang, William Haller, and Gregory Ramshaw, 'Diaspora Tourism and Homeland Attachment: An Exploratory Analysis', *Tourism Analysis* 18, no. 3 (August 2013): 285, http://dx.doi.org/10.3727/108354213X1367339861069.

a growing number of people are interested in exploring their cultural heritage. The digitisation of the government's birth, death, marriage, and immigration records and the rise of genealogical websites such as ancestry.com.au, myancestors.com.au, and findmypast.com.au have made searching for ancestors' records much easier. People interested in their family history can also hire a professional genealogist to help search for the official records,[6] or they can follow step-by-step guides to gather oral or archival information about their ancestors themselves.[7] Companies such as 'My China Roots' also offer 'commodified' village exploration tours. People can join a package tour to travel to their ancestral villages with a professional genealogist to track down their family history. Those embarking on a hometown journey of their own may engage a guide with local knowledge of genealogy searches, for example Douglas Lam,[8] or request assistance from the local branch of the government's Overseas Chinese Affairs Office.

In this chapter, we adopt an 'embodied transnational approach'[9] to shed light on the differentiated experiences of diaspora tourism by Chinese Australians and explore how their travels relate to their place attachment and diasporic identities. Rather than assuming movements between places are 'frictionless', we give weight to personal and affective engagement with places, and the 'sticky embeddedness' that can attach to more than one place.[10] We examine three cases of homeland visits made by Australian-born Chinese whose ancestors migrated from Zhongshan in the late nineteenth century. None of these people had visited their ancestral homeland during their childhood. Their socio-economic backgrounds, family upbringing, and the time that they travelled to Zhongshan were different; they also had different experiences of place through their social and material engagements (people, villages, buildings, and objects) during their visits. Focusing on their embodied encounters with their families' material heritage and social relations through a transnational lens, we make sense of the impact of these travels on their place attachment and their self-identities.

Diaspora Tourism and Transnationalism

This chapter frames diaspora tourism through the lens of transnationalism, defined as 'the process by which immigrants build social fields that link together their

---

6. See family history research services by professional genealogists offered by My China Roots.com, accessed 16 September 2021, https://www.mychinaroots.com/services/research/village-exploration.
7. Chinese Museum, 'Guide to Chinese-Australian Family Research', accessed 16 September 2021, https://www.chinesemuseum.com.au/Handlers/Download.ashx?IDMF=10baa807-34f4-480a-9f57-ab093ad13dbc.
8. See Chapter 3 of this volume for Douglas Lam's life story.
9. Kevin Dunn, 'Embodied Transnationalism: Bodies in Transnational Spaces', *Population, Space and Place* 16, no. 1 (2010): 4–7, https://doi.org/10.1002/psp.593.
10. Dunn, 'Embodied Transnationalism', 7.

country of origin and their country of settlement.[11] In Nina Glick Schiller's words, the transnational social field is a global space where 'simultaneous social-cultural, economic and political process of local and cross-border participation, sociality, membership, connection and identification' occurs.[12] This transnational space enables diaspora members to 'take actions, make decisions and feel concerns and develop identities within social networks that connect them to two or more societies simultaneously'.[13]

In this framing, diaspora tourism can be regarded as one form of transnational practice that connects a migrant's homeland and place of settlement. The concept of transnationalism also has different implications for the affective dimension for early and contemporary migrants' homeland travels.[14] While earlier migrants may have been motivated by 'longing for home', with a sense of belonging to a singular place or national identity, contemporary migrants often maintain transnational ties with their home country even though they have successfully integrated with the host country.[15] Their transnational connections and belongings are more complicated than the conventional understanding of place attachment and identities of earlier migrants based on the division of 'home' and 'host' countries. Besides, these transnational migrants, even those coming from the same country, never represent a homogeneous group.[16] Their perceptions, actions, and identities are shaped by individual experiences and the political, social, and economic contexts in their homeland and place of settlement as well as a 'diasporic state of mind' – a fragmented, shifting, and mixed-up consciousness constituted by migrants' practices of remembrance, territorial attachments, and sense of belonging.[17] As a result, contemporary migrants' identities are not static or fixed but constantly evolve and are mediated through interwoven social relations and processes in the transnational social field in a movement between 'home and away'.[18]

---

11. Nina Glick Schiller, Linda Basch, and Cristina Blanc-Szanton, 'Transnationalism: A New Analytic Framework for Understanding Migration', *Annals of the New York Academy of Sciences* 645, no. 1 (1992): 1, https://doi.org/10.1111/j.1749-6632.1992.tb33484.x.
12. Nina Glick Schiller, 'Transnationality and the City', in *The New Blackwell Companion to the City*, ed. Gary Bridge and Sophie Watson (Malden, MA: Blackwell Publishing, 2011), 179, https://doi.org/10.1002/9781444395105.ch16.
13. Schiller, Basch, and Blanc-Szanton, 'Transnationalism', 1–2.
14. Wei-Jue Huang, Gregory Ramshaw, and William C. Norman, 'Homecoming or Tourism? Diaspora Tourism Experience of Second-Generation Immigrants', *Tourism Geographies* 18, no. 1 (2016): 61–62, https://doi.org/10.1080/14616688.2015.1116597.
15. See also Chapter 3 of this volume.
16. Laurence Ma, 'Space, Place and Transnationalism in the Chinese Diaspora', in *The Chinese Diaspora: Space, Place, Mobility, And Identity*, ed. Laurence J. C. Ma and Carolyn Cartier (Lanham, MD: Rowman and Littlefield, 2003), 5.
17. Ien Ang, 'Unsettling the National: Heritage and Diaspora', in *Cultures and Globalization: Heritage, Memory and Identity*, ed. Helmut Anheier and Yudhishthir Raj Isar (London: SAGE, 2011), 6.
18. Ang, 'Unsettling the National', 6.

Homeland Travel, Place Attachment, and Diasporic Identity

Unlike usual forms of travel in which visitors tend to cast a 'tourist gaze' on a foreign culture,[19] diaspora tourism is usually associated with a sense of diasporic 'homecoming'.[20] Paul Basu, in his research on visits of overseas Scots to the Scottish highlands, notes that the diaspora's journey generally contains three facets: a sense of 'homecoming', 'seeking the indeterminate', and 'pilgrimage'.[21] This means that a migrant's or their descendants' return to the original homeland is generally motivated by a desire to discover their family history or heritage, and that these travels are usually regarded as a 'sacred journey' with symbolic meanings attached to it. They can be understood as a manifestation of the diaspora's search for a sense of belonging through the physical movement of visiting ancestral homelands.[22] As Basu remarks, these journeys have 'the capacity to effect personal transformation', rendering them quite literally 'life-changing experiences for many participants'.[23]

Research on homeland travel is mainly found in the tourism literature. A strand of research on diaspora tourism is devoted to the study of the affective elements of diaspora tourism, including place attachment and self-identity. Place attachment refers to the 'affective bonds' that individuals develop with their physical environment.[24] Some research has shown a complex relationship between diaspora tourism and emotional attachment to homelands. For example, Monica Iorio and Andrea Corsale's study of Transylvanian Saxons' homeland tours revealed that these journeys played an 'ambivalent' role in the (re)definition of the meaning of home and homeland and contributed to reaffirming a sense of belonging to Transylvania and Germany at the same time.[25] A quantitative study of Chinese diaspora tourism found evidence that hometown visits can lead to nostalgic memory and affective arousal, influencing diaspora tourists' hometown attachment.[26] A study by Ellen Oxfeld in southeast China highlighted the moral dilemmas associated with diaspora hometown visits for local communities, which were caused by the returnees' donations to the village, the fanfare to welcome their visits, and their impact on families without overseas connections.[27]

---

19. John Urry, *The Tourist Gaze*, 3rd ed. (Los Angeles: SAGE, 2011), 15.
20. Huang, Ramshaw, and Norman, 'Homecoming or Tourism', 60.
21. Paul Basu, 'Route Metaphors of "Roots-Tourism" in the Scottish Highland', in *Reframing Pilgrimage: Cultures in Motion*, ed. Simon Coleman (London: Routledge, 2004), 157.
22. Basu, 'Route Metaphors', 175.
23. 'Basu, 'Route Metaphors', 157.
24. Ning Chen, Michael Hall, and Girish Prayag, 'Place Matters! Introduction to Sense of Place and Place Attachment in Tourism', in *Sense of Place and Place Attachment in Tourism*, ed. Ning Chen, Michael Hall, and Girish Prayag (Abingdon: Routledge, 2021), 3.
25. Monica Iorio and Andrea Corsale, 'Diaspora and Tourism: Transylvanian Saxons Visiting the Homeland', *Tourism Geographies* 15, no. 2 (2013): 199, https://doi.org/10.1080/14616688.2012.647327.
26. Zou, Meng, and Li, 'Chinese Diaspora Tourists', 10.
27. Ellen Oxfeld, *Drink Water, but Remember the Source: Moral Discourse in a Chinese Village* (Berkeley: University of California Press, 2010), 152–71.

Another strand of research on diaspora tourism focuses on the experiences of the diaspora's second or later generations.[28] Studies have shown that their emotional responses and homeland attachments were different from those of first-generation migrants.[29] Wei-Jue Huang, Gregory Ramshaw, and William Norman note that the homeland attachment of second-generation Chinese migrants was not rooted in a specific locale, as they can also feel emotional attachments to their family's place of origin without actually visiting there.[30] This implies that these descendants of migrants are not looking for an actual home through their homeland travels, but for an imaginary homeland or just 'moments of home'.[31] Proficiency in their parents' language by the second or later generation of migrant visitors was found to be a primary factor for positive or negative experiences in their homeland travels.[32] In related research, Huang, Kam Hung, and Chun-Chu Chen have shown that homeland ties vary from generation to generation and that later diaspora generations tend to express stronger attachment to the home country rather than their specific ancestral hometown. However, this study showed that social bonds developed during a visit could help maintain hometown attachment and lead to repeat visitation in future.[33]

The relations between homeland travel and diasporic identity have also received much attention in the diaspora tourism literature. Duval's study of return visits of Eastern Caribbean diasporas in Toronto found that homeland visits enabled them to physically reconnect with people and culture and to develop social ties. This helped them 'renew, reiterate and solidify' their cultural norms and values and maintain their diasporic identities.[34] A study by Carl Iain Cater, Katja Poguntke, and Wyn Morris found that diaspora tourism can bring visitors to a setting that enables them to connect with and reflect on their cultural identity, thus leading to identity development.[35] Similarly, Nigel Bond and John Falk have argued that diaspora tourism is motivated by people's self-identity and desire to connect with their cultural heritage by visiting the homeland. Their tourist experience may be reflected upon and lead to processes of 'identify development', 'identity maintenance', or 'identity moderation

---

28. Z. Xiang, W. Huimin, and F. Huaxiu, eds, *Finding Family Roots: Youth of Chinese Descent from USA and Canada Visit Xinhui and Enping Counties* (Beijing: Great Wall Books, 1983).

29. Zou, Meng, and Li, 'Chinese Diaspora Tourists', 10.

30. Huang, Ramshaw, and Norman, 'Homecoming or Tourism', 60.

31. Mitra Etemaddar, Tara Duncan, and Hazel Tucker, 'Experiencing "Moments of Home" through Diaspora Tourism and Travel', *Tourism Geographies* 18, no. 5 (2016): 513–14, https://doi.org/10.1080/14616688.2016.1220973.

32. Huang, Ramshaw, and Norman, 'Homecoming or Tourism', 73.

33. Wei-Jue Huang, Kam Hung, and Chun-Chu Chen, 'Attachment to the Home Country or Hometown? Examining Diaspora Tourism across Migrant Generations', *Tourism Management* 68 (2018): 61–62, https://doi.org/10.1016/j.tourman.2018.02.019.

34. David Timothy Duval, 'Conceptualising Return Visits: A Transnational Perspective', in *Tourism, Diasporas, and Space*, ed. Tim Coles and Dallen Timothy (London: Routledge, 2004), 59.

35. Carl Iain Cater, Katja Poguntke, and Wyn Morris, 'Y Wladfa Gymreig: Outbound Diasporic Tourism and Contribution to Identity', *Tourism Geographies* 21, no. 4 (2019): 665–86, https://doi.org/10.1080/14616688.2019.1571095.

and reconstruction'.[36] Diaspora tourism can be seen as a means through which those 'aspects of identity that have been previously cast aside can be rediscovered, or re-imaged in a way that accounts for changes in the individual's need and circumstance or context'.[37]

Chinese Australians and Their Ancestral Homeland Visits

In the following section, I provide three case studies to explore the spatial and emotional dimensions of the travels made by Australian Chinese migrant descendants to their ancestors' hometowns in Zhongshan. The discussion mainly draws on interviews with these returning descendants and family members who travelled with them on homeland visits. I start with a brief biographical narrative of each descendant focusing on their family backgrounds, as identities can be passed down to next generations through 'the transmission of knowledge, traditions, money and other cultural practices with families and institutions'.[38] Next, I outline their hometown travel experiences, including both material and non-material encounters in their ancestral villages. Finally, I describe how they reflect on what the travels meant to them, including their diasporic identities.

Denise Ma: 'I'm equally proud of being Australian and Chinese'

Denise Ma (馬詠賢 Ma Wing Yin) was born in 1953 in Sydney. She is a third-generation Chinese Australian of the Ma family from Sha Chong village (沙涌村) in Zhongshan. Her grandfather Joseph (馬祖容 Ma Joe Young) was the brother of Ma Wing Charn (馬永燦, 1863–1938) and the cousin of Ma Ying Piu (馬應彪, 1860–1944), the two founders of the Sincere Department Store. Joseph Ma was involved in the early management of Wing Sang & Co. (永生) and later became the Hong Kong director of Sincere.

Denise Ma's father Thomas (馬顯維 Ma Hin Wai) was born in Hong Kong in 1916. He was the sixth child of Joseph Ma. Thomas came to Sydney in 1935 when he was nineteen years old to work in the family business Wing Sang & Co. In 1963, he bought a subsidiary of the company, Wing Tiy & Co. (永泰果欄), and operated the business until his retirement in the late 1970s. Denise's mother Lily Chan (陳英保 Chan Ying Bow) was born in Darwin in 1923. Lily returned to China with her family for three years to receive a Chinese education when she was five years old.

---

36. Nigel Bond and John Falk, 'Tourism and Identity-Related Motivations: Why Am I Here (and Not There)?', *International of Tourism Research* 15 (2013): 436–37, https://doi.org/10.1002/jtr.1886.
37. Bond and Falk, 'Tourism and Identity', 440. Probably 're-imagined' was intended, not 're-imaged'.
38. Mette Louise Berg and Susan Eckstein, 'Introduction: Re-imagining Migrant Generation', *Diaspora* 18 (2015): 7, https://doi.org/10.1353/dsp.2015.0001.

Denise and her brothers grew up in Strathfield, a suburb in the inner west of Sydney. Denise recalled that she and her siblings were brought up in a traditional 'Chinese' way. 'We had a very, very Chinese upbringing . . . It was all about family. It was all about respect.'[39] Denise's parents insisted that she speak Chinese (Cantonese) at home, and one of her family's rituals was to visit Rookwood Cemetery every Sunday to pay tribute to her ancestors. Growing up in Australia in the 1960s and 1970s, Denise faced racial discrimination when she was a child, although it was quite 'covert'. She conceded that she felt embarrassed to acknowledge her Chinese heritage. 'You did everything possible to hide the fact [her Chinese heritage], you can't hide your looks but just in every other thing you did, you just weren't Chinese', she said.

Being third-generation Australian Chinese, Denise admitted that she did not have a connection with Zhongshan. Although she had visited Hong Kong with her father when she was a child, she had never been to Zhongshan. As she said, 'the extent of the connection for me was that I always knew that my family came from Zhongshan. If I ever spoke to someone, "Oh, your family's from Zhongshan," I had no idea. I just knew that it was in the south of China. Somewhere in Guangdong Province.'

Denise's first hometown visit was in 1983. She booked a one-day tour to Zhongshan with her husband and young child and asked the tour guide to take her to Sha Chong village (沙涌村). When she arrived at the village for the first time, she felt 'blown away' and she developed a bond with the villagers almost instantly:

> There were people there who were colleagues of my uncle. They said they remember my grandfather and grandmother. They remember my uncle, who was younger than dad. But they didn't remember dad because dad left Hong Kong at nineteen. But they knew of dad. What blew me away was the fact that I was meeting these people. They were all Mas, and secondly, they understood me because I had to speak in Chinese. That blew me away; that they knew my family, and I could actually converse with them in Chinese.

After this one-day tour, Denise always wanted to return to the village again, but it was not until 2011 that she went on a trip with her two brothers Jonathan Ma and Matthew Ma and a cousin who had been to the village before. During this trip, they visited the humble house where their grandfather Joseph Ma was born. Although the house has been turned into a clinic, Denise still felt a connection to the building: 'That's where all the Mas – our grandfather and his brothers were born.'

Denise and her brothers visited several mansions in Sha Chong. One was a grand two-storey mansion built by their great-grandfather Ma Yung Joong (馬恩

---

39. Denise Ma, Jonathan Ma, and Matthew Ma, interview by Ien Ang, Christopher Cheng, and Alexandra Wong, 16 October 2017. All unreferenced quotes attributed to Denise Ma, Jonathan Ma, and Matthew Ma in this chapter are taken from this interview.

Figure 4.1: Mansion built by Denise's great-grandfather Ma Yung Joong (馬恩重) in Sha Chong village (沙涌村). Photo by Denis Byrne.

重). She instantly recognised the connection of this mansion to her grandparents' residence in Hong Kong, as the interiors of the two mansions were very similar.[40] Ma Yung Joong's mansion was unoccupied for a long time and has been turned into a cultural centre for martial arts practices in recent years. Denise and her brothers also went into the two mansions that belonged to Ma Ying Piu and Ma Wing Charn and met with Mar Lok Shan (馬樂山), a distant relative and famous mould maker of Charles Schulz's Snoopy cartoon characters.[41]

---

40. Denise's grandfather Joseph Ma had a mansion at 1 Duke Street, Kowloon, in Hong Kong. The mansion was a replica of Ma Yung Joong's mansion in Sha Chong. Denise Ma visited the mansion in Hong Kong when she was eleven and later recognised that the rooms in the Sha Chong mansion were in the same pattern as those in the building in Hong Kong.
41. Mar Lok Shan started making moulds for Charles Schulz from the 1970s after Schulz failed to find mould makers who could make his characters to his satisfaction. Mar taught cartoon mould-making at in Zhongshan Polytechnic, where there is now a museum to house his work. Mar Lok Shan passed away in 2014.

In addition to Sha Chong, Denise and her brothers also visited the Xiangshan Commercial Culture Museum (香山商業文化博物館) in Shekki (石岐, Shiqi), where they learned about the history of the Sincere Department Store and saw a model of the Sincere Department Store in Shanghai. They felt a sense of pride in their family history: 'Our grandfather and his brothers and cousin created that company. It grew – it would have been at its peak in the thirties and forties', Jonathan said.

Denise and her brothers enjoyed the time they spent in Zhongshan. 'It's just so exciting', Denise said; she attributed this partly to their ability to speak Chinese. She said, 'they weren't critical of the fact that your Chinese isn't good, in fact in many ways they tried to understand us . . . it makes you feel good because you think "Wow they can really understand me"'. Talking about the value of this homeland visit, Denise and her brothers thought the trip gave them 'a sense of history'. By going there and seeing the place, they were 'making a connection to their past'. As Matthew Ma said, 'Mum always talked to me about different things and mentioned these things. But I never made the connections . . . I heard about the house, but I did not know the connections back to Zhongshan and Sha Chong. This [visit] made it the stronger connection now.'

When we asked Denise about her cultural identity, she explained, 'when you are Chinese born in Australia – and we are third-generation Australians – you're neither Chinese nor Australian'. However, as the policy of Australia has changed to multiculturalism, Denise now sees herself as 'Australian-born Chinese' and emphasised that she is 'equally proud of being Australian as I am of my Chinese heritage'.

This trip helped renew Denise and her brothers' interest in their family heritage. In 2018, Denise went back to Sha Chong with nine people of the extended Ma family from Sydney. During this trip, Denise interviewed an elder of the village and learned more about the long history of her family, dating back to the 1200s. After that trip, Denise changed her last name back to 'Ma' (previously she went by her married name, 'Denise Flockton'). She explained, 'it was on this trip that I decided to reclaim my Ma (馬) birth name, due to the increased link I feel to my Zhongshan heritage'.[42] In November 2019, Denise organised a gathering of some one hundred Australia-based descendants of Joseph Ma in Sydney's Bicentennial Park for a family photo to commemorate the 150th anniversary of his birth.[43] The family photo can be seen as serving the purpose of giving 'material' reality of their heritage to the Ma clan in Sydney,[44] and it continued the traditional practice among Chinese since the nineteenth century of taking a family photo on a transnational scale.[45]

---

42. Email correspondence with Denise Ma, 17 April 2019.
43. Email correspondence with Denise Ma, 12 December 2019.
44. Connor Graham and Mark Rouncefield, 'Photo Practices and Family Values in Chinese Households' (Proceedings of the Workshop on Social Interaction and Mundane Technologies, 2008), accessed 25 September 2021, https://citeseerx.ist.psu.edu/viewdoc/download?doi=10.1.1.483.2583&rep=rep1&type=pdf.
45. Régine Thiriez, 'Photography and Portraiture in Nineteenth-Century China', *East Asian History (Canberra)* 17, nos. 17–18 (1999): 93.

Figure 4.2: The Ma clan photo (馬氏家族合照) taken in Sha Chong village (沙涌村) in 1917. Ma Wing Charn (馬永燦) is fifth from the left, Denise's grandfather Ma Joe Young (馬祖容) is sixth from left, Ma Ying Piu (馬應彪) is fourth from the left. Denise's grandmother is seated third from the right, with Denise's father Ma Hin Wai (馬顯維) on her knee. Photo courtesy of Denise Ma.

Figure 4.3: Descendants of Ma Joe Young (馬祖容) on the 150th anniversary of his birth; photo taken in 2019 in Sydney. Photo courtesy of Denise Ma.

William and Nancy Lee: 'We have become too Westernised'

William Lee (李惠林) was born in Sydney in 1934, the son of Lee Wah Hook (李華福) and Doris Gay (雷彩回). William's grandfather Lee Chee Win (李紫雲) came to Australia from Zhongshan in the late nineteenth century and established a grocery store in Sydney's Chinatown, named Yet Shing & Co. (日昇公司). His ancestral village was Xincun (新村), located just south of Shekki. William's father was born in Zhongshan in 1911. He was sent to study in Honolulu, Hawaii, before he came to Sydney in 1931 to work at the family store. William's mother Doris was born in Rose Bay, Sydney. Her father, George Louis Gay (雷鷄), was also from Zhongshan. He married Ada Hong (李紫洪), who was half Chinese and operated a market garden in Guildford in Western Sydney.

William lived with his family in Ultimo, which was close to the family grocery store in Chinatown. William attended the Ultimo Public School and later the Fort Street High School in Petersham and helped out in the family store when he was young. He met Nancy Logan, who is from an Irish family, when he was studying at the University of Sydney. They married in 1959 and have four children. Nancy was the one who kept all the historical records for the Lee (李) family. She researched and wrote biographies of William's ancestors. In our interview with them, Nancy often spoke for them both as William was hard of hearing.

Figure 4.4: William and his mother Doris at their family general store Yet Shing & Co. (日昇公司) in Sydney's Chinatown (雪梨唐人街). Photo courtesy of Nancy and William Lee.

According to Nancy, they did not have any connection with Zhongshan. This was because William's mother Doris did not want them to have these connections. Doris was three-quarters Chinese and did not really see herself as Chinese: 'She looked Chinese and she had a Chinese father, and she might know some words of Chinese, but she didn't speak Chinese.'[46] In fact, she 'didn't like the Chinese side much' and 'didn't have that feeling of "this is the clan" sort of thing'. William recalled that he often escaped from the Chinese school at the Chinese Presbyterian Church (雪梨華人長老會) near Chinatown on Saturdays and went to the movies instead when he was young. He cannot read or write Chinese, although he can speak a little bit of Cantonese. As Nancy said, 'William has lost a lot of Chineseness by marrying me' and 'we're not a Chinese family'.

The first time William and Nancy went to Zhongshan was in the late 1980s. When asked what motivated them to visit William's ancestral hometown, Nancy said it was curiosity. 'This is my family; I want to know who I am ... But I didn't have anybody to tell it, so I went out to get it.' They took advantage of a cheap airfare when a new airline was introduced in Australia. She said, 'it was an interest in China. We tried to get into China in the early 1980s, but it was not open to Australians, only certain people could go from Australia to China ... But when it became more open, we took our cheap fare to Guangdong.'

Nancy and William's journey was very much an exploration as William did not have much information about his ancestral village. 'We had to find our way to this village', Nancy said. She talked about the difficulties of travelling in Zhongshan: 'We were very wary about travelling in China. We had to hire a car, a government car. We had to have a government interpreter. We didn't know where we stood as we drove through the villages. At the towns, we would be stopped by the police.' After driving around a different village, they finally found Xincun (新村, lit. new village). Nancy described how they found the village:

> Finally, in the second last village at the end of the unmade road, and Bill got out of the car, and he said my name is so and so, and my father's name was so and so, do any of you remember them? One old guy said – there's a picture of him – he said, 'I drank wine at your father's wedding festival.'

While in Xincun village, William and Nancy discovered that William's ancestral house had been bombed by the Japanese during the war and that the site was now used as a pigsty. Nancy said, 'we might have been more interested if there was a family house there, but there wasn't'. Besides, they realised all their close family had already left the village or migrated elsewhere and only a distant cousin was still here. Although the people in the village were very welcoming to Nancy and William, Nancy did not feel very comfortable in the village:

---

46. William and Nancy Lee, interview with Denis Byrne and Alexandra Wong, 6 October 2017. All unreferenced quotes attributed to William and Nancy in this chapter are taken from this interview.

There was always a feeling of suspicion. We didn't want to be held as the rich, Australians. We kept out of their way so we wouldn't have to keep them. Because remember, our attitudes towards China were given by my mother-in-law, who didn't like the way that she was being treated by the Chinese parents . . . Our attitudes were given by Bill's three-quarter Chinese mother.

William's grandfather Lee Chee Win had a shop on one of Shekki's main streets (Yuelai Road 悦來路) and built a house nearby, both of which are still standing and owned by the Lee family. However, Nancy and William did not see the houses when they were in Shekki because they did not know the addresses at the time. Nancy said their visit to Zhongshan was very short, and as she said, 'I was on edge all the time, I didn't feel free' and 'our car kept getting stopped [by the police] along the way'. They left the village quickly: 'We'd seen what we wanted to see and we got out.' When asked whether they would go back again, Nancy said they were 'not interested'. 'There's nobody there we want to know, no buildings we want to see. We wanted to know this is what it was like, but that's all.'

Although Nancy and William have not returned to Zhongshan since that trip, their youngest child Geoff Lee (a minister of the New South Wales State government since 2019 and the Liberal Party member for Parramatta since 2011) made a

Figure 4.5: The shop owned by William's grandfather Lee Chee Win (李紫雲) in Yue Lai Road, Shekki (石岐悦來路), in 2017. Photo by Denis Byrne.

trip to Zhongshan in 2016 and managed to track down the two houses in Shekki. However, Nancy said they wanted to give the houses away.

> It's a building made of bricks and stone, why leave it there when it can be used by other people? So Geoffrey's idea is to donate it to the Chinese government on the condition it's used for charity, and who knows? He doesn't want [it], we don't want the house – nobody wants it, nobody wants to go back.

Speaking about William's identity, Nancy said, 'we've become too Westernised' and referred to her family as 'the very Western end of the family'. Nancy said her children have little identification with China and do not see themselves as Chinese. She did not believe the family's connection with Zhongshan would continue into the next generation. It would seem that William and Nancy's homeland visit has reinforced William's Australianness rather than his Chineseness.

Mabel Lee: 'I don't see the need of having any tag'

Mabel Lee (陳順妍) is the sister of Stanley Hunt (陳沛德, 1927–2019), mentioned in Chapters 2 and 7 of this volume. Mabel's grandfather was from Zhongshan. He came to Sydney during the 1890s and established an import/export business. Mabel's father Harry Hin Hunt (陳欣) was born in Sydney in 1902, but he was taken back to Zhongshan as a baby and grew up in Mashan village (馬山村) before returning to Sydney at the age of seventeen. He later operated a general store in Warialda, a small town in the Northern Tablelands of New South Wales. Mabel's mother Leong Wun-Ginn (梁雲娟), who was from Doumen (斗門), joined Harry, along with Stanley and two young children, from China in 1939, and Mabel was born in Warialda

Figure 4.6: Mabel Lee (陳順妍) (right) and her sisters in Merrylands, Sydney. Photo courtesy of Mabel Lee.

the same year. In 1945, when Mabel was five years old, the family left Warialda for Sydney, opening a fruit shop in Merrylands, and lived upstairs above the shop. Mabel recalled helping out in the family fruit shop with all her siblings every day after school and on weekends.

Mabel grew up in a period when Chinese were often subject to discrimination, but she never worried about her Chinese identity.[47] She recalled that when she was a child, other children called her 'Ching Chong Chinaman', but she would fight back. 'I was born a tough fighter, bully or whatever you like, I won't tolerate anything.'[48] Mabel attended Parramatta High School and then entered the University of Sydney in 1957 on a scholarship. After obtaining her Bachelor of Arts with first class honours in 1962, she went on to complete her PhD in 1966 with a thesis on Chinese political and economic thought in the late nineteenth and early twentieth centuries. Mabel joined the University of Sydney after she graduated and taught Chinese Studies for thirty years until she retired in 2000, but she is still active as an Adjunct Professor.[49] One of her most well-known achievements was her translation of 2000 Nobel Prize winner Gao Xingjian's (高行健) novel *Soul Mountain* (靈山) into English.

Mabel's father believed that his children should maintain their Chinese identity and insisted that they speak Chinese at home. He taught her some Chinese when she was young. 'My father was pleased that I was studying China and studying Chinese [at the University of Sydney]. My parents came to both my BA and my PhD [graduations]. And both of them were proud, particularly because I was doing Chinese history.'[50] Mabel's parents maintained connections with people from Zhongshan in Sydney. She remembers how her father helped some young boys from Zhongshan to come to Sydney to get an education, and her parents used to go to the Mandarin Club in Chinatown to socialise with people from Zhongshan in their older age. However, her parents did not tell her much about the home village when she was young as they 'didn't have time'.

The first time Mabel visited China was with a group of Chinese academics from Sydney in 1965. Two years later, she went to China again with an Australian delegation of teachers. She spoke about her early experiences of travelling to China:

> It was very interesting because it was during the Cultural Revolution, and you know, you'd have to listen to the lectures, and they said, 'Before China was liberated, it was a struggling', et cetera, et cetera. And then the next time I went was like two years after, and they said, 'it was more free.' So I went two times before the Cultural Revolution ended.

---

47. J. V. D'Cruz, interview with Mabel Lee, *Overland*, no. 179 (Winter 2005): 65–68.

48. Mabel Lee, interview with Ien Ang, Denis Byrne and Alexandra Wong, 12 December 2018. All unreferenced quotes attributed to Mable Lee in this chapter are taken from this interview unless stated otherwise.

49. Chinese Studies Association of Australia (CSAA), 'Interview: Adjunct Professor Mabel Lee', *Chinese Studies Association of Australia (CSAA) Newsletter*, no. 40 (August 2010): 10–13, accessed 10 September 2021, http://www.csaa.org.au/wp-content/uploads/2014/04/CSAA_Newsletter_40.pdf.

50. CSAA, 'Interview', 10–13.

During these two trips, she only went to big cities such as Shanghai, Guangzhou, Hangzhou, and Xi'an, but not Zhongshan. She first visited Zhongshan in the late 1970s. She went there mainly because her father wanted to go: 'He would say, "If you don't take me, I'll be dead." So I said, "Okay, I'll take you." So every year, at the end of the year, I would try to take him [to Zhongshan].' When Mabel and her father were in Zhongshan, they stayed in a hotel in Shekki, and her relatives from Mashan village would meet them there. After the opening up of China, she took her father to Guangzhou or Zhongshan whenever she could.

Figure 4.7: Sung-Sun Hall of Learning in Mashan School (馬山小學崇信教學樓) in 2017. The building was demolished in 2018 to make way for a new school building to be constructed with earthquake-resistant materials. Photo by Denis Byrne.

Mabel has only been to the ancestral village of Mashan once. In 1983 she travelled with her father and all her siblings to Mashan village for the official opening of Mashan Primary School (馬山小學). The school was donated by her brother Stanley Hunt. It can house 800 students, and the primary teaching building, the 'Sung-Sun Hall of Learning' (崇信教學樓), was named after their father (Harry Hunt's Chinese name is Chan Sung-Sun 陳崇信).[51] However, Mabel did not have a pleasant memory of this visit. She remembers: 'The time I went to Mashan, it scared me, people taking me by the hand and saying, "Please look after my daughter, take my daughter, or my son [to Australia]" . . . they were desperate to give their kids the opportunity of an education.'

Mabel's father Harry Hunt had an ancestral home in Mashan, but he had given the house to a distant relative after he left his home village. The ancestral home had been vacant since the occupants had moved away in the 1980s and has since collapsed.[52]

Mabel's father passed away in 1990, and she has not been to Mashan or Zhongshan since because she feels there is no reason for her to go there. Mabel's daughter who sees herself as 'Australian', travelled to China with her a couple of times but, Mabel said, 'she hated it. She can't stand the crowds.' Mabel does not see her connections with Zhongshan continuing into the next generation. As she conceded, 'I'm not connected with Zhongshan'.

Although Mabel regards her connections with her ancestral hometown as finished, she still maintains a very strong connection with China, in particular through her academic career. She used to go to China every two years, staying in Shanghai for a couple of weeks and then travelling to Taiwan for a few weeks. Apart from teaching Chinese Studies, Mabel co-owned a publication company, Peony Press, and published eighteen books under the University of Sydney East Asian series, including books on Japanese, Chinese, and Korean academic writing and a poetry series by Australian poets of Asian backgrounds. 'Our mission is to promote Chinese or East Asian culture to the English-speaking world', she says. Her translation works served the same purpose. She believes she has played an important role in making contemporary Chinese writings accessible to English readers.[53]

When asked about her identity, Mabel responded, 'I wouldn't see the need of having any tags . . . Why does one need to be identified?' She continued, 'I would say "I'm of Chinese heritage, born in Australia" rather than say, "I'm Chinese Australian" or "Australian Chinese"'. This response seems to be in line with Mabel's sense of belonging, which is no longer defined narrowly by where her family comes from or where she lives but is mediated through her attachment to Chinese history and

---

51. For details of Stanley Hunt's contributions to schooling in Mashan, see Chapters 2 and 7 of this volume.
52. Fieldwork notes by the author in Mashan village, Zhongshan on 18 December 2017.
53. D'Cruz, 'Interview', 65–68.

literature. In this sense, her 'homeland' cannot be reduced to Mashan or Zhongshan but has become a much wider, imaginative place.

Discussion

This chapter explores the links between mobility, place, and identity in contemporary homeland travel by Chinese Australians. The above three cases show how 'roots' travel experiences can be very different in terms of motivation, experience, and resulting attachments to place. Denise Ma and her brothers went to Zhongshan with a desire to make sense of their family's past, while William and Nancy Lee went out of curiosity about where William's ancestors came from, taking advantage of cheap flights as China opened up. Mabel Lee's return, meanwhile, took place mainly because of filial piety and her obligation to take her father back to Zhongshan.

The embodied transnational lens helps us understand how family memories and cultural practices inherited from their respective families intersect with the political and social circumstances of the ancestral place at a specific point in time and how they acted upon their engagement with Zhongshan.[54] For instance, in Denise Ma's case, her proficiency in the Chinese language was due to her family's 'Chinese' way of bringing up their children, enabling her to communicate comfortably with the people she met during her visits, which facilitated the development of social bonds with people from Sha Chong and contributed to her pleasurable experience in Zhongshan. Her visit also coincided with government policy that promoted inbound tourism,[55] and a social atmosphere that has welcomed foreigners since the 1990s. William and Nancy, by contrast, attributed their feelings of 'wariness' in Xincun village to William's mother's negative attitude towards China and her 'Chineseness', as well as the political and social circumstances of China in the 1980s, when the government still maintained an attitude of 'mistrust' towards foreign visitors after the Cultural Revolution. Similarly, Mabel's interests in China and Chinese culture may in part be attributed to her family's emphasis on maintaining their Chinese identity. Her experience in Mashan, when villagers asked her to take their children to Australia, was a reflection of the political and social context of that time – peasants from the village were eager to 'go abroad' for a better life shortly after the opening of China in the early 1980s. The embodied transnational lens enables us to understand these people's subjective experiences as constituted by the 'complex interconnections' of migrants' past/present and here/there, which intertwine and mutually condition each other during their homeland visits,[56] complicating the traditional understanding of diaspora based on a clear distinction

---

54. Berg and Eckstein, 'Introduction', 7.
55. Yanyun Zhao and Bingjie Liu, 'The Evolution and New Trends of China's Tourism Industry', *National Accounting Review* 2, no. 4 (2020): 344, https://doi.org/10.3934/NAR.2020020.
56. Nicola Piper, 'The Complex Interconnections of the Migration-Development Nexus: A Social Perspective', *Population, Space and Place* 15, no. 2 (2009): 100, https://doi.org/10.1002/psp.535.

between 'home' and 'host' countries and a one-way conception of migration and settlement.

The material aspect of homeland visits also deserves our attention. Drawing on insights from the 'material turn' in migration studies, which emphasises the interpretation of 'human affections, desires and identities not in isolation from the material world but through things',[57] we can see how material objects, in particular the ancestral home, have impacted these Chinese migrant descendants' emotions and place attachments through an embodied engagement with these houses.[58] The three cases also demonstrated very different emotions and attachments in their engagement (or disengagement) with family heritage objects. The case of Denise and her brothers highlights how a visit to her ancestral village was more than a purely antiquarian venture to identify and visit sites and buildings. At an experiential level, Denise's exploratory travel was deeply emotional. When she arrived at the site where her grandfather was born, she was 'blown away' and could 'feel the connections'. Objects such as her great-grandfather Ma Yung Joong's grand mansion, the family lineage records book (家譜 *jiapu* in Mandarin) presented to her, and the model of the Sincere Department Store displayed in the Xiangshan Museum of Commercial Culture rekindled her feeling of family pride and had a powerful affective resonance for her. Rather than being passive objects of discovery and observation, these material objects facilitated Denise's 'symbolic attachment' to the hometown. Her organisation of a clan photo with one hundred extended Ma family members further made her attachment to the Ma clan and her ancestral homeland materially tangible.

When William and Nancy went to Zhongshan, they found that William's ancestral house in Xincun village had been destroyed. The absence of the material building may mean that no affective arousal was developed. Even though, at a later stage, their son was able to find the two buildings owned by William's grandfather in Shekki, they conceded no attachment to them; as Nancy said, 'no one wants them'. William and Nancy's intention to donate the ancestral homes also symbolises their desire to end their family's connections with Zhongshan. Similarly, in Mabel's case, her encounter with the material building of Mashan Primary School, a large school recently donated by her brother with a teaching building named after her father, did not seem to have any affective resonance for her and she will not return to Mashan again. The materiality of heritage objects can resonate with people in very different ways.

These three different cases of diaspora return travel throw light on the complexity of Chinese diasporic senses of identity and belonging. Too often, migrants from the same country are lumped together into a singular 'essentialised' collective

---

57. Cangbai Wang, 'Introduction: The "Material Turn" in Migration Studies', *Modern Languages Open* (2016): 3, https://doi.org/10.3828/mlo.v0i0.88.
58. See Chapter 5 of this volume for a discussion of affective resonances around homes and built structures in the village.

identity based on their country of origin, such as 'Chinese'. However, these three cases show that the self-identities of Chinese diasporic subjects can be sharply different from each other and from societal conceptions of identity. In Denise's case, her ancestral homeland visit put her in a setting to reconnect with her 'Chineseness'. She developed connections and bonds with the local people and material heritage, which helped reinforce her Chinese identity.[59] Among the three cases, Denise is the only person who developed stronger links with Zhongshan after the visit, and now she regards it as her 'hometown'. The strengthening of her Chinese identity was manifested in her action to change her last name to 'Ma'. It is interesting to note the evolution of Denise's identity – from ambivalence about her Chineseness, to being 'neither Chinese nor Australian', to claiming to be 'equally proud of her Australian and Chinese heritages'. It seems her homeland visits have enabled her to reflect on her identity and caused an iterative identity development process. Denise's sense of belonging to both Australia and Zhongshan has resulted in her hybrid identification as 'Australian-born Chinese'. This echoes Peggy Levitt and Nina Glick Schiller's argument that 'assimilation and enduring transnational ties are neither incompatible nor binary opposite'.[60] Denise feels a sense of belonging to Zhongshan even though she does not share a common territory with the people there. In this sense, identity development is not geographically bounded but is a flexible and non-static process of negotiation and evolution.

William and Nancy's experience of homeland travel to Zhongshan was in stark contrast to Denise's case. William did not inherit much 'Chinese' identity from his family. Nancy explained that this was because William's mother, who was from a mixed heritage background, did not like her 'Chineseness' and did not want her son to retain a Chinese identity. Growing up with this family background, William did not read or speak Chinese. William and Nancy rejected the claim of being a 'Chinese family', referring to themselves as 'the very Western end of the family'. William's case reflects the importance of family in passing down cultural identity to the next generation.[61] William and Nancy did not develop any attachment to Zhongshan, neither to its material heritage (their ancestral home was destroyed) nor to the people in Xincun village (their close relatives had all left and they had a feeling of suspicion towards the villagers). Instead of reconnecting William to his 'Chineseness', their disconcerting experiences during their visit to Zhongshan seemed to reinforce his 'Australian' identity. William and Nancy were not interested in returning to the ancestral village again, and their plan to donate the two houses in Shekki signify their intention to end their last connections with Zhongshan. The

---

59. Duval, 'Conceptualising Return Visits', 50–61.
60. Peggy Levitt and Nina Glick Schiller, 'Conceptualizing Simultaneity: A Transnational Social Field Perspective on Society', *The International Migration Review* 38, no. 3 (2004): 1002, https://doi.org/1002. 10.1111/j.1747-7379.2004.tb00227.x.
61. Berg and Eckstein, 'Introduction', 7.

difference in attachment to Zhongshan between Denise and William shows that the importance of a specific ancestral location varies among individuals.

Again, Mabel's case demonstrated a very different self-identification and place attachment. Mabel inherited a strong Chinese identity from her parents, who grew up in China and retained strong connections with Zhongshan while they were in Sydney. Mabel's 'Chineseness' has also formed a salient aspect of her identity in her professional career as a globally well-known scholar of Chinese Studies. However, unlike Denise, Mabel does not seem to have ambivalent or unsettled feelings about her Chinese and Australian identities. She never worries about her Chinese identity and would not tolerate any discrimination against her Chinese background. As in William's case, her ancestral homeland visit did not strengthen her connection with Zhongshan. She developed no bonding with either the material heritage or the people in Mashan village. Mabel made just one visit to Mashan out of family obligation but has no interest in returning. However, this does not mean she does not have a connection with China. In fact, Mabel has frequently travelled to China and other countries in the Sinophone world; taught Chinese language, literature, and history to students in Australia; and promoted understanding of Chinese and Asian writings to the English-speaking world through writing and publishing ventures. In this sense, Mabel's attachment is not restricted to her home village but is to a bigger world of 'Chineseness' exemplified through Chinese literature and history. Mabel's broader, symbolic conceptualisation of 'homeland' resonates with her self-described identity: 'I'm of Chinese heritage, born in Australia.' Rather than asserting her Australian identity or Chinese identity or acknowledging a hybrid identity, she eschews 'the need to have any tags'. Her cosmopolitan identity transcends the geographical boundaries of 'host' and 'home' countries for a much bigger, de-territorialised transnational world.

Conclusion

Diaspora tourism refers to diasporic community members' visits to ancestral homelands to get in touch with their 'roots'. This chapter has provided three cases of homeland travels by descendants of Zhongshan migrants in Australia that took place in the last two decades. Adopting an embodied transnational approach, we focused on the interaction between their experience of homeland travel and their identity development, and we explored how their travel experience reflected upon or shaped their diasporic identities. The material and affective aspects of their visits were given equal attention.

This chapter highlights the heterogeneity among diaspora members. Even though they share Zhongshan as their ancestral home, they are vastly different in terms of cultural knowledge, family memories, and identities. At an experiential level, homeland travels can be quite emotional, as heritage objects such as the ancestral house and the lineage records book can have a powerful affective resonance for visitors. However, rather than assuming that heritage sites or objects have uniform impacts on the diaspora, this chapter has shown that they act upon diaspora members in very different ways.

Different experiences of homeland travel also have different impacts on place attachment. Of the three cases, only one developed a deeper connection with Zhongshan. This returnee now goes to Zhongshan often and considers it her 'hometown' as she develops a stronger place attachment. However, in the other two cases the homeland travels were more disconcerting experiences, leading to the decision not to return to Zhongshan again.

The chapter has also examined the subtle and complex relations between diaspora tourism and diasporic identity. Homeland travel played a role in the reflexive process of identity development of the returnees, leading to very different emotional ties and identification with their ancestral homeland. In one case, homeland travel reaffirmed Denise's 'Chineseness' and resolved the ambivalences of her hybrid Australian Chinese identities. However, in the second case, the homeland visit reaffirmed William's 'Australianness' rather than 'Chineseness'. The final case of Mabel also throws light on generational differences in diasporic identities. While first-generation migrants have a stronger attachment to a specific place such as their home village or hometown, the second or later generations' attachment has broadened to the home country or a 'de-territorialised' Chinese culture and heritage in a transnational social space. While in all three cases the interviewees' 'Chineseness' is mixed up with their Australianness, their identity reconstruction or reaffirmation process may yield very different outcomes for their diasporic identities. This further confirms the fluidity of 'Chineseness', which is not fixed but in a continual process of change – constantly being reflected upon and reflexively shaped by individual diasporic members, giving rise to diverse notions of 'Chineseness'.[62]

Public discourse in Australia tends to see the Chinese community as one 'homogeneous ethnic group' with a fixed identity. The three cases revealed the hybridity of Chinese identities, which evolve and change over time. The general assumption that members of the Chinese diaspora are either 'loyal and attached to their homelands' or 'assimilated into the host country' is inadequate to capture the complexity of diasporic identities. The case studies show that attachment to homeland and country of settlement are not mutually exclusive. Increased mobility and transnational networks may cause diaspora subjects to feel a sense of attachment to both their country of residence and their ancestral homeland.

---

62. See further Chapter 3 of this volume on the variations of identification among Chinese Australians. For a discussion of Chineseness as a flexible signifier, see Ien Ang, *On Not Speaking Chinese: Living between Asia and The West* (London: Routledge, 2001), Chapter 1.

Bibliography

Ang, Ien. *On Not Speaking Chinese: Living Between Asia and the West*. London: Routledge, 2001.

Ang, Ien. 'Unsettling the National: Heritage and Diaspora'. In *Cultures and Globalization: Heritage, Memory and Identity*, edited by Helmut Anheier and Yudhishthir Raj Isar, 2–14. London: SAGE, 2011.

Basu, Paul. 'Route Metaphors of "Roots-Tourism" in the Scottish Highland Diaspora'. In *Reframing Pilgrimage: Cultures in Motion*, edited by Simon Coleman, 153–78. London: Routledge, 2004.

Berg, Mette Louise, and Susan Eckstein. 'Introduction: Reimagining Migrant Generations'. *Diaspora* 18, no. 1 (2009): 1–23. https://doi.org/10.1353/dsp.2015.0001.

Bond, Nigel, and John Falk. 'Tourism and Identity-Related Motivations: Why Am I Here (and Not There)?' *The International Journal of Tourism Research* 15, no. 5 (2013): 430–42. https://doi.org/10.1002/jtr.1886.

Cater, Carl Iain, Katja Poguntke, and Wyn Morris. 'Y Wladfa Gymreig: Outbound Diasporic Tourism and Contribution to Identity'. *Tourism Geographies* 21, no. 4 (2019): 665–86. https://doi.org/10.4324/9780203458389-9.

Chen, Ning, Michael Hall, and Girish Prayag. 'Place Matters! Introduction to Sense of Place and Place Attachment in Tourism'. In *Sense of Place and Place Attachment in Tourism*, edited by Ning Chen, Michael Hall, and Girish Prayag, 1–16. Abingdon: Routledge, 2021.

Chinese Museum. 'Guide to Chinese-Australian Family Research'. Accessed 16 September 2021, https://www.chinesemuseum.com.au/Handlers/Download.ashx?IDMF=10baa807-34f4-480a-9f57-ab093ad13dbc.

Chinese Studies Association of Australia (CSAA). 'Interview: Adjunct Professor Mabel Lee'. CSAA newsletter, no. 40 (August 2010): 10–13. Accessed on 10 September 2021. http://www.csaa.org.au/wp-content/uploads/2014/04/CSAA_Newsletter_40.pdf.

Couchman, Sophie, and Kate Bagnall. 'Memory and Meaning in the Search for Chinese Australian Families'. In *Remembering Migration: Oral Histories and Heritage in Australia*, edited by Kate Darian-Smith and Paula Hamilton, 331–46. Cham: Palgrave Macmillan, 2019.

D'Cruz, J. V. 'Interview with Mabel Lee'. *Overland*, no. 179 (Winter 2005): 65–68.

Dunn, Kevin. 'Embodied Transnationalism: Bodies in Transnational Spaces'. *Population, Space and Place* 16, no. 1 (2010): 1–9. https://doi.org/10.1002/psp.593.

Duval, David Timothy. 'Conceptualising Return Visits: A Transnational Perspective'. In *Tourism, Diasporas, and Space*, edited by Tim Coles and Dallen Timothy, 50–61. London: Routledge, 2004.

Etemaddar, Mitra, Tara Duncan, and Hazel Tucker. 'Experiencing "Moments of Home" through Diaspora Tourism and Travel'. *Tourism Geographies* 18, no. 5 (2016): 503–19. https://doi.org/10.1080/14616688.2016.1220973.

Glick Schiller, Nina. 'Transnationality and the City'. In *The New Blackwell Companion to the City*, edited by Gary Bridge and Sophie Watson, 179–92. Malden, MA: Blackwell Publishing, 2011. https://doi-org.ezproxy.uws.edu.au/10.1002/9781444395105.ch16.

Glick Schiller, Nina, Linda Basch, and Cristina Blanc-Szanton. 'Transnationalism: A New Analytic Framework for Understanding Migration'. *Annals of the New York Academy of Sciences* 645, no. 1 (1992): 1–24. https://doi.org/10.1111/j.1749-6632.1992.tb33484.x.

Graham, Connor, and Mark Rouncefield. 'Photo Practices and Family Values in Chinese Households'. (Proceedings of the Workshop on Social Interaction and Mundane Technologies, 2008). Accessed 25 September 2021. https://citeseerx.ist.psu.edu/viewdoc/download?doi=10.1.1.483.2583&rep=rep1&type=pdf.

Huang, Wei-Jue, William Haller, and Gregory Ramshaw. 'Diaspora Tourism and Homeland Attachment: An Exploratory Analysis'. *Tourism Analysis* 18, no. 3 (August 2013): 285–96. http://dx.doi.org/10.3727/108354213X1367339861069.

Huang, Wei-Jue, Kam Hung, and Chun-Chu Chen. 'Attachment to the Home Country or Hometown? Examining Diaspora Tourism across Migrant Generations'. *Tourism Management* 68 (2018): 52–65. https://doi.org/10.1016/j.tourman.2018.02.019.

Huang, Wei-Jue, Gregory Ramshaw, and William C. Norman. 'Homecoming or Tourism? Diaspora Tourism Experience of Second-Generation Immigrants'. *Tourism Geographies* 18, no. 1 (2016): 59–79. https://doi.org/10.1080/14616688.2015.1116597.

Iorio, Monica, and Andrea Corsale. 'Diaspora and Tourism: Transylvanian Saxons Visiting the Homeland'. *Tourism Geographies* 15, no. 2 (2013): 198–232. https://doi.org/10.1080/14616688.2012.647327.

Levitt, Peggy, and Nina Glick Schiller. 'Conceptualizing Simultaneity: A Transnational Social Field Perspective on Society'. *The International Migration Review* 38, no. 3 (2004): 1002–39. https://doi.org/10.1111/j.1747-7379.2004.tb00227.x.

Ma, Laurence. 'Space, Place and Transnationalism in the Chinese Diaspora'. In *The Chinese Diaspora: Space, Place, Mobility, and Identity*, edited by Laurence J. C. Ma and Carolyn Cartier, 1–50. Lanham, MD: Rowman and Littlefield, 2003.

McGreevy, Ronan. 'Plans for Global Irish "Homecoming"'. *Irish Times*, 7 October 2011. https://www.irishtimes.com/news/plans-for-global-irish-homecoming-1.884890.

My China Roots.com. Accessed 16 September 2021, https://www.mychinaroots.com/services/research/village-exploration.

Oxfeld, Ellen. *Drink Water, but Remember the Source: Moral Discourse in a Chinese Village*. Berkeley: University of California Press, 2010.

Piper, Nicola. 'The Complex Interconnections of the Migration–Development Nexus: A Social Perspective'. *Population, Space and Place* 15, no. 2 (2009): 93–101. https://doi.org/10.1002/psp.535.

Thiriez, Régine. 'Photography and Portraiture in Nineteenth-Century China'. *East Asian History (Canberra)* 17, nos 17–18 (1999): 77–102.

Urry, John. *The Tourist Gaze*. Third edition. Los Angeles: SAGE, 2011.

VisitScotland. 'Scotland's Themed Years'. Accessed 8 September 2021, https://www.visitscotland.com/about/themed-years/.

Wang, Cangbai. 'Introduction: The "Material Turn" in Migration Studies'. *Modern Languages Open*, 2016. https://doi.org/10.3828/mlo.v0i0.88.

Xiang, Z., W. Huimin, and F. Huaxiu, eds. *Finding Family Roots: Youth of Chinese Descent from USA and Canada Visit Xinhui and Enping Counties*. Beijing: Great Wall Books. 1983.

Zhao, Yanyun, and Bingjie Liu. 'The Evolution and New Trends of China's Tourism Industry'. *National Accounting Review* 2, no. 4 (2020): 337–53. https://doi.org/10.3934/NAR.2020020.

Zou, Yongguang, Fang Meng, and Qianghong Li. 'Chinese Diaspora Tourists' Emotional Experiences and Ancestral Hometown Attachment'. *Tourism Management Perspectives* 37 (2021): 100768. https://doi.org/10.1016/j.tmp.2020.100768.

Part 2

Sites in the Heritage Corridor

5

Making Heritage

The Mar Family and Sha Chong

Glenn Mar and Phillip Mar

This chapter presents a case study of one Sydney family's experience of heritage and place as they retraced their origins in Zhongshan. Mar See Poy (馬社培) came to Sydney from Zhongshan in 1914 but was forced to return to China in 1926. The authors are two grandsons of See Poy, two of the six children of See Poy's son Raymond Mar (馬勵文). In the first section Glenn Mar, who with his cousin Gary Mar (a son of Raymond's younger brother James Mar 馬啟華) took the lead in researching the family's history, describes the family background and the slow process of filling in small pieces of information about our family history, leading to the family's visit in 2015 to Sha Chong (沙涌村), Mar See Poy's home village. In the second section Phillip Mar, who has a background in anthropology and social research, reflects on family members' emotional engagement with the village, based on interviews about their personal experiences of the visit.

Two voices – the first more personal, the second more analytical – offer distinct perspectives on our family's quest. This layering of voices will show 'migrant heritage' to be a deeply relational – and sometimes contested – process, in which concrete places and things are entwined with complicated emotional relations arising from a combination of cultural background and family dynamics.

To Sha Chong and Back: A Personal Account (Glenn Mar)

I grew up and spent most of my adult life in suburban Sydney, disconnected from my family's Chinese heritage. This heritage came to life only recently, resulting in a visit to our grandfather's house in a village near Zhongshan. By lucky coincidence, our engagement with our family's past also led to the discovery of the life of our maternal grandfather's extraordinary life in early twentieth-century Australia and China.

A Chinese Australian family in suburban Sydney

It is natural to think that our stories start when we are born, especially in modern Western societies. I suppose in traditional Chinese families of times past it was less about 'me' and more about 'us', the family, with pictures of ancestors on the wall and daily and annual rituals celebrating the ancestors and reminding us of where we belong. My five siblings and I grew up thinking our place was in suburban Sydney, living the 'Australian' way of life. Our Chineseness was in our faces but very little in the way we lived or thought of ourselves. We never learned Cantonese, as my mother did not speak it, and Dad had discouraged us from learning. In our childhood years we lived in suburban Ryde, our house a short walk from our parents' accountancy office. The office was part of a building that was really a terrace house and behind the shopfront office was where our grandmother lived until she died there in her sleep one day in 1986.

My father Raymond Mar was born in Sydney in 1923. In our lifetimes he had not travelled outside of Australia; holiday trips were car trips to the Gold Coast or spots within a few hours' drive of Sydney, or train trips to Melbourne with Mum to visit her relatives. We knew Dad had spent his school years in Hong Kong but not much else. He was not a talkative man, and we did not have the sense to ask him more about his early life when we had the opportunity. However, in his later years he showed signs of opening up, sometimes talking Cantonese with my wife Jackie, a native of Hong Kong. He died from bowel cancer in 1997, diagnosed so late there were only a few days of illness before death. At age seventy-three he was still working in his small accountancy practice, so he was robbed of his well-earned retirement. We can speculate that had he lived to enjoy that retirement in his garden out in Oakville on the outskirts of Sydney, we may have got around to getting him to talk about his early life. Jackie, then pregnant with our first child, got Dad talking Cantonese probably for the first time since his mother died.

In Ryde Primary in the 1960s there was only one other Chinese family. In high school there were only a few Chinese faces, some of whom were boarders, including one whose family lived in New Guinea. There was a Jonathan Ma. At the time I did not know that we shared more than the same Chinese surname.

So there we were – six children with Chinese faces in suburban Sydney. We were not close to the families of my father's two brothers (uncles Jimmy and Arthur) even though they also lived in Sydney. We were not part of any Chinese social groups. Our Chinese cultural practice was limited to Mum's Chinese cooking once a week, occasionally visiting our 'Por Por' (婆婆, paternal grandmother in Zhongshan vernacular) and sampling her cooking, and once or twice a year heading to Chinatown for a Chinese meal. We were an example of an assimilated Chinese family, perhaps more completely assimilated than most other Chinese Australian families. We were even unaware of Chinese New Year, let alone celebrating it, while nowadays no one living in Sydney would not know about Lunar New Year.

Our consciousness of Chinese culture was probably heightened more from without than from within our family as we grew up and began to enter adulthood. The opening up of China, China in the media, and now of course China in geopolitics means everyone is at least aware of China and thinks they know at least a few things about Chinese people, history, and culture. Chinese places in Sydney are so much more numerous now than they were in our childhoods. There was always Chinatown in the Haymarket; my father would dutifully take Por Por to the Chinese Church in Surry Hills every Sunday followed by a visit to a Chinese grocery shop in Campbell Street. Now there are many suburban Sydney Chinatowns, eat streets, and Chinese grocery shops.

My father apparently made a conscious decision to sever ties with his Chinese past. My late Uncle Jimmy told us that when Dad's Hong Kong friends wrote to him after he returned to Sydney, he did not reply. He also told us that our Dad had been accomplished in Chinese calligraphy and playing Chinese instruments but did not pursue these things at all here in Sydney, instead taking up the cello and gardening. Dad vetoed Mum's suggestion that we learn Chinese (or try).

My mother was also born in 1923. She died in 2009 after a stroke. Mum was a quiet woman, busy raising six kids. She was active in our school tuckshops (even after we had left school), a churchgoer, and known for her baking efforts for the school or church cake stall, while working as an accountant with my father in their small Ryde office. Mum's relatives were like us, very assimilated, a big clan down in Melbourne, where we often holidayed at Christmas.

In 1993 I married my wife Jackie and by 1999 our two daughters were born. Jackie was a Hong Konger so now there was Cantonese in our house, but I was unable to pick up the language as my two young daughters did. Jackie and her three sisters were first-generation Hong Kongers, their parents having fled Dongguan (東莞), Guangdong in the late 1950s. Jackie went back to see her family regularly, so I also went several times, getting to know Hong Kong quite well, and a few times we went into China as tourists: Beijing, the Great Wall, Harbin.

Home was Sydney, but now there were extra roots in Hong Kong.

One grandfather's story and White Australia

A get-together in 2012 with the family of Dad's brother Uncle Jimmy was the catalyst for cousin Gary Mar and I to start putting together respective family trees. At Easter 2013 Gary hosted a 'Wong-Yee-Mar family get together'. Yee (余) was our paternal grandmothers' family name, while Gary's mother's family was Wong (王). A highlight was the meeting of two Yee half-brothers who had not met before. Cousin Gary had done a lot of legwork to chase up as many relatives as he could for the reunion, and now his family tree is a comprehensive document complete with pictures.

My family tree research was more sporadic. One day in early 2015 I discovered the 'Name Search' tool on the National Archives website. Searching on my grandfather's name 'Mar See Poy' gave no results. However, browsing through other Chinese Australian files showed the potential of what could be discovered, particularly in the 'Immigration' category of the records, so I persisted with searching in the hope that another spelling might yield results. A file 'Mar Sha Poi' appeared.

The file was my grandfather's 114-page immigration file. From this I learned that Mar See Poy was able to come to Sydney in 1914 as a substitute manager for the firm Wing Sang (永生果欄) at the age of twenty-two (see Figure 5.1). The 1901 Immigration Restriction Act regulations had at some stage been changed to allow substitutes in categories such as 'merchants' to come in to replace naturalised Chinese Australians leaving Australia for an extended period. At this time, the senior managers of Wing Sang were heading back to China following Ma Ying Piu (馬應彪), who had set up the Sincere store in Hong Kong in 1900, the first department store in China, using his Sydney experience of stores such as Anthony Hordern. Sincere (先施百貨) was the oldest of what are known in southern China and Hong Kong as the 'Four Great Companies' 四大公司 (Wing On 永安百貨, The Sun 大新百貨, and Sun Sun 新新百貨 being the other three). These businesses would grow into

Figure 5.1: Managers of Wing Sang & Co. (永生果欄), 1924. Mar See Poy (馬社培) is seated in the front row, centre. Photo courtesy of City of Sydney Archives, donated by Gordon Mar.

diversified conglomerates headquartered in Hong Kong, and in Shanghai the early twentieth-century department store buildings still stand in Nanjing Road (南京路). Mar See Poy was proposed as a substitute for Joe Young Ma (馬祖容), who, it turns out, was my old school friend Jonathan Ma's grandfather. Both families came from the same village of Sha Chong near Shekki, the city centre of Zhongshan.

Mar See Poy's Australian life depended on the bureaucracy that supported the White Australia laws granting his yearly extension to stay there. After ten years, in 1924, a customs officer reported that Mar See Poy sometimes helped load bananas on trucks at the Wing Sang store he managed at 96 Hay Street, Sydney. This was enough to result in a decision not to extend his permission to stay, as the interpretation was that he could be here only as a merchant but not do duties as a storeman. Despite entreaties from the Chinese Consul and the manager of Wing Sang William Liu (劉光福, 1893–1983), the extension was rejected by the Minister for Home and Territories, the Labor Senator George Pearce, even though the department secretary's recommendation was to allow the extension. By this time See Poy had fathered a daughter, lost his first wife, remarried, and had two Sydney-born sons – a Chinese Australian family.

Defeated and facing deportation, Mar See Poy wrote to the Department simultaneously questioning the decision, thanking the government for his stay, claiming he had to leave Australia for family reasons, and asking for a small extension. By leaving on his own terms, Mar See Poy could at least save a bit of face, I suppose.

Now we knew much more of our grandfather's family's story, courtesy of the immigration file. But the file only said Mar See Poy was from 'Canton', the ubiquitous place of origin for almost all Chinese coming to Australia for decades.

Mar See Poy left Australia in April 1926 with his family, including my father and his brother Arthur, aged one, and settled in his home village of Sha Chong. Mar See Poy's fate was to die in 1928 in some misadventure on a short trip away in a very unstable China, leaving his wife pregnant with third son James.

For widow Daisy Mar, life in the Mar village was difficult. As a single woman in the village, isolated from her Yee family's village, she would have been without allies. Matchmakers and suitors knew that marrying Daisy would yield the prize of the family's house, farmland, and company shares (in Sincere, Wing On, and other companies valued at £5,500 according to the immigration file). To escape from these pressures she took her family out of the village around 1931 and went to Hong Kong, first staying in the house of Joe Young Ma, a mansion built with some of the wealth of the Sincere company. This part of the story was told by my grandmother Daisy to her sons, and Uncle Jimmy relayed it to us.

They stayed until the spectre of Japanese invasion loomed, and so my father – by then a teenager – completed the circle by returning to Sydney in 1938. Daisy and her two younger sons Arthur and Jimmy followed in October 1940, while her stepdaughter, now an adult, stayed in Hong Kong (and would later also return to Sydney after the death of her Hong Kong husband).

So, there is the life of Mar See Poy and his family's story. We can only wonder whether during his Sydney life he imagined that Sydney would be his family's permanent home, or whether he dreaded the denial of the right to remain in Sydney that was his eventual fate.

A trip to grandfather's village

In 2013 my Uncle Jimmy, cousin Gary Mar, and I met with Douglas Lam. Douglas had emigrated from China as a fourteen-year-old on a student visa in the early 1960s, and Jimmy had known Douglas's shopkeeper uncle. Recently Douglas had started taking annual trips back to his family village of Antang (安堂村) near Zhongshan city.[1] Douglas agreed to help Jimmy locate his father's house in Sha Chong. In earlier years there was an arrangement that a relative would reside in the house so there was someone looking after it, but this ended when that relative passed away. Uncle Jimmy was born in the village in 1927, the year his father See Poy died.

During his trip in 2014, Douglas had focused on getting to know a key village elder, Mar King-Hung (馬敬洪), who had a copy of the Ma/r clan genealogy book, or 'juk pou' (族譜, as pronounced in Cantonese). (He turned out to be Mar See Poy's closest surviving relative.) After a few twists and turns, Douglas's persistence yielded success; the family home was located. In July 2015, Jimmy, Gary, and I met with Douglas to talk about a potential trip to the village. Happily, it turned out all my five siblings, Uncle Jimmy and his three sons, along with some partners and children, a party of eighteen in total, plus Douglas as our guide, were able to travel to Sha Chong via Hong Kong. Soon we were standing in Mar See Poy's house and meeting our relatives who had lived in the village their whole lives.

I remember the first day we visited the ancestral home. Mar King-Hung was explaining the process to re-establish possession of an ancestral house – apparently all that was needed was an application and approval from at least three village elders (there was also the need to pay all outstanding taxes, we were told later). For a fleeting moment I imagined doing this and funding the necessary work to restore the house, which was in poor repair and standing empty. The next-door house was a duplex of Mar See Poy's, originally inhabited by my great-grandfather, now modernised and lived in by relatives. Then reality kicked in, as I realised the practical difficulties of such a venture.

The highlight of the trip was watching elderly Uncle Jimmy entering our grandfather's house and returning home to his birthplace. We shared several meals with relatives and at a banquet in his honour Uncle Jimmy was presented with a copy of his family's *juk pou*, where he could trace his ancestors back twenty generations. We all felt things were an order of magnitude more significant for him and his generation.

---

1. See Ien Ang, Chapter 3 of this volume, for more about Douglas Lam's life and his connection to Zhongshan.

Since then, side trips from our Hong Kong visits have enabled several brief returns to the village, including a memorable day when my wife's (陳 Chan) relatives from Dongguan (also recently re-united with Jackie's elderly mother) met my Sha Chong Mar relatives.

On that first trip to the village, we could feel and touch our family's past, and see parallel lives in our village relatives, similar faces with different homes but a shared genealogy.

Another grandfather comes to light

While this chapter is part of a book focused on Sydney–Zhongshan links, my family's story would be incomplete without including the story of my maternal grandfather Wong Shee Ping, whose story is more a Sze Yup–Melbourne one. It is believed he hailed from a village in Kaiping (開平), one of the 'Four Counties' (四邑 Sze Yup). The village may be Yongan (永安, Wing On in Cantonese) in the Kaiping World Heritage area.

Our family knew the name of our grandfather Joseph Wong Shee Ping (黃樹屏), that he was a preacher,[2] and that he returned to China when our Mum was very young. That was all we knew, and for some reason none of our efforts at family research had looked into this man – until historian Michael Williams, one of the authors of this book, rang me in July 2018. After asking if I was a son of Bonnie Mar, to which I responded in the affirmative, Michael informed me that Wong Shee Ping had been discovered to be the author of a work of fiction originally published anonymously in a Chinese-language newspaper in 1909 and 1910. Michael was part

Figure 5.2: Wong Shee Ping (黃樹屏), 1920. Photograph courtesy of Mar family.

---

2. Wong Shee Ping had trained in China as a preacher in the Church of Christ. See Michael Williams, 'Wong Shee Ping', in Wong Shee Ping, *The Poison of Polygamy* (多妻毒): *A Social Novel*, trans. Ely Finch (Sydney: Sydney University Press, 2019).

of a team, along with translator Ely Finch and historian Mei-Fen Kuo, whose project was to publish Wong's novel *The Poison of Polygamy* (多妻毒).[3]

Wong Shee Ping, also known as Wong Yue Kung (黃右公),[4] had been brought to Australia in 1908 to work for the *Chinese Times* newspaper (愛國報), which was originally published in Melbourne, later in Sydney. The aim of the *Chinese Times* and its backers was the promotion of Chinese Republicanism and reform. Wong Shee Ping was a preacher and must have received an excellent Chinese literary education, as Ely Finch reveals many intricacies in his annotations to Shee Ping's work of fiction. He was a leading figure in establishing branches of the Kuomintang (國民黨) (KMT) around Australia in the early 1920s.

It seems certain that grandfather Mar See Poy would have known grandfather Wong Shee Ping, as they both had a role in the Sydney branch of the KMT, and with Mar See Poy being a backer of the Sydney edition of the *Chinese Times* when Wong Shee Ping was its editor. In the archives there is the large group photo of the 1920 Sydney KMT convention with the two grandfathers: Wong Shee Ping front and centre, and tall Mar See Poy at the back. It is a happy embarrassment that it had taken a team of dedicated historians working on publishing the earliest known Chinese Australian novel to bring to light the life of this grandfather, as I soon found there was quite a lot written about Wong Shee Ping.

Our family knows little about the relationship between Wong Shee Ping and my grandmother, Louisa Ellen Sam or 'Cissy'. She was living with one her brothers, Albert Charles Sam in 1923. Albert Charles Sam was the husband of Maud Gunter, whose story as the madam of a brothel empire in Melbourne is just now emerging. Perhaps Wong Shee Ping was a house guest of the Sams and met my grandmother there. We know little more than what the records show: a marriage in January 1923, my mother's birth in February 1923, and Wong Shee Ping's departure for China in December 1923 to attend the first party congress of the KMT in Canton (Guangzhou) as the Australasian delegate. Whether he had intended to return to Australia when he left, we do not know – but he never did. Michael Williams and Ely Finch's research has found he held various posts in Republican China up to 1930 or so. In 2020, Mei-fen Kuo unearthed an article about Wong Shee Ping's death, so now we at least know he died in 1948 and something of the circumstances of his later life in China.

I look forward to some point in the future when I will visit the home ground of this grandfather, while counting myself so fortunate to be able to get some understanding of this part of my family's history through both specific knowledge of people like grandfather Wong Shee Ping as well as associated learnings of those

---

3. Wong Shee Ping, *The Poison of Polygamy* (多妻毒): *A Social Novel*, trans. Ely Finch (Sydney: Sydney University Press, 2019).
4. Or Wong Yau Kung (黃又公); he appears in various histories of Chinese Australia under these names. See Williams, 'Wong Shee Ping', 1.

pivotal times in the late nineteenth and early twentieth centuries for China and Australia.

China on my mind

So that is my family's Chinese Australian story: two grandfathers who were born in China, lived in Australia for key parts of their lives, but didn't die there; two single mums as grandmothers. Stories we didn't hear from our parents: instead they were revealed through archival records, the work of historians, and field research in Zhongshan by Douglas Lam. I wonder what the Chinese episodes of my father's and grandfathers' lives were like, and I can guess a little of what hopes they had for China in that moment in history after the fall of imperial rule, both having experienced Western life in Sydney.

Not speaking Chinese is the biggest barrier for me to see Sha Chong village as 'home' in any present sense, as it is to becoming closer to newly met Chinese relatives, mine or my wife's. I was able to get friendly with these relatives but only to the extent that not sharing a language allowed. Having been to a place and knowing about it are two elements of belonging, but knowing the language of the place is a vital missing link.

For me, the Sydney–Zhongshan corridor has the significant extra stop, Hong Kong, with that port always the terminus of the international part of voyages, with separate short journeys required to get to and from there. While Sydney remains home, I feel that I now know Sha Chong, Zhongshan, and Hong Kong well enough as places explored as well as to a fair extent understood.

My family history is an opportunity to know more about where we are from, how we got from there to here, and what links two or more places. I am keen to keep learning of the times of my recent ancestors. It is amazing to realise that a time span of two or three generations covers a fair slab of Australia's post-Cook history and all of China's modern history.

On Homecoming: Emotion and Place in a Visit to Our Grandfather's Village (Phillip Mar)

In October 2015, we visited Sha Chong, the home village of our grandfather Mar See Poy. The village is now absorbed within Zhongshan city. Our party of eighteen members of the Mar family was multi-generational, including James Mar (Uncle Jimmy), nine of See Poy's grandchildren (three sons of Jimmy Mar and six children of Raymond Mar, including both of us), and four great-grandchildren, the youngest being three years old.

Our family's search for our heritage was conditioned by historical and social contexts, most obviously the displacement and rupture caused by the White

Australia policy and assimilationist policies in twentieth-century Australia that contributed to our lack of cultural knowledge and physical connection to our Cantonese family background. While 'heritage' in Australia is mostly understood to mean the significant buildings and artefacts that mark Australia as a settler nation, our heritage-making foray was taking place against the grain of the conventional one-way story of migrant settlement. Our journey to Sha Chong was a direct consequence of our grandfather See Poy's unjust removal from Australia in the 1920s, an event that conditioned our very existence.

How we felt about it was conditioned by differences in family dynamics and access to family stories. How migration is remembered is an important question for migrant heritage, as the complexity of people's experience is often subordinated to a national narrative of Australia as a 'welcoming haven' for one-way immigrants. Our cultural inheritance has been constituted in terms of 'post-memory', or 'absent memory', where migration stories were not passed on by parents who had succumbed to an assimilationist view that 'too many memories' would complicate 'adjustment' and making a 'fresh start'.[5] Raymond, our father, rarely spoke of his past life and connections to China and the diaspora, whereas James (Jimmy) was active in researching and arranging to return to his place of birth. Fatherly relationships are key to this story of emotions, amplified by the patrilocal character of the village.

Here I focus on our first encounter with Sha Chong village and the ancestral house in October 2015, as these events were the most vividly remembered. Our feelings were grounded in the excitement of 'discovery' of what we understood as a place of origin, an experience that was at once collective and personal. As with pilgrimages, ours was both an 'external' (physical) and an 'internal' (psychological) journey.[6] I describe some key scenes from the visit and provide an interpretation of the emotional responses to key places we visited. For this purpose I interviewed four of Mar See Poy's grandchildren (my siblings and cousins) and asked them to recall the emotions of their visit to Zhongshan.

The village

While we made several visits to Sha Chong, the first encounter most strongly resonated with us. For Glenn, 'the highlights in that sense, emotionally, were entering the village, the village main street, just entering the village. And then, of course, seeing the actual house.'

On our first visit we travelled by local bus from Zhongshan's centre, uncertain of the precise location of Sha Chong. We alighted on an arterial road and walked a

---

5. Kate Darian-Smith and Paula Hamilton, 'Remembering Migration', in *Remembering Migration: Oral Histories and Heritage in Australia*, ed. Kate Darian-Smith and Paula Hamilton (Cham: Palgrave Macmillan 2019), 3, 6.
6. Laura Sanchini, 'Visiting La Madre Patria: Heritage Pilgrimage among Montreal Italians (Notebook)', *Ethnologies* 32, no. 2 (2010): 235–56, https//doi.org/10.7202/1006311ar.

Figure 5.3: Family photo at Sha Chong village gate (沙涌牌坊). Photo courtesy of Gary Mar 2015.

short way until we could see the entrance to the village, now marked by an arched gateway. We experienced a Eureka moment, a shared sense that 'this is it'.

This was the first of many group photoshoots. These would constitute an important ritual to mark significant moments, build group solidarity at key sites and events, and provide an important *aide-mémoire* for the future. Some people prepared for interviews by viewing the stockpile of photos and videos, reconnecting to feelings at the time, and realigning the narratives of our memories.

My sister Lea describes the 'liminal' feeling of moving through the gateway: 'It's like we are moving now into a clan village, which is where our forebears lived. It was like the entryway, like the grand entryway' [Lea Mar].

Beyond this gateway was a small commercial area. For Glenn, 'it showed that the village was something more than a museum piece, that the village was a living thing. It was the atmosphere; the days before we were in the city, but now we spend time in a Chinese village' [Glenn Mar].

Lea recalls 'beginning to realise that the whole makeup of their lives is totally different; it's a bit like stepping back in time because the village life there is very different to our lives in Australia'. We were experiencing Sha Chong as a discrete 'village' rather than as a suburb within a contemporary urban space. We could at that moment imagine Sha Chong as embodying Chinese traditions, linked to an historical past. Sha Chong felt like a newly discovered place that we could both separate from our (Australian) selves, as well as 'own' – at least in thought – as 'our' village, as directly associated with our family (we remembered it as 'the clan village' or 'the Mar village'). Of course, we did not actually think that Sha Chong was objectively stuck in the past and somehow historically distanced from present realities. But this imagining of the village as a past in the present was a way in which we could reconcile those parts of our fragmented identities – Chinese and Australian – that in our lives were so difficult to bring together. We desired a place in which we could imagine our grandfather living and our fathers playing as young children (James Mar lived there until he was three years old, Raymond Mar until he was eight).

We met up with contacts in the village who would be our guides: Mar King-Hung (馬敬洪) and his great-nephew Kit-Leung (馬傑良), who had a job in local administration and whom we dubbed 'The Mayor'. In the streets of Sha Chong we were greeted by curious people. For Lea, this evinced a feeling of 'homecoming' as these Sha Chong people seemed to recognise us as relations: 'We came round the corner, and then there were some other men, three men in fact, and they all sat down. Jimmy had a photo taken with them. I think they were clan relatives' [Lea Mar].

This feeling of homecoming necessarily took place at a remove. Firstly, engagements were necessarily mediated by translation. Apart from Douglas Lam and Jimmy, no one had more than a miniscule grasp of Cantonese or the local dialect. Messages reaching us were haphazard and fragmented, given the size of our party and the need for interpretation of events as they occurred. Secondly, our affective responses at the time were very much 'channelled' through Uncle Jimmy, who had been born in the village and was the only returnee. Jimmy's presence was essential to our experience of the village as homecoming. We were 'sharing Jimmy's elation really. He didn't know these people, and he's hugging them, embracing them. It was through him, the connection was through Jimmy' [Lea Mar].

It was not just that Jimmy's personality was gracious and generous and tended to lighten moments. By observing and monitoring Jimmy we gained a sense of what was happening in a confusing situation. The psychologist Silvan Tomkins uses the notion of affective 'contagion' to describe the ways in which feelings spread in a group, for instance through bodily comportment, facial expressions, even chemically.[7] They were also the result of an openness of feeling and communication that had developed between our two families.

We spent some time at a recently constructed temple. For Glenn this was not so interesting, as it was 'not original, and not connected to Jimmy', that is, not of the time of our fathers' life in Sha Chong. While architectural authenticity is important

---

7. Silvan Tomkins, *Exploring Affect: The Selected Writings of Silvan S. Tomkins* (Cambridge: Cambridge University Press; Editions de la Maison des sciences de l'homme, 1995).

in conceptions of 'heritage', what was of emotional interest for us, by contrast, were the parts of the village that existed at the time our grandfather lived there, that Jimmy and Raymond would have known.

Our memories of places we visited such as the pagoda and community centre were largely consistent in factual terms but they differed in their emotional 'colouring'. Lea was very positive about the experience of that first visit to Sha Chong; it was significant to her that Sha Chong was a 'clan village where all our forebears lived'. (Sha Chong fits the category of a single-surname village where 'a single lineage is the dominant status'.)[8] She could identify with and 'own' the village as a whole entity, as the 'Mar village'. For Lea, village life is vital and distinctly Chinese: 'the whole makeup of their lives is totally different.' She felt Sha Chong was a lively place; that the temple we visited was important in everyday life, that it played a role similar to temples in other Asian places she had visited.

By contrast, my brother Tim Mar remembered the village as 'a bit of a ghost town', recalling it as 'dark and gloomy' with few people around except in the main shopping area; 'it was almost like no one was there'. He described the buildings as 'dark and closed', 'like fortresses, with walls with glass shards, little holes like peep-holes'.

A key organiser of the trip, Gary Mar, Uncle Jimmy's eldest son, had an intense interest in the village. At first, he wanted to 'capture it all' by videoing and photographing 'anything and everything' he came across. 'I was recording it because I wanted to capture everything about it; that's how intense I was inside; this meant a lot to me.' For instance, he videoed a man emerging from his house with a bicycle. 'He was the only person I could see (laughing); he must be a Mar as well, the whole village was Mars.' But Gary's ultimate aim was to find the house where his father Jimmy had been born. He had a restless feeling of 'hurry up, let's just keep going'. He wanted to get to the house, which he felt was the 'central point' in Sha Chong, and then to move out to explore places his father could have been familiar with. The village was a radiating space of lived experience centred on our grandfather's house.

These contrasting renderings of the built environment of the village are expressive of emotions that were powerfully felt at the time, albeit filtered by shifting memory. At the same time, we all 'empathically' shared a sense of excitement at this homecoming experience. Video footage conveys an overarching atmosphere of discovery, even if simultaneously there may have been doubts or misgivings. Glenn distinguished our visit from a tourist's experience: 'It's not as if we were just a group of tourists going to the souvenir shop or something; certainly we were visitors, but at least in some sense it was *our* village.'

---

8. Li Xiuguo, 'Social Implications of the Resurgence of Lineage Culture: The Case Study of a Single-Surname Village in Guangdong within the Currents of Industrialization' (PhD diss., Hong Kong Polytechnic University, 2000).

The house

Grandfather See Poy's house had been surrounded by rice fields; deeds for the rice fields were passed on to his three sons when the land was divided on See Poy's death. The surrounding land has long been filled in by housing.

The house we visited is half of a one-storey duplex building with a party wall dividing the building in two.[9] The house has a door at the front but no windows. As with typical Chinese houses of this period, internal spaces were divided by panels rather than structural walls. The house consisted of the entrance and two main rooms, with an 'open-air courtyard' (天井) behind the house. The house had been vacant for some time and was now used for storage.

Our visit to the house occurred after some hours of walking in Sha Chong, eating a meal at the restaurant, and visiting the home of Mar King-Hung, our main contact in the village. We were not certain of what was happening until we actually arrived. Lea recalls wandering the streets before coming to a locked gate and thinking, 'Oh, are we going to be able to get in, and then, is this really the house, how do we know if this is actually the house?' There had been some confusion about which house it was as we had received photos depicting a different house. When we reached the house Jimmy led the way to the front door. This moment

Figure 5.4: James Mar (馬啟華, 'Uncle Jimmy') at the door of the house, Sha Chong village (沙涌村). Photo courtesy of Gary Mar 2015.

---

9. This configuration was locally known in Zhongshan in Cantonese as 'heng dai uk' 兄弟屋 (lit. fraternal house).

was remembered as an emotional 'high point', albeit with accompanying feelings of disbelief.

Once we could enter, we set about exploring the interior of the house with its two main rooms separated by a screen. Memories of this exploration show a layering of emotions that accompanied the general atmosphere of excitement. We were looking for traces of what the building would tell us about our grandfather's life and Uncle Jimmy's early life, for some verification of continuity with our own lives.

People were curious about the house's construction and its present condition. Differing memories of the building and its condition ranged from concerns about it being 'in ruins', run-down and termite-infested, or having water damage to the roof, to being 'quite sound' and 'having no structural issues'. Descriptions of the house also reflected a desire to assess the status of our forebears. For Lea it was:

> quite a substantial house, it had very high ceilings, and the way the roofing was done with the timber, beams and battens. It was certainly a very solid place, so he [See Poy] obviously was a man of means in his time, if he had a house like that.

Tim also had a sense of the house as 'grand' and remembered it being built of stone, implying that the family 'would have had a certain stature in the village'.

The house was being used by other families to store various objects; these were of importance in our imaginings of the house. The first thing we noticed on entering the house was a child's bike. Des Mar, one of Jimmy's sons, exclaimed to his father: 'Here's your bike, Jimmy!' The joke – made by our party's chief jester – ironically shows that we were seeking concrete artefacts to connect us to the place and to our forebears. But this artefact was out of place in terms of what we imagined we would find; it was obviously not an old bike. The joke also implied the imagining of a pristine historical environment, as if our forebears had just left the house undisturbed. We were engaged in a fantasy somewhat like heritage reconstructions where everything is in its 'original' place, despite intervening years.[10] Other objects, a toy gun and framed family photos, similarly disturbed the excitement of finding the house.

Glenn felt slightly disappointed that the house had been used for storage and was 'not in such good nick'. For Gary, the effect of these objects was more disruptive:

> Then you see that toy gun, going into the bedroom and that. And all run down, ruins, I didn't feel that excitement as much, I felt more confusion. That threw me off . . . you look at a whole lot of other things and then you think, I don't think that's from Dad's family, that looks too modern. Other people's stuff is in here. And then you have a look at the old photos and they're of KH (Mar King-Hung), his family stuff. [Gary Mar]

These objects – 'other people's belongings' – had affective weight because they interrupted or tarnished expectations. They disturbed an imaginary or ideal image of

---

10. See Denis Byrne, Chapter 9 of this volume, on paradoxes of heritage restoration.

Figure 5.5: Child's bike, Sha Chong house. Photo courtesy of Peter Mar 2015.

Figure 5.6: Toy gun, Sha Chong house. Photo courtesy of Peter Mar 2015.

Figure 5.7: Another family's photos, Sha Chong house. Photo courtesy of Peter Mar 2015.

home and place of origin, threatening the sense of continuity and authenticity we expected to feel. Here again, we looked to Jimmy's demeanour as an emotional indicator of the genuineness of our experience. For Lea, when we went into the house there was still the question, 'is this *the* house or is it just *a* house?'

> Going in, we were still not really sure. But once we went in . . . Jimmy had recognition of the house. It became obvious that it was the house and Jimmy had recall of it and we all wandered through, quite interested in the actual building and its design and whatever. [Lea Mar]

Lea also drew on the feelings evoked by a group photograph taken slightly later at the house with Jimmy sitting at the front. 'It felt like, "Look at this, this is where I come from."' This sense of Jimmy's 'transmitted' emotion convinced Lea that this was where Jimmy was born and where our father [Raymond] lived.

Gary Mar also looked to his father for confirmation of the house's authenticity. But for Gary, the house 'didn't spark any memories' for Jimmy. Gary hoped to encounter an original 'scene' of his father's childhood in the house. When I suggested that this might not be surprising given Jimmy's young age when he left, Gary countered that, although he was only very young, Jimmy could 'remember the ringing of the bell from the pagoda tower, he could remember his farm, running around, this is what he did, and when people would come and invade, the bell would ring and they would all go and hide'.[11] His father's lack of recall led Gary to question the authenticity of the house as his father's house: 'At the time, yeah, it was elation. But it's clouded because you walk in there and you see other people's belongings . . . this is not our house.'

Clouding and disappointment coexisted with the elation collectively felt by the group. Gary's feelings would change, particularly after further discussions with his father. As mentioned earlier, Gary's family could draw on a greater familiarity with stories about the village, as Jimmy was more forthcoming in sharing details of the family's history than our father Raymond. This included knowledge about relations with relatives in Sha Chong, including the difficulties encountered by our (paternal) grandmother Daisy Mar in remaining in the village after the death of Mar See Poy. The house had been a key stake in these conflicts.

Glenn, on the other hand, while having doubts about the differing photos of the house, was convinced our relatives in Sha Chong had eventually identified the correct house of our grandfather. He surmised that they may have sent the wrong photos due to a mistake in reading the clan records (*juk pou*), which they later corrected. He was willing to give the benefit of the doubt to the relatives, who, realising our visit was imminent, corrected their error. Glenn's sense of attachment to the house would extend to thoughts of possibly making a claim on the house. He

---

11. It is possible that the sound Jimmy recalled was the bell from the primary school built by diaspora funds that was quite close to the house. See Chapter 7 of this volume.

had heard from Douglas and King-Hung that there was a procedure whereby three 'elders' from the village could support a claim for rights to a house.

The question of how connected or 'attached' we were to the house relied on our belief in its authenticity as the house in which our ancestors lived. But personal affiliation in the present was also very important for an emotional link to be made with the house, most particularly this was centred on Jimmy. For Lea, attachment to the house was secured 'because it was grandpa's house, and because Jimmy was there particularly as well. If Jimmy hadn't been there, I don't think it would have been the same.'

Jimmy's three sons were a close-knit group supporting their father, who was frail and found travel physically demanding. Yet Jimmy was always friendly, generous, and happy to talk about his experience in China. For the family of Raymond Mar, Jimmy stood in for our late father, who had largely disavowed his Chinese background and who rarely spoke of his past in the village or encouraged interest in it. As the living connection to the house and the village, Jimmy acted as a 'governor' of the affective environment; his openness provided a viable channel for our feelings.

Our positive attachment to the house was grounded in our sense of Jimmy's seemingly happy state, which we associated with his recognition of the house as his childhood home, hence a recognition of the event as a homecoming. For most of us, the experience of the visit to Sha Chong and to the house was self-validating, that is, it was enough to have made the journey.

Tim Mar, however, was less able to strongly connect to the house. While it was 'so good to see Jimmy's emotions' at the house, he was also dubious about it being the right house. He could not visualise our father Raymond living there; this was related to his anger towards him for having cut off any knowledge of or connection to his life in China. While he felt that the visit was an 'amazing experience that I had never expected', it also demonstrated a lack of strong connection.

There were practical limits to attachment to the house: the limited extent of our engagement with the past, the cultural and linguistic distance from our assimilated Australian lives, the many gaps in our knowledge. For instance, we still did not know what had happened to our grandfather, where he had died or was buried. We were largely happy to accept these limits, without desiring or expecting any further outcome of the visit. Glenn, however, wanted to extend his attachment to the house, proposing to make a claim on the house with a view to repairing it; he also suggested putting money into the village to help establish a stronger foothold in Sha Chong. There was tension at the time, as most of us did not want to commit to this kind of investment.

Gary and Jimmy's family had more tangible aims, including finding See Poy's grave and establishing ongoing connections with some relatives in the village. But doubts about the house would lead them to 'walk away' from further engagement with the relatives in Sha Chong. The intensity of attachment to the house was associated with the intensity of the investment one had made in it and was also relative to expectations – the greater the expectation, the higher the emotional stakes. Gary acknowledged the vulnerability of being highly invested in the visit to the house, contrasting his own feelings with those of others who had a lesser investment: 'If you don't expect much, you just enjoy it.'

Whatever the actual status of the house, it exerted a very strong emotional focus for all of us. It was a tangible entity at the centre of our desires to connect with our history and lineage, and as such it provided a test of these imaginings and desires.

Homecoming in Sha Chong? Emotion and heritage

Heritage as a living process implies emotional connection and identification; indeed, emotions and affect must be vital constituents of heritage experience.[12] Our visit to Sha Chong, an attempt to recover a ruptured lineage, exemplifies 'heritage in the making'. The visit was characterised by a shared depth of feeling, empathic processes, and affective flows – often mediated through Jimmy. Concern with the authenticity of spatial complexes, notably the Chinese village and house, was an important emotional focus. Differing perceptions of places and things were influenced by psychological aspects, especially internal relations with father figures.

Our emotional and affective investment in objects (other bodies, things, or places) allows them to act as 'agents' of emotion in ways that could seem independent of us.[13] Emotional investment intensifies the significance of objects; in their circulation they 'produce the very surfaces and boundaries that allow the individual and the social to be delineated as objects'.[14] Object relations theory focuses on the ways in which things can mediate transitions in our emotional worlds, from our mother's breast to toys and later 'transitional objects' able to stand in for our developing desires and act as sources of security.[15] Things in the village and the house became animated as emotional objects. Our feelings were reactions to the ways in which we could imagine a homecoming, the forms it might take. Thinking psychoanalytically, we can conceive of these feelings as an encounter with an imaginary of home; our engagement with things can be viewed in terms of 'what makes an object become desirable, . . . how it becomes confused with this more or less structured image which, in diverse ways, we carry with us'.[16]

---

12. Laurajane Smith and Gary Campbell, 'The Elephant in the Room: Heritage, Affect, and Emotion', in *A Companion to Heritage Studies*, ed. William Logan, Máiréad Nic Craith, and Ullrich Kockel (Hoboken, NJ: John Wiley & Sons, 2015).

13. Denis Byrne, 'Love & Loss in the 1960s', *International Journal of Heritage Studies* 19, no. 6 (2013): 601, https://doi.org/10.1080/13527258.2012.686446.

14. Sara Ahmed, *The Cultural Politics of Emotion*, second edition (New York: Routledge, 2015), 10.

15. Donald W. Winnicott, *Playing and Reality* (London: Routledge, 1991 [1971]).

16. Jacques Lacan, *The Seminar of Jacques Lacan*, Book 1: *Freud's papers on technique (1953–1954)* (New York: W. W. Norton, 1988), 141.

For Gaston Bachelard, the form of a house is integral to a primal experience of containment, shelter, and intimacy, providing a basis for subjective development and imaginative capacities.[17] Experiences of homeliness, security, and intimacy are repeated in transitions to new homes and places. But the house can also be a scene of negative emotions regarding belonging and security, of a sense of 'unhousing'.[18] Small wonder that the house in Sha Chong occupied such an important emotional focus in our search for family 'roots'. But the house itself provided materials for doubt and other unsettling emotions; its state of disrepair, its use for storage, and the presence of objects disrupting a pristine imaginary of home. *But – hold on – is this house a home?*

At the same time, our visit to the village and the house could still provide us with a strong normative validation of our origins and identity. Our visit to Sha Chong disclosed a complicated layering of emotional experience and the coexistence of apparently contradictory emotions. While we all shared in happy feelings of adventure and discovery, we could simultaneously harbour doubts and anxious feelings. Emotions, as practices, can be socially mobilised, communicated, and regulated.[19] Positive emotions were developed through many small rituals that built up our sense of the shared purpose of our trip – family reunions, sharing meals, joking, playing with children, group photos – forming an empathic social environment enabling our cross-cultural exploration to take place. Other emotional currents, less explicit and often subconscious, were related to familial psychologies, particularly relations with fathers, which gained an added historical and cross-cultural complexity.

I have suggested that there is an important link between *heritage* – places and things we collectively consider important in our formation, and *inheritance* – what we have received from our forebears. Our trip to Zhongshan was an exploration of what *our* heritage – with its culturally ambiguous historical trajectory – is, or might be. Emotions are fundamental to this sense of our heritage.

Diagrammatically, kinship has been conventionally represented by the genealogical model of the family tree, an abstract structure in which 'kinship is made to look as though its lines connect'.[20] This image of a whole structure is daunting for us; the lines did not and could not all connect, given the historical ruptures shaping our particular situations. Moreover, material things and places age, decay and change, knowledge is lost; fabrics fray, to extend Ingold's metaphor of kinship as a 'meshwork'.[21] The work of Gary, Glenn, and Douglas to uncover details of our ancestry might appear to be backward-looking, always pointing to the past. Certainly, we

---

17. Gaston Bachelard, *The Poetics of Space* (Boston, MA: Beacon, 1969).
18. See Jennifer Rutherford, 'Undwelling: Or Reading Bachelard in Australia', in *Halfway House: The Poetics of Australian Spaces*, ed. Jennifer Rutherford and Barbara Holloway (Crawley, WA: UWA Publishing, 2010), 114.
19. Monique Scheer, 'Are Emotions a Kind of Practice (and Is That What Makes Them Have a History)? A Bourdieuian Approach to Understanding Emotion', *History and Theory* 51, no. 2 (2012): 193–220, https://doi.org/10.1111/j.1468-2303.2012.00621.x.
20. Tim Ingold, *Lines: A Brief History* (London: Routledge, 2016), 154.
21. See Denis Byrne, Chapter 2 of this volume.

were looking for a place where we could imagine a history in the past. But the actual making of inheritance is a live activity, very much in the present, full of immanent imaginings and feelings, and engaging afresh with concrete things and places, and with each other. Our making of heritage/inheritance continues as a living, ongoing process, in movement, like 'eddies in a stream'.[22] *We* are an energetic centre making our heritage.

Bibliography

Ahmed, Sara. *The Cultural Politics of Emotion*. Second edition. New York: Routledge, 2015.

Bachelard, Gaston. *The Poetics of Space*. Boston, MA: Beacon, 1969.

Byrne, Denis. 'Love & Loss in the 1960s'. *International Journal of Heritage Studies* 19, no. 6 (2013): 596–609. https://doi.org/10.1080/13527258.2012.686446u.

Darian-Smith, Kate, and Paula Hamilton. 'Remembering Migration'. In *Remembering Migration: Oral Histories and Heritage in Australia*, edited by Kate Darian-Smith and Paula Hamilton, 1–14. Cham: Palgrave Macmillan, 2019.

Ingold, Tim. *Lines: A Brief History*. London, New York: Routledge, 2016.

Lacan, Jacques. *The Seminar of Jacques Lacan. Book 1: Freud's Papers on Technique (1953–1954)*. Translated by John Forrester. New York: W. W. Norton, 1988.

Li, Xiuguo. 'Social Implications of the Resurgence of Lineage Culture: The Case Study of a Single-Surname Village in Guangdong within the Currents of Industrialization'. PhD diss., Hong Kong Polytechnic University, 2000.

Rutherford, Jennifer. 'Undwelling: Or Reading Bachelard in Australia'. In *Halfway House: The Poetics of Australian Spaces*, edited by Jennifer Rutherford and Barbara Holloway, 113–31. Crawley, WA: UWA Publishing, 2010.

Sanchini, Laura. 'Visiting La Madre Patria: Heritage Pilgrimage among Montreal Italians (Notebook)'. *Ethnologies* 32, no. 2 (2010): 235–56.

Scheer, Monique. 'Are Emotions a Kind of Practice (and Is That What Makes Them Have a History)? A Bourdieuian Approach to Understanding Emotion'. *History and Theory* 51, no. 2 (2012): 193–220. https://doi.org/10.1111/j.1468-2303.2012.00621.x.

Smith, Laurajane, and Gary Campbell. 'The Elephant in the Room: Heritage, Affect, and Emotion'. In *A Companion to Heritage Studies*, edited by W. Logan, Máiréad Nic Craith, and Ullrich Kockel, 467–84. Hoboken, NJ: John Wiley & Sons, 2015.

Tomkins, Silvan S. *Exploring Affect: The Selected Writings of Silvan S. Tomkins*. Cambridge: Cambridge University Press, 1995.

Williams, Michael. 'Wong Shee Ping'. In Wong Shee Ping, *The Poison of Polygamy* (多妻毒): *A Social Novel*, 1–10. Sydney: Sydney University Press, 2019.

Winnicott, Donald W. *Playing and Reality*. London: Routledge, 1991 [1971].

Wong Shee Ping. *The Poison of Polygamy* (多妻毒). Translated by Ely Finch. Sydney: Sydney University Press, 2019.

---

22. Ingold, *Lines*, 154–55.

6
Remittance Houses in Zhongshan

Denis Byrne

To say that the built environment of migration constitutes a zone of continuity stretching between the migrant's origin place and their destination place is, of course, to say that migration brings into being a transnational social field. This is a field populated by what might be referred to as the extended community of migration, consisting of those who emigrate and those who stay behind and by the long-distance interaction between them, as well as the emotional and economic interdependency that fuels this interaction. The material heritage of migration consists of the physical manifestation of this cross-border social field, which is to say the part of its material footprint which endures into the present. In examining the built heritage of the Zhongshan–Australia migration corridor in this chapter, I strive to stay close to the past community of migration that generated it. In other words, I will strive to avoid falling into the error of allowing the 'stuff' – the buildings and the things they contain – to become mere antiquities whose aesthetic charm or technical qualities eclipse the lived histories of the people it represents.

I begin, in the following section, with an account of the 'remittance houses' (僑房 *kiu fong* in Cantonese) of Zhongshan, a term employed for the houses built in the home villages of migrants with funds remitted back there by those who migrated to Australia. The term is, however, used expansively here to include those houses built by migrants returning to their village on a visit or by those who returned permanently, using money repatriated rather than remitted from Australia. A typology of Zhongshan remittance houses is presented which attempts to show how different styles of houses reflect key changes in the lifestyle of the villages, the architectural fashions of the wider world, and the social aspirations of migrant builders and their village-based families. Attention then shifts from the architecture of the houses to their affective valency, which is to say to their capacity to precipitate affective experiences, such as pride and shame, in those associated with them. This is followed by a section on the early twentieth-century adoption by the builders of remittance houses in Zhongshan of a hybrid version of European neoclassical style. Finally, the chapter considers the fate of the houses during the Mao era, which represents a three-decade hiatus in migration and which, more than that, brought with it catastrophic change in the lives of villagers with migrant associations and in the 'lives' of the buildings which migration had produced and sustained.[1]

This chapter describes the houses constructed in the villages of Zhongshan county by those who had migrated from there to Australia. As I will show, the houses have their architectural origins in the vernacular houses of southern China, but by the end of the nineteenth century they began to incorporate self-consciously modern design elements. Indeed, the houses reflect the aspirational modernity that so inflected the lives of those who left Zhongshan for overseas destinations. The very act of leaving demonstrated a desire for a better life, which at this time in history was virtually synonymous with a modern life.

The houses were built in the last decades of the Qing dynasty (1644–1911) and during the Republican era (1912–1949), though a few were constructed after the Japanese occupied the Pearl River Delta in 1938. They often stood on the same village streets as houses built by those who had migrated to Hawaii, California, Cuba, or Canada. Migrant destination locales maintain a presence in the villages partly via the habit villagers have of referring to particular houses using the terms 'Australian house', 'Hawaiian house', and so on. The scale of remittance building in southern China in the early twentieth century was truly impressive, one commentator observing that in the city of Xiamen in Fujian province more than 5,300 new homes were built in the period 1928–1931, over 90 per cent of them with overseas Chinese capital.[2] As Michael Williams has described, remittances from overseas were a major factor in changing the built environment of Zhongshan, including in the form of new houses.[3] Many of these houses are also likely to have been constructed by migrants who had returned permanently to live in their home villages in Zhongshan, with such returnees, according to Williams, constituting a significant proportion of the population of some emigrant villages.[4]

Rather than effacing the homeland from their consciousness, most migrants maintain a dual orientation to their origin and destination locales. They might be said to simultaneously 'face' in the direction of both locales.[5] Like the bodies of migrants, the material objects and places of migration also have this dual orientation. The remittance houses in the emigrant villages of Zhongshan were oriented simultaneously towards the villages in which they stood and towards those buildings

---

1. See also Chapter 9 of this volume.
2. James A. Cook, 'Reimagining China: Xiamen, Overseas Chinese, and a Transnational Modernity', in *Everyday Modernity in China*, ed. Madeleine Yue Dong and Joshua Lewis Goldstein (Seattle: University of Washington Press, 2008).
3. Michael Williams, *Returning Home with Glory: Chinese Villagers around the Pacific, 1849 to 1949* (Hong Kong: Hong Kong University Press, 2018).
4. Michael Williams, Chapter 1 of this volume.
5. Sara Ahmed, *Queer Phenomenology: Orientations, Objects, Others* (Durham, NC: Duke University Press, 2006).

and places in San Francisco or Sydney where Chinese migrants dreamt of them, planned them, and laboured to earn money to construct them. As well as providing accommodation for family members who have stayed behind in the villages, remittance houses act as placeholders for absent migrants themselves, lending them a 'proxy presence' there.[6] This *presencing* aspect of the remittance house goes beyond what in heritage practice is known as the associative value of a heritage place, which refers to the connections a certain place has to particular people or events in the past.[7] I argue that the migrant builder is not merely associated or connected with the remittance house, but rather and more pointedly that the house is a material instantiation or embodiment of the migrant. The remittance house in Zhongshan is woven into the same transnational 'meshwork' as the houses, shops, and market gardens that Zhongshan folk occupied in Australia.[8]

Zhongshan Remittance Houses 1890s–1940s: A Typology

Zhongshan's remittance houses of the pre-1940s era, in their various types, form a remarkably intact array, partly as a result of the hiatus in house-building activity during the Mao era, discussed at the end of this chapter. This contrasts with situations in some other migrant-sending countries. In Greece, for example, houses built in their home villages by those who had departed to places abroad in the period 1890 to 1924 were mostly destroyed in the Second World War and the Greek Civil War which followed.[9]

In the early years of Chinese migration to Australia, remittances were often sent home to relatives in the form of gold entrusted to friends and clansmen, but by the 1930s it was common for payments to be made to Chinese shop owners in Australia who consolidated small payments into drafts on Hong Kong banks. Some of these banks had branches in Shekki (石岐, Shiqi), Zhongshan's county town.[10] The first priority of emigrants was the support of relatives left behind; the proportion of remittances devoted to house-building in Zhongshan was in the order of 20 per cent.[11] Remittances were also used for buying agricultural land, either for farming or as the site for a new house. A survey of land holdings carried out around

---

6. Dimitris Dalakoglou, 'Migrating-Remitting-"Building"-Dwelling: House-Making as "Proxy" Presence in Postsocialist Albania', *The Journal of the Royal Anthropological Institute* 16, no. 4 (2010), https://doi.org/10.1111/j.1467-9655.2010.01652.x.

7. See, for example, L. Harold Fredheim and Manal Khalaf, 'The Significance of Values: Heritage Value Typologies Re-examined', *International Journal of Heritage Studies* 22, no. 6 (2016): 473, https://doi.org/10.1080/13527258.2016.1171247.

8. Tim Ingold, *Lines: A Brief History* (London: Routledge, 2007). See also discussion of meshwork in Chapter 2 of this volume.

9. Kostis Kourelis, 'Three Elenis: Archaeologies of the Greek American Village Home', *Journal of Modern Greek Studies* 38, no. 1 (2020): 88, 89.

10. Williams, *Returning Home with Glory*, 100–103.

11. Williams, *Returning Home with Glory*, 78.

1950 in the emigrant areas of Guangdong, including Zhongshan, found that overseas families owned between 0.5 and 3.2 acres of land compared with only 0.2 to 0.3 acres among non-migrant families.[12] For Guangdong as a whole, between 1862 and 1949 real estate acquisition (including commercial properties) is estimated to have absorbed more than half of remittances.[13]

The houses described in what follows were identified in the field using information provided by the descendants of Zhongshan emigrants in Australia and with the aid of village officials, elderly residents of the villages, and the staff of the Zhongshan office of the Bureau of Overseas Chinese Affairs (僑辦 *kiu baan* in Cantonese). The houses have been ordered into four types based on their architectural attributes. The typology represents an overlapping temporal sequence: Type 1 first appeared in the late 1800s, followed by Type 2 in the 1910s, Type 3 in the 1920s, and Type 4 in the 1930s. Except for the Type 1 house, which seems not to have been built after about 1900, the house types were being produced simultaneously up to the 1940s, the difference between them reflecting the different means and ambitions of their creators. While the houses embody an imaginative effort that was for the most part distributed and shared across the span of migration corridors, we must acknowledge that migration is experienced differently by different people. We know, for example, that by no means all Chinese immigrants in Australia built houses in their ancestral villages, whether that was because they could not afford the expense or because they simply had no desire to build them.

Prior to setting off for overseas destinations, Zhongshan emigrants had overwhelmingly been farmers, cultivating their own few fields or renting fields from landlords. They lived in small houses that were mostly on rectangular plots of land measuring about four metres wide by fifteen metres deep. These differed from vernacular houses in some other parts of China in their lack of an internal courtyard.[14] The houses were separated by narrow spaces or were conjoined to form rows of houses lining the typically narrow lanes of the village. The village was usually a compact cluster of houses, with one or two temples and ancestral halls set among them, surrounded by rice fields. The single-storey vernacular houses, which represented the baseline from which remittance houses departed, had walls of sun-dried mud bricks and gabled roofs covered with straw thatch or ceramic tiles.[15] The walls of the houses of some of the better-off peasant farmers were made of kiln-fired red brick or a combination of red brick for the lower wall and mud brick for the higher portion. The façade had a central doorway but no windows, and the ridge of the gabled roof paralleled the façade. In some of the poorer, non-emigrant villages of

---

12. Glen Peterson, *Overseas Chinese in the People's Republic of China* (London: Routledge, 2012), 44.
13. Peterson, *Overseas Chinese*, 43.
14. For an account of the vernacular house in China, see Ronald G. Knapp, *Chinese Houses: The Heritage of a Nation* (Tokyo: Tuttle, 2006).
15. Interview with Gan Jian-Bo (甘建波), conducted in Zhongshan, 9 May 2018.

the Pearl River Delta this type of house was still standard up to the 1970s.[16] Today, very few survive in Zhongshan, even as ruins.

Before embarking on a detailed account of the four house types, a few words about the socio-economic class of the builders are in order. There were migrants who never made enough money overseas to allow them to build houses in Zhongshan, even if they desired them, and there were others who did accumulate enough wealth but chose not to use it to build houses. However, in the early decades of the twentieth century, many of the houses being built by migrants in Zhongshan were on a scale of grandeur that clearly separated them, in terms of class, from those who built more modest Type 1 and Type 2 houses. The apogee of the grand migrant-built house in Zhongshan took the form of the two mansions (my Type 4 house) that were constructed by members of an emergent diasporic mercantile elite, an elite for which Peter Hamilton has coined the term *kuashang*.[17] The class distinction that was a product of transnational migration came to an abrupt end in 1949 with the advent of the Chinese Communist Party's (CCP) land reform programme and its campaign against class enemies of the early 1950s, both of them aimed at instituting a classless society in China.

Type 1: The stretched traditional house

By the 1890s a recognisably distinct remittance house had emerged that was a larger version of the vernacular house described earlier, though built using a more durable and expensive type of brick, grey in colour, that had been favoured by the elite in Zhongshan since Ming times. Built on the same plots of land as the older houses they replaced, the new houses could only be larger by virtue of being higher. While some of the older houses had a loft, reached by a ladder, extending over the back half of the front room, in the Type 1 house this loft grows to become a mezzanine in a front room that has approximately doubled in height. A semi-transparent wooden screen wall separates the mezzanine from the front room. Back from the mezzanine in some of the houses are upper-storey bedrooms under a second gable. Effectively this is a two-storey house fitted into the template of the single-storey traditional house, but its two-storey interior is disguised from the street by a façade that is identical to that of the former except that it is higher (Figure 6.1). The same style of doorway is present but is stretched higher in accord with the heightened façade.

---

16. Anita Chan, Richard Madsen, and Jonathan Unger, *Chen Village: Revolution to Globalization*, 3rd ed. (Berkeley: University of California Press, 2009), 256.
17. Peter E. Hamilton, *Made in Hong Kong: Transpacific Networks and a New History of Globalization* (New York: Columbia University Press, 2021), 3.

This type of house, staying within the conventions of the vernacular while stretching the template, might be said to be simultaneously an expression of sameness and an assertion of difference. While it represents the flow of new money into the emigrant village, this money does not translate as architectural ostentation. From a heritage, and indeed an archaeological perspective, the importance of this house type lies in it being one of a series of types that together tell a story of increasing wealth flowing through the migration corridor into Zhongshan.

Figure 6.1: Type 1 house, built in Caobian village (曹邊村) by a migrant based in Queensland. Photo by Denis Byrne 2018.

Type 2: The large two-storey house

This is a fully realised two-storey house which, while stylistically continuous with Type 1, is significantly larger and internally more elaborate. Emerging in the 1910s, almost all these houses are free-standing, the larger of them being located on what would then have been the edge of their villages where fields had been purchased for their construction (Figure 6.2). Many adopt a duplex form, built to accommodate the families of brothers in accord with an embedded social ideal that brothers should remain close residentially,[18] something that in northern China would have been achieved by extending the father's single-storey 'courtyard house' (四合院) laterally. The façade typically features two high doors along with small windows on the upper level. As with the Type 1 house, the front room is an open space spanning the full height of the house, from the floor (of wooden boards or, alternatively, ceramic tiles on concrete) to the exposed roof beams above.

In common with the Type 1 house, these houses have decorative friezes under the eaves, consisting of stucco relief mouldings and paintings of auspicious fruit, flowers, animals, and non-figurative symbols. A range of landscape motifs commonly appear on the panels of the wooden screen walls of the interior. By the 1920s and 1930s, steamships and motor buses, emblems of mobility and modernity (the two were elided), sometimes feature in these landscapes (Figure 6.3). The screen walls often also have 'panels' of textured coloured glass, 'reverse painted' with symbols and landscape scenes, along with unpainted glass mirrors.[19] Glass mirrors were being imported to China by the 1880s and were mass-produced there during Republican times.[20]

Some Type 2 houses incorporate watchtowers, or *diaolou* (碉樓, in Mandarin), rising two or more levels above the roof. They were used for refuge during attacks by bandits attracted to emigrant villages by their remittance-fuelled wealth. Such attacks became widespread in Zhongshan in the 1920s and 1930s.[21] The towers are smaller and less elaborate than those of Kaiping county, 60 kilometres southwest of Zhongshan, an array of which were included on the World Heritage list in 2007.[22]

Modernity is also represented in these houses in the form of light. Glazed windows were typically installed on both floors. Flat glass (also known as 'plated' glass) had been adopted by the elite in China from the mid-nineteenth century and by Republican times had been taken up by the lower classes, with hundreds of new

---

18. This configuration was locally known in Zhongshan in Cantonese as '*heng dai uk*' 兄弟屋 (lit. fraternal house).
19. Reverse painting on glass was a decorative art that developed in the context of China's trade with the West in the eighteenth and nineteenth centuries but was absorbed into the domestic market for decorative arts, particularly in coastal China. See David S. Howard, *A Tale of Three Cities: Canton, Shanghai & Hong Kong; Three Centuries of Sino-British Trade in the Decorative Arts* (London: Sotheby's, 1997).
20. Frank Dikötter, *Things Modern: Material Culture and Everyday Life in China* (London: Hurst, 2007), 185–86.
21. Williams, *Returning Home with Glory*, 90–91.
22. For Kaiping *diaolou*, see the UNESCO World Heritage list, https://whc.unesco.org/en/list/1112/, accessed June 2021.

Figure 6.2: Type 2 house, Caobian village (曹邊村). The house was constructed in duplex (兄弟屋) form and is likely to have accommodated the families of two brothers. Photo by Denis Byrne 2018.

Figure 6.3: A detail of an interior panel painting in an early twentieth-century Type 2 house in Caobian village (曹邊村), showing a motor bus. Steamboats are depicted in the background above the bus (see also Figure 6.4). Crazing has resulted from the shrinkage of the paint layer over time. Photo by Denis Byrne 2018.

glass factories springing up in China to cater to the demand.[23] The windows tended to be small, but they brought light into spaces where the only other source of illumination was the oil lamp. Equating light with modernity in China, Frank Dikötter notes that increased illumination permitted such modern activities as reading (with the spread of modern schooling, literacy increased dramatically at this time) and the crafting of clothing in new styles using foot-pedal sewing machines, which quickly became de rigueur items in remittance houses.[24] The British had installed an electric power plant in Canton (Guangzhou) by 1901,[25] and in Zhongshan oil lamps were superseded by electricity in some remittance houses by around the 1910s. Jan See-Chin (鄭泗全, 1858–1937), who migrated to Queensland from Zhongshan and returned to his native home of Hou Tau village (濠頭村) in 1915, in the 1920s drew on the wealth he had accumulated from his Queensland sugar plantations to build an electric power plant for the village.[26]

The architectural vernacular is strongly apparent in these houses and yet they also clearly materialise particular modern ideas and practices. The houses are hybrid entities that defy understanding in terms of the conventional traditional-modern dualism. The entwinement or 'confusion' of the traditional and the modern in them parallels that found in indigenous architecture in late colonial India.[27] Because of their overall size and height, they would have been standout structures in the emigrant villages of the early twentieth century, making a clear gesture to the relative affluence of those at the other end of the migration corridor whose wealth enabled their construction.

Type 3: The portico-balcony house

By the 1920s in Zhongshan county's emigrant villages a larger version of the Type 2 house appeared, rendered dramatically distinctive by the grafting onto its front of a portico and first floor balcony in a style bearing strong similarities to European neoclassical architecture (Figure 6.5). Neoclassical influence may have first filtered through to Zhongshan from the foreign enclave in Canton, where it was in evidence from the eighteenth century.[28] Closer to Zhongshan, in Hong Kong by the late 1800s the neoclassical style was dominant in the architecture of public and commercial buildings as well as in many of the houses of the Chinese and Western elite.

The architectural ostentation of the neoclassical-style façades of the Type 3 houses allowed their owners to display the wealth their offshore lives had brought

---

23. Dikötter, *Things Modern*, 156.
24. Dikötter, *Things Modern*, 165.
25. Michael Tsin, 'Canton Remapped', in *Remaking the Chinese City: Modernity and National Identity, 1900–1950*, ed. Joseph W. Esherick (Honolulu: University of Hawai'i Press, 2001), 25.
26. Pamela Lee Wong, *The Mystery Aussie Jan See Chin* (Palo Alto, CA: PWL Publishing, 2018), 144.
27. Jyoti Hosagrahar, *Indigenous Modernities: Negotiating Architecture and Urbanism* (London: Routledge, 2005).
28. Johnathan A. Farris, *Enclave to Urbanity: Canton, Foreigners, and Architecture from Late Eighteenth to the Early Nineteenth Centuries* (Hong Kong: Hong Kong University Press, 2007), 15.

Figure 6.4: A bed compartment and panel paintings on the first floor of an early twentieth-century Type 2 house in Caobian village (曹邊村). The painting of a bus, shown in Figure 6.3, is located immediately above the bed compartment. Photo by Denis Byrne 2018.

them and to make implicit claims to an elevated status in the village. In reality, the building of these houses sometimes overextended the migrant's finances. As Adam McKeown observes, most migrants failed to tell villagers at home how difficult their lives were abroad: 'Rather, they devoted much of their time at home to conspicuous consumption, providing entertainment and banquets for friends and villages, renovating their homes, showing off the sewing machines, radios and cameras they brought for their families.'[29]

It was common for the interior walls and the ceilings of these houses to be painted with auspicious symbols and landscape scenes, similar to those in the more elaborate Type 2 houses, except here the landscapes tended to be painted in Western

---

29. Adam McKeown, *Chinese Migrant Networks and Cultural Change: Peru, Chicago, Hawaii, 1900–1936* (Chicago, IL: University of Chicago Press, 2001), 74.

rather than traditional Chinese perspective (Figure 6.3). The tiled gable roof of the Type 1 and 2 houses is retained, except where the front gable has been replaced with a flat, reinforced concrete roof. While a few of the Type 2 houses have concrete floor plates, here they are prevalent and the entire portico-balcony element is of stucco-rendered reinforced concrete, including the neoclassical-style columns. In the larger houses the entire structure is based on a reinforced-concrete frame. Most of the internal walls are of brick and plaster, though wooden screen walls are also used. The provision of masonry interior walls, according to Dikötter, reflects changing notions of the privacy of individuals within the family in Republican China

Figure 6.5: Type 3 portico-balcony house, built in Hou Tau village (濠頭村) by Jan See-Chin (鄭泗全), a migrant who had returned from Queensland. Photo by Denis Byrne 2018.

and of the home as a 'repository of the individual'.[30] But in contrast to the inward-looking traditional houses, the balconies of this type of house represent a semi-opening of the house to the outer world. Where they existed, the flat portions of the roof were used recreationally and for sun-drying grain, vegetables, and meat. Along with the windows in the upper floors, the flat roofs afforded the novelty of being able to observe village life from above. In more contemporary times, Xiaoyang Zhu has referred to the flat roofs (天台, *tiantai* in Mandarin) of post-1990s houses near Kunming, Yunnan, as 'sky patios' that represent the relocation upwards of the old-style internal courtyard.[31]

In terms of the Western architectural canon, the grafting of a neoclassical façade onto a semi-vernacular gable-roofed house might seem to render the design incoherent, but as Jyoti Hosagrahar points out, the unsettling of architectural certainties has been an essential element of indigenous modernities in the Global South.[32] The portico-balcony houses of Zhongshan, with their radically novel façades, the sheer stylistic variety of those façades, and their inclusion of reinforced concrete and terrazzo, called for new construction skills that are likely to have been sourced from Hong Kong, whose construction labour force came mainly from neighbouring areas of the Pearl River Delta to which these skills are in turn likely to have filtered back.[33] In at least a few cases, architects were retained from Hong Kong to design the houses; otherwise they were designed by their owners and by local builders.[34] The standardisation of building form and technology, which had been a hallmark of traditional Chinese architecture,[35] was giving way in the new houses to a diversification in such things as the dimensions and arrangement of rooms and internal and external decoration. This bestowed a greater individualism on them than is seen in the Type 1 or Type 2 house, in accord with Dikötter's observation that in China at this time, 'new materials and new ideas allowed enormous diversification of the architectural landscape in design, layout and substance'.[36]

By the 1920s, a number of the migrant-built portico-balcony houses in Zhongshan were connected to the local electricity grid and to the piped water network, infrastructure which, so emblematic of modernity, was only possible to install in emigrant villages and in Shekki town because of the wealth flowing from overseas Zhongshanese. It changed the pattern of domestic life but it also meant that the previously autonomous house became networked into and dependent upon an

---

30. Dikötter, *Things Modern*, 160–61.
31. Xiaoyang Zhu, *Topography of Politics in Rural China: The Story of Xiaocun* (Singapore: World Scientific Publishing, 2014), 127.
32. Hosagrahar, *Indigenous Modernities*, 7.
33. Moira M. W. Chan-Yeung, *Lam Woo: Master Builder, Revolutionary, and Philanthropist* (Hong Kong: Chinese University of Hong Kong Press, 2017), 73.
34. Interviews with migrant descendants in Zhongshan and Australia attest to the involvement of architects in the design of some of these houses.
35. Edward Denison, *Architecture and the Landscape of Modernity in China before 1949* (Abingdon: Routledge, 2017), 94, https://doi.org/10.4324/9781315567686.
36. Dikötter, *Things Modern*, 187.

Type 4: The mansion house

On a larger and grander scale than any of the other houses built in Zhongshan were two mansions constructed there by department store tycoons. Ma Ying Piu (馬應彪, 1860–1944), one of the founders of the Sincere chain of department stores (先施百貨), in 1929 retained a Hong Kong architect to build a three-storey Palladian-style house in his native village of Sha Chong (沙涌村). A few years later, the Kwok (郭氏兄弟) brothers, founders of the Wing On chain (永安集團), built a three-storey Art Deco-style mansion in Chuk Sau Yuen (竹秀園, Zhuxiuyuan), their ancestral village (Figure 6.6). Each of the 'Four Great Companies' (Sincere 先施百貨, Wing On 永安百貨, The Sun 大新百貨, and Sun Sun 新新百貨) that ran department stores in Hong Kong, Shanghai, and some other Chinese cities in the first half of the twentieth century had their origins in the business activities of men from Zhongshan who migrated to Sydney in the last decades of the nineteenth century and became successful fruit and vegetable traders there.[38] The Sincere and Wing On companies modelled their department stores on the modern style and modern retailing strategy of the large Anthony Hordern & Sons department store that was located only a few blocks from Sydney's Chinatown.[39]

The Ma family mansion in Sha Chong, built by Ma Ying Piu,[40] was in keeping with the neoclassic style, while the 'Kwok mansion' reflected the Art Deco style of the Wing On company's twenty-one-storey apartment block in Shanghai, Wing On Mansions.[41] Both houses have large ground floor reception rooms and numerous bedrooms and bathrooms on the floors above, equipped with modern plumbing. They have reinforced-concrete frames and floor plates and dispense with gables in favour of flat reinforced-concrete roofs. Wall paintings are conspicuously absent and there is an almost studied avoidance of traditional referents in general, something that may be partly explained by their builders having converted to Christianity while in Australia. The exception is where they reimported Chinese design in the form of European Art Deco motifs that had absorbed 'Chinese' design elements, as

---

37. Tsin, 'Canton Remapped'.
38. Wellington K. K. Chan, 'Personal Styles, Cultural Values and Management: The Sincere and Wing On Companies in Shanghai and Hong Kong', *The Business History Review* 40 (1996), https://doi.org/10.2307/3116879; John Fitzgerald, *Big White Lie: Chinese Australians in White Australia* (Sydney: UNSW Press, 2007), 190–99. See also Chapter 8 of this volume for a discussion of Wing Sang, the fruit company in Sydney which formed the basis of the wealth that led to the development of the department stores established by Ma Ying Piu and others.
39. Fitzgerald, *Big White Lie*, 194.
40. See also Chapter 5 of this volume.
41. Edward Denison and Guang Yu Ren, *Modernism in China: Architectural Visions and Revolutions* (London: Wiley, 2008), 181.

Figure 6.6: Art Deco mansion built by the Kwok brothers in Chuk Sau Yuen village (竹秀園 Zhuxiuyuan) after their return from Australia. The 'sunburst' motif on the parapet was a design element commonly occurring in Art Deco buildings worldwide in the 1930s and early 1940s. Photo by Denis Byrne 2017.

seen in the case of the Kwok mansion's internal glass doors with their lattice screen pattern and in the pagoda in the stained-glass panel above one of the doors (Figure 6.7). The Chinese influence on Art Deco continued a pattern set by the Art Nouveau movement of the late 1800s and early 1900s.[42]

Art Deco, which was also a design influence in some Type 3 houses, was as transnationally mobile and adaptive as the migrant actors who deployed it in Zhongshan. As Vandana Baweja observes of Art Deco, 'as it spread across the

---

42. Clay Lancaster, 'Oriental Contributions to Art Nouveau', *The Art Bulletin* 34 (1952): 297–310.

Figure 6.7: Ground floor of 'Kwok mansion' (沛勳堂), showing 'lattice screen' style doors and a stained-glass window featuring a pagoda and a man fishing from a sampan. The ceramic floor tiles are a recent addition. Photo by Denis Byrne 2017.

globe it absorbed and synthesised various geographical and temporal influences that included ancient Egyptian, German modernist, Streamlining, Mayan, Aztec, Babylonian, and African'.[43] The 'aerodynamic aesthetic' of architectural streamlining discussed by Baweja in relation to Art Deco buildings in Bombay and other Indian cities emerged out of the enthusiasm for speed that gripped many in the early decades of the twentieth century as ever faster motorcars, airplanes, and ships came into use.[44] It had a particular resonance for those diaspora Chinese of the Pearl

---

43. Vandana Baweja, 'Messy Modernisms: Otto Koenigsberger's Early Work in Princely Mysore, 1939–41', *South Asian Studies* 31, no. 1 (2015): 6, https://doi.org/10.1080/02666030.2015.1008806.
44. Baweja, 'Messy Modernisms', 6.

River Delta who had modern ocean liners depicted in wall paintings in houses they built in their home villages. In practical terms, these new steamships dramatically reduced travel time between migrant origin and destination locales. Their speed was depicted in the paintings by horizontal streams of smoke trailing out from the ships' funnels. At the same time, the paintings were a status claim on the part of owners and occupants of the houses, announcing their belonging to the modern world of international travel. Their equivalent in today's world includes the remittance houses in the Punjab that have large models of jumbo jets mounted on their roofs.[45] As a heritage object, the remittance house is a placeholder in the local landscape for the absent (or only occasionally present) migrant, but it also gives material substance and support to new identities being constructed around claims to wealth, social status, cosmopolitanism, and global connectivity.

For all their grandeur, the mansions were infrequently occupied, family members being kept busy running their businesses in Hong Kong and Shanghai. Like the department stores themselves, the houses were the acme of modernity. They were dramatic expressions of wealth and status but critically, along with the modern schools endowed by these families in their ancestral villages,[46] they were material expressions of the continued importance placed on maintaining ties to the ancestral place and membership of that place's *in situ* and diasporic community. Other members of the Ma family had similar though smaller houses in Sha Chong village, and more distant lines of the same lineage who had also sent migrants to Australia built Type 1 and 2 remittance houses there. By employing hundreds of fellow villagers in their department stories in Canton (Guangzhou), Hong Kong, and Shanghai, the Ma and Kwok families helped network clanspeople from these villages into their business empires.[47]

The mansions were requisitioned by the Japanese during their 1937–1945 occupation of Guangdong and after 1949 were appropriated to the state by the Communist government under Mao, ownership later being restored to the Ma and Kwok families based in Hong Kong and elsewhere outside China's then borders.[48] Now protected as heritage properties, the mansions are a source of pride for family descendants, including those in Australia, and are fixtures of the itineraries of those Zhongshan migrants and their descendants in Australia who make return visits to Zhongshan.[49] Many Zhongshanese in Australia continued to hold shares in the

---

45. Steve Taylor, "'Home Is Never Fully Achieved . . . Even When We Are in It': Migration, Belonging and Social Exclusion within Punjabi Transnational Mobility', *Mobilities* 10, no. 2 (2015): 200, https://doi.org/10.1080/17450101.2013.848606.

46. Christopher Cheng, 'Beacons of Modern Learning: Diaspora-Funded Schools in the China-Australia Corridor', *Asian and Pacific Migration Journal* 29, no. 2 (2020): 139–62, https://doi.org/10.1177/0117196820930309.

47. Fitzgerald, *Big White Lie*, 199.

48. Hong Kong Island and the Kowloon Peninsula were ceded to Britain in 1842 and 1860 respectively. In 1898 Britain extended the Crown Colony by obtaining a ninety-nine-year lease from the Qing government.

49. Information from interviews conducted with Zhongshan migrants and migrant descendants in New South Wales. See also Alexandra Wong, Chapter 4 of this volume.

Figure 6.8: A watchtower house (碉樓 *diaolou*) in Jinjiangli village, Kaiping County (開平縣錦江里村), Guangdong. Such houses were constructed by migrants in the early decades of the twentieth century using reinforced concrete and brick. Photo by Denis Byrne 2013.

'Four Great Companies' into the late twentieth century. The mansion houses are attention-grabbing objects in the China–Australia heritage corridor, the equivalent, say, of the tower houses (碉樓 *diaolou*) built in Kaiping county by people who had migrated to America, Canada, and elsewhere (Figure 6.8),[50] but in terms of providing a well-rounded survey of remittance house types in Zhongshan, they are no more significant than the other houses covered here.

---

50. Selia Jinhua Tan, 'Kaiping Diaolou and Its Associated Villages: Documenting the Process of Application to the World Heritage List' (PhD thesis, University of Hong Kong, 2007); Selia Jinhua Tan, *A Research on the Ornamentation of Kaiping Diaolou and Its Associated Villages* (in Chinese) (Beijing: Overseas Chinese Publishing House, 2013).

Affective Entanglements

We experience old things and places by way of sense, affect, and emotion, at least as much as by an intellectual apprehension of them. Our attachment to them can be expected to accrue at least as much from our histories of embodied experience as from deliberative thought. In this respect, the well-known definition of affect coined by Gregory Seigworth and Melissa Gregg is worth citing.

> Affect arises in the midst of in-between-ness: in the capacities to act and be acted upon. Affect is an impingement or extrusion of a momentary or sometimes more sustained state of relation *as well as* the passage (and duration of passage) of forces or intensities. That is, affect is found in those intensities that pass body to body (human, non-human, part-body, and otherwise), in those resonances that circulate about, between, and sometimes stick to bodies and worlds.[51]

The kind of in-betweenness they refer to here holds good over a larger space-time scale than those very intimate and immediate settings in which affect is mostly seen to be situated. In the migration context, we might think of it as a body-mind state of being that involves intimate relations with things that may be separated from those that experience them by a great distance. It is the play of the intensities of affect and emotion across this distance that partly characterises the lived experience of transnational migration.

A study of the ways in which recent migrants from Lebanon relate to a national park in suburban Sydney illustrates the long-distance dynamic of affect.[52] Take, for example, the act of fishing at the edge of the river that flows through the park. For Lebanese immigrant recreational fishers, the specific weight of the Lebanese fishing rod they held in their hands was precisely the same as that of the rods they used to fish with back home, back then. Also the same, or very similar, were the repetitive motions involved in baiting the hook, casting out the line, and hauling it in.[53] What gives the rod its *affective* weight is a combination of one's personal history of holding similar rods in Lebanon, the propensity of one's body to remember the sensations which go with that, and the 'vibrancy' of the matter constituting the rod.[54] Objects are known to play an active role in triggering 'embodied memories'.[55] Our affective entanglement with them is consonant with the symmetry of human–non-human

---

51. Gregory J. Seigworth and Melissa Gregg, 'An Inventory of Shimmers', in *The Affect Theory Reader*, ed. Melissa Gregg and Gregory J. Seigworth (Durham, NC: Duke University Press, 2010), 1.
52. Denis Byrne and Heather Goodall, 'Placemaking and Transnationalism: Recent Migrants and a National Park in Sydney, Australia', *Parks: The International Journal of Protected Areas and Conservation* 19, no. 1 (2013): 63–72, https://doi.org/10.2305/IUCN.CH.2013.PARKS-19-1.DB.en.
53. Heather Goodall, Stephen Wearing, Denis Byrne, and Allison Cadzow, 'Fishing the Georges River: Cultural Diversity and Urban Environments', in *Everyday Multiculturalism*, ed. Amanda Wise and Selvaraj Velayutham (Houndmills: Palgrave Macmillan, 2009), 183.
54. Jane Bennett, *Vibrant Matter: A Political Ecology of Things* (Durham, NC: Duke University Press, 2010).
55. Paul Connerton, *How Societies Remember* (Cambridge: Cambridge University Press, 1989).

relations argued for by Bruno Latour,[56] and the non-hierarchical positioning of humans and objects in Levy Bryant's 'flat ontology'.[57] Julie Chu's book *Cosmologies of Credit* provides a wonderful ethnographic setting in which to think of remittance houses in this way, particularly in their guise as a form of cultural capital that accrues status both to the migrant abroad and to his or her relatives at home.[58]

Chu observes how in the village of Longyan, the site of her research in Fujian, a new generation of houses with reinforced-concrete frames and red-brick walls were built between 1978 and 1985, reflecting the new prosperity of the post–Mao Reform Era. But between the mid-1980s and the mid-1990s these houses came to be surrounded by larger houses with ceramic tile-covered exteriors built by those in the village receiving remittances from relatives in the United States.[59] The formerly proud owners of the red-brick houses, which in their time were 'shining symbols of new prosperity', now found themselves dwelling in structures that, outshone by the tiled houses around them, had morphed into 'the ramshackle signs of low living among newly imaginative structures of modern and cosmopolitan dwelling'.[60]

Now seen as 'hopelessly crammed, dilapidated, and backward', the newly passé red-brick houses of Longyan may seem but passive victims of changing human fashion.[61] But are they mere objects of embarrassment for human subjects or have they assumed a new mode of agency in relation to those subjects? Where once, a mere decade previously, they caused their owners to swell with pride, now they cause them to shrink with shame. I use these common English descriptors of shame's affects – 'swell' and 'shrink' – because they capture the corporeality of affect. The implications of this affective relationality for the turnover of built fabric in Longyan suggest that we may need to think of the temporality of the built heritage of migration as framed not in terms of migrant generations (the first-generation, second-generation interval, for example) but of generations of built fabric and of the temporality of successive waves of building fashion that washed through diasporic space.

The causal sequence wherein the red-brick house acquires its capacity to embarrass is initiated, one might guess, in village society's tendency to assign social status partly according to the houses people occupy. The houses' agency thus derives from a particular social situation, but this in no way lessens the capacity of the red-brick houses of Longyan to cause their owners to cringe with embarrassment. These are real embodied affects triggered by real physical things.

---

56. Bruno Latour, *We Have Never Been Modern*, trans. Catherine Porter (Cambridge, MA: Harvard University Press, 1993).
57. Levy Bryant, *The Democracy of Objects* (Ann Arbor, MI: Open Humanities Press, 2011), http://dx.doi.org/10.3998/ohp.9750134.0001.001.
58. Julie Y. Chu, *Cosmologies of Credit: Transnational Mobility and the Politics of Destination in China* (Durham, NC: Duke University Press, 2010).
59. Chu, *Cosmologies of Credit*, 41–46.
60. Chu, *Cosmologies of Credit*, 45.
61. Chu, *Cosmologies of Credit*, 46.

For Chu, locality is 'a structure of feeling'.[62] The process of migration stretches this structure such that houses in emigrant villages become actors imbricated in causal sequences of transnational scope. Village members overseas have laboured for the new houses and the social status they confer, and it is only by means of this labour that they and their relatives at home can escape the embarrassing, status-diminishing effects of the superseded 'old' houses, houses that in effect demand to be renovated, rebuilt, or replaced. It is misleading to think of them as mere 'products' of the phenomenon of migration, a point that is also at the heart of Iván Sandoval-Cervantes's ethnographic study of remittance houses in Zegache village in Oaxaca, Mexico.[63] While the houses may nourish what Miller refers to as a 'myth of return' on the part of the emigrant,[64] for those left behind they may be sites of 'active waiting'.[65] Drawing on Lauren Berlant's concept of 'cruel optimism', Sandoval-Cervantes describes how such houses, especially those in an unfinished state, promise the return of those who initiated them.[66]

For relatives at home, including mothers of migrant sons, caring for the house built by the absent one is an aspect of active waiting and longing in which they are exposed to and respond to the affective intensities of the house.[67] The absentee's presence is materialised in the fabric of the house. 'The daily lives of the families of transnational migrants are constantly informed by actions and emotions that emerge from unfinished houses, active awaiting, and the hopeful aspirations of the ever-present possibility of return migration and family reunification, as migrants build houses that seem to indicate their desire to return.'[68] At least some of the early twentieth-century remittance houses of South China that have been the subject of my own research are likely, in a similar way, to be embodiments of active waiting, but the turmoil and catastrophe of the mid-twentieth century in China have made it virtually impossible to reconstruct this aspect of their meaning. From a heritage studies perspective, what is important about the work of Chu and Sandoval-Cervantes is that it at least alerts us to the range of possible meanings that such buildings (many of them now passing into the realm of public heritage) have had for people living with them in the past and how these buildings spoke to them.

In proposing the migration heritage corridor as a useful concept in heritage practice, I do so on the understanding that we think of it as (in addition to its other characteristics) a structure of feeling. The relevance of feeling and affective

---

62. Chu, *Cosmologies of Credit*, 35.
63. Iván Sandoval-Cervantes, 'Uncertain Futures: The Unfinished Houses of Undocumented Migrants in Oaxaca, Mexico', *American Anthropologist* 119, no. 2 (2017): 209–22, https://doi.org/10.1111/aman.12864.
64. Daniel Miller, 'Migration, Material Culture and Tragedy: Four Moments in Caribbean Migration', *Mobilities* 3, no. 3 (2008): 407, https://doi.org/10.1080/17450100802376712.
65. Sandoval-Cervantes, 'Uncertain Futures', 210.
66. Lauren Berlant, *Cruel Optimism* (Durham, NC: Duke University Press, 2011).
67. Sandoval-Cervantes, 'Uncertain Futures', 212.
68. Sandoval-Cervantes, 'Uncertain Futures', 215–16.

relationality is not unappreciated in the heritage studies field as a whole.[69] But these insights have so far failed to penetrate migration heritage as a field of study, where they might call into question the very idea of the bordered, nation-state container approach to the conservation and interpretation of that heritage.

Embracing the Neoclassical in Zhongshan

As described earlier, many of Zhongshan county's remittance houses built in the 1920s and 1930s were distinctive for their neoclassical-style façades featuring porticoes and balconies supported by Greek columns. Zhongshan emigrants would have had plenty of opportunity to observe and frequent neoclassical buildings in Australia and yet there is no evidence that the neoclassical houses they built in Zhongshan were directly inspired by those buildings rather than by examples of neoclassical architecture closer to Zhongshan itself. In the late nineteenth and early twentieth centuries in Macao, Hong Kong, and the treaty ports of China, such as Shanghai and Xiamen (Amoy), Western architects created neoclassic buildings, including houses, that provided 'architectural familiarity' for Western nationals resident there and that symbolised the West's dominance in colonial or crypto-colonial space.[70] The situation was comparable to British India where, according to Thomas Metcalf, neoclassical architecture was deployed to express the spirit of empire and the relations of power that went with imperial subjugation.[71]

The nature of this influence remains, however, debatable. Arguing that neoclassical architecture in China was not so much a direct import from the West as representative of an architecture of the larger colonial zone, Peter Rowe and Seng Kuan note that the 1908 railway station in Shanghai had 'close stylistic parallels' not just with its 'counterpart' in Bombay but also with Victorian public buildings in Melbourne and Hong Kong.[72] By extension, it seems likely the migrant builders of neoclassical-style houses in Zhongshan were drawing inspiration not from Australia as a country and, from 1901, a nation, but from a colonial architectural milieu in which Australia participated. The relation of the houses to Australian architecture was likely one of simultaneity rather than of a unilinear flow of influence. The neoclassical architectural milieu of the British Empire was a hybrid of metropolitan style and local influences, including among the latter the important element of climate.

---

69. Denis Byrne, 'Love & Loss in the 1960s', *International Journal of Heritage Studies* 19, no. 6 (2013): 596–609, https://doi.org/10.1080/13527258.2012.686446; David Crouch, 'Affect, Heritage, Feeling', in *The Palgrave Handbook of Contemporary Heritage Research*, ed. Emma Waterton and Steve Watson (Houndmills: Palgrave Macmillan, 2015), 177–90; Divya Tolia-Kelly, Emma Waterton, and Steve Watson, eds, *Heritage, Affect and Emotion: Policies, Practices and Infrastructures* (London: Routledge, 2017).

70. Peter G. Rowe and Seng Kuan, *Architectural Encounters with Essence and Form in Modern China* (Cambridge, MA: MIT Press, 2002), 30.

71. Thomas Metcalf, *An Imperial Vision: Indian Architecture and Britain's Raj* (Berkeley: University of California Press, 1989).

72. Rowe and Kuan, *Architectural Encounters*, 33.

These considerations caution against thinking of the China–Australia migration heritage corridor (of which the Zhongshan heritage corridor forms a strand) in a narrowly delineated manner. The Zhongshan–Australia corridor was certainly not insulated from colonial Southeast Asia, Britain's larger empire, or from the global Chinese diaspora, but it retains sufficient coherence to be useful as a concept.

We should not think of those migrant-built houses in Zhongshan which have neoclassical-style façades as a *version* of the European neoclassical. Whatever the nature and degree of Western architectural influence on the houses, they represent a hybrid that is a local invention insofar as the migrant builders reworked the neo-classical style to create a house form unique to their area of the Pearl River Delta. They thus represent an architecture that is authentic in its own right; one that in its departure from the European neoclassical style might even be described as repre-senting a *resistance* to that style, following Yuan Shu's reasoning in his discussion of Indigenous epistemologies in Asia.[73]

British architecture in Hong Kong appears to have had a significant influence on the builders of Zhongshan remittance houses, but their engagement with it took the form of a complex cultural exchange. People from Zhongshan had traded with and worked in Hong Kong since the Crown Colony's inception in 1841. Many became important players in its economy and their mostly poorer relatives were among those who migrated to Australia. Almost all Zhongshan emigrants departed from Hong Kong port, and when making return visits to China or returning to settle, they disembarked there en route to their home villages in Zhongshan. Many permanent returnees opted to settle in Hong Kong while maintaining close contact with their home villages. Hong Kong was indeed a key node or 'knot', to use Tim Ingold's terminology, on migrant lifelines transecting the Zhongshan–Australia corridor, and it seems reasonable to think that architectural trends there were influ-ential among those building remittance houses in nearby Zhongshan.[74]

Under the British, Hong Kong was a racially segregated society, a situation illustrated by the law that between 1902 and 1946 prevented Chinese living on Victoria Peak, a British residential enclave where colonial privilege was expressed in the neoclassical style of many of its houses.[75] The colonial administration saw Chinese houses and European houses as 'mutually exclusive building types' belong-ing to clearly distinguished residential districts.[76] In the pre-1940s era, the Chinese 'house' (唐樓 *tong lau* in Cantonese) in Hong Kong took the form of a three- or four-storey row house that was long and narrow in plan, typically with a shop on

---

73. Yuan Shu, 'Introduction', in *Oceanic Archives, Indigenous Epistemologies, and Transpacific American Studies*, ed. Yuan Shu, Otto Heim, and Kendall Johnson (Hong Kong: Hong Kong University Press, 2019), 2–3.
74. Ingold, *Lines*.
75. John M. Carroll, *A Concise History of Hong Kong* (Lanham, MD: Rowman and Littlefield, 2007); Lawrence W. C. Lai, 'Discriminatory Zoning in Colonial Hong Kong: A Review of the Post-war Literature and Some Further Evidence for an Economic Theory of Discrimination', *Property Management* 29, no. 1 (2010): 50–86, https://doi.org/10.1108/02637471111102932.
76. Lai, 'Discriminatory Zoning', 53–55.

the ground floor and accommodation on the upper floors, often in the form of tenements occupied by recent migrants from the Chinese mainland.[77] Cecelia Chu describes these buildings as a hybrid of the 'traditional townhouses of South China' and a modern commercial style designed by their builders (mostly Chinese) to take advantage of the opportunities of Hong Kong's rapidly expanding economy while at the same time complying with the colony's discriminatory zoning regulations.[78] The colonial zoning laws in Hong Kong determined that only the 'European' type house, typically a detached dwelling surrounded by gardens, could be built in Hong Kong Island's 'hill district', which included The Peak, and while Chinese were permitted to buy properties there, which many did, they could only live in them with the consent of the government, which up to 1946 was never granted.[79]

Key to explaining the neoclassical influence of migrant-built houses in Zhongshan is the fact that while wealthy Chinese residents in Hong Kong, including returned migrants, could not live in areas reserved for white colonists, there was nothing to stop them appropriating the 'architecture of privilege' found in those zones for the houses they built for themselves in areas outside them. For example, James Choy Hing (1869–1957), a returned migrant from Australia and co-founder of the Sincere department store chain, in 1915 built himself a grand neoclassical mansion at No. 2 Park Street in the Mid-Levels on Hong Kong Island that easily rivalled in neoclassical grandeur the houses of the British on The Peak.[80] According to Selina Chan, Hong Kong was a place that was constantly hybridising the other.[81] Beyond symbolising white privilege, within local Chinese society in Hong Kong, neoclassical style came to symbolise wealth and success. While in the emigrant villages of Zhongshan county neoclassical style stood for wealth and success gained through migration, it also carried the cachet of the new and the modern.

But in highlighting the degree of agency shown by Chinese in Hong Kong and migrant builders in Zhongshan in their appropriation and reworking of neoclassical style, we must be wary of understating the extent to which this style was imbued with the power relations of colonialism. It would be naïve to think that the Chinese adoption of elements of the neoclassical style, however reworked, was the outcome of a neutral choice, any more than that it was a matter of neutral choice that Chinese migrants in Sydney adapted themselves to existing Anglo-Australian architecture rather than constructing buildings more amenable to their lifestyle. In Hong Kong, wealthy Chinese were almost obliged to live in neoclassical-style

---

77. Cecilia Chu, 'Between Typologies and Representation: The *Tong Lau* and the Discourse of the "Chinese House" in Colonial Hong Kong', in *Colonial Frames, Nationalist Histories: Imperial Legacies, Architecture, and Modernity*, ed. Mrinalini Rajagopalan and Madhuri Desai (Farnham: Ashgate, 2012), 255.
78. Chu, 'Between Typologies and Representation'.
79. Lai, 'Discriminatory Zoning', 58.
80. David Bellis, 'Breezy Point, 2 Park Road', *Gwulo: Old Hong Kong*, blog accessed July 2021, https://gwulo.com/node/23308#14/22.2839/114.1826/Map_by_ESRI-Markers/100.
81. Selina Ching Chan, 'Tea Cafés and the Hong Kong Identity: Food Culture and Hybridity', *China Information* 33, no. 3 (2019): 311–28.

houses if they wanted to elevate their social status; in Sydney, anti-Chinese senti-ment among Anglo-Australians seems likely to have meant that Chinese migrants, to avoid standing out, were more inclined to assimilate themselves to the local archi-tecture than to produce a distinctive architecture of their own. For their domestic and business accommodation they mostly rented existing buildings constructed by white Australians, but even where they commissioned new buildings, as in the case of the Kwong War Chong (廣和昌) building built by Phillip Lee Chun (李臨春, 1865–1935) in 1910 in Sydney's Haymarket district, they chose designs that were indistinguishable from those generally fashionable in Australia at the time.[82] Neither in Hong Kong nor in Sydney was the built environment a level playing field for Chinese striving to better themselves.

Sara Ahmed, drawing on the work of Edmund Husserl and Franz Fanon, lays out an argument for the way non-white bodies become oriented to a world that colonialism has constructed.[83] 'Colonialism makes the world "white", which is of course a world "ready" for certain kinds of bodies, as a world that puts certain objects within their reach.'[84] In Ahmed's account, the way whiteness works is by creating an environment – for present purposes this can be taken to include the *built* environment – that is amenable to and comfortably 'reachable' by white people but not to or by white people without an effort. It is a world oriented to the needs and habits of whites, but it requires a *re*-orientation on the part of non-whites if they want to succeed in it. In Ahmed's words, 'white bodies are comfortable *as they inhabit spaces that extend their shape.* The bodies and spaces point towards each other.'[85] Ahmed's 'phenomenology of whiteness' is useful in thinking through the specifics of how neoclassical architectural style was appropriated and reworked by those Chinese in Hong Kong who wanted to succeed in colonial space and soci-ety.[86] Writing of the neoclassical houses built by wealthy Chinese in British colonial Malaya, David Kohl proposes that although Chinese migrants there may not have appreciated the architectural association of those houses with ancient Greek and Roman culture, they did understand the weighty connotations of social status that this style carried.[87] This is not to say that they, or Chinese house-builders in Hong Kong and Zhongshan, became helpless imitators, but rather that what they built gives material form to a complex tension between local agency and colonial power.

But to explain how a hybrid neoclassical style came to exist in the emigrant vil-lages of Zhongshan county, outside the colonial space of Hong Kong, requires further explanation. I suggest it was the outcome of a process in which the neoclassical had

---

82. For the Kwong War Chong company, see Chapter 8 of this volume.
83. Sara Ahmed, 'A Phenomenology of Whiteness', *Feminist Theory* 8, no. 2 (2007): 149–68, https://doi.org/10.1093/acprof:oso/9780199734771.001.0001.
84. Ahmed, 'A Phenomenology of Whiteness', 154.
85. Ahmed, 'A Phenomenology of Whiteness', 158 (italics in the original).
86. Ahmed, 'A Phenomenology of Whiteness'.
87. David G. Kohl, *Offshore Chinese Architecture: Insights on Five Centuries of Overseas Chinese Building Practices* (Portland, OR: One Spirit, 2018).

become, in Claude Lévi-Strauss's terms, a 'floating signifier'.[88] By this I mean that while in the colonial setting the architecture signified racial status and the subversion of that by Chinese subalterns, by the time it reached Zhongshan's emigrant villages it had been emptied, or largely emptied, of this specificity and simply signified social status accrued through migration. Whereas in Hong Kong, the neoclassicism of the Chinese entrepreneur's house made a direct allusion to white status and power, in Zhongshan this allusion was weak or non-existent. This also appears to have been true of houses built by migrants in their home villages in Fujian in the 1930s.[89] Through their donations towards the building or repair of ancestral halls, schools, and other community infrastructure, migrant families by the early 1900s were assuming something of the role and status of the old gentry class of China.[90] This work of sponsorship elevated their social status. But the house, and particularly its façade, could function in the village setting as a more direct material statement of the status, or aspirant status, of an individual or family. It acted to 'showcase their overseas wealth'.[91]

As argued at the beginning of this chapter, the heritage landscape of Chinese migration is constituted in assemblages of human and non-human agents that are transnational in scope. Part of the complex meaning of neoclassical style in Western culture was carried into remittance houses in Zhongshan partly via the agency of their builders and partly via the agency invested in architectural elements such as Greek-style pillars and porticoes as floating signifiers of race-related social status. The houses, which at face value may seem to be no more than heritage objects representing specific migrant trajectories, must also be credited as embodiments of broader transnational flows and forces, including those of colonialism.

An Unstable Legacy: Migrant Houses in the Mao Era and Beyond

A fundamental tenet of Maoist policy from the 1950s until Mao's death in 1976 was prioritisation of industrial growth and its entailment in the rigid regime of food extraction from the countryside.[92] With heavy industry concentrated in the cities, rural areas were given over almost exclusively to food production. Even the emigrant areas of the Pearl River Delta, such as Zhongshan, which in the previous several decades had achieved a level of prosperity and modernity in some ways comparable to cities such as Canton and Shanghai, were transformed into a condition concomitant with a near-subsistence peasant economy. Where the foreign

---

88. Jeffrey Mehlman, 'The "Floating Signifier": From Lévi-Strauss to Lacan', *Yale French Studies* 48 (1972): 10–37.
89. Ta Chen, *Emigrant Communities in South China: A Study of Overseas Migration and Its Influence on Standards of Living and Social Change* (New York: Institute for Pacific Relations, 1940).
90. In relation to schools, see Cheng, 'Beacons of Modern Learning'; Williams, *Returning Home with Glory*, 88–89.
91. Glen Peterson, *Overseas Chinese*, 44.
92. Robert Ash, 'Squeezing the Peasants, Grain Extraction, Food Consumption and Rural Living Standards in Mao's China', *The China Quarterly* 188 (2006): 182, https://doi.org/10.1017/S0305741006000518.

connections and remittance income of the families who had members living overseas had once been the envy of other villagers, now, particularly with the onset of the Korean War in June 1950, the taint of foreignness that such ties carried put these families at great political risk. And where remittances had allowed them to leave off labouring in the fields, Maoism, in many cases, sent them back there.

The redistribution of land to favour poor peasants had been a key plank of Communist policy since the early 1930s when it was implemented in territory under CCP control in northern China.[93] On the ground, it was typically accompanied by brutality; in 1947 alone 250,000 rich peasants and landlords were killed in northern China.[94] When land reform was rolled out in southeastern China immediately after the Communist victory in 1949, village officials were found to be opposed to stringent enforcement of the policy and the government replaced them with cadres from northern China.[95] A government survey conducted in 1953, when land reform was considered complete, reported that 5 per cent of overseas Chinese in Guangdong had been classified as landlords.[96] Many of them were killed and many others fled to Hong Kong. The same survey reported that up to 90 per cent of houses owned by migrant families in Guangdong had been confiscated.[97] The confiscated houses were distributed to villagers classed as poor peasants and landless labourers, the larger houses often being divided up to accommodate multiple families or used as government offices, military accommodation, or for other public purposes.

Land reform was, however, just one part of what Glen Peterson refers to as 'social and economic levelling'. The land purchased and the houses built by these families helped to distinguish them. As proposed in the previous section, the neo-classical style adopted for many of the houses can be seen as part of a deliberate effort by these families to elevate their social status. They were one of an array of signs of social distinction. As Peterson observes:

> The visible everyday markers of Overseas Chineseness included grand 'foreign-style' houses; the foreign words and phrases that peppered their speech; foreign clothing and hairstyles; even the food that Overseas Chinese ate and *how much* they ate compared to other villagers; lavish consumption of all kinds; and the idle, remittance-fuelled lifestyles that some transnational families were able to lead.[98]

The lifestyle and property that had once provoked pride among their owners and the envy of many poorer villagers without migrant ties, now, in the 1950s and 1960s, intimated bourgeois decadence and counter-revolutionary leanings. The affective capacity of the newly unfashionable remittance houses in Chu's Fujian study to

---

93. Brian DeMare, *Land Wars: The Story of China's Agrarian Revolution* (Stanford, CA: Stanford University Press, 2019).
94. DeMare, *Land Wars*, 113.
95. DeMare, *Land Wars*, 67.
96. Peterson, *Overseas Chinese*, 44.
97. Peterson, *Overseas Chinese*, 44.
98. Peterson, *Overseas Chinese*, 50.

provoke shame in their owners, discussed earlier, finds a comparison in the situation in early 1950s Guangdong when it can be imagined that the very 'foreignness' of the houses of overseas Chinese families triggered anxiety in their owners. However, in this case the houses might be expected to have provoked real fear rather than shame.

From the outset in 1949, the People's Republic of China had made serious efforts to try to stem the decline of remittances and investment by the diaspora in the Chinese economy. Since it was understood that the flow of funds from the diaspora depended on those overseas having confidence that their relatives in China would have access to the remittances, from 1953 'preferential treatment' measures were adopted for overseas families.[99] Families classified as 'landlords' (地主 *dizhu* in Mandarin) and 'rich peasants' (富農 *funong* in Mandarin) could now apply to be reclassified as ordinary peasants, and an effort was made to return ownership rights of houses to them, although in many cases the new occupants of houses simply refused to vacate them.[100]

Few of the houses of overseas Chinese families, however, appear to have suffered serious damage during the Mao era, beyond that occasioned simply by lack of maintenance. Very few new houses were constructed during this period, meaning that when the death of Mao and the downfall of the Gang of Four in 1976 were followed by economic liberalisation, an enormous surge of housing construction swept through China. In Fujian, for example, a third of all rural households constructed new houses at this time.[101] In Zhongshan, the neoclassicism of the pre-1949 remittance houses gave way to freestyle concrete construction in the pattern of what has come to be called Third World Modernism.[102] In the emigrant villages, these houses typically form a band around the periphery of the old village core where the pre-1940s remittance houses, temples, and lineage halls are concentrated. As far as remittance houses from the pre-1949 period are concerned, having morphed during the land reform years and the Cultural Revolution from being a source of pride and status to being a liability, by the end of the twentieth century the pendulum had swung back: the houses were now protected and celebrated as a proud legacy of Zhongshan's history of diasporic connections.

---

99. Peterson, *Overseas Chinese*, 56.
100. Peterson, *Overseas Chinese*, 60.
101. Ronald G. Knapp, 'Rural Housing and Village Transformation in Taiwan and Fujian', *China Quarterly* 147 (1996): 782, https://doi.org/10.1017/S0305741000051791. See also Khun Eng Kuah-Pearce, 'Collective Memories as Cultural Capital: From Chinese Diaspora to Emigrant Hometowns', in *At Home in the Chinese Diaspora: Memories, Identities and Belongings*, ed. Khun Eng Kuah-Pearce and Andrew P. Davidson (New York: Palgrave Macmillan, 2008), 124.
102. Duanfang Lu, ed., *Third World Modernism: Architecture, Development and Identity* (London: Routledge, 2011).

Bibliography

Ahmed, Sara. *Queer Phenomenology: Orientations, Objects, Others.* Durham, NC: Duke University Press, 2006.

Ahmed, Sara. 'A Phenomenology of Whiteness'. *Feminist Theory* 8, no. 2 (2007): 149–68. https://doi.org/10.1093/acprof:oso/9780199734771.001.0001.

Ash, Robert. 'Squeezing the Peasants, Grain Extraction, Food Consumption and Rural Living Standards in Mao's China'. *The China Quarterly* 188 (2006): 959–98. https://doi.org/10.1017/S0305741006000518.

Baweja, Vandana. 'Messy Modernisms: Otto Koenigsberger's Early Work in Princely Mysore, 1939–41'. *South Asian Studies* 31, no. 1 (2015): 1–26. https://doi.org/10.1080/02666030.2015.1008806.

Bellis, David. 'Breezy Point, 2 Park Road'. *Gwulo: Old Hong Kong*, blog. Accessed July 2019, https://gwulo.com/node/23308#14/22.2839/114.1826/Map_by_ESRI-Markers/100.

Bennett, Jane. *Vibrant Matter: A Political Ecology of Things.* Durham, NC: Duke University Press.

Berlant, Lauren. *Cruel Optimism.* Durham, NC: Duke University Press, 2011.

Bryant, Levy. *The Democracy of Objects.* Ann Arbor, MI: Open Humanities Press, 2011. http://dx.doi.org/10.3998/ohp.9750134.0001.001.

Byrne, Denis. 'Love & Loss in the 1960s'. *International Journal of Heritage Studies* 19, no. 6 (2013): 596–609. https://doi.org/10.1080/13527258.2012.686446.

Byrne, Denis, and Heather Goodall. 'Placemaking and Transnationalism: Recent Migrants and a National Park in Sydney, Australia'. *Parks: The International Journal of Protected Areas and Conservation* 19, no. 1 (2013): 63–72. https://doi.org/10.2305/IUCN.CH.2013.PARKS-19-1.DB.en.

Carroll, John M. *A Concise History of Hong Kong.* Lanham, MD: Rowman and Littlefield, 2007.

Chan, Anita, Richard Madsen, and Jonathan Unger. *Chen Village: Revolution to Globalization*, 3rd ed. Berkeley: University of California Press, 2009. https://doi.org/10.2307/3116879.

Chan, Selina Ching. 'Tea Cafés and the Hong Kong Identity: Food Culture and Hybridity'. *China Information* 33, no. 3 (2019): 311–28.

Chan, Wellington K. K. 'Personal Styles, Cultural Values and Management: The Sincere and Wing On Companies in Shanghai and Hong Kong'. *The Business History Review* 40 (1996): 141–66. https://doi.org/10.2307/3116879.

Chan-Yeung, Moira M. W. *Lam Woo: Master Builder, Revolutionary, and Philanthropist.* Hong Kong: Chinese University of Hong Kong Press, 2017.

Chen, Ta. *Emigrant Communities in South China: A Study of Overseas Migration and Its Influence on Standards of Living and Social Change.* New York: Institute for Pacific Relations, 1940.

Cheng, Christopher. 'Beacons of Modern Learning: Diaspora-Funded Schools in the China–Australia Corridor'. *Asian and Pacific Migration Journal* 29, no. 2 (2020): 139–62. https://doi.org/10.1177/0117196820930309.

Chu, Cecilia. 'Between Typologies and Representation: The *Tong Lau* and the Discourse of the "Chinese House" in Colonial Hong Kong'. In *Colonial Frames, Nationalist Histories:*

Imperial Legacies, Architecture, and Modernity, edited by Mrinalini Rajagopalan and Madhuri Desai, 253–83. Farnham, UK: Ashgate, 2012.

Chu, Julie Y. *Cosmologies of Credit: Transnational Mobility and the Politics of Destination in China*. Durham, NC: Duke University Press, 2010.

Connerton, Paul. *How Societies Remember*. Cambridge: Cambridge University Press, 1989.

Cook, James A. 'Reimagining China: Xiamen, Overseas Chinese, and a Transnational Modernity'. In *Everyday Modernity in China*, edited by Madeleine Yue Dong and Joshua Lewis Goldstein, 156–94. Seattle: University of Washington Press, 2008.

Crouch, David. 'Affect, Heritage, Feeling'. In *The Palgrave Handbook of Contemporary Heritage Research*, edited by Emma Waterton and Steve Watson, 177–90. Houndmills, UK: Palgrave Macmillan, 2015.

Dalakoglou, Dimitris. 'Migrating-Remitting-"Building"-Dwelling: House-Making as "Proxy" Presence in Postsocialist Albania'. *Journal of the Royal Anthropological Institute* 16, no. 4 (2010): 761–77. https://doi.org/10.1111/j.1467-9655.2010.01652.x.

DeMare, Brian. *Land Wars: The Story of China's Agrarian Revolution*. Stanford, CA: Stanford University Press, 2019.

Denison, Edward. *Architecture and the Landscape of Modernity in China before 1949*. Abingdon: Routledge, 2017. https://doi.org/10.4324/9781315567686.

Denison, Edward, and Guang Yu Ren. *Modernism in China: Architectural Visions and Revolutions*. London: Wiley, 2008.

Dikötter, Frank. *Things Modern: Material Culture and Everyday Life in China*. London: Hurst, 2007.

Farris, Johnathan A. *Enclave to Urbanity: Canton, Foreigners, and Architecture from Late Eighteenth to the Early Nineteenth Centuries*. Hong Kong: Hong Kong University Press, 2007.

Fitzgerald, John. *Big White Lie: Chinese Australians in White Australia*. Sydney: UNSW Press, 2007.

Fredheim, L. Harold, and Manal Khalaf. 'The Significance of Values: Heritage Value Typologies Re-examined'. *International Journal of Heritage Studies* 22, no. 6 (2016): 466–81. https://doi.org/10.1080/13527258.2016.1171247.

Goodall, Heather, Stephen Wearing, Denis Byrne, and Allison Cadzow. 'Fishing the Georges River: Cultural Diversity and Urban Environments'. In *Everyday Multiculturalism*, edited by Amanda Wise and Selvaraj Velayutham, 177–96. Houndmills, UK: Palgrave Macmillan, 2009.

Hamilton, Peter E. *Made in Hong Kong: Transpacific Networks and a New History of Globalization*. New York: Columbia University Press, 2021.

Hosagrahar, Jyoti. *Indigenous Modernities: Negotiating Architecture and Urbanism*. London: Routledge, 2005.

Howard, David S. *A Tale of Three Cities: Canton, Shanghai & Hong Kong; Three Centuries of Sino-British Trade in the Decorative Arts*. London: Sotheby's, 1997.

Ingold, Tim. *Lines: A Brief History*. London: Routledge, 2007.

Knapp, Ronald G. 'Rural Housing and Village Transformation in Taiwan and Fujian'. *China Quarterly* 147 (1996): 779–94. https://doi.org/10.1017/S0305741000051791.

Knapp, Ronald G. *Chinese Houses: The Heritage of a Nation*. Tokyo: Tuttle, 2006.

Kohl, David G. *Offshore Chinese Architecture: Insights on Five Centuries of Overseas Chinese Building Practices*. Portland, OR: One Spirit, 2018.

Kourelis, Kostis. 'Three Elenis: Archaeologies of the Greek American Village Home'. *Journal of Modern Greek Studies* 38, no. 1 (2020): 85–108.

Kuah-Pearce, Khun Eng. 'Collective Memories as Cultural Capital: From Chinese Diaspora to Emigrant Hometowns'. In *At Home in the Chinese Diaspora: Memories, Identities and Belongings*, edited by Khun Eng Kuah-Pearce and Andrew P. Davidson, 111–27. New York: Palgrave Macmillan, 2008.

Lai, Lawrence W. C. 'Discriminatory Zoning in Colonial Hong Kong: A Review of the Post-war Literature and Some Further Evidence for an Economic Theory of Discrimination'. *Property Management* 29, no. 1 (2010): 50–86. https://doi.org/10.1108/0263747111 1102932.

Lancaster, Clay. 'Oriental Contributions to Art Nouveau'. *The Art Bulletin* 34 (1952): 297–310.

Latour, Bruno. *We Have Never Been Modern*. Translated by Catherine Porter. Cambridge, MA: Harvard University Press, 1993.

Lu, Duanfang, ed. *Third World Modernism: Architecture, Development and Identity*. London: Routledge, 2011.

McKeown, Adam. *Chinese Migrant Networks and Cultural Change: Peru, Chicago, Hawaii, 1900–1936*. Chicago, IL: University of Chicago Press, 2001.

Mehlman, Jeffrey. 'The "Floating Signifier": From Lévi-Strauss to Lacan'. *Yale French Studies* 48 (1972): 10–37.

Metcalf, Thomas. *An Imperial Vision: Indian Architecture and Britain's Raj*. Berkeley: University of California Press, 1989.

Miller, Daniel. 'Migration, Material Culture and Tragedy: Four Moments in Caribbean Migration'. *Mobilities* 3, no. 3 (2008): 397–413.

Peterson, Glen. *Overseas Chinese in the People's Republic of China*. London: Routledge, 2012.

Rowe, Peter G., and Seng Kuan. *Architectural Encounters with Essence and Form in Modern China*. Cambridge, MA: MIT Press, 2002.

Sandoval-Cervantes, Iván. 'Uncertain Futures: The Unfinished Houses of Undocumented Migrants in Oaxaca, Mexico'. *American Anthropologist* 119, no. 2 (2017): 209–22. https://doi.org/10.1111/aman.12864.

Seigworth, Gregory J., and Melissa Gregg. 'An Inventory of Shimmers'. In *The Affect Theory Reader*, edited by Melissa Gregg and Gregory J. Seigworth, 1–25. Durham, NC: Duke University Press, 2010.

Shu, Yuan. 'Introduction'. In *Oceanic Archives, Indigenous Epistemologies, and Transpacific American Studies*, edited by Yuan Shu, Otto Heim, and Kendall Johnson, 2–10. Hong Kong: Hong Kong University Press, 2019.

Tan, Selia Jinhua. 'Kaiping Diaolou and Its Associated Villages: Documenting the Process of Application to the World Heritage List'. PhD thesis, University of Hong Kong, 2007.

Tan, Selia Jinhua. *A Research on the Ornamentation of Kaiping Diaolou and Its Associated Villages* (in Chinese). Beijing: Overseas Chinese Publishing House, 2013.

Taylor, Steve. '"Home Is Never Fully Achieved . . . Even When We Are in It": Migration, Belonging and Social Exclusion within Punjabi Transnational Mobility'. *Mobilities* 10, no. 2 (2015): 193–210. https://doi.org/10.1080/17450101.2013.848606.

Tolia-Kelly, Divya, Emma Waterton, and Steve Watson, eds. *Heritage, Affect and Emotion: Policies, Practices and Infrastructures*. London: Routledge, 2017.

Tsin, Michael. 'Canton Remapped'. In *Remaking the Chinese City: Modernity and National Identity, 1900–1950*, edited by Joseph W. Esherick, 19–29. Honolulu: University of Hawai'i Press, 2001.

Williams, Michael. *Returning Home with Glory: Chinese Villagers around the Pacific, 1849 to 1949*. Hong Kong: Hong Kong University Press, 2018.

Wong, Pamela Lee. *The Mystery Aussie Jan See Chin*. Palo Alto, CA: PWL Publishing, 2018.

Zhu, Xiaoyang. *Topography of Politics in Rural China: The Story of Xiaocun*. Singapore: World Scientific Publishing, 2014.

7

From Ancestral Halls to Modern Schools

Diaspora-Funded Education in Zhongshan

Christopher Cheng and Phillip Mar

Introduction

Chinese Australians have a history of supporting education in their home regions in China from the late 1800s to the present. Sometimes this took the form of making modest contributions to funding campaigns for the building and staffing of schools in China organised by Chinese community groups in Australia; at other times it involved affluent Chinese Australians founding and funding such schools entirely from their own resources. In either case, the schools have come to constitute an important aspect of the heritage of the Zhongshan–Australia migration corridor.[1]

Conditions in China from the late nineteenth century created the need for a fundamental shift in educational models from the elite focus on training classical scholar-officials towards modern, universal education based on national citizenship. Schooling had been based largely on classical texts that effectively excluded the mass – perhaps 90 per cent – of the population from peasant, artisan, and trading backgrounds as well as most women, in favour of a scholar-official class.[2] Imperial China had never developed a concept of mass literacy,[3] and while there was a strong cultural valorisation of learning, there was not a 'modern' (现代 *xiandai* in Mandarin) notion of education linked to citizenship.

In the last years of the Qing dynasty there was a widespread realisation of the need to fundamentally change Chinese education, which had been tied for millennia to the system of civil service examinations. Even before the collapse of the Qing dynasty there had been efforts to reform the traditional education system

---

1. Even in the latter case, there were usually contributions from small donors in the diaspora and sometimes from returnees in China.
2. Benjamin Elman, 'The Civil Service Examination', in *Berkshire Encyclopedia of China: Modern and Historic Views of the World's Newest and Oldest Global Power*, ed. Linsun Cheng (Great Barrington: Berkshire Publishing, 2009), Vol. 5, 405–10.
3. Evelyn Sakakida Rawski, *Education and Popular Literacy in Ch'ing China* (Ann Arbor: University of Michigan Press, 1979), 1.

along modern lines.[4] This epochal shift also meshed with the needs of migrants and sojourners at the time; as this chapter will show, a concern with educational reform was central to the historical experience of the Zhongshan–Australia migration corridor.[5]

Funding from the Chinese diaspora played a significant role in effecting educational change in areas that saw high levels of emigration, including in the rural emigrant villages or *qiaoxiang* (僑鄉) of Zhongshan. Public and clan-funded charitable village schools (義學 *yixue* in Mandarin) were established and assisted by emigrant funds paid for by remittances.[6] Diaspora-funded school-building in China occurred most strongly in two periods where the opportunity was greatest: the early twentieth century, from when the Qing state was disintegrating into the decades of Republican China; and in the years following the introduction of the 'Open Door' policies from 1978 (see Figure 7.1 for a map of Australian diaspora-funded schools built in Zhongshan in the twentieth century). The first period would later be recognised as the golden age of diaspora-funded schools.[7] American Chinese funding and initiatives were able to provide most school-age children with primary school education in villages in Taishan county (台山縣) to the south of Zhongshan, a considerable achievement for the early twentieth century.[8] In the 1920s and 1930s, many new-style schools (新式學堂) were built in the lineage-dominated rural regions associated with high emigration, such as the Pearl River Delta.

What were the factors that motivated migrants from Zhongshan, the majority of whose original members were uneducated, to make significant contributions to education in China? The answer to this question appears to lie partly in the experience or condition of migrancy itself. While life in the peasant rural villages of Zhongshan in the century between the 1840s and the 1940s was viable – at least at a certain level – without the acquisition of literacy or other attributes of a formal education, economic and social success in the context of migration was a different matter. This led some Chinese migrants in Australia to better themselves by enrolling in English-language schools run by Christian churches. It also led to an enthusiasm for the education of their children in the Australian school system, while also, very often, sending them back to their home counties in China for periods of time, not only to learn to write Chinese and to speak local dialects such as Cantonese (廣東

---

4. See Glen Peterson and Ruth Hayhoe, 'Introduction', in *Education, Culture, and Identity in Twentieth-Century China*, ed. Glen Peterson, Ruth Hayhoe, and Yongling Lu (Hong Kong: Hong Kong University Press, 2001), 1–22; Elizabeth R. VanderVen, *A School in Every Village: Educational Reform in a Northeast China County, 1904–1931* (Vancouver: University of British Columbia Press, 2012).

5. See Christopher Cheng, 'Beacons of Modern Learning: Diaspora-Funded Schools in the China-Australia Corridor', *Asian and Pacific Migration Journal* 29, no. 2 (2020): 139–62, https://doi.org/10.1177/0117196820930309.

6. Rawski, *Education and Popular Literacy*, 28. Renqiu Yu, 'Chinese American Contributions to the Educational Development of Toisan 1910–1940', *Amerasia* 10, no. 1 (1983): 47–72.

7. Glen Peterson, *The Power of Words, Literacy and Revolution in South China, 1949–95* (Vancouver: University of British Columbia, 1997), 24.

8. Yu, 'Chinese American Contributions', 66.

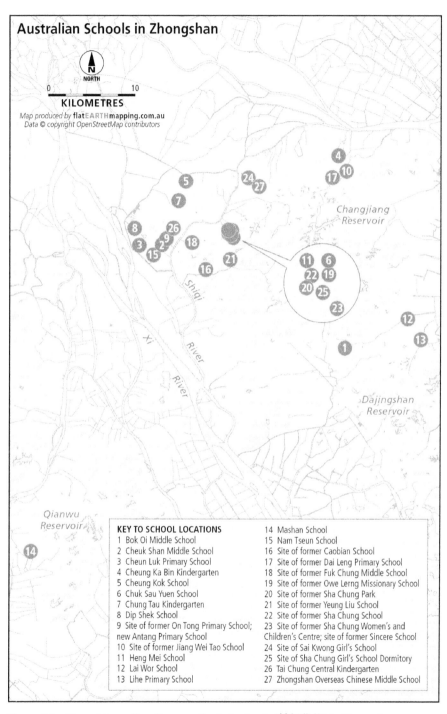

Figure 7.1: Map of Australian diaspora-funded schools (僑捐學校) in Zhongshan.

話) or Longdu (隆都話), but also to get to know their relatives in China and become familiar with the cultural practices of their parents' homeland.[9] What this highlights is the importance of education for the circulatory flows that occurred along the China–Australia migration corridor and that made Chinese migration a transnational affair, especially before 1949, when Australian citizenship was generally inaccessible to Chinese migrants due to the 'White Australia Policy'. The sending of one's children – most often male children – for schooling in China may be considered a manifestation of the sense of dual belonging that many Chinese migrants and their children experienced, a sense that also motivated many of them to want to invest in the education of those in their home villages who had not migrated.

The migration corridor concept and the companion concept of the heritage corridor, both central to this book, do not merely describe pathways of migration exchanges; they imply common projects and a shared temporality – degrees of contemporaneity in lived time – between people at different points in the corridor.[10] The notion of a transnational heritage corridor allows us to analyse what could be *brought together* through living relations and flows of things and ideas in an ongoing engagement between places. The research that informs this chapter attempts to capture these flows and highlights the transnational dynamics of educational initiatives and experiences of education.[11]

The Significance of Education in the Context of Chinese Migration

In areas of rural southern China such as Zhongshan, prior to mass emigration from the 1850s, there had been little practical reason for literacy, except in the case of those aspiring to officialdom. Villagers in China's agricultural economies had lived in a relatively stable space–time continuum for centuries,[12] relying on the few educated villagers for administrative advice and assistance, which was far easier than learning to read classical Chinese.[13] Emigration changed village life: now there were letters (僑批 *qiaopi*) to read and write, newspapers and magazines (僑刊 *qiaokan*) to read about the wider world opened up by emigration, and calculations to be made

---

9. For instance, see Malcolm Oakes, 'William Lee: First Barrister of Chinese Descent Admitted to the New South Wales Bar', *Bar News: The Journal of the New South Wales Bar Association* (Winter 2015): 73–76.

10. See Eugene Minkowsi, *Lived Time: Phenomenological and Psychopathological Studies*, trans. Nancy Metzel (Evanston: Northwestern University Press, 1970).

11. The research was conducted in the context of research towards Christopher Cheng's PhD thesis, 'Australian Migrant Heritage in South China: The Legacy of Diaspora-Funded Schools in 20th century Zhongshan' (PhD Diss, Western Sydney University, in process). The research included interviews in Australia and China and site visits to document the materiality of schools donated by Australian Chinese. A total of 21 schools (kindergarten, primary, and middle schools) were visited in villages and towns across present-day Zhongshan and Zhuhai, Guangdong province.

12. Philip A. Kuhn, *Chinese among Others: Emigration in Modern Times* (Lanham, MD: Rowman and Littlefield, 2008), 25.

13. Fei Xiaotong, 'Bringing Literacy to the Countryside', in *From the Soil: The Foundations of Chinese Society*, ed. and trans. Gary G. Hamilton and Zheng Wang (Berkeley: University of California Press, 1992), 45–52.

about remittances, credit, and investment. Kin from the *qiaoxiang* or emigrant village were often enlisted in business ventures within the diaspora, necessitating the acquisition of new skills.[14] The resultant widening of horizons contributed to a vision of a literate future that was grounded both in the practical demands of migration and in newly acquired perspectives of modernity.

As Zhongshan migrants 'made good' in Australia, new economic structures and elite groups emerged; the wealth of Zhongshan sojourners who had made fortunes in Australia in the late nineteenth and early twentieth centuries generated capital that could be utilised for philanthropic purposes beyond the normal levels of remittances flowing back to *qiaoxiang* regions.[15] In addition, new civil solidarities developed in Australia. Many prominent Zhongshan merchants converted to Christianity, including Ma Ying Piu (馬應彪, 1860–1944), the principal investor in the Sincere department store (先施百貨); his brother-in-law Ma Wing Charn (馬永燦, 1863–1938) and other founders of Wing Sang, the prominent fruit trading company; and George Bew (郭標 Kwok Bew) and James Gocklock (郭樂, 1870–1957), the latter two being founders of Wing On department store (永安百貨). These members of an emerging commercial elite were all parishioners of the Chinese Presbyterian Church in Sydney (雪梨華人長老會) under the ministry of the Reverend John Young Wai (周容威), who came to the Victorian goldfields in 1867 but later devoted his life to the church, and who was an avowed supporter of the republican cause in China.[16] The church ran a night school from 1893 that both taught Cantonese to children and provided a means for uneducated people from rural backgrounds to improve their English and to acquire skills and contacts to deal effectively with Westerners. The school and church community were important in encouraging Zhongshan Chinese in Sydney to participate in areas of life apart from their businesses.[17] It was in this period – from the 1890s – that a 'diasporic identity' began to take shape, as Mei-fen Kuo argues. Newly modernised elite groups responded to political dilemmas at both ends of the corridor, namely through the emerging political nationalism of groups seeking modern ways of being Chinese and responding to the discriminatory environment of 'White Australia'.[18] The missionary work that began at Sydney's Chinese Presbyterian Church would have resonances throughout the corridor as churches and associated schools were founded in Zhongshan. (These also had their roots in older missionary schools and churches in China, particularly in the treaty ports.) The Zhongshanese founders of the four great department stores were all active philanthropists – and arguably

---

14. Fitzgerald, *Big White Lie*, 199–200.
15. See Ien Ang, Chapter 8 of this volume.
16. Adrian Chan, 'Young Wai, John (1847–1930)', *Australian Dictionary of Biography*, https://adb.anu.edu.au/biography/young-wai-john-9222.
17. Mei-fen Kuo, 'The Making of a Diasporic Identity: The Case of the Sydney Chinese Commercial Elite, 1890s–1900s', *Journal of Chinese Overseas* 5, no. 2 (2009): 340–41, https://doi.org.10.1163/179303909X12489373183091.
18. Kuo, 'Making of a Diasporic Identity', 337.

forerunners of contemporary philanthrocapitalism[19] – which would be significant for economic development across the corridor and beyond, for instance in preparing young people of the home region for employment in burgeoning commercial enterprises. Rather than simply doing what Chinese businesses are known for, that is, capitalising for 'private benefit' (私義 *siyi* in Mandarin), a homeland link provided a 'higher order' of public benefit (公益 *gongyi* in Mandarin).[20] Philanthropy at that time could both serve progressive commitments to the new nation and mobilise pre-existing ties to ancestral localities.[21]

Education was a primary target for this philanthropy, schooling being the most favoured form of donation. For Williams, education philanthropy 'probably had the greatest impact on the *qiaoxiang* in the long term'[22] through financial support for students and the building of new schools. There is evidence that diaspora funding for schools had a significant effect on educational attainment in China; in Taishan county, southwest of Zhongshan, the number of schools expanded from five in 1850 to 47 in 1911, and school attendance levels reached 75 per cent of children in 1935.[23]

The age-old imperial examination system was officially disbanded in 1905, but the new educational requirement for 'a school in every village'[24] would not be attainable for more than a century. Nevertheless, the vision of a literate future was embedded in China's emerging political movements. Sun Yat-sen (孫中山), a Zhongshan native and leader of the Xinhai Revolution of 1911, was one beneficiary of missionary school education and a Christian. Christian schools in China founded by foreign missionaries from the 1840s represented a transitional schooling sector. By 1906, around 2,000 primary schools and 400 secondary schools were operated by Western missionaries in China.[25] While these schools supported a colonialist goal to 'Christianise the Chinese empire' and were understandably distrusted by most Chinese, they also pioneered some key elements of 'modern' education such as schooling for girls, free tuition, purpose-built school buildings, and new curricular areas such as science and foreign languages.[26] The educational philanthropy

---

19. Jessica Sklair and Luna Glucksberg, 'Philanthrocapitalism as Wealth Management Strategy: Philanthropy, Inheritance and Succession Planning among the Global Elite', *The Sociological Review* 69, no. 2 (2021): 314–29, https://doi.org/10.1177/0038026120963479.

20. John Fitzgerald, 'Building Trust: Private Charity (*cishan*) and Public Benefit (*gongyi*) in the Associational Life of the Cantonese Pacific, 1850–1949', in *Chinese Diaspora Charity and the Cantonese Pacific, 1850–1949*, ed. John Fitzgerald and Hon-ming Yip (Hong Kong: Hong Kong University Press, 2020), 193–210.

21. Madeline Y. Y. Hsu, *Dreaming of Gold, Dreaming of Home: Transnationalism and Migration between the United States and South China, 1882–1943* (Stanford, CA: Stanford University Press, 2000), 96.

22. Michael Williams, *Returning Home with Glory: Chinese Villagers around the Pacific, 1849 to 1949* (Hong Kong: Hong Kong University Press, 2018), 82.

23. Hsu, *Dreaming of Gold*, 47.

24. VanderVen, *A School in Every Village*, 209.

25. Deng Peng, *Private Education in Modern China* (Westport, CT: Praeger, 1997), 32.

26. Deng Peng, *Private Education in Modern China*, 31, 32, 34, 69.

of Zhongshan migrants in Australia emerged from the turn of the twentieth century as a result of Nationalist and Christian influences.[27]

The new schools helped to equip the younger generation for the kinds of employment that were emerging in the migration corridor by the beginning of the twentieth century, principally in expanding forms of commerce. For villagers, education enabled a life beyond farming, where recording business transactions as well as writing letters in Chinese and English were the 'daily rice' of the early twentieth-century commercial world. The businesses established by Chinese migrants in Australia could and did provide desirable employment for educated villagers able to make the journey.[28] Education was integral to a migration ecology that was self-supporting: within the corridor's emerging commercial economy, schooling enabled the teaching of new skills to match the needs of migrant businesses and the new jobs in those businesses located in Australia and other parts of the diaspora, in turn generating remittances that were able to further support village infrastructure, including schools.

Diaspora-Funded Modern Schools in Zhongshan to 1937: Buildings, Materials, Memories

The first diaspora-funded school (僑捐學校) in Zhongshan was founded in 1872 by Yung Wing (容閎, 1828–1912), a sojourner in America who was the first Chinese graduate of an American university.[29] Architecturally, the school building resembled other premodern structures in southern China, such as study halls and temples. There is evidence of Australian diaspora-supported schools being established as early as 1895 in Shekki (石岐) and Long Du (隆都), Zhongshan.[30] A Chinese survey found that 41 new schools were founded in Zhongshan before 1949, eight of them being primarily Australian Chinese initiatives.[31]

Having touched on the ideas and values that informed thinking about education in early twentieth-century China and the Chinese diaspora and the way that this thinking meshed into a functioning transnational ecology, the remainder of

---

27. On the convergence of Christian and Republican advocacy, Yong noted that 'it is striking that nearly all the top leaders of the Chinese Nationalist Party in Victoria and New South Wales in the years 1910–1930 were associated with Churches'. C. F. Yong, *The New Gold Mountain: The Chinese in Australia 1901–1921* (Richmond, S. Australia: Raphael Arts, 1977), 206.

28. Janis Wilton, 'Histories of the Chinese in Regional NSW 1859–1950', *Journal of the Royal Australian Historical Society* 105, no. 1 (2019): 59.

29. Yin Xiao-huang, 'A Case Study of Transnationalism: Continuity and Changes in Chinese American Philanthropy to China', *American Studies* 45, no. 2 (2004): 68.

30. Williams, *Returning Home with Glory*, 83.

31. This number does not include smaller but significant donations to educational projects that were not Australian Chinese initiated or funded. See Zhongshan Overseas Chinese Affairs Bureau (中山市外事僑務局), *Zhongshanshi huaqiao zhi* 中山市華僑志 [Annals of Zhongshan Overseas Chinese Affairs], ed. Chen Diqiu (陳迪秋) (Guangzhou: Guangdong's People's Press, 2013), 349–50. (Individual authors' names not given.)

the chapter will focus more concretely on the material flows and changes that contributed to school-building across the twentieth century, and in particular on diaspora-funded schools in Zhongshan. These diaspora-funded private schools were significant contributors to a gradual shift from traditional to modern education, pitched against the historical conditions that affected material and communicative flows within the migration corridor.

Before the advent of mass schooling in Europe, schools did not usually have purpose-designed buildings; they were typically housed in places of worship, production, or residence. Schooling was an extension of communities and social hierarchies.[32] The situation in the British colonial world was somewhat similar; in nineteenth-century colonial India, for example, indigenous schooling took place in teachers' or parents' houses, in mosques, temples, or gardens. Colonial reports frequently criticised such culturally embedded schooling; the critical subtext of these reports was that there were no 'proper school buildings' in India.[33] From this perspective, 'proper' or modern school buildings should be purpose-built, specialised, standardised, and separated from local cultural 'worlds', and embodying specific forms of modern discipline and technology. In China, too, the modernisation of schooling meant a gradual transition to purpose-built schools, but this development took longer in rural areas, not least due to lack of resources. In the emigrant villages of the Pearl River Delta, diaspora philanthropy was an important source of funding for the building of schools.

Close to Zhongshan, in Hong Kong's New Territories, schools were typically located in temples, village offices, or ancestral halls.[34] Private study halls, or, in Cantonese, *sishu* (私塾), or more frequently ancestral halls (祠堂), were the most common location for educational institutions in Guangdong province. Voluntary donations and collective lineage funds (stemming from agriculture) paid for the construction of ancestral halls and the recruitment of tutors to teach in them. Schooling took place in the presence of plaques commemorating meritorious ancestors and recording the success of lineage members in imperial examinations.[35] These traditional Chinese schools embodied both local and imperial hierarchies. An example of diaspora support for traditional schools is the Chik Kwai Study Hall (植桂書室) in the Lai Uk Tsuen area (黎屋村), New Territories, Hong Kong, built around 1899 by Tommy Ah Kum (黎金泰 Lai Kam Tai), who had sojourned in Queensland, Australia. The building is a typical example of a Qing dynasty two-hall,

---

32. Ian Grosvenor and Catherine Burke, *School* (London: Reaktion, 2008), 11, 13.
33. Nita Kumar, 'Learning Modernity? The Technologies of Education in India', *Autrepart* 18, no. 2 (2001): 85–100, https://doi.org/10.3917/autr.018.0085.
34. Tom K. C. Ming 明基全, ed., *From Study Hall to Village School* [教不倦：新界傳統教育的蛻變] (Hong Kong: Urban Council, 1996), 30 (in Chinese and English).
35. Ming, *From Study Hall*, 12.

one-courtyard building with elaborate wood carving throughout, which still maintained the duality of ancestor worship and the education of young clansmen.[36]

The modernisation of schools in Zhongshan would demand more thoroughgoing material changes. In the following, we present three examples of school projects supported by diaspora funds; these were all associated with Ma Wing Charn (馬永燦) – a co-founder of the Wing Sang company in Sydney – who supported the modernisation of schooling in his home village of Sha Chong (沙涌) in the early twentieth century through successive interventions to upgrade traditional schooling, establish a missionary school, and build a modern self-contained school.

The first intervention grew from the extension of the village's small ancestral hall from one to three rooms (Figure 7.2). As it was only used for occasional rituals, Sha Chong villagers proposed that the ancestral hall could be used as a school. But even with three rooms the building was not adequate. A contemporary elderly resident of the village describes the situation:

> There were [only] three halls, how many classrooms could there possibly be? The last hall displayed [ancestral] tablets. The two open-air courtyards were susceptible to sun and rain so could not be ordinarily used. The remaining space on either side [of the hall] was all the space we had for makeshift classrooms.[37]

Our second example of a school built on the edge of Sha Chong was the outcome of Christian philanthropy stemming from the conversion of Zhongshan men in Sydney, including Ma Wing Charn. This was the Owe Lerng Missionary School (歐亮福音堂學校), named after its prime instigator Owe Lerng (歐亮), a sojourner who had returned from Sydney in 1909.[38] The school was housed on the ground floor of the church building, designed pro bono by Hong Kong architect Ho Wingkin (何永乾), while the upper floor served as a chapel.[39] A stone plaque records that Ma Wing Charn laid the foundation stone on behalf of the board of directors in 1918 (Figure 7.3). The stone plaque can be seen as a convergence of the tradition of memorialisation of donors to the building of Chinese temples and ancestral halls[40] and of the foundation stones (or cornerstones) that have a long tradition in Western churches and civic buildings.

The Owe Lerng School resulted from a missionary initiative to build churches in Zhongshan led by directors of the Wing On and Sincere companies, who were

---

36. Alison Choy Flannigan, *Chinese Whispers – In Search of Ivy: An Australian Gold Rush Story Told by Generations of an Australian Chinese Family* (Sydney: Black Quill, 2018); Ho Puay-peng, Henry Ka-Yu Lo, and Heidi Sze-Man Lam, 'Consultancy for Conservation Study of Chik Kwai Study Hall at Pat Heung' (Hong Kong: Antiquities and Monuments Office, 2008).

37. Interview with Ma Yin-Chiu (馬彥昭) by Christopher Cheng, Sha Chong, Zhongshan, 2 January 2019.

38. *Chinese Republic News* 民國報, 22 December 1917, 3.

39. Sohu 搜狐, 'Shangtangcun: Danghuaguangdian yu Shang Liangdoutang qimiao de "huaxue fanying" fashengle' 上塘村：當華光殿遇上良都堂，奇妙的 "化學反應" 發生了 [Sheung Tong Village: When Wah Kwong Temple meets Liangdu Church a wonderful 'reaction' occurs], last modified 9 March 2019, accessed 9 August 2021, http://www.sohu.com/a/300186097_258296.

40. See Byrne, Chapter 9 of this volume.

Figure 7.2: Sketch of the Ma ancestral hall (馬氏大宗祠) in Sha Chong village (沙涌村) (now demolished) with three rooms/halls. Source: Sha Chong – Ma genealogy book (中山沙涌馬氏族譜).

Figure 7.3: Foundation stone of Liangdu Church (良都堂), laid in 1918, present-day South District (南區). Photo by Denis Byrne, December 2017.

appointed as directors of the board of the Heung San Presbyterian Self-Governance Church (香山長老自理會). Around 1905, they had purchased shares, including Sincere and Wing On, and used the annual dividends to fund the operating expenses of missionary churches, which also incorporated schools, and other philanthropic ventures. A church was built by returning migrants in 1906 in Shekki, Zhongshan's commercial centre.[41] When the Shekki church was completed in 1906, it was named the Heung San Self-Governing (Chinese) Presbyterian Church, to distinguish it from Western missionary-controlled churches.[42]

The sequence of actions in Zhongshan reflected the priorities of the Australian Chinese returnees. These Christian converts began by nurturing a Christian community in their home region, then building churches, which usually included educational facilities.[43] They may have been influenced by the night school in John Young Wai's Presbyterian church in Sydney; another donor, Philip Gockchin (郭泉, 1875–1966) of the Wing On department store, acknowledged his Sydney pastor John Young Wai through lifelong philanthropic activity in Sydney, Zhongshan, Hong Kong and Shanghai.[44] Liao considers that the Shekki church 'contributed substantially to primary education in Zhongshan during the first half of the 20th century'.[45] The Shekki church housed the Kwong Gee Citizens' School (廣智國民學校) and the Pui Gan Kindergarten (培根幼稚園), possibly the first kindergarten in Zhongshan county. Ongoing funding from share dividends enabled the church to fund further churches and schools. The church in Shekki later seeded the Liangdu Church (良都堂) near Sha Chong in 1918 that housed the Owe Lerng School, and later supported other schools, the Commoners' School (平民学校) in Longdu district and the Sai Kwong Girls' School (世光女子高等小學), one of the first girls' schools in Zhongshan.[46]

Our final example is the standalone primary school in Sha Chong (沙涌學校), completed in 1923. Funding for this school project was apparently being pooled by the Ma clansmen from 1907.[47] The difficulties of constructing the building in what was then an undeveloped rural area were described by an elderly Sha Chong resident in 2019:

---

41. Heritage Corridor website: 'Christian Churches Sydney', https://www.heritagecorridor.org.au/heritage-connections/christian-churches-sydney.

42. Liao Hongyue, 'Shang and Shan: Charitable Networks of the "Four Great Department Stores" and Their Associated Chinese-Australian Families 1900–1949,' (PhD thesis, Swinburne University, 2018), 121.

43. In Zhongshan they include Tai Ping Church (太平堂) in Shekki in 1905 and Liang Du Church (良都堂) (present-day South District 南區) in 1918 (Kuo 2013: 49–50; interview with Li Xiangping (李向平), South District, Zhongshan, 15 December 2017). A neoclassical church, Hop Yat (合一堂), was also built in Hong Kong in 1926.

44. Fitzgerald, *Big White Lie*, 207.

45. Liao, 'Shang and Shan', 121.

46. Liao, 'Shang and Shan', 121.

47. *Tung Wah Times* 《東華新報》, 'Lv aozhou mujuan Shachong Mashi xuetang jingfei shulie' 旅澳洲募捐沙涌馬氏學堂經費數列 [Contributions from Australia for a Ma clan school in Sha Chong enumerated], 4 May 1907, 8.

Most likely roads were being laid as the materials were transported by foot into the village. China was so backward at the time . . . construction materials came from Hong Kong . . . The whole lot came by boat . . . shipments arrived at Shekki River (岐江河), and then the laborious task of unloading cargo onto hand-pushed trolleys to be transported to the village began . . . That's why it took so long [to build everything].[48]

The Sha Chong School was a two-storey building supported by a reinforced-concrete frame, with red-brick walls and handsome masonry lintels, a rooftop cupola that housed the school bell,[49] and a portico entrance flanked by cement columns. Kiln-fired red bricks were then novel in rural southern China, where the norm was tapped earth or grey bricks.[50] It is possible that the use of ferro-concrete was influenced by the Chinese builder Lam Woo (林護), who was employed for a period with the Wing Sang firm (永生果欄) in Sydney.[51] While working with the Canton-based Australian architectural firm Purnell and Paget, Lam Woo had developed expertise in working with ferro-concrete technology; he went on to become a significant Hong Kong builder and educational philanthropist.[52]

The interior non-structural walls of Sha Chong School were made of concrete reinforced with bamboo, a cheaper and readily available substitute for steel reinforcing bars. This mixing of building techniques was an example of a 'hybrid modernity' in rural China. Outside Zhongshan, in other migrant-sending areas of the Pearl River Delta, a number of newly constructed schools were built in a style that became known as 'adaptive Chinese' or 'Chinese Renaissance' architecture, characterised by combining modern Western technology and a 'Chinese palatial look', typically with a glazed terracotta gable roof on a Western building frame.[53] By contrast, Australian diaspora-funded schools in Zhongshan at that time did not seek to project a Chinese 'style'; they were initially more akin to the remittance houses in the region, distinctive in their neoclassical influences and features such as columns, portico balconies, and rooftop cupolas drawn from colonial architecture of the time.[54]

The form and style of school buildings provide some clues to the engagement with the changing requirements of 'modern' education in the Chinese context. The three examples of schools built with diaspora funds in Sha Chong exemplify

---

48. Interview with Ma Yin-Chiu (馬彥昭) by Christopher Cheng, Sha Chong, Zhongshan, 2 January 2019.
49. Figure 7.6 shows the rooftop in a dilapidated state, photographed in 2018. Figure 7.5 shows the building from the front at the time.
50. Shu Changxue, 'Towards Western Construction in China: Shanghai Brickwork and Printed Technical Resources 1843–1936', *Construction History* 33, no. 1 (2018): 102.
51. Moira M. W. Chan-yeung, *Lam Woo: Master Builder, Revolutionary, and Philanthropist* (Hong Kong: Chinese University Press, 2017), 86.
52. Chan-yeung, *Lam Woo*, 54, 121, 124, 177.
53. Ho Yin Lee and Lynne D. DiStefano, 'Chinese Renaissance Architecture in China and Hong Kong', *Context* 145 (2016): 17–20.
54. For a discussion of neoclassical elements in Zhongshan in the early twentieth century, see Denis Byrne, Chapter 6 of this volume.

successive shifts in conceptions of schooling and how it could be materially embedded in village life. Improvements to the ancestral hall brought into question the adequacy of *sishu* schooling – with its more intimate and ritualised tutoring model – for a more general conception of education for all. The Owe Lerng School, as a representative of the missionary school model, was physically embedded in a Christian church and hence remained reliant on church staffing and appointments. Finally, the Sha Chong primary school, as an autonomous, purpose-built modern school, allowed for larger numbers of pupils, including children sent back from Australia for education.[55]

While the building of new schools in Zhongshan introduced a repertoire of new construction technologies, they also cultivated new elements of modern life, traceable in a fragmentary way through the memories of those who attended them. Interviews in Zhongshan with former students show how material objects could trigger not just isolated memories but also connected 'object biographies', particularly about new social experiences introduced to village life.[56] Stairs are a case in point; in rural China stairs were ladder-like, steep and without handrails. The modern-style staircases of the new schools were thus a novelty in rural Zhongshan. A former student of Sha Chong School recalled his teacher outlining the etiquette of using the stairs.

> The lower grade students were astonished. They kept running up and down [the stairs], chasing each other, doing cartwheels on the balcony, so the school decided to set up rules. The rooftop was out of bounds . . . On the first day [of school], we were told: 'You cannot climb onto the rails.' The [first floor] balcony rail was one meter high, so our teacher instructed: 'If you fall over the edge, you'll kill yourself for sure! Also, you shall not run on the stairs. When going down, keep to the right. When going up, keep right. Staying on the right all the time, you'll never bump into anyone. There will be no collisions, and you should never ever chase after your classmates either up or downstairs.'[57]

School bells provided another novel experience. Two former pupils of Sha Chong recalled their school bell ringing the class times. Describing the bell tower on top of the school, Mr Ma spread his hands to indicate an invisible bell, over half a metre in diameter. Punctuality became a desirable trait for modern subjects, contributing to the inculcation of 'modern time discipline'.[58]

---

55. For example, the village school built in 1911 in Dai Leng village (大嶺村), Zhongshan, accommodated up to 300 children. Au-yeung Chow, *Zhongshan Dailengcun qiaoshi* 中山大嶺村僑志 [Dai Leng Village overseas history, Chung-shan] (Macau: New Hip Hing Printing, 2001), 42.

56. See Janet Hoskins, 'Agency, Biography and Objects', in *Handbook of Material Culture*, ed. Christopher Tilley, Webb Keane, Susanne Kuechler, Mike Rowlands, and Patricia Spyer (London: SAGE, 2006), 74–84.

57. Interview with Ma Yin-Chiu (馬彥昭) by Christopher Cheng, Zhongshan, 2 January 2019.

58. Sally Borthwick, *Education and Social Change in China: The Beginning of the Modern Era* (Stanford, CA: Hoover Institution Press, 1983), 15; Timothy Mitchell, 'Introduction', in *Questions of Modernity*, ed. Timothy Mitchell (Minneapolis: University of Minnesota Press, 2000), xxviii.

The diaspora-funded schools brought striking new settings to the village, both for its students and for villagers, exposing them to aspects of material modernity. Diaspora philanthropy and fundraising across the China–Australia migration corridor was used to develop schooling to support the needs of *qiaoxiang* communities that were increasingly connected economically to Australia, Hong Kong, and other parts of China through commercial and labour flows. It is more difficult, however, to assess the longer-term educational legacy of the diaspora-funded schools in Zhongshan. The following section shows how disruptions to the flow of goods and communications within the China–Australia corridor had serious implications for educational interventions.

Diaspora-Funded Schools from the Japanese Occupation to the Mao Era: Material Tides

The peak period of diaspora-funded schooling was from the turn of the twentieth century and the Republican period until the beginning of the Japanese invasion of Guangdong in 1939. During the Japanese occupation (1938–1945), schooling was largely suspended and school property was often ravaged. In one school in Longdu, 'the desks of teachers and students were used as firewood, and 40,000 books were burned to ashes'.[59] After the end of the Second World War, some overseas migrants returned to their families and started rebuilding their homes and revamping schools.[60] The Kwok (郭) family of Wing On Co. collectively contributed to the restoration of Chuk Sau Yuen school (竹秀園學校), in addition to making schooling there free. Yet, a shortfall of funds saw some schools close, such as the Lai Wor School (禮和學校, as pronounced in Cantonese) in Ngoi Sha (外沙) or Waisha village, present-day Zhuhai, which was unable to continue as the Canton (Guangzhou) business of its elderly benefactor James Choy Hing (蔡興) had been destroyed by fire.[61]

With the founding of the People's Republic of China in 1949, Western individualist educational philosophy was rejected in order to 'flatten the educational pyramid'.[62] Fees were abolished and classes were made larger. But universal education was not readily achievable; shortages of state funding meant that government subsidies for schools remained minimal, leaving schools chronically starved of

---

59. Williams, *Returning Home with Glory*, 94.
60. Williams, *Returning Home with Glory*, 94; Zhongshan East District Overseas Chinese Committee 中山市東區僑聯會, *Qiaoxiang kuchongcun shi* 僑鄉庫充村史 [*Qiaoxiang* Koo Chung village history] (Zhongshan: Zhongshan East District Overseas Chinese Committee and East District Koo Chung Village Committee, 1999).
61. Interview with Ms Sheng Lai-Kum (盛麗金) by Christopher Cheng, Ngoi Sha village, Zhuhai, 29 November 2018.
62. Jonathan Unger, 'Severing the Links Between School Performance and Careers: The Experience of China's Urban Schools, 1968–1976', *Comparative Education* 20, no. 1 (1984): 94.

support and teachers poorly paid.[63] As student and teacher loads exceeded capacity, educational quality suffered drastically.

During the 1950s, 'community run' or *minban* (民辦, pronounced in Mandarin) schools were introduced. According to Peterson, unlike state schools, 'the operative principle of *minban* schooling was to build schools "out of nothing" (白手起家 *baishou qijia*)';[64] hence they were often lacking in basic facilities and equipment, poorly staffed, and located in abandoned temples, ancestral halls, sheds, or warehouses – hardly modern or 'proper' schools. These mostly rural schools were indeed commonly described as 'not like real schools' (不如學校 *buru xuexiao*),[65] implying that they were outside the norms and standards of modern or 'proper' schooling that had been supported by government since the late Qing. Literacy levels dropped, even in Guangdong; while regular schools aimed at quality, the *minban* schools often lacked funds for staff and furniture. Unqualified or under-qualified teachers and a watered-down curriculum produced a 'second-rate alternative to real education'.[66]

In general, the *qiaoxiang* schools in Zhongshan were affected negatively by the closing down of borders and flows of remittances that ensued after 1949. Nevertheless, there were some cases of diaspora-assisted education in the early years of the PRC. The Zhongshan Overseas Chinese Middle School (中山華僑中學) was founded in Shekki in 1954, supported mainly by Nanyang (南陽), or Southeast Asian Chinese returnees, for the education of their own children, with contributions from a small number of returnees from Australia.[67] In this period, many diaspora-funded schools were subject to the forces of decay and dilapidation as funds for maintenance dried up. Private school buildings were often confiscated and used for other purposes by the government or villagers, along with other *huaqiao* properties.

Construction and maintenance of diaspora-funded schools largely ceased in this period as the flows of people and remittance funds along the corridor were cut off.[68] During the Cultural Revolution (1966–1976), almost all schools were classified as *minban*, resulting in expansion of access to schooling but a dramatic loss of quality. School programmes aimed to combine work and study and to solve 'real-world problems' – the factory and the farm were regarded as an extension of the

---

63. I.E. [initials only given], 'Education in Communist China', *World Today* 8, no. 6 (1952): 258.
64. Glen Peterson, 'State Literacy Ideologies and the Transformation of Rural China', *The Australian Journal of Chinese Affairs* 32 (1994): 119.
65. Peterson, 'State Literacy Ideologies', 119.
66. See Suzanne Pepper, *Radicalism and Education Reform in 20th-Century China: The Search for an Ideal Development Model* (New York: Cambridge University Press, 1996), 306; Edward Vickers and Xiaodong Zeng, *Education and Society in Post-Mao China* (Abingdon: Routledge, 2017), 205.
67. Interview with historian Ms Chen Diqiu (陳迪秋) by Christopher Cheng, Zhongshan, 8 August 2018.
68. See Denis Byrne, Chapter 9 of this volume, for an account of the visible effects on the Zhongshan landscape.

classroom – and teachers were often untrained.[69] Education became ideological at every level; children learned Chinese by memorising Chairman Mao's quotations. To tackle unemployment, excess urban labour was transferred to the countryside. Millions of secondary school graduates were, for example, assigned to the countryside in the 1960s and 1970s regardless of their school performance.[70] During the Cultural Revolution, the building that had housed the Liangdu Church and Owe Lerng school was turned into a factory; church services were not resumed until 1983.[71]

Nonetheless, education levels were increasing nationally. In 1974, China's educational programme was described as 'the closest to the World Bank's model program for a developing country'.[72] China's primary school system expanded enormously, with nearly 400 million students graduating between 1949 and 1982, and secondary education became more attainable.[73] But schooling in their home counties remained a great concern for diaspora Chinese. While there had been educational improvement in the PRC, there were widening equity gaps, particularly between urban and rural schools. In 1985, when universal education had become the norm for urban children aged between six and sixteen, in rural areas of the Pearl River Delta, many of them rapidly urbanising, universal *primary* schooling was not achieved until 1986.[74]

In the post–Maoist Open Door period from 1978, it was recognised that new knowledge and skills were required; education was a key component of Deng Xiaoping's 'Four Modernisations' (四個現代 *si ge xiandai* in Mandarin).[75] China's remarkable economic expansion in the last two decades of the twentieth century not only enabled educational expansion, it also changed the expectations of Chinese people about modern education. In the Pearl River Delta, this period was characterised by migrant returnees funding new projects to modernise their ancestral localities, including in the realm of education.

---

69. Han Dongping, 'Impact of Cultural Revolution on Rural Education and Economic Development: The Case of Jimo County', *Modern China* 27, no. 1 (2001): 74, https://doi.org/10.1177/009770040102700102.

70. Exactly how many urban secondary school graduates were sent to the countryside is uncertain. Estimates of the number of people sent down to the countryside between 1968 and 1975 range from 12 to 17 million. See Thomas P. Bernstein, *Up to the Mountains and Down to the Villages: The Transfer of Youth from Urban to Rural China* (New Haven, CT: Yale University Press, 1977); Xu Bin, 'Intergenerational Variations in Autobiographical Memory: China's "Sent-Down Youth" Generation', *Social Psychology Quarterly* 82, no. 2 (2019): 134–57, https://doi.org/10.1177/0190272519840641.

71. Site visit to Liangdu Church, Zhongshan, by Heritage Corridor Research Team on 15 December 2017.

72. Pepper, *Radicalism and Education Reform*, 1.

73. Peterson, 'State Literacy Ideologies', 120.

74. Peterson, *The Power of Words*, 172.

75. The four fields included agriculture, industry, defence, and science and technology. See Vickers and Xiaodong Zeng, *Education and Society*, 15; Sun Hong and David Johnson, 'From *ti-yong* to *gaige* to Democracy and Back Again: Education's Struggle in Communist China', *Contemporary Education* 61, no. 4 (1990): 213.

Second Wave: Diaspora-Funded Schooling in Zhongshan after 1978

After a long period of insufficiency of rural education, opportunities for diaspora investment in education in Zhongshan began to open up after 1978. Chinese Australians such as Robert Yuen (阮祖裕)[76] and Stanley Hunt (陳沛德, 1927–2019)[77] felt compelled to build new schools in their native villages after they were able to revisit China. The global initiatives of the Chinese diaspora – of which Chinese Australians from Zhongshan were a small part – produced numerous new schools in the *qiaoxiang* during the 1980s and 1990s, from kindergartens to primary and secondary schools.

From 1984, legal ownership of properties of overseas Chinese that had been confiscated or expropriated after 1949 was restored.[78] New policies encouraged return to and investment in the *qiaoxiang* areas by overseas Chinese.[79] In Sha Chong, where diaspora-funded schools had long ceased operations, the Hong Kong management of Sincere department store (先施百貨公司) agreed to pay for much-needed renovation, including the conversion of the former Women and Children's Centre (婦兒院) (previously occupied by the Japanese and later the People's Liberation Army) to the Sincere Primary School (先施學校) in 1983.[80]

Some restorations were funded by descendants of the original benefactors, but there were also schools built by new benefactors. Stanley Hunt funded a school in his ancestral village of Mashan (馬山村) in Doumen district (斗門區) of Zhuhai in 1983.[81] Hong Kong–based Australian businesswoman Cheng Wai-kwan (鄭慧君) donated one million RMB to establish Bok Oi Middle School (博愛中學)[82] in her ancestral village of Yongmo (雍陌村), San Heung town (三鄉鎮), in 1983. In 1986, Mrs Eileen Lai (黎李杏華, née Lee Hing-Wah) and her late husband, Alen Lai (黎錦鴻), owners of the Lean Sun Lowe café (聯新樓) and Eastern Restaurant (東山酒家) in Dixon Street of Sydney's Chinatown, founded a kindergarten in Chung Tau village (涌頭村). Following a return trip to Zhongshan, Alen (who is not from Zhongshan but of Dongguan 東莞 origins) proposed to build a kindergarten in his wife's natal Zhongshan village, and Eileen agreed because she had grown up with little education and saw the need to free village women from parental duties.[83]

---

76. Diana Giese, *Astronauts, Lost Souls & Dragons: Voices of Today's Chinese Australians* (St Lucia: University of Queensland Press, 1997), 177–78.

77. Stanley Hunt, *From Shekki to Sydney* (Sydney: Wild Peony, 2009), 183–86.

78. See Ien Ang, Chapter 3 of this book.

79. Mette Thunø, 'Reaching Out and Incorporating Chinese Overseas: The Transterritorial Scope of the PRC by the End of the 20th Century', *China Quarterly* 168 (2001): 915, 918–19, https://doi.org/10.1017/S0009443901000535.

80. Interview with Ma Yin-Chiu (馬彥昭) by Christopher Cheng, Sha Chong, Zhongshan, 2 January 2019.

81. Hunt, 'From Shekki to Sydney', 183. See also Byrne, Chapter 2 of this volume.

82. *Bok oi* (博愛), in Cantonese, literally means 'universal love', after Dr Sun Yat-sen's Christianised slogan advocating equality. See Zhongshan Overseas Chinese Affairs Bureau, 中山市華僑志, 366.

83. Interview with Eileen Lai (黎李杏華) by Christopher Cheng, North Sydney, 24 April 2018.

To encourage funding from the diaspora, the government matched funds from overseas donors.[84] Stanley Yee (余金晃 Yee Kum Fung), another Sydney-based Chinatown restaurateur, collaborated with fellow clansmen to fund the expansion of Cheuk Shan Middle School (卓山中學) in Tai Chung (大涌, Dachong). From 1987 to 1994, Stanley and his relations in Fiji, Australia, Hong Kong and Macau provided over RMB six million for a RMB 12.3 million school project in Dachong under the fund-matching scheme.[85]

In many *qiaoxiang* areas after 1978, diaspora funds supported not only new kindergartens but also middle schools, in addition to expanding primary schools funded by the diaspora prior to 1949 – most of the known 41 diaspora-funded schools in Zhongshan from that period were primary schools.[86] However, the second wave of diaspora funding produced 49 new kindergartens, 91 new primary school buildings and 33 new middle school buildings funded by the Zhongshan diaspora worldwide.[87]

There was greater emphasis by diaspora funders on supporting specialised learning, as evidenced by the school equipment donated by migrants and migrant descendants to enhance depleted schools. Items donated included books (English-language textbooks for teachers and encyclopaedias for the school library), musical instruments (Yamaha keyboards, pianos, accordions, and drum kits), sports equipment (basketballs), and electronic goods (fans and computers).[88] A former student of Sincere School claimed that in the 1990s his village was 'the first and only school in Zhongshan to have computers'.[89]

Some of the new diaspora schools featured neo-traditional architectural styles. Whereas the flat, steel-reinforced concrete roof had been a defining feature of diaspora-funded schools in the earlier part of the century, several new schools incorporated traditional-style gable roofs, with classic green or yellow ceramic tiles representing bamboo, a symbol of ever-growing prosperity (see Figure 7.4). The neo-traditional flavour of the new school architecture may be attributed to the changing cultural perspectives of the donors. In the previous era, the schools were largely funded by those sojourning overseas, expecting to retire in China; they were among the first people in many emigrant villages to embrace Western ideals, so the schools they funded were also influenced by Western architecture, including neoclassical styles. In the years after 1978, however, the donors were firmly settled overseas with houses and established businesses in the places to which they had

---

84. Jiangang Zhu (朱健剛) and Yanchun Jing (景燕春), 'Push and Pull: A Case Study of the Dynamics of Chinese Diaspora Philanthropy', *The China Nonprofit Review* 11, no. 2 (2019): 302, https://doi.org/10.1163/18765149-12341366.

85. Zhongshan Overseas Chinese Affairs Bureau, 中山市華僑志, 366.

86. Zhongshan Overseas Chinese Affairs Bureau, 中山市華僑志, 349.

87. See Zhongshan Overseas Chinese Affairs Bureau, 中山市華僑志, 359–67; Yu, 'Chinese American Contributions', 66.

88. Data gathered from interviews at schools in Zhongshan and with donor families in Australia.

89. Interview with Ma Kit-Leung (馬傑良) by Christopher Cheng, Sha Chong, Zhongshan, 12 June 2018.

Figure 7.4: Chuen Luk School (全祿學校), Dachong town (大涌鎮), Zhongshan, completed in 1991. Photograph by Christopher Cheng, 2018.

migrated. These buildings reflected a pride in being Chinese, consonant with multicultural attitudes in places such as Australia.[90]

But many school buildings from the 1980s had been quickly erected, using poor materials and local, low-skilled labour. In 1983, Stanley Hunt had built a school in Mashan with a two-storey block containing 16 classrooms (named the Sung-Sun Hall of Learning 崇信教學樓 after his father). But the quality of the building was compromised by the shortage at that time of materials such as cement, steel reinforcing bars, and even ready-made blackboards. As Hunt commented, regarding the 16-classroom school he founded:

> Inferior building materials were the only kind available at the time, and this was often combined with poor workmanship. After only fifteen years the building was in a shocking state. Part of the foundation had subsided, and the window frames had all warped. I donated another large sum of money to have the whole building renovated. The wooden frames were replaced with aluminium ones.[91]

The building would eventually be demolished in 2020 for failing to comply with earthquake regulations. Meanwhile, the government had responded to this

---

90. See Ien Ang and Alexandra Wong, Chapter 8 of this volume, for the oriental featurism in Sydney and other Chinatowns that emerged with multiculturalism.
91. Hunt, *From Shekki to Sydney*, 186.

situation, and to growing student numbers, by building a much larger classroom block in 2012, located on higher ground close to the 1983 building, and seeming to dwarf the original school built by Hunt.[92] The fate of Stanley Hunt's building exemplifies the complexity of assessing the legacy of diaspora philanthropy in rapidly changing circumstances. Hunt's initiative was a response to the lack of adequate schooling in 1980s Zhongshan, yet the diaspora-funded school now seemed to have been eclipsed by the state school in a literal (material) sense.

The 'second wave' of diaspora funding for schools eventually faded as economic growth and urbanisation altered the regional environment in Zhongshan.[93] As the population growth rate plateaued and then declined with the one child policy and young people left rural areas to work in cities, some village authorities found it more profitable to rent out school buildings for other purposes rather than continuing to run the schools at a loss. Village leaderships converted many disused schools into factories 'overnight', meaning donor families in Australia were often not aware it had occurred. The long period of isolation of the home villages from diaspora communities during the Mao era meant many such families had become distanced from the schools that their elders or ancestors had contributed to. For instance, in the post-reform era, the Sha Chong Primary School was converted into a shoe factory (Figure 7.5). A visit to the site in December 2018 revealed that Chinese migrant workers typically slept on the premises; the rooftop cupola, which once housed the school bell, was now strung with clotheslines for factory workers (Figure 7.6).[94]

In some areas of Zhongshan, an influx of internal 'migrant workers' (農民工 *nongmin gong* in Mandarin) and their families from other parts of China during the rapid growth of the factory economy in the 1980s and 1990s, combined with out-migration of Zhongshanese, meant that the existing schools no longer catered primarily to the *qiaoxiang*, at least if we understand this term to be grounded in kinship and cultural identification.[95] An important factor in the slowing of this wave of diaspora support for schools was also the eventual achievement of higher levels of educational provision in Zhongshan as a result of increased government funding. For Williams (see Chapter 1 of this volume), Chinese economic development reduced the prosperity gap between Zhongshan and the diaspora; hence, the period of reliance on diaspora capital was a 'relatively brief' one. The growing wealth of China transformed 'the once remittance-dependent county into a wealth-generating one'.

---

92. Denis Byrne, *The Heritage Corridor: A Transnational Approach to the Heritage of Chinese Migration, 1880s–1940s* (London: Routledge, 2022), and Chapter 2 of this volume.
93. See Michael Williams, Chapter 1 of this volume.
94. Site observation by Christopher Cheng, December 2018.
95. This 'primordial' understanding of *qioxiang* linkages has been recently contested, as in the period since 1978 kinship and shared background seem less crucial for *qioxiang* linkages than economic contributions and business calculation. See Yow Cheun Hoe, *Guangdong and Chinese Diaspora: The Changing Landscape of Qiaoxiang* (Abingdon: Routledge, 2013), 2.

Figure 7.5: The former Sha Chong School 沙涌學校 (舊址) in a dilapidated condition, used as a factory building. Photograph by Denis Byrne, December 2018.

Figure 7.6: Rooftop cupola of former Sha Chong School 沙涌學校 (舊址), with flag post on top; note clothes lines. Photograph by Denis Byrne, December 2018.

Caobian School: Material Stories and Intergenerational Legacies

One way to illustrate the achievements and challenges of educational interventions by Zhongshan Chinese in the diaspora is to focus on material changes over time in a particular place. The school in Caobian, a village associated with the Leong/Leung/Liang (梁) clan, exemplifies the material changes effected by the trajectory of historical events in the twentieth century. Completed in 1929, the Caobian school (曹邊學校) was built during the golden period of the construction of remittance-funded schools. It is of particular interest as one of the few Australian diaspora-built schools before 1949 that did not include donations from the wealthy Zhongshanese department store owners. Major donors to the school included more modestly affluent owners of grocery stores in regional areas of Queensland, such as the Leong clansmen associated with the Houng Yuen & Co. store (洪源) in Ingham and Tip Hop and Co. in Hughenden, who had strong *qiaoxiang* links. These Queensland businesses were able to coordinate financial transfers to Caobian through Fook War Shing (福和盛, pronounced in urban Cantonese), a business enterprise with a branch in Zhongshan's urban centre, Shekki, that handled remittances and other financial dealings for many clients in Queensland.[96] Remittance payments were conveyed through Chinese stores, as described by a relative of a store owner in Townsville, Queensland:

> When Chinese migrants in Australia accumulated savings, not knowing a word of English, they dared not use the post office. They sent money home through my father-in-law instead. It first went to Tong Shan[97] through Hong Kong using an address in English, and from Hong Kong's Yuet Cheong Lung (悦昌隆), redirected to Chung Shan. Fook War Shing not only served Caobian people but all Chung Shan folk. I heard from my late husband that it was a bustling hive of activity . . . My father-in-law brought a basket and visited each family in the village, distributing remittances and writing letters.[98]

Fook War Shing's network in Queensland made it possible for the coordination of a large project at the Zhongshan end of the Caobian–Queensland migration corridor, namely the construction of the Caobian village school, which opened in 1929.

The Leong clansmen who ran a store called Houng Yuen & Co. in Ingham, Queensland,[99] were major donors to the school. They included the stores' partners Charlie Hong (梁瑞榮 Leong Jui Jung, 1882–1943) and George Leong (梁業榮 Leong Yip Wing, 1877–1950), who supported the 1920s village school. Charlie's

---

96. According to Caobian village historian Anthony Leong and several senior Cantonese-speaking Townsville descendants from that village.

97. The vernacular Cantonese expression *Tong Shan* (唐山), literally meaning 'Tang mountains', refers to the glorious days of the Tang dynasty, and specifically the homeland in Guangdong.

98. Interview with Mrs Wenney Leong by Christopher Cheng, Townsville, 17 April 2018.

99. Sandi Robb and Joe Leong, 'Casting Seeds to the Wind: My Journey to North Queensland', in *Rediscovered Past: Chinese Network*, ed. Gordon Grimwade, Kevin Rains, and Melissa Dunk (East Ipswich, Qld.: China Inc, 2016), 1–6.

son, Zhongshan-born William Leong (梁門教, 1905–1992), who had been sent to Australia to acquire further education, eventually took over the store. Following his father's example, William continued to contribute to village infrastructure. In commemoration of the family's generosity, a classroom was named after Charlie Hong and George Leong in the 1929 Caobian school, while their sons, William and Richard (George's son), also had classrooms named after them in a new kindergarten classroom block built in the 1980s. As in almost all cases of school-building in Zhongshan villages, naming buildings and spaces created a 'proxy presence' for the donor in the village, as with remittance houses.[100]

The two-storey school was completed in 1929, occupying a prominent position facing the village square. The grandeur of its neoclassical façade, as well as its size – until the late twentieth century it was the largest building in the village – testified

Figure 7.7: Interior courtyard (天井) of the former Caobian school 曹邊學校 (舊址). Photograph by Denis Byrne 2018.

---

100. See Denis Byrne, Chapter 6 of this volume, on remittance houses.

to the importance of education to the villagers in the early twentieth century and to their relatives overseas. The building has an interior courtyard that would have allowed cool air to circulate to the classrooms, all of which opened onto the courtyard (see Figure 7.7). A cupola on the roof of the school is topped by a flagpole. Like the Sha Chong primary school, reinforced concrete was used in the school's construction, a technology that was becoming widespread in the Pearl River Delta by the 1920s and which had become a symbol of modernity. The floors, roof, and pillars are made of reinforced concrete, while the interior and exterior walls consist of brick covered with cement render and plaster. Like the multi-storey flat-roofed remittance houses that had begun to appear in the villages of Zhongshan in the 1920s, the school had a flat roof (天台 *tiantai* in Mandarin) from which one could look down across the village, introducing new perspectives to village life. Former pupils and children of pre-school age at that time have recalled playing around the school building and on the school's flat rooftop. A female former pupil reminisced about 'shouting games', where a student stood on the roof of the school yelling to their classmates on the ground below, and remembered boys flying kites and paper planes from the roof.[101]

A brass bell hangs from the ceiling of the front balcony. If the bell was an original feature of the school, it would have been rung to mark out the intervals of the school day. The sound of the school bell would have been one of the many ways in which modernity and overseas migration reconfigured the village environment.[102]

After more than three decades of educational use, under Mao the school building was occasionally requisitioned as a storehouse. A Shanghai resident who had been 'sent down'[103] to his native home of Caobian in the 1960s recalled peanuts being laid out to dry on the school's roof terrace.[104] During the wet typhoon seasons, the large two-storey school building kept the harvest dry at a time when many residents lived in single-storey dwellings prone to seasonal flooding.[105]

When overseas Chinese finally returned to China from 1978, they could witness the effects of the disruptions and shortcomings of the Maoist period. The reform and opening of China (改革開放 *gaige kaifong* in Mandarin) from 1978 encouraged new contributions from the diaspora to restore the built environment of *qiaoxiang* villages that had effectively been isolated from the diaspora for thirty years. Leung Man Hon (梁维漢, 1916–2001), who returned to visit Caobian in the 1970s for the

---

101. Phone interview with Brisbane resident Felicia Seeto (梁淑彥) by Christopher Cheng, 74, 28 June 2020.
102. See description of the Caobian Village School on https://www.heritagecorridor.org.au/places/caobian-village-school-zhongshan.
103. This campaign, also known as 'Up to the mountains, down to the villages' (上山下鄉), was designed to eliminate urban unemployment, reform youths according to communist ideology, assist in rural development, and ease the mayhem created by the Red Guards during the Cultural Revolution. See Bernstein, *Up to the Mountains*, 33.
104. Interview with Anthony Leong (梁正衡) by Christopher Cheng, Caobian village, Zhongshan, 8 May 2018.
105. Interview with Paul Liang (梁文泰) by Christopher Cheng, Sun Doo Restaurant, Townsville, 17 April 2018; phone interview with Felicia Seeto of Brisbane (梁淑彥), 20 October 2020.

first time since leaving for Queensland over a decade earlier, observed the dilapidation of infrastructure in the village including the old school, which was run-down and in need of repair.[106] Man Hon and his childhood friend Philip Leong (梁華立 Leong Wah Lup, 1917–1999), who had also attended the Caobian school and who later also emigrated to Queensland, turned their attention to raising funds for improvements to their home village. Besides raising funds to repair roads and the village gate, they assisted in the renovation of the Caobian school and the building of a new classroom block to be used as a kindergarten in 1987.[107]

Some thirty years after its renovation, the Caobian school is no longer used for educational purposes. The building now houses village offices and a small museum, an example of 'adaptive reuse' conservation. Considerable care has been taken to retain the architectural integrity of the building, which is now regarded as a heritage item by villagers, members of the diaspora, and the government, and it is a stopping place on 'roots tourism' tours by diaspora members. The building has been maintained as a public space, accessible to villagers and visitors alike.

The Caobian school illustrates the changing material circumstances of schooling initiatives funded through the Australian diaspora. Strong connections between Caobian and businesses in Queensland had enabled the building of the school in 1929. The school was then an impressively modern building that became a central feature in the village landscape, introducing new building technologies, educational standards, and imperatives of modernity. The building survived in relatively good condition considering the loss of diaspora support in the decades after 1949. Its educational role was restored in the 1980s when diaspora ties were renewed and philanthropic flows were resumed by former students, some of whom were descendants of the original school benefactors. Today, the building still serves the village, though no longer as a school. This attests to the strength of lifelines across the migration corridor.[108]

Conclusion

This chapter has highlighted the importance of educational initiatives in the Zhongshan–Australia heritage corridor and in the context of the Cantonese Pacific diaspora generally. Diaspora-funded schools in Zhongshan occupy a central place in transnational migrant history. We explored the practices and dilemmas of sustaining the legacies of diaspora schools through an investigation of their material history and the recollections of people at both ends of the migration corridor. The building of schools in Zhongshan from the early twentieth century was fuelled by a convergence of commercial success and philanthropic initiative that went beyond

---

106. Phone interview with Felicia Seeto (daughter of Leung Man Hon), 5 August 2020.
107. Phone interview with Felicia Seeto, 5 August 2020.
108. See Denis Byrne, Chapter 9 of this volume.

local reinvestment in places of origin and the support of remittances from workers in the diaspora. Supporting modern education became increasingly important in a context of the transnational commercial economy that developed along the corridor, an economy that required literacy and numeracy, cultural adaptability, and a wider sense of the world. Investment in educational innovation was also supported by the urgency of Nationalist politics in China during the Republican era and by the Christian perspectives of many key philanthropists.

The commercial success of a new elite of entrepreneurs originating from Zhongshan would support opportunities for young people in their home county, particularly in commerce and trade, and their capacities to adapt to the new cultural circumstances of transnational life. But the instability of conditions in China from the late 1930s to the late 1970s created a severe lacuna in educational provision in Zhongshan that these diaspora-funded schools could not overcome as the conditions for material and human connectivity across the corridor were eroded. Nevertheless, a 'second wave' of educational philanthropy flowing from the diaspora demonstrated the strength of connective lifelines in spite of the long period of blockage of social and economic networks. However, this renewal of educational initiatives also outlined the sharp differences between the *qiaoxiang* networks of the early twentieth century and contemporary transnational relations. These include widening cultural gaps, especially the loss of local knowledge and language of diaspora philanthropists, suggesting limits to the *qiaoxiang*'s sustainability.

From this distance in time, the diaspora-funded schools can be assessed in terms of their historical significance and their value and potential as material heritage. China now considers *qiaoxiang* buildings, including schools, as significant heritage items that should be preserved (see Denis Byrne, Chapter 9 of this volume). The schools we have discussed sometimes present difficulties for conventional heritage practice due to the changing uses of school buildings and the fact that, given the subtropical climate of the region, buildings can deteriorate rapidly without ongoing maintenance. Should these buildings be restored (where feasible), written off or ignored, or recognised as mutable objects subject to entropic processes of alteration and decay? The latter course may allow for the telling of more complex transnational and even more-than-human stories.[109]

For its part, Australia could also begin to recognise the transnational (not merely unidirectional) trajectories of material heritage through long migratory movements. While this would entail a major conceptual and policy change in the approach to heritage beyond that of national settlement, this could take place with a gradual shift towards more collaborative and international practices of heritage classification and management, and through more expansive and imaginative

---

109. For instance, rats collected many items of everyday human use in their nests at Sydney's Hyde Park Barracks; the form of these collections was maintained in a museum display. See Caitlin DeSilvey, 'Observed Decay: Telling Stories with Mutable Things', *Journal of Material Culture* 11, no. 3 (2006): 334, https://doi.org/10.1177/1359183506068808.

approaches to historical narrative and material heritage by museums and other heritage institutions. Schooling and education should be accorded an important place in such an understanding of the material heritage of transnational migration.

Bibliography

Au-yeung Chow. *Zhongshan Dailengcun qiaoshi* 中山大嶺村僑志 [Dai Leng village overseas history, Chung-shan]. Macau: New Hip Hing Printing, 2001.

Bernstein, Thomas P. *Up to the Mountains and Down to the Villages: The Transfer of Youth from Urban to Rural China*. New Haven, CT: Yale University Press, 1977.

Borthwick, Sally. *Education and Social Change in China: The Beginning of the Modern Era*. Stanford, CA: Hoover Institution Press, 1983.

Byrne, Denis. 'The Need for a Transnational Approach to the Material Heritage of Migration: The China–Australia Corridor'. *Journal of Social Archaeology* 16, no. 3 (2016): 261–85. https://doi.org/10.1177/1469605316673005.

Byrne, Denis. *The Heritage Corridor: A Transnational Approach to the Heritage of Chinese Migration, 1880s–1940s*. London: Routledge, 2022.

Chan-yeung, Moira M. W. *Lam Woo: Master Builder, Revolutionary, and Philanthropist*. Hong Kong: Chinese University Press, 2017.

Cheng, Christopher. 'Beacons of Modern Learning: Diaspora-Funded Schools in the China–Australia Corridor'. *Asian and Pacific Migration Journal* 29, no. 2 (2020): 139–62. https://doi.org/10.1177/0117196820930309.

Choy Flannigan, Alison. *Chinese Whispers – In Search of Ivy: An Australian Gold Rush Story Told by Generations of an Australian Chinese Family*. Sydney: Black Quill, 2018.

Deng, Peng. *Private Education in Modern China*. Westport, CT: Praeger, 1997.

DeSilvey, Caitlin. 'Observed Decay: Telling Stories with Mutable Things'. *Journal of Material Culture* 11, no. 3 (2006): 318–38. https://doi.org/10.1177/1359183506068808.

Elman, Benjamin. 'The Civil Service Examination'. In *Berkshire Encyclopedia of China: Modern and Historic Views of the World's Newest and Oldest Global Power*, Vol. 5, edited by Linsun Cheng, 405–10. Great Barrington: Berkshire Publishing, 2009.

Fei, Xiaotong. 'Bringing Literacy to the Countryside'. In *From the Soil: The Foundations of Chinese Society*, edited and translated by Gary G. Hamilton and Zheng Wang, 45–52. Berkeley: University of California Press, 1992.

Fitzgerald, John. *Big White Lie: Chinese Australians in White Australia*. Sydney: UNSW Press, 2007.

Fitzgerald, John. 'Building Trust: Private Charity (*cishan*) and Public Benefit (*gongyi*) in the Associational Life of the Cantonese Pacific, 1850–1949'. In *Chinese Diaspora Charity and the Cantonese Pacific, 1850–1949*, edited by John Fitzgerald and Hon-ming Yip, 193–210. Hong Kong: Hong Kong University Press, 2020.

Giese, Diana. *Astronauts, Lost Souls & Dragons: Voices of Today's Chinese Australians*. St Lucia: University of Queensland Press, 1997.

Grosvenor, Ian, and Catherine Burke. *School*. London: Reaktion, 2008.

Han, Dongping. 'Impact of Cultural Revolution on Rural Education and Economic Development: The Case of Jimo County'. *Modern China* 27, no. 1 (2001): 59–90. https://doi.org/10.1177/009770040102700102.

Ho Puay-peng, Henry Ka-Yu Lo, and Heidi Sze-Man Lam. 'Consultancy for Conservation Study of Chik Kwai Study Hall at Pat Heung'. Hong Kong: Antiquities and Monuments Office, 2008.

Hoskins, Janet. 'Agency, Biography and Objects'. In *Handbook of Material Culture*, edited by Christopher Tilley, Webb Keane, Susanne Kuechler, Mike Rowlands, and Patricia Spyer, 74–84. London: SAGE, 2006.

Hsu, Madeline Y. Y. *Dreaming of Gold, Dreaming of Home: Transnationalism and Migration between the United States and South China, 1882–1943*. Stanford, CA: Stanford University Press, 2000.

Hunt, Stanley. *From Shekki to Sydney: An Autobiography*. Sydney: Wild Peony, 2009.

I.E. [initials only provided]. 'Education in Communist China'. *World Today* 8, no. 6 (1952): 257–68.

Kuhn, Philip A. *Chinese among Others: Emigration in Modern Times*. Lanham, MD: Rowman and Littlefield, 2008.

Kumar, Nita. 'Learning Modernity? The Technologies of Education in India'. *Autrepart* 18, no. 2, (2001): 85–100. https://doi.org/10.3917/autr.018.0085.

Kuo, Mei-fen. 'The Making of a Diasporic Identity: The Case of the Sydney Chinese Commercial Elite, 1890s–1900s'. *Journal of Chinese Overseas* 5, no. 2 (2009): 336–63. https://doi.org.10.1163/179303909X12489373183091.

Kuo, Mei-fen. *Making Chinese Australia: Urban Elites, Newspapers and Chinese–Australian Identity during Federation*. Clayton, Victoria: Monash University, 2013.

Lee, Ho Yin, and Lynne D. DiStefano. 'Chinese Renaissance Architecture in China and Hong Kong'. *Context* 145 (2016): 17–20.

Liao, Hongyue. 'Shang and Shan: Charitable Networks of the "Four Great Department Stores" and Their Associated Chinese-Australian Families 1900–1949'. PhD thesis, Swinburne University of Technology, 2018.

Ming, Tom K. C. 明基全, ed. *From Study Hall to Village School* [教不倦：新界傳統教育的蛻變]. Hong Kong: Urban Council, 1996.

Minkowsi, Eugene. *Lived Time: Phenomenological and Psychopathological Studies*. Translated by Nancy Metzel. Evanston, IL: Northwestern University Press, 1970.

Mitchell, Timothy. 'Introduction'. In *Questions of Modernity*, edited by Timothy Mitchell, xi–xxviii. Minneapolis: University of Minnesota Press, 2000.

Oakes, Malcolm, SC. 'William Lee: First Barrister of Chinese Descent Admitted to the New South Wales Bar'. *Bar News: The Journal of the New South Wales Bar Association* (Winter 2015): 73–76.

Pepper, Suzanne. *Radicalism and Education Reform in 20th-Century China: The Search for an Ideal Development Model*. New York: Cambridge University Press, 1996.

Peterson, Glen. 'State Literacy Ideologies and the Transformation of Rural China'. *The Australian Journal of Chinese Affairs* 32 (1994): 95–120.

Peterson, Glen. *The Power of Words, Literacy and Revolution in South China, 1949–95*. Vancouver: University of British Columbia Press, 1997.

Peterson, Glen, and Ruth Hayhoe. 'Introduction'. In *Education, Culture, and Identity in Twentieth-Century China*, edited by Glen Peterson, Ruth Hayhoe, and Yongling Lu, 1–22. Hong Kong: Hong Kong University Press, 2001.

Rawski, Evelyn Sakakida. 1979. *Education and Popular Literacy in Ch'ing China*. Ann Arbor: University of Michigan Press.

Robb, Sandi, and Joe Leong. 'Casting Seeds to the Wind: My Journey to North Queensland'. In *Rediscovered Past: Chinese Network*, edited by Gordon Grimwade, Kevin Rains, and Melissa Dunk, 1–6. East Ipswich, Qld.: China Inc, 2016.

Shu, Changxue. 'Towards Western Construction in China: Shanghai Brickwork and Printed Technical Resources 1843–1936'. *Construction History* 33, no. 1 (2018): 83–110.

Sklair, Jessica, and Luna Glucksberg. 'Philanthrocapitalism as Wealth Management Strategy: Philanthropy, Inheritance and Succession Planning among the Global Elite'. *The Sociological Review* 69, no. 2 (2021): 314–29. https://doi.org/10.1177/003802612096 3479.

Sun, Hong, and David Johnson. 'From *ti-yong* to *gaige* to Democracy and Back Again: Education's Struggle in Communist China'. *Contemporary Education* 61, no. 4 (1990): 209–14.

Thunø, Mette. 'Reaching Out and Incorporating Chinese Overseas: The Transterritorial Scope of the PRC by the End of the 20th Century'. *China Quarterly* 168 (2001): 910–29. https://doi.org/10.1017/S0009443901000535.

Unger, Jonathan. 'Severing the Links between School Performance and Careers: The Experience of China's Urban Schools, 1968–1976'. *Comparative Education* 20, no. 1 (1984): 93–102.

VanderVen, Elizabeth R. *A School in Every Village: Educational Reform in a Northeast China County, 1904–1931*. Vancouver: University of British Columbia Press, 2012.

Vickers, Edward, and Xiaodong Zeng. *Education and Society in Post-Mao China*. Abingdon: Routledge, 2017.

Williams, Michael. *Returning Home with Glory: Chinese Villagers around the Pacific, 1849 to 1949*. Hong Kong: Hong Kong University Press, 2018.

Wilton, Janis. 'Histories of the Chinese in Regional NSW 1859–1950'. *Journal of the Royal Australian Historical Society* 105, no. 1 (2019): 49–69.

Xu, Bin. 2019. 'Intergenerational Variations in Autobiographical Memory: China's "Sent-Down Youth" Generation'. *Social Psychology Quarterly* 82, no. 2 (2019): 134–57. https://doi.org/10.1177/0190272519840641.

Yin, Xiao-huang. 'A Case Study of Transnationalism: Continuity and Changes in Chinese American Philanthropy to China'. *American Studies* 45, no. 2 (2004): 65–99.

Yong, C. F. *The New Gold Mountain: The Chinese in Australia 1901–1921*. Richmond, S. Australia: Raphael Arts, 1977.

Yow, Cheun Hoe. *Guangdong and Chinese Diaspora: The Changing Landscape of Qiaoxiang*. Abingdon: Routledge, 2013.

Yu, Renqiu. 'Chinese American Contributions to the Educational Development of Toisan 1910–1940'. *Amerasia* 10, no. 1 (1983): 47–72.

Zhongshan East District Overseas Chinese Committee 中山市東區僑聯會. *Qiaoxiang kuchongcun shi* 僑鄉庫充村史 [Qiaoxiang Koo Chung village history]. Zhongshan: Zhongshan East District Overseas Chinese Committee and East District Koo Chung Village Committee, 1999.

Zhongshan Overseas Chinese Affairs Bureau 中山市外事僑務局. *Zhongshan shi huaqiao zhi* 中山市華僑志 [Annals of Zhongshan Overseas Chinese Affairs], edited by Chen Diqiu (陳迪秋). Guangzhou: Guangdong's People's Press, 2013.

Zhu, Jiangang (朱健剛), and Yanchun Jing (景燕春). 'Push and Pull: A Case Study of the Dynamics of Chinese Diaspora Philanthropy'. *The China Nonprofit Review* 11, no. 2 (2019): 282–303. https://doi.org/10.1163/18765149-12341366.

Interviews

Anthony Leong 梁正衡, Caobian, Zhongshan, 8 May 2018.
Ms Chen Diqiu 陳迪秋, Zhongshan, 8 August 2018.
Mrs Eileen Lai 黎李杏華, North Sydney, 24 April 2018.
Ma Kit-Leung 馬傑良, Sha Chong, Zhongshan, 12 June 2018.
Mrs Wenney Leong, Townsville, 17 April 2018.
Ma Yin-Chiu 馬彥昭, Sha Chong, Zhongshan, 2 January 2019.
Li Xiangping 李向平, Chuk Sau Yuen School, Zhongshan, 15 December 2017.
Paul Liang 梁文泰, Sun Doo Restaurant, Townsville, 17 April 2018.
Mrs Felicia Seeto 梁淑彥, 28 June 2020, 5 August 2020, 20 October 2020.
Ms Sheng Lai-Kum 盛麗金, Ngoi Sha village, Zhuhai, 29 November 2018.

8
Zhongshan in Sydney's Chinatown

Ien Ang and Alexandra Wong

The Emergence of Chinatown in Sydney

When Chinese men from southern China – among them many from Zhongshan county – first began to make their three- to four-week voyage to Australia in large numbers in the mid-nineteenth century, many disembarked in Sydney. Thousands of Chinese indentured labourers arrived in the colony of New South Wales (NSW) from 1848 onwards, recruited by Sydney entrepreneurs who undertook to ship these workers as cargo from China to serve the labour requirements of the colony, particularly in the pastoral industry.[1] Although some of these indentured labourers were deployed in Sydney, most of them were placed in rural districts, where they were paid below market standards for their hard work. This indenture system soon broke down, not least because of the discovery of gold in the 1850s, when many workers simply walked away from unsatisfactory positions and joined men of all nationalities in the search of gold. News of gold also spread quickly to the villages around Canton (Guangzhou), which propelled Chinese (probably Cantonese) businessmen in Hong Kong to ship as many men as they could to Australia under a system of credit tickets, with fares repayable when fortunes were made. By 1861 there were almost 13,000 Chinese in New South Wales.[2]

Only small numbers of these migrants stayed in Sydney in the early days, but in the following decades there was a steady drift of Chinese from rural areas to the city. Between 1861 and 1871 the number of Chinese in Sydney rose from a tiny 189 to 336, but by 1878 there were 960 Chinese in the port city, rising to 1,321 in 1888. Although these numbers were still small, the increase was visible because of a tendency among the Chinese to congregate in just a few areas in the city, such as around Circular Quay and Lower George Street in The Rocks, which

---

1. Shirley Fitzgerald, *Red Tape Gold Scissors: The Story of Sydney's Chinese* (Ultimo: Halstead Press, 2008), 31.
2. Fitzgerald, *Red Tape*, 35–36.

saw the beginnings of a Chinatown of sorts.[3] The large number of Chinese people milling around the wharves contributed to a moral panic among white locals, who expressed fears of being 'swamped' by the Chinese – a racist sentiment that has recurred regularly throughout modern Australian history – overlooking the fact that many of these Chinese would only spend a short time in town, and that many were in fact passing through only to take boats back to China. This was part of the sojourning pattern of frequent coming and going that has, over time, created a Zhongshan–Sydney heritage corridor, a key focus of this book. In what C. Y. Choi has described as a commuting migration system,[4] Chinese migrants would, when circumstances allowed, return to their home villages every few years to be with their family and come back to Australia for a further stint of work, and so on. The New South Wales Customs Department calculated that between 1872 and 1881, 15,574 Chinese arrived, but 8,491 departed via the port of Sydney.[5]

Although the number of Chinese was relatively small, anti-Chinese attitudes in Australia steadily hardened. In 1881 the New South Wales Parliament introduced the Influx of Chinese Restriction Act in an effort to exclude Chinese from entering the country by imposing a poll tax and restricting entry to one Chinese for every one hundred tons of shipping.[6] And in 1901, when the six separate British self-governing colonies of New South Wales, Queensland, Victoria, Tasmania, South Australia, and Western Australia agreed to unite and form the Commonwealth of Australia, the new national government enacted its Immigration Restriction Act, which did not mention Chinese (and other people of colour) specifically but was expressly designed to keep non-whites out through an infamous 'dictation test'.[7] Such restrictive White Australia measures made it increasingly hard for Chinese to enter Australia, and for those already in the country to continue their frequent commute back and forth that had been part of their transnational lifestyle. While some of them decided to stay, many others decided permanently to return to their homeland.[8] By 1901 there were only 29,627 Chinese in Australia, whereas at one time there were believed to have been between 45,000 and 50,000.[9] In the following decades numbers declined further: census figures showed that the total number of Chinese in Australia fell from 21,858 in 1911 to 6,594 in 1947.[10] However, while the national Chinese population dwindled, the number of Chinese in Sydney remained more or less stable throughout the first half of the twentieth century. By 1947, 3,300 Chinese lived in Sydney, more than half of Australia's total Chinese population. The steady migration of Chinese from other cities and rural areas towards Sydney was,

---

3. Fitzgerald, *Red Tape*, 37.
4. C. Y. Choi, *Chinese Migration and Settlement in Australia* (Sydney: Sydney University Press, 1975).
5. Fitzgerald, *Red Tape*, 42.
6. Fitzgerald, *Red Tape*, 41.
7. Michael Williams, *Australia's Dictation Test: The Test It Was a Crime to Fail* (Leiden: Brill, 2021).
8. Fitzgerald, *Red Tape*, 46.
9. Choi, *Chinese Migration*, 27.
10. Fitzgerald, *Red Tape*, 57.

as historian Shirley Fitzgerald notes, 'a measure of the contraction of opportunities for the Chinese population in general'.[11]

Sydney was thus a central place to which many of Australia's Chinese converged. On Lower George Street in The Rocks, many Chinese businesses emerged soon after the start of the gold rush to cater to the needs of those passing through, for example boarding houses and shops to provide temporary lodgings, supplies, and shipping news.[12] By the late nineteenth century the number of Chinese establishments in The Rocks had multiplied, indicating that some Chinese were no longer just passing through but were becoming settled in the city. There was a substantial rise in the number of furniture makers among the Chinese: by the mid-1880s Chinese furniture workshops accounted for a quarter of all furniture workshops in Sydney, providing furnishings for the city's growing population at that time.[13] Other urban occupations included laundering, vegetable and fruit distribution, general dealing and hawking, grocery retailing, cooking, and running cafés.[14]

At the same time, many Chinese had also set themselves up in Sydney's surrounding suburbs as market gardeners and fishermen, two occupations that provided opportunities for the Chinese as they tended to be spurned by British settlers.[15] These poorer Chinese tended to congregate in the southern end of the city spreading from Haymarket to Surry Hills, especially after the relocation of Sydney's fruit and vegetable markets to the Belmore Markets, on the site of the present Capitol Theatre, in 1869.[16] Here, market gardeners from the suburbs could find cheap lodgings when they stayed overnight in the city. Although The Rocks was the location of Sydney's first Chinese concentration because of its vicinity to the wharves, after a further market relocation in 1910 the Haymarket area eventually became known as Sydney's 'Chinatown' (雪梨唐人街). While many wealthier merchants preferred to reside in The Rocks or move to a suburban location, many ordinary Chinese were drawn to the Haymarket, with many businesses relocating there from The Rocks.[17] By 1900, the Sydney City Council reported that of the 1,440 Chinese living in the city, 14 per cent lived in The Rocks, while 86 per cent lived in Haymarket.[18]

---

11. Fitzgerald, *Red Tape*, 58.
12. Fitzgerald, *Red Tape*, 90.
13. Fitzgerald, *Red Tape*, 90–91, 106; Choi, *Chinese Migration*, 32. The fortunes of Chinese furniture manufacturing were short-lived: by the 1940s it had virtually disappeared, according to Choi (*Chinese Migration*, 53) due to labour restrictions imposed by discriminatory laws which prohibited Chinese furniture makers from recruiting workers for their businesses. A recent in-depth study of the Chinese furniture factories of this time suggests that bankruptcies were also due to market downturns, limited capital, and high workers' wages. See Peter Gibson, 'Made in Chinatown: Chinese Furniture Factories in Australia, 1880–1930', *Australian Economic History Review* 61, no. 1 (2021): 102–8, https://doi.org/10.1111/aehr.12211.
14. Choi, *Chinese Migration*, 33.
15. Fitzgerald, *Red Tape*, 91–92; Michael Williams, *Chinese Settlement in NSW: A Thematic History. Report for the NSW Heritage Office of NSW* (Sydney: NSW Heritage Office, 1999).
16. Fitzgerald, *Red Tape*, 91.
17. Fitzgerald, *Red Tape*, 112–18.
18. Fitzgerald, *Red Tape*, 120. There were a further 1,657 Chinese living in the suburbs on the periphery of metropolitan Sydney, according to the 1901 census.

By the 1920s, Haymarket had become the centre of Chinese community life in the city, especially along and around Dixon Street (德信街) – still the core of Sydney's official Chinatown to this day.[19] At that time, it was one of the poorest districts in the city. Many Chinese families moved into the area, especially after their houses in neighbouring Surry Hills (莎莉山), such as those in Wexford Street, were demolished in the name of slum clearance and better traffic management.[20] Small traders set up financially marginal grocery stores or restaurants in premises rented from the city council, which progressively lowered the rates, rents, and insurance premiums to keep the markets functioning, while market traders, fruit merchants, and wholesale importers moved into warehouses in the area.[21] Between 1910 and 1920 large Chinese wholesale fruit distributing firms, including Wing On (永安果欄), Wing Sang (永生果欄), and Tiy Sang & Co. (泰生果欄), dominated this sector.[22] The Chinese merchant class had become wealthy enough to purchase real estate in the area. Buildings on Dixon Street, Campbell Street, Goulburn Street, Ultimo Road, and surrounding streets were bought up by clan and native-place associations, retail firms, and other Chinese-owned businesses, amounting to concentrated Chinese ownership in the greater Haymarket district.

A range of Chinese organisations founded before the Second World War still have their premises in Haymarket today. This includes the Kuomintang (KMT) building on 75 Ultimo Road, which was purchased by supporters of Dr Sun Yatsen's Chinese Nationalist Party in 1921 and opened in May 1922 as the Party's Australian headquarters (中國國民黨部大樓).[23] The Nationalists had wide support in Australia after the overthrow of the last Qing emperor and the brief transition to Republican rule from 1911; the KMT achieved rule over the whole of China by 1928, by then under Chiang Kai-shek.

China was thrown into crisis by the Japanese invasion in 1937, followed by civil war with the Chinese Communist Party, which ended with the defeat of the Nationalists and the retreat of Chiang Kai-shek to Taiwan in 1949, to the consternation of many KMT supporters in Australia and elsewhere. When the Australian government under Gough Whitlam finally recognised the People's Republic of China in 1972, a Sydney KMT activist went to the party rooms in Ultimo Road and hanged himself.[24]

---

19. According to long-time Sydney resident Douglas Lam, Haymarket was always known to Cantonese speakers as 'maa git' 孖結, which sounded like the English word 'market', the latter 'git' as in guitar. The current term 'hey see' 禧市 is relatively new.
20. Fitzgerald, *Red Tape*, 157.
21. Fitzgerald, *Red Tape*, 154–55.
22. Choi, *Chinese Migration*, 53.
23. Fitzgerald, *Red Tape*, 146. For a history of the Kuomintang in Australia, see Mei-fen Kuo and Judith Brett, *Unlocking the History of the Australasian Kuo Min Tang* (North Melbourne: Australian Scholarly Publishing, 2013).
24. Fitzgerald, *Red Tape*, 149.

Another key Chinese organisation with premises in Haymarket is the Chinese Youth League (澳洲僑青社, CYL). Established in 1939 and located on Dixon Street, this organisation began as a Chinese Youth Dramatic Association with the aim to raise money for China through dramatic performances.[25] But the CYL was also involved in direct political work, particularly with the Chinese Seamen's Union, supporting Chinese seamen stranded in Sydney during the Pacific War. During the Cold War in the 1950s and 1960s, the CYL was suspected of spying for the People's Republic of China by ASIO, Australia's security intelligence organisation.[26] Today, the CYL remains one of the most active Chinese organisations in Sydney, dedicating itself primarily to the promotion of Chinese cultural activities such as lion and dragon dancing, Cantonese opera, *wushu* (武術, lit. martial arts), and dragon boat racing.[27]

The White Australia policy (白澳政策) made life difficult for Chinese in the first half of the twentieth century. The Chinese population declined to its lowest level by mid-century as many returned to China, especially those aged sixty and above, suggesting that they tended to return to their ancestral home to retire.[28] Some were unable to return, as it became increasingly difficult after 1937 due to the Japanese invasion and the civil war between the Nationalists and the Communists in China; ageing market gardeners and labourers retired to boarding houses in the Haymarket where they could be cared for by the Chinese benevolent associations.[29] These were the so-called left-over men, forced to spend their lonely final days in meagre lodgings in the Chinese enclave.[30] Death and emigration resulted in the decline of the area, whose population was increasingly dominated by old men.

After the Second World War the decline of the Chinese population over the period from 1901 to 1947 was compensated for by new arrivals. Political change in China in 1949 resulted in a stream of refugees from the mainland, some of whom ended up in Australia. There was also a gradual increase in the entry of students of Chinese heritage, who came to Australia via Hong Kong,[31] or from Southeast Asian countries such as Malaysia and Singapore, who were allowed in ostensibly as part of Australia's Colombo Plan from 1951, though most were self-funded.[32] While many of these students later returned to their home countries, a significant number came to stay. More generally, immigration restrictions were gradually relaxed from

---

25. Fitzgerald, *Red Tape*, 174.
26. Drew Cottle and Angela Keys, 'Red-Hunting in Sydney's Chinatown', *Journal of Australian Studies* 31, no. 91 (2007): 28, https://doi.org/10.1080/14443050709388125.
27. Chinese Youth League website, http://www.cyl.org.au/.
28. Choi, *Chinese Migration*, 45.
29. Choi, *Chinese Migration*, 51–52.
30. Fitzgerald, *Red Tape*, 153.
31. Both Douglas Lam and Kam Louie, whose life stories are told in Chapter 3 of this volume, came to Australia as students in the early 1960s.
32. The Colombo Plan was a post-colonial Commonwealth initiative launched in 1951 to boost Asian economic and social development through cooperative ventures, including scholarships for students from Asian countries to study in Australia.

the 1950s onwards, making it easier for local Chinese merchants to facilitate the entry of assistants in their businesses, substitutes (of employees who had returned to China), cooks, and dependants. When the Australian government decided to grant naturalisation rights to the Chinese in 1956, many more women also began to arrive.[33]

These developments resulted in a significant increase in Sydney's Chinese population, which rose from 3,300 in 1947 to 9,943 in 1966.[34] However, most of the increase was absorbed not into the urban centre, but into the outer zones of the city. Wealthy merchants and their families relocated to the suburbs, and new arrivals tended to bypass the traditional gateway locations in the inner city and also moved straight to the suburbs.[35] This suburbanisation of the Chinese led to a process of assimilation where they adopted, to all intents and purposes, the Australian way of life.[36] Many of these Chinese were not at all connected to the city's de facto Chinatown in Haymarket.[37] By the mid-1960s, only about 15 per cent of Chinese residents lived in the inner city, down from almost 50 per cent in 1947. The Dixon Street area still hosted Chinese organisations, such as the Chinese Youth League and the Kuomintang on Ultimo Road, but otherwise it was quite moribund, with a residential population that consisted mostly of the old, least assimilated, and least 'successful'. The area was certainly not a thriving Chinatown at that time. As a city council official commented, 'one does admit to a sense of shame when one shows a San Franciscan our version of a "Chinatown"'.[38] Things only started to change in the 1970s, when Australia adopted policies of multiculturalism. The Haymarket area, with Dixon Street as its core, was transformed into what is today's Chinatown – with its characteristic Chinatown gates and stereotypical Orientalist paraphernalia such as green upturned roofs, pagodas, and red lanterns that mark 'Chinatownness' the world over – as part of the city council's effort to revitalise the precinct, in collaboration with Haymarket Chinese businesspeople.[39] It was only then that the label 'Chinatown' became the official name for this revamped inner city Sydney district, opened by Lord Mayor Nelson Meers to great fanfare in 1980.

---

33. Choi, *Chinese Migration*, 64–66.
34. Choi, *Chinese Migration*, 70.
35. Choi, *Chinese Migration*, 70.
36. Glenn Mar, who grew up in the Sydney suburb of Ryde, describes his family's assimilation into Australianness in Chapter 5 of this volume.
37. Fitzgerald, *Red Tape*, 185.
38. Quoted in Fitzgerald, *Red Tape*, 186–87.
39. For a critical analysis of this redevelopment of 'Chinatown', see Kay Anderson, '"Chinatown Re-oriented": A Critical Analysis of Recent Redevelopment Schemes in a Melbourne and Sydney Enclave', *Australian Geographical Studies* 28, no. 2 (1990): 137–54, https://doi.org/10.1111/j.1467-8470.1990.tb00609.x.

Zhongshan Merchants in Chinatown

As described in this book's Introduction, sojourners and migrants from Zhongshan county made up a large portion of the Chinese who came to Sydney from the mid-nineteenth century onwards. Not surprisingly, they were also heavily represented in Haymarket, and the material traces of their once dominant presence are still visible in today's Chinatown. Choi refers to data indicating that in the first decades of the twentieth century, those originating from Toi Shan (台山, also known as Taishan) and Sun Wui (新會, also known as Xinhui) dominated in Melbourne, while in Sydney and Brisbane the majority of the Chinese were from Zhongshan.[40] An important reason for such differentiated regional concentration was the impact of chain migration or sponsored arrivals. This intensified under the 1901 Immigration Restriction Act, where the dictation test constituted an insurmountable barrier to entry unless one was granted an exemption. Several categories of Chinese migrants were exempted from the dictation test, such as students and merchants. Moreover, merchants were allowed to bring in assistants and special clerks to assist them in their businesses, while assistants and 'substitutes' for local traders and market gardeners, as well as chefs and café workers, were exempted and allowed in on temporary permits from 1934.[41] However, the system of exemptions was a complicated bureaucratic process and required the active sponsorship of a merchant or employer already in Australia, which reinforced the entry of people from the same hometowns or lineages. However, the Act disallowed the entry of wives and dependants, except those of merchants and well-established families.[42] At the time of Federation (1901), Chinese merchants already occupied important positions in the fruit and vegetable markets and import/export trade and had gained respect for 'their capacity for commerce and their more tidy-looking European dress'.[43] In Sydney's Haymarket, a very large number of these merchants had Zhongshan roots.[44]

These merchants and entrepreneurs built their businesses as family firms on the strength of their native-place links and lineage ties, but they also actively expanded their networks beyond the limited circles of kinship and place. As John Fitzgerald has stressed, networks of trust based on lineage and native-place connections were supplemented in Sydney by broader, more inclusive civic networks from the late nineteenth century. The New South Wales Chinese Chamber of Commerce, for example, established in 1903, welcomed representatives of Chinese firms based in

---

40. Choi, *Chinese Migration*, 78.
41. Choi, *Chinese Migration*, 41.
42. Choi, *Chinese Migration*, 45.
43. Choi, *Chinese Migration*, 34.
44. One reason for this could be Zhongshan's unique geographic position adjacent to the entrepôts of Macau and Canton (Guangzhou), and not too far from Hong Kong, exposing people from Zhongshan early to trade and commerce. Many Zhongshan men became compradors. See Pui Tak Lee, 'Business Networks and Patterns of Cantonese Compradors and Merchants in Nineteenth-Century Hong Kong', *Journal of the Hong Kong Branch of the Royal Asiatic Society* 31 (1991): 1–39.

NSW drawn from every region in China. Around sixty firms joined the chamber over its first year of operation.[45] Other important organisations that transcended familial and regional boundaries include the Sydney Presbyterian Chinese Mission, the Chinese Masonic Society, and the Australasian KMT. It is noteworthy, however, that while the KMT was officially a national political party, open to all Chinese residents, its Sydney headquarters on Haymarket's Ultimo Road was dominated by a small coterie of leading merchant families with strong nativist links with Zhongshan. These Zhongshan merchants were particularly drawn to Sun Yat-sen's KMT because Sun's home village was in Heung Shan (Zhongshan), but they were also astute in using the KMT's extensive party networks, not just in Australasia but reaching out to the Pacific and back to Hong Kong and South China, as springboards for their entrepreneurial endeavours, thus mixing business and politics. John Fitzgerald quotes the journalist Vivian Chow, himself of Dongguan (東莞) parentage, who complained in 1933 that 'the Sydney Kuo Min Tang is dominated by the Heungshan [香山, Zhongshan] natives or descendants of men from there', at the expense of people from other counties.[46] Such tensions between parochialism and nationalism highlight the intimate entanglement of local and trans-local loyalties and connections that provided Zhongshan merchants in Haymarket with the networks that enabled them to operate highly successful businesses, starting out in the Haymarket area but from there spreading out to become large, transnational enterprises, while maintaining strong connections with their ancestral districts in Zhongshan.

Many of these merchants purchased properties in the Haymarket district for their businesses, and some of these still exist today, although they have long ceased operating in their original form. Such properties constitute part of the Sydney end of the transnational heritage corridor that links Zhongshan with Australia; their histories bear witness to the circulation of people, money, goods, and ideas across the condensed zone of flows generated within the corridor. Far from having only local meaning in the Sydney context, therefore, the significance of these properties must be understood in the light of the expansive transnational connections and diasporic networks that they accommodated. Here, we will focus on two businesses in Haymarket which epitomise the vitality and dynamism of the Zhongshan–Sydney corridor throughout much of the twentieth century: the Kwong War Chong (廣和昌) general store and trading company, and the Wing Sang banana and fruit company (永生果欄).

---

45. John Fitzgerald, *Great White Lie: Chinese Australians in White Australia* (Sydney: UNSW Press, 2007), 181–85.

46. Fitzgerald, *Great White Lie*, 161–62. As a contrast to the 1930s, by the second half of the twentieth century, one of Cheng's informants (see Chapter 7 of this volume) ran a hugely popular 'long and short soup' (wonton noodle soup) shop, the Lean Sun Lowe café (聯新樓) in Chinatown. It was a successful case of an intermarriage and fruitful business cooperation between a Dongguan man and a Zhongshan woman.

Kwong War Chong (廣和昌)

Community networks among Chinese before the Second World War were to a large extent organised through kinship ties and native-place associations, and less through the generic identification of 'Chinese'. Dialect and village or district of origin played a substantial role in migrants' distinct senses of fellowship and belonging, and they formed the basis for regionally organised 'native-place associations' (同鄉會 *tongxianghui* in Mandarin). These associations were essentially self-help organisations through which migrants maintained links with their villages back home, but they were also gathering places to network for partnerships in stores and market gardens, to borrow money, and – importantly – to arrange remittance letters back home and even marriages, as well as the return of bones of deceased migrants. These were exclusive organisations: one could become a member only if one hailed from the relevant district.[47] In Sydney's budding Chinatown, the Goon Yee Tong (澳洲東莞同鄉會公義堂), formed by Chinese from the Dongguan district of Guangdong, and the Loong Yee Tong (聯義堂), a joint association for migrants from Dongguan and Zengcheng (增城), acquired newly built premises on 50 Dixon Street in 1917, which are still owned by these associations.[48]

Interestingly, however, a Zhongshan native-place society no longer exists in the core of Chinatown. A specific Long Du society,[49] the Heung Yup Long Du Tong Sen Tong (香邑隆都同善堂), was established in 1906, but it appears to have been dissolved by the 1930s.[50] It is not known why this happened, but it could be speculated that as many Zhongshan people became merchants and there were fewer market gardeners among them, general stores could handle issues such as remittances and other matters without the need for a more formal organisation.[51] These Chinese Australian stores had also founded their businesses on a 'native place' basis, and as such they acted as social hubs for people of the same district, where they could share gossip and news in their own dialect. In this way the stores were assured of a loyal customer base and generated handsome profits for store owners by providing a range of services to assist the migrants in maintaining their links with the home village or *qiaoxiang* (僑鄉). By the 1920s, the main Zhongshan firms in Sydney, such as Wing On, On Yik Lee (安益利), and Kwong War Chong, not only provided remittance and letter writing services but also paid fares back to China, purchased tickets, arranged Immigration Restriction Act–related paper work, provided accommodation, and even lent money for a migrant's first remittance home.[52] These

---

47. Michael Williams, *Returning Home with Glory: Chinese Villagers around the Pacific, 1849 to 1949* (Hong Kong: Hong Kong University Press, 2018), 114–17.
48. Fitzgerald, *Red Tape*, 157.
49. Long Du is a district of Zhongshan, consisting of eighty villages and speaking the distinctive Long Du dialect.
50. Williams, *Returning Home with Glory*, 116, note 114. More recently, the Chung Shan Society of Australia was established in 1982, with premises in Albion Street, Surry Hills.
51. Michael Williams, email communication, 1 July 2021.
52. Williams, *Returning Home with Glory*, 117–18.

Sydney-based stores were able to provide these services because they were part of a network of stores related by ownership and/or common partners in Hong Kong and the home districts.

The Kwong War Chong was a very prominent store for Long Du (隆都) people. It was a general store and trading company established by Phillip Lee Chun (李臨春, 1865–1935) with several business partners in 1883. Lee Chun was born in the village of Chung Tau (涌頭村) in Zhongshan's Long Du district (present-day Shaxi town 沙溪鎮) and came to Australia in 1875. According to his descendants he landed at Cooktown in Northern Queensland at the end of the Palmer River gold rush and from there made his way to Sydney.[53] By the 1900s, Lee Chun was one of Sydney's most successful Chinese merchants. In 1907, for example, celebrations for his fiftieth birthday were extensively reported on in the *Chinese Australian Herald* (廣益華報), along with a family photograph with his wife and two of his children, all dressed in traditional Chinese attire. Two hundred well-wishers participated in the celebrations with food, music, and firecrackers.[54] He was a naturalised British subject, signalling his relative standing in white Australia and giving him privileges that many other Chinese in Australia did not have, such as bringing his wife into the country.

Lee Chun was one of the first Chinese merchants who bought land on Dixon Street soon after the city council's decision to relocate the produce markets in 1909. Here he erected what were then known as the Canton Buildings, a three-storey brick building in Edwardian style consisting of two premises side by side, which became 82–84 Dixon Street.[55] In November 1910 the Kwong War Chong store was moved into no. 84 from its original location at 46 Campbell Street, while no. 82 was tenanted to a restaurant, the Moon Hoon Jam (滿香棧). This restaurant also relocated from Campbell Street, and it offered accommodation in its upstairs rooms. By this time Lee Chun was the controlling partner of Kwong War Chong; he eventually bought out all his partners and converted it into a family business.

Phillip Lee Chun was a leading member of the Heung Yup Long Du Tong Sen Tong, the Long Du native-place society. In fact, his Kwong War Chong store functioned as a central hub for the community of Long Du people; members of the community often met on the third floor of 82 Dixon Street.[56] For many years a photograph of one such meeting, featuring a dozen members including Phillip

---

53. Malcolm Oakes SC, 'William Lee: First Barrister of Chinese Descent Admitted to the New South Wales Bar', *Bar News: The Journal of the New South Wales Bar Association* (Winter 2015): 73, https://nswbar.asn.au/docs/webdocs/BN_022015_lee.pdf.

54. As reported in the *Chinese Australian Herald*, 23 March–13 April 1907, https://trove.nlaf.gov.au/newspaper/article/168794703. Information and translation provided by Ely Finch, 'Summary of Australian Chinese-Language Newspaper Content That Relates to the Sydney Firm of Kwong War Chong', commissioned by the Chinese Australian Historical Society, Melbourne (August 2020).

55. Hector Abraham Architects, *82–84 Dixon Street, Haymarket Heritage Assessment for City of Sydney Council* (15 July 2019), 4, https://meetings.cityofsydney.nsw.gov.au/documents/s33419/Attachment%20A2%20-%20Planning%20Proposal%20Appendix%201%20-%20Heritage%20Assessment.pdf.

56. Williams, *Chinese Settlement in NSW*, 57.

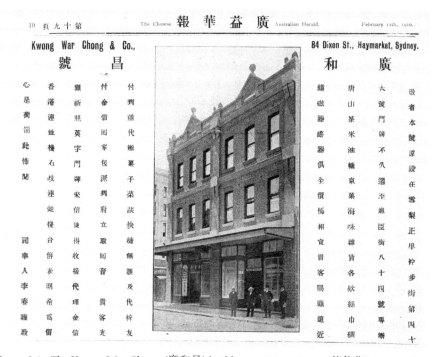

Figure 8.1: The Kwong War Chong (廣和昌) building in Dixon Street (德信街), Haymarket (孖結／禧市) in 1910.

Lee Chun himself, hung on one of the walls of the Kwong War Chong shop.[57] The Kwong War Chong also hosted Sunday lunches for Long Du market gardeners. The gardeners would stay overnight in upstairs dormitories after selling vegetables at the markets on Saturday, and the Sunday lunches were an important opportunity for them to socialise before returning to their often isolated gardens.[58] In this way, the Kwong War Chong combined community service with a highly profitable commercial enterprise, providing not just imported Chinese groceries and products but also remittances and all services related to the arrangements of going from and back to the home villages. In 1916, for example, the Kwong War Chong was reported to be the Sydney store that issued the most ship tickets for Chinese people returning to China.[59]

By the 1930s Phillip Lee Chun's connections were so successful that he had not only established partnerships with similar remittance stores in Hong Kong and Long Du, as was usual among overseas Chinese merchants, but had also founded

---

57. This photograph is reproduced in Shirley Fitzgerald's book *Red Tape Gold Scissors* on pages 72–73. It is unknown where the photograph is today.
58. Williams, *Returning Home with Glory*, 119.
59. *Chinese Australian Herald*, 30 September 1916, in Ely Finch, 'Summary'.

branch stores in both Hong Kong and the Zhongshan county capital of Shekki (石岐).[60] These branches were a key component in the arrangement of remittances to Chinese families in the home villages. A small commission would be charged for each individual remittance, a standard letter written to the family to accompany the payment, and a bank draft drawn to be sent to the Hong Kong branch of the Kwong War Chong, and from there sent to the Shekki branch, which would then distribute the money to the families. A receipt, including a letter back to Sydney, would be signed and returned to the shop in Dixon Street, where it was put on a rack in the front window for the recipient to collect.[61]

Lee Chun's prominence and influence as a community leader extended beyond Sydney and the Long Du/Zhongshan community. For example, he was a member of the Chinese Merchants Anti-Opium League, which was instrumental in having opium banned in NSW, and he was a part-owner of the Chinese-language newspaper the *Chinese Republic News* (民國報). He often participated in official Chinese Australian delegations and was actively involved in diasporic Chinese politics, for example in relation to an international boycott of Japanese goods as part of China's efforts to assert its independence against colonial powers, and in fundraising for the Republican cause of Sun Yat-sen's Kuomintang. Lee Chun also donated generously to philanthropic causes in Zhongshan, for example for the construction of a *diaolou* (碉樓, fortified tower, pronounced in Mandarin) in his home village of Chung Tau as protection against bandits, and for Zhongshan's Oi Wai Hospital (愛惠醫院).[62]

Michael Williams notes that merchants such as Phillip Lee Chun performed their important leadership roles through their ability to in some measure cross the racial boundaries that made life so difficult for ordinary Chinese residents. Kwong War Chong's store managers and clerks were sufficiently familiar with English and European ways to overcome some of the ruling racial biases.[63]

Lee Chun returned to Hong Kong with his wife and children in 1932, where he died a few years later. His only daughter, Lily Lee, accompanied the body back to the ancestral village, where he was buried. His sons Harry and William Lee stayed in Sydney to look after the business, but William, who had spent much of his youth in Hong Kong studying Chinese, was anxious to get out and went to study law at Sydney University. He became the first barrister of Chinese descent in New South Wales in 1938.[64] Their brother Norman Lee later took over from Harry in running the business and attended the shop for many decades until it was closed in 1987. After that, 84 Dixon Street was turned into a tea house and gift shop named Live Craft Centre, where Norman could still be found giving assistance to those in need

---

60. Williams, *Returning Home with Glory*, 86.
61. Michael Williams, 'Historical Notes on 82–84 Dixon Street', 2018, Chinese Australian Historical Society website, https://cahsociety.files.wordpress.com/2018/05/84-dixon-st-heritage.pdf.
62. Finch, 'Summary'.
63. Williams, 'Historical Notes', 5.
64. Oakes, 'William Lee', 73.

even in his retirement. The building's façade and original shop front remained in place. 82 Dixon Street was rented out over the years to various entities, and from 1971 it was the home of Hingara Chinese Restaurant, run by Eva Lee, widow of Harry Lee, and So Lin Wang Pang.[65] When the restaurant closed in 2017 after forty-six years in business, it was described in the media as a 'stalwart' of the Chinatown restaurant scene.[66]

When the Lee family sold 82–84 Dixon Street for A\$20 million in 2017 after more than a century's ownership, it marked the end of an era in the history of Chinese Sydney and, more particularly, the history of Zhongshan presence in Chinatown. Sydney's Chinese community went into action when it was reported that the new owner intended to demolish and redevelop the site, threatening to destroy this precious material link to history. In response, the city council made an interim heritage order to assess the heritage significance of the property in March 2019. An independent heritage assessment was conducted by Hector Abraham Architects in July 2019, and submissions were made by the Chinese Australian Historical Society (CAHS) and others to convince the council and the public that this building had heritage significance and needed to be preserved. The council agreed, arguing that 'the retention and potential adaptive reuse of the Edwardian building at 82–84 Dixon Street will maintain links to the Chinese-Australian community and has the potential to enhance the character by contributing to the distinct sense of place of Chinatown'.[67] In April 2020, the NSW Government's Department of Planning, Industry and Environment approved the listing of the building on the State Heritage Inventory. The statement of significance declares that the former Kwong War Chong building is representative of 'the history of Sydney's Chinatown and twentieth century Chinese Australian commerce and settlement in Sydney', which is 'embodied in the intact exterior of the whole building and in the interior architecture of 84 Dixon Street'. The statement mentions a range of material features of the building, as well as objects and ephemera that were found inside it: original façade, shop front, partitions, doors, stairs, and hand-operated goods lift, as well as packing-crate furniture, washing machines, bathtubs, calendars, crockery, merchandise, and personal effects. In summary, the statement confirmed that the Kwong War Chong building satisfied all the criteria of the Heritage Council for local heritage significance. The recommendation was made that much of the building and its contents should be conserved, and that a museum should be considered,

---

65. Sydney City Council, *Heritage Inventory for Former Kwong War Chong & Company Buildings, Including Interiors and Contents of No. 84*, 20 November 2019, https://meetings.cityofsydney.nsw.gov.au/documents/ s37143/Attachment%20D%20-%20Heritage%20Inventory%20for%20Former%20Kwong%20War%20 Chong%20Company%20Building%20Including%20Interiors.pdf. The store signage suggests its Chinese name was '*Sing sin zau ka*' 聖膳酒家, but Cantonese-speaking patrons such as Douglas Lam knew it better as '*hung ya*' 幸雅.
66. Scott Bolles, 'Chinatown Stalwart Hingara Restaurant Serves Last Dumplings', *Good Food*, 27 July 2017, https:// www.goodfood.com.au/eat-out/news/chinatown-stalwart-to-serve-last-dumplings-20170721-gxfucw.
67. Sydney City Council, 'Heritage Inventory'.

'demonstrating domestic and commercial life of the Chinese diaspora people living in Sydney in the early mid-twentieth century'.[68]

This official recognition of the heritage significance of the Kwong War Chong provides a measure of protection against demolition, paving the way for this 'rare surviving link to early Chinatown' to play a role in keeping alive the memory of a time when the Chinese Australian community went through a period of cultural isolation as a consequence of the White Australia policy, and the legacy of Zhongshan merchants such as Phillip Lee Chun in establishing an enduring Chinese footprint in the architectural and cultural-historical fabric of Sydney. Moreover, it is important to stress that the economic, cultural, and community functions of the Kwong War Chong were critical not just for the local history of the Chinese in Sydney, but also for their history of transnational interconnectedness and mobility that linked them to other places, in particular their home villages in Zhongshan. In other words, the Kwong War Chong is a valuable landmark in the Zhongshan–Sydney heritage corridor.

Wing Sang & Co. (永生果欄)

The case of the Kwong War Chong highlights the importance of the remittance trade in the Zhongshan–Sydney corridor. This trade thrived on the social networks and native-place associations that linked merchants and migrants in a quasi-familial relationship of trust that underpinned the profitability of the business. This close link between commercial transactions and native-place loyalties was central to the business model of stores such as the Kwong War Chong, which provided the remittance service through networks of trade that linked the shop in Chinatown with the villages in Zhongshan. The connection with the *qiaoxiang*, in short, was the cultural rationale sustaining these business activities.

However, some Zhongshan entrepreneurs in Sydney went much further in their business pursuits than capitalising on their countrymen's attachment to their families and home villages. Wing Sang & Co. was one of the most prominent cases in this regard. Wing Sang (永生 meaning 'Eternity' in Chinese) was founded in 1890, originally as a fruit store, by a group of Chinese who all came from Zhongshan: George Bew (郭標), Choy Hing (蔡興), Ma Ying Piu (馬應彪), and Mark Joe (also known as Ma Wing Charn) (馬永燦). The company's fortunes were derived from the highly profitable Australian banana trade, over which Wing Sang – together with other large Chinese Australian fruit firms such as Tiy Sang (泰生果欄 established in 1893) and Wing On (永安果欄 established in 1898) – had majority control by the turn of the century. The firm began to trade with Queensland banana growers

---

68. Former Kwong War Chong & Company building, including interiors and contents of No. 84, Statement of Significance, https://apps.environment.nsw.gov.au/dpcheritageapp/ViewHeritageItemDetails.aspx?ID= 5067050.

in 1894, and by 1899 it handled 7,000 bunches of bananas per week from Northern Queensland.[69] But the Sydney Chinese fruit traders also aspired to exploit the banana industry in Fiji, where they saw greater potential than in Queensland. In 1902 three firms, Wing Sang, Wing On, and Wing Tiy, amalgamated to form Sang On Tiy and Co. (生安泰), which cultivated and shipped bananas from Fiji to Sydney at a rate of at least 2,000 bunches a week, adding dramatically to these traders' wealth but also increasing anti-Chinese sentiment due to the formidable competition they posed to European traders.[70] The involvement of these fruit merchants in the banana industry in Fiji allowed them to prosper despite disasters such as the cyclone that destroyed a large part of the banana crop in Queensland in 1906. By the end of that year, they monopolised the banana trade.[71] They also sponsored large numbers of Zhongshan natives to enter Fiji and establish local small businesses there that became part of their burgeoning transnational business networks.[72] At the same time, they arranged the remittances of these Fijian Chinese back to Zhongshan.[73] In this way, Fiji became a significant node in the Zhongshan–Sydney corridor.

Thus, the wealth generated by Wing Sang and similar companies was based not only on the banana trade, but also on the remittance business. As Mei-fen Kuo has suggested, the remittance trade had economic pay-offs that far transcended the parochial interests of native-place associations. Kuo notes that from the 1890s until the 1910s Chinese Australian remittances benefited from the currency exchange market because of Australia's economic wealth at that time, together with British imperial power, as Australia complied with London's adherence to the gold standard on the exchange market.[74] During this period, Sydney Chinese sent huge amounts of gold to Hong Kong, which was converted into cash at highly lucrative exchange rates, providing them with capital to invest in new businesses. In other words, the remittance network enabled Sydney Chinese merchants to circulate capital in order to expand their enterprises. As these merchants were aware that any expansion of their businesses in Australia would be stymied by White Australia restrictions, they sought opportunities to expand their Sydney family companies in Hong Kong and China.[75] In the process, they turned their companies into sprawling transnational firms in a burgeoning capitalist world economy, foreshadowing the flexible

---

69. Mei-fen Kuo, *Making Chinese Australia: Urban Elites, Newspapers and the Formation of Chinese-Australian Identity, 1892–1912* (Clayton, Victoria: Monash University Publishing, 2013), 107–8.

70. Kuo, *Making Chinese Australia*, 54, 107–8.

71. Kuo, *Making Chinese Australia*, 152.

72. Fitzgerald, *Big White Lie*, 163.

73. Mei-fen Kuo, '*Jinxin*: The Remittance Trade and Enterprising Chinese Australians, 1850–1916', in *The Qiaopi Trade and Transnational Networks in the Chinese Diaspora*, ed. Gregor Benton, Hong Liu, and Huimei Zhang (New York: Routledge, 2018), 160.

74. Kuo, '*Jinxin*', 158. Kuo describes how, over the 1914–1916 period, the Australian government targeted the Chinese gold exports and introduced a limit to gold exports of £50 per person, putting an end to the lucrative gold-based remittance trade. This led to the transfer of remittances to mail and telegram (159).

75. Fitzgerald, *Big White Lie*, 179.

citizenship practices that Chinese diaspora entrepreneurs adopted across the Asia-Pacific a century later in the most recent era of globalisation.[76]

Central to this was the role of Hong Kong as a hub for the massive flow of people and goods (and money) from and to South China that had evolved as a result of the emigration of men to far-flung corners of the world.[77] So-called Gold Mountain firms (金山莊 *jinshanzhuang* in Mandarin) sprung up in Hong Kong to cater to the needs of these emigrants. These firms began in Hong Kong as grocery exporters, especially to the large overseas Chinese communities in California, but they grew in response to the desire of customers overseas to maintain contact with their families and native places, expanding their businesses to include postal, banking, and remittance activities.[78]

Sydney Chinese merchants adopted the *jinshanzhuang* model in their business expansions, but they also transcended this model. For example, Ma Ying Piu (1868–1944), one of Wing Sang's founders, made several journeys from Sydney to Hong Kong, where he eventually settled and set up his new business, the Wing Chong Tai (永昌泰) *jinshanzhuang*, as early as 1894.[79] The lucrative yield from gold exports in the Chinese Australian remittance trade was considerable at a time when gold exports from San Francisco were declining.[80] The accumulated capital was invested over time in new business ventures that were transnational in scope, most famously in the 'big four' department stores (四大公司) that the founders of Wing Sang variously spawned: Sincere (先施百貨), Wing On (永安百貨), The Sun (大新百貨), and Sun Sun Company (新新百貨).[81] Ma Ying Piu established the first of these, the Sincere department store, in Hong Kong in 1900, calling on his long-standing business partners at Wing Sang in Sydney (including Choy Hing and George Bew) and others to raise the necessary funds. By 1916 the company boasted paid-up capital of HK$2 million raised from small investors in Australasia and North America, and branches were opened in Canton (1912), Singapore (1917), and Shanghai (1917). The grandest department store, The Sun Company store in Shanghai, was established by Wing Sang co-founder Choy Hing and his brother Choy Chong (蔡昌) in 1936.[82] The link to the ancestral villages in Zhongshan was not forgotten: the Sincere and Wing On department stores also had branches in Shekki, Zhongshan's urban

---

76. Aihwa Ong, *Flexible Citizenship: The Cultural Logics of Transnationality* (Durham, NC: Duke University Press, 1999).

77. Elizabeth Sinn, 'Hong Kong as an In-Between Place in the Chinese Diaspora, 1848–1939', in *Connecting Seas and Connected Ocean Rims*, ed. Donna R. Gabaccia and Dirk Hoerder (Leiden: Brill, 2011), 225–47.

78. Madeline Hsu, 'Trading with Gold Mountain: *Jinshanzhuang* and Networks of Kinship and Native Place', in *Chinese American Transnationalism: The Flow of People, Resources, and Ideas between China and America during the Exclusion Era*, ed. Sucheng Chan (Philadelphia, PA: Temple University Press, 2006), 22–33.

79. Fitzgerald, *Big White Lie*, 195; Kuo, '*Jinxin*', 160.

80. Kuo, '*Jinxin*', 162.

81. Fitzgerald, *Big White Lie*, 194–99.

82. Fitzgerald, *Big White Lie*, 196–97.

centre,[83] and all these department stores employed hundreds of villagers from their founders' ancestral homes in their Shanghai and other big-city branches.[84]

Wing Sang is thus an outstanding example of how some market gardeners from Zhongshan became local and regional fruit merchants in Sydney, and from there went on to establish large transnational enterprises. As Mei-fen Kuo notes, 'their experience in the banana trade inspired and equipped the Sydney businessmen to join an international-level financial elite'.[85] In 1919 Wing Sang in Hong Kong became a limited liability company and in 1921 it became Wing Sang's head office.[86] The original founders of the company had long since moved to Hong Kong and China, but they retained their branch in Sydney. George Bew (1868–1932), one of Wing Sang's founders, became the general manager of Wing On in Shanghai in 1917 and was a highly successful entrepreneur in China in the 1920s and 1930s, but as Kuo describes, quoting his daughter, he liked to reminisce about his early life as a banana trader in Sydney.[87]

The Sydney branch of Wing Sang continued to be a successful fruit and banana company, and it is this part of Wing Sang that had a long-standing presence in Chinatown. From 1918 it was managed by Mar Sun Gee (馬辛巳), who belonged to the same clan from Sha Chong village (沙涌村), Zhongshan, as Wing Sang founders Ma Ying Piu and Ma Wing Charn.[88] After Sun Gee's death in 1937 the management of the company was passed on to his son Harry Mar (馬亮華 Mar Leong Wah), and when the latter retired in the late 1970s, his son Gordon Mar (馬國棟) took over. Gordon arranged the relocation of Wing Sang to Flemington, a suburb in Western Sydney, where the Sydney produce market had moved from its Haymarket location in 1975. In 1984, Gordon sold the company, marking the end of Wing Sang, saying that the present generation of his family was no longer interested in the banana trade.[89]

In Haymarket, Wing Sang operated at several locations at different times during its almost one hundred years in existence.[90] The company's first premises, at 26–28 Campbell Street, was opposite the Belmore growers' market. In 1895, the company rented the larger part of a three-storey commercial building at 18–22 Campbell Street; this Victorian Federation–style building still stands today. Around 1909, Wing Sang expanded to a grand warehouse on 90 Hay Street, close to where the markets had relocated, and in 1912, the company leased a three-storey warehouse

---

83. Williams, *Returning Home with Glory*, 86.
84. Fitzgerald, *Big White Lie*, 199.
85. Kuo, *Making Chinese Australia*, 153.
86. Kuo, '*Jinxin*', 162.
87. Kuo, *Making Chinese Australia*, 153–54.
88. As Glenn and Phillip Mar write in Chapter 5 of this volume, their grandfather Mar See Poy was also a manager for Wing Sang, arriving in Sydney in 1914 but forced to return to China in 1926.
89. Gordon Mar, interview by Ien Ang and Alexandra Wong, 21 September 2018. See Chapter 3 of this volume for a longer discussion of Gordon Mar's life trajectory.
90. See the entry on the Wing Sang & Co. buildings, Sydney, on the Heritage Corridors project website, https://www.heritagecorridor.org.au/places/the-wing-sang-co-buildings-sydney.

Figure 8.2: The Wing Sang & Co. (永生果欄) building on the corner of Sussex and Hay Streets. Courtesy of City of Sydney Archives, circa 1910.

at 58 Hay Street from the city council as its head office and banana ripening plant, occupying it until 1975, when the company moved to Flemington near the new growers' market. As was common practice among Chinese businesses in the area, the upper floors of the building were turned into accommodation for employees, many of whom had migrated from Zhongshan, especially from the Ma/r clan (馬氏) of Sha Chong village, sponsored by Wing Sang. 58 Hay Street was demolished in 1980 to make way for Sydney's new Entertainment Centre.

Wing Sang's footprint is thus no longer part of Sydney Chinatown's built environment and heritage landscape. Gordon Mar salvaged some moveable items from Wing Sang's premises before he closed the business, such as an advertising sign, an abacus, and two fruit merchant's aprons, and he has donated these to the Museum of Applied Arts and Sciences, which has made these items accessible on its website as part of its digital collection.[91] These are the few remaining material

---

91. https://collection.maas.museum/object/380436; https://collection.maas.museum/object/380446; https://collection.maas.museum/object/380423.

traces of this remarkable business which contributed so much to the dynamics of the Zhongshan–Sydney heritage corridor, exemplifying an expansive transnational reach and impact that marks an enduring legacy of Australia's connection with China.

Zhongshan in Chinatown from the 1950s to the Present

In the 1950s and 1960s the Dixon Street area was in relative decline, but it was still a preferred site for new migrants to set up their businesses. Some of these went on to shape the emergence of a properly recognised 'Chinatown' in the 1970s. They also played an important part in the continuation of the Zhongshan–Sydney connection in the post-war era.

Say Tin Fong (方瑞田) was born in Duntao village (敦陶村) in Zhongshan and migrated to Fiji in 1932, where he ran a mixed grocery store and milk bar. He embodied the significant place of Fiji as a node in the Zhongshan–Sydney corridor. At the end of the Second World War, Fong decided to return to Zhongshan with his wife and children. As the first leg of their journey they were allowed to travel to Sydney on an American warship that was picking up American soldiers from the base near their Suva shop. They arrived in Sydney on 18 March 1946. But when Fong learned that civil war had broken out in China between the Communists and the Nationalists, he decided to stay in Australia on a 'merchant status' visa, which required him to import or export goods valued at £10,000 per year for fifteen years before the family could obtain permanent residency in Australia. Fong rented premises at 56–58 Dixon Street in Haymarket in 1949 and opened Say Tin Fong & Co., selling Chinese groceries, kitchenware, and arts and crafts. He purchased the building a few years later and renovated the upper levels into a lodging house for Chinese boarders. There were ninety-two rooms, each three by three metres in size.[92]

Say Tin Fong's son King Fong (方勁武), born in Fiji in 1938, took over as general manager in 1958 and ran the business until he retired in 1986. He sold the building, which was turned into what is today the Sussex Centre, a modern Asian-style shopping mall in the heart of Sydney's Chinatown. King Fong has been an active leader in Sydney's Chinese community since the 1960s and was a member of the Dixon Street Chinese Committee, which worked with Sydney City Council to redevelop Chinatown in the 1970s. He helped organise fundraising campaigns to build the Chinese-style ceremonial archways (with stone lions) at both ends of Dixon Street and a Chinese-style pavilion, which were officially opened in 1980. As a descendant of a Zhongshan family, King was also an active member of the Chung Shan Society

---

92. Say Tin Fong's story was told by his son King Fong, interview by Ien Ang, Denis Byrne, and Alexandra Wong, 17 March 2017.

of Australia (澳洲中山同鄉會), founded in 1982 and located on Albion Street in nearby Surry Hills, of which he was the president between 2000 and 2005.

Another Zhongshan migrant who has contributed greatly to Chinatown's rejuvenation is Stanley Yee (余金晃 Yee Kam Fong), who was born in the 1940s in Chuen Luk village (全祿村, Quanlucun), Dachong district (大涌), in Zhongshan. His family fled to Macau to escape the political turmoil after Mao came to power in 1949, where he studied as a youngster before travelling to Sydney. Stanley was part of the cohort of young Chinese people who came to Sydney as high school students in the early 1960s. While studying Stanley worked part-time in one of Haymarket's banana wholesale companies and as a kitchen hand, and from 1972 he was active in the Chinatown restaurant industry. In 1979 he opened Emperor's Garden (皇冠海鮮酒樓), a Cantonese-style seafood restaurant located on the corner of Dixon and Hay Street, now right next to Chinatown's southern ceremonial arch. The restaurant benefited from Chinatown's new status as a tourist destination and helped introduce traditional Cantonese delicacies (點心 *dim sum* in Cantonese) in the form of *yum cha* (飲茶) to a larger Sydney customer base. Two major expansions in the 1980s saw the restaurant grow from a small, eighty-seat space to a two-storey restaurant seating 350 (see Figure 8.3). Yee also established a number of other businesses in the Chinatown area, including a Chinese bakery, a butchery, and a tofu factory. When he retired in 1999, management of the business was handed over to his sons Valentine (余威麟) and Jonathan Yee (余威達).

While firmly established in Sydney and Australia, the Yee family has retained strong connections with Zhongshan. Stanley has returned regularly to Macau, where he spent part of his childhood, and to his ancestral village in Zhongshan, donating generously for infrastructure such as a school, a community centre, and a kindergarten.[93] In 2004 he was awarded the Honorary Citizen of Zhongshan (中山市榮譽市民) title for his contributions to his hometown. He was also offered the title of Honorary Life President of the Chung Shan Society of Australia (澳洲中山同鄉會永遠榮譽會長). His Sydney-born son Jonathan, meanwhile, is also active in the Chung Shan Society of Australia (澳洲中山同鄉會), serving as its president for several years. He sees the association's role especially as a cultural one, promoting Zhongshanese culture, especially its dialects. One of the things he has been trying to do is to expand the membership of the organisation to a younger generation, which, he says, means 'forty and above'.[94] He has also promoted tours for Australian-born Zhongshanese children to Zhongshan, where they are introduced to Chinese cultural traditions such as the lion and dragon dance, tea culture, and Chinese calligraphy. In this he has received organisational and financial support from the Overseas

---

93. Stanley Yee was a significant educational philanthropist, contributing to a number of schools in Zhongshan. See Chapter 7 of this volume.

94. Jonathan Yee, interview with Ien Ang, Christopher Cheng, and Alexandra Wong, 15 September 2017.

Figure 8.3: The Emperor's Garden Restaurant (皇冠海鮮酒樓), Stanley Yee's restaurant on the corner of Dixon and Hay Streets, Chinatown. Photo by Denis Byrne 2021.

Chinese Affairs Office in Zhongshan (僑務辦公室), with which the Chung Shan Society of Australia has a close relationship.

People such as King Fong, and Stanley and Jonathan Yee, demonstrate that the Zhongshan–Sydney corridor has been kept alive by a determination to maintain the links that bind these sites together. Chinatown has been a particularly important hub, where the signature of businesses set up by migrants from Zhongshan is still prominent, representing a distinctly southern Chinese, Cantonese cultural imprint. However, this prominence is likely to diminish as time passes. In recent decades, Sydney's Chinatown has thrived, but in the process it has become a much more hybrid, multi-Asian precinct, where Chinese-origin venues are now complemented by Thai, Malaysian, Korean, Japanese, and other Asian businesses.[95] Most importantly, in the past two decades large numbers of Chinese from other parts of mainland China have migrated to Australia, with many settling in Sydney, including Haymarket.[96] The 2016 census showed that 20 per cent of Haymarket residents who spoke a language other than English at home spoke Mandarin, compared with

---

95. Kay Anderson, Ien Ang, Andrea Del Bono, Donald McNeill, and Alexandra Wong, *Chinatown Unbound* (London: Rowman and Littlefield, 2019), especially Chapters 4, 5, and 7.
96. Barry Li, *The New Chinese: How They Are Changing Australia* (Milton, Qld: Wiley, 2017); Alexandra Wong and Ien Ang, 'From Chinatown to China's Town? The Newest Chinese Diaspora and the Transformation of Sydney's Chinatown', in *New Chinese Migrations: Mobility, Home, Inspirations*, ed. Yuk Wah Chan and Sin Yee Koh (London: Routledge, 2018), 21–38.

5 per cent who spoke Cantonese.[97] This shift is also reflected in the diversification of culinary outlets, with many regional cuisines such as Sichuan, Yunnan, and Uyghur competing with the traditional Cantonese fare served by restaurants such as Emperor's Garden. In fact, Emperor's Garden decided to adapt its menu to cater to the changing face of its customers by adding northern Chinese dishes such as chilli chicken, pig ears, steamed buns, and Peking duck.[98] And, Jonathan Yee adds, while waiting staff in the past were required to speak Cantonese, it is now imperative that they speak Mandarin. Such developments are indicative of a diminishing Zhongshanese – and, more broadly, Cantonese – influence in Chinatown's make-up. Stanley Yee, meanwhile, has plans to knock down his restaurant and build a high-rise in its place, hoping to christen the new building 中山大廈 ('Chung Shan tai ha', meaning 'Zhongshan tower'). With this name, he wishes to remind people of the long-standing contributions of Zhongshan people to Sydney, especially Chinatown.[99]

Conclusion

Many Chinese migrants to Australia in the one hundred years from the mid-nineteenth century hailed from the villages of Zhongshan county. They formed a significant proportion of Chinese who ended up in Sydney. They congregated in areas in the city that were conducive to their livelihoods, first in The Rocks, close to the harbour, and later in and around Dixon Street in the Haymarket district, where the city's produce markets were located. Restrictions imposed by the White Australia policy, which favoured commercial activity as grounds for exemption, were an important reason why the merchant class came to dominate in the Sydney Chinese community. Their businesses were highly successful, and some of these merchants became fabulously wealthy through their establishment of iconic transnational enterprises. At the same time, they maintained their connections with their ancestral villages in Zhongshan by sending remittances, conducting trade, or sponsoring fellow villagers to come to Australia. Many of them operated from their premises in Haymarket, where their stores, warehouses, and boarding houses were concentrated. Their class privilege also enabled them to put a defining stamp on the social and material fabric of the Haymarket district, which was later officially named Sydney's Chinatown.[100]

---

97. Australian Bureau of Statistics. '2016 Census Quick Stats: Haymarket', https://quickstats.censusdata.abs.gov.au/census_services/getproduct/census/2016/quickstat/SSC11877?opendocument.

98. Jason Liu and Heidi Han, 'What's Happening to Chinatown's Cantonese Restaurants?', SBS Mandarin Radio, 13 July 2017, https://www.sbs.com.au/chinese/english/what-s-happening-to-chinatown-s-cantonese-restaurants.

99. Interview with Stanley Yee by Christopher Cheng, 11 March 2022.

100. It should be pointed out that the bias in Chinese diaspora heritage towards merchants and their lineages is amplified by their ability to materialise their legacy in enduring architectural presences, which labourers and other working-class Chinese could not. The strong focus on merchants is also partly due to historians'

By the early twenty-first century, however, the Zhongshanese presence in Chinatown's built environment has begun to disappear, marked by the sale of the Kwong War Chong building and the closure of the Hingara restaurant in 2017. While the remnants of this venue may be preserved for posterity as a result of its eleventh-hour local heritage designation, this would only signify that the dynamic intensity of Zhongshan–Sydney interaction has gradually become a thing of the past. Precisely at this juncture, the Sydney City Council has recognised the significance of this history in the formation not just of Chinatown, but of the entire metropolis of Sydney. It has recently allocated a three-storey heritage building in Haymarket, which was occupied by the Haymarket library, for a new Museum of Chinese in Australia (MOCA).[101] As Lord Mayor Clover Moore declares, 'Haymarket is the home of our city's oldest and largest Chinatown, so it's fitting that this is where we will create a centre for the preservation of our Chinese history'.[102] Tellingly, however, as the name of this new museum suggests, the anticipated scope of this museum, and the history and heritage it will display, is defined by a national focus in a dual sense: it highlights 'the Chinese' in 'Australia'. The Zhongshan–Sydney heritage corridor, which fundamentally transcends the national by encompassing both local and transnational dimensions, should be a central narrative in the stories this museum in Chinatown will tell.

Bibliography

Anderson, Kay. '"Chinatown Re-oriented": A Critical Analysis of Recent Redevelopment Schemes in a Melbourne and Sydney Enclave'. *Australian Geographical Studies* 28, no. 2 (1990): 137–54. https://doi.org/10.1111/j.1467-8470.1990.tb00609.x.

Anderson, Kay, Ien Ang, Andrea Del Bono, Donald McNeill, and Alexandra Wong. *Chinatown Unbound: Trans-Asian Urbanism in the Age of China*. London: Rowman and Littlefield, 2019.

Australian Bureau of Statistics. '2016 Census Quick Stats: Haymarket'. https://quick-stats.censusdata.abs.gov.au/census_services/getproduct/census/2016/quickstat/SSC11877?opendocument.

Barlass, Tim. 'Sydney to Get Museum of History of Chinese Settlement'. *Sydney Morning Herald*, 15 May 2020. https://www.smh.com.au/national/sydney-to-get-museum-of-history-of-chinese-settlement-20200515-p54t9k.html.

Bolles, Scott. 'Chinatown Stalwart Hingara Restaurant Serves Last Dumplings'. *Good Food*, 27 July 2017. https://www.goodfood.com.au/eat-out/news/chinatown-stalwart-to-serve-last-dumplings-20170721-gxfucw.

---

reliance on surviving written sources as well as a Chinese cultural tendency to highlight the prominent in terms of material success and prosperity.

101. See https://www.moca.com.au.

102. Tim Barlass, 'Sydney to Get Museum of History of Chinese Settlement', *Sydney Morning Herald*, 15 May 2020, https://www.smh.com.au/national/sydney-to-get-museum-of-history-of-chinese-settlement-2020 0515-p54t9k.html.

Choi, C. Y. *Chinese Migration and Settlement in Australia*. Sydney: Sydney University Press, 1975.

Cottle, Drew, and Angela Keys. 'Red-Hunting in Sydney's Chinatown'. *Journal of Australian Studies* 91 (2007): 25–33. https://doi.org/10.1080/14443050709388125.

Finch, Ely. *Summary of Australian Chinese-Language Newspaper Content That Relates to the Sydney Firm of Kwong War Chong*. Commissioned by the Chinese Australian Historical Society. Melbourne, August 2020 (unpublished).

Fitzgerald, John. *Big White Lie: Chinese Australians in White Australia*. Sydney: UNSW Press, 2007.

Fitzgerald, Shirley. *Red Tape Gold Scissors: The Story of Sydney's Chinese*. Ultimo: Halstead Press, 2008.

Gibson, Peter. 'Made in Chinatown: Chinese Furniture Factories in Australia, 1880–1930'. *Australian Economic History Review* 61, no. 1 (2021): 102–8. https://doi.org/10.1111/aehr.12211.

Hector Abraham Architects. *82–84 Dixon Street, Haymarket Heritage Assessment for City of Sydney Council*. City of Sydney, 15 July 2019. https://meetings.cityofsydney.nsw.gov.au/documents/s33419/Attachment%20A2%20-%20Planning%20Proposal%20Appendix%201%20-%20Heritage%20Assessment.pdf.

Hsu, Madeline. 'Trading with Gold Mountain: *Jinshanzhuang* and Networks of Kinship and Native Place'. In *Chinese American Transnationalism: The Flow of People, Resources, and Ideas between China and America during the Exclusion Era*, edited by Sucheng Chan, 22–33. Philadelphia, PA: Temple University Press, 2006.

Kuo, Mei-fen. *Making Chinese Australia: Urban Elites, Newspapers and the Formation of Chinese-Australian Identity, 1892–1912*. Clayton, Victoria: Monash University Publishing, 2013.

Kuo, Mei-fen. '*Jinxin*: The Remittance Trade and Enterprising Chinese Australians, 1850–1916'. In *The Qiaopi Trade and Transnational Networks in the Chinese Diaspora*, edited by Gregor Benton, Hong Liu, and Huimei Zhang, 153–68. New York: Routledge, 2018.

Kuo, Mei-fen, and Judith Brett. *Unlocking the History of the Australasian Kuo Min Tang*. North Melbourne: Australian Scholarly Publishing, 2013.

Lee, Pui Tak. 'Business Networks and Patterns of Cantonese Compradors and Merchants in Nineteenth-Century Hong Kong'. *Journal of the Hong Kong Branch of the Royal Asiatic Society* 31 (1991): 1–39.

Li, Barry. *The New Chinese: How They Are Changing Australia*. Milton, Qld: Wiley, 2017.

Liu, Jason, and Heidi Han. 'What's Happening to Chinatown's Cantonese Restaurants?' SBS Mandarin Radio, 13 July 2017. https://www.sbs.com.au/chinese/english/what-s-happening-to-chinatown-s-cantonese-restaurants.

Oakes, Malcolm, SC. 'William Lee: First Barrister of Chinese Descent Admitted to the New South Wales Bar'. *Bar News: The Journal of the New South Wales Bar Association* (Winter 2015): 73–76.

Ong, Aihwa. *Flexible Citizenship: The Cultural Logics of Transnationality*. Durham, NC: Duke University Press, 1999.

Sinn, Elizabeth. 'Hong Kong as an In-Between Place in the Chinese Diaspora, 1848–1939'. In *Connecting Seas and Connected Ocean Rims*, edited by Donna R. Gabaccia and Dirk Hoerder, 225–47. Leiden: Brill, 2011.

Sydney City Council. *Heritage Inventory for Former Kwong War Chong & Company Buildings, Including Interiors and Contents of No. 84*. 20 November 2019. https://meetings.cityofsydney.nsw.gov.au/documents/s37143/Attachment%20D%20-%20Heritage%20Inventory%20for%20Former%20Kwong%20War%20Chong%20Company%20Building%20Including%20Interiors.pdf.

Williams, Michael. *Chinese Settlement in NSW: A Thematic History. Report for the NSW Heritage Office of NSW*. Sydney: NSW Heritage Office, 1999.

Williams, Michael. 'Historical Notes on 82–84 Dixon Street'. Chinese Australian Historical Society, 2018. https://cahsociety.files.wordpress.com/2018/05/84-dixon-st-heritage.pdf.

Williams, Michael. *Returning Home with Glory: Chinese Villagers around the Pacific, 1849 to 1949*. Hong Kong: Hong Kong University Press, 2018.

Williams, Michael. *Australia's Dictation Test: The Test It Was a Crime to Fail*. Leiden: Brill, 2021.

Wong, Alexandra, and Ien Ang. 'From Chinatown to China's Town? The Newest Chinese Diaspora and the Transformation of Sydney's Chinatown'. In *New Chinese Migrations: Mobility, Home, Inspirations*, edited by Yuk Wah Chan and Sin Yee Koh, 21–38. London: Routledge, 2018.

9
Making Heritage in the Migration Corridor

Denis Byrne

The foregoing chapters of this volume have all in their different ways highlighted the transnational nature of the heritage of Chinese migration to Australia. This chapter looks first at the disparity between, on the one hand, the two-way transnational flow of people, ideas, goods, and money along the China–Australia migration corridor between the 1840s and the 1940s, and, on the other hand, the efforts of the Chinese and Australian governments to interpret and manage the heritage of migration in a nation-centric manner. These efforts come under the category of what I will call 'heritage from above', which is to say the official version of heritage – what Laurajane Smith calls 'authorised heritage' – produced by state actors and heritage experts retained by governments.[1] The second half of the chapter then turns to consider 'heritage from below', a term which refers to the activities of individuals and community groups engaging with their own material past, drawing on particular sites and objects from the past in the framing of their identity and often working to achieve public and official recognition of these things *as heritage*. I take two particular areas of activity as examples of 'heritage from below', the first being the quest that many Chinese Australians have embarked on to locate their ancestral houses (祖屋 *joe uk* in Cantonese) in Zhongshan, Guangdong, and the second being the engagement of overseas Chinese, many of them migrant descendants, in the restoration of the ancestral halls (祠堂 *chee tong* in Cantonese) of their home villages in Zhongshan.

Heritage from below equates with the term 'heritage-making', adopted by many to describe community-based heritage activity.[2] Heritage-making is not dissimilar from the much better-known concept and practice of placemaking, which refers to the way individuals or groups signify and become attached to (hence the idea of place attachment) particular places in their local environment. The work of making

---

1. Laurajane Smith, *Uses of Heritage* (Abingdon: Routledge, 2006).
2. Hamzah Muzaini, 'Informal Heritage-Making at the Sarawak Cultural Village, East Malaysia', *Tourism Geographies* 19, no. 2 (2017): 244–64, https://doi.org/10.1080/14616688.2016.1160951; Iain J. M. Robertson, ed., *Heritage from Below* (London: Routledge, 2016).

Denis Byrne 241

places out of spaces is seen to be a fundamental priority of human life.³ What is particular about heritage-making is that it is directed at places and objects from the past, inscribing them with meaning that is particular to individuals or groups in the present. In so doing, these things from the past are incorporated into the landscape of the present.

Heritage-making is generally thought of as a practice that takes place in local settings and in the context of what Emma Waterton and Modesto Gayo refer to as personal, vernacular, or everyday genres of heritage.⁴ But this should not be taken to imply that governments and institutions do not also *make* heritage. Heritage, it might be argued, is a particular way of valuing old things; old things become heritage via those particular kinds of discourse and practice that in the 1980s and early 1990s became the focus of the new academic field of critical heritage studies. Attention was directed at the manner in which old things such as ancient monuments and archaeological sites were mobilised to do certain kinds of work, such as helping finesse a nation's continuity with the past or a person's membership of the upper class.⁵ One of the most prevalent kinds of state-level heritage-making is the compiling of lists of heritage sites that are held to represent a nation's history and legacy. It is worth noting that what I am referring to as 'heritage from above' includes the activities of heritage professionals who, while not state actors as such, tend to follow state definitions and categorisations of heritage.

Constructing the Heritage of Migration from Above

Turning to the particular context of the China–Australia migration corridor, I look in what follows at the way its heritage has been 'made', which is to say constructed, in very different ways by the Australian and the Chinese nation-states. When it comes to heritage, nation-states have overwhelmingly concentrated their attention on old places and objects lying within their territorial boundaries. This material legacy is held to tell the story of the nation as a spatially and temporally coherent entity.⁶

Australia: The official heritage of migration

Opting for a bordered framing of its heritage, Australia has produced a distorted representation of the heritage of migration, one that turns its back on the

---

3. Edward S. Casey, *Getting Back into Place: Toward a Renewed Understanding of the Place-World* (Bloomington: Indiana University Press, 1993).
4. Emma Waterton and Modesto Gayo, 'The Elite and the Everyday in the Australian Heritage Field', in *Fields, Capitals, Habitus: Australian Culture, Inequalities and Social Division*, ed. Tony Bennett, David Carter, Modesto Gayo, Michelle Kelly and Greg Noble (London: Routledge, 2020), 66.
5. Smith, *Uses of Heritage*.
6. In the case of Australia, see, for example, Denis Byrne, 'Deep Nation: Australia's Acquisition of an Indigenous Past', *Aboriginal History* 20 (1996): 82–107.

circulatory, cross-border fluidity of the migrant experience in favour of a one-way narrative of migration that privileges sites of migrant arrival and settlement.[7] This resonates with Michael Williams's critique of the way the nation-bounded framing of histories of Chinese migration produced in Australia and the United States both effaces the evidence of multiple ongoing flows between these destinations and the home villages and towns in China and produces a false impression that permanent settlement in the destination country was a goal of Chinese migrants.[8]

Australia's first programme of mass immigration, begun in the late 1940s and shaped by a government post-war reconstruction policy that aimed to boost demographic and economic growth by facilitating migration from Britain and war-torn Europe, idealised one-way migration, permanent settlement in the host country, and rapid assimilation of migrants into Australian society.[9] From 1949, significant government resources went into social welfare programmes aimed at keeping migrants from departing.[10] Prior to the introduction of multiculturalist policies in the 1970s, the emphasis was on assimilating non-British migrants to an Australian society that was conceived as being ethnically and culturally British. Before the 1970s, Australia's material heritage was conceived in terms of those sites, such as white settler homesteads and mansions, courthouses, grand commercial buildings, and the infrastructure of bridges and railways, which testified to the narrative of white colonial settlement of the continent. To the extent that the archaeological remains of indigenous Australian occupation were known of, they were not included under the category of heritage until the 1960s, when they began to be reimagined as providing the Australian nation with a deep past.[11]

Given this background, it is no surprise that when, under the imprimatur of multiculturalism, the category of migration history gained currency in the 1980s, its focus was not on the heritage of migration as such – this would have meant including the material record of sojourning, return migration, and transnational place-making – but on a heritage of immigrant *settlement*. It reflected the government's post-war adherence to an inside-outside binary in which arrival meant permanent settlement and departure meant permanent alienation. This masked the reality that many migrant departures from Australia took the form of visits to the homeland, often undertaken on a regular basis, followed by return to Australia, a pattern that

---

7. Denis Byrne, 'Heritage Corridors: Transnational Flows and the Built Environment of Migration', *Journal of Ethnic and Migration Studies* 42, no. 14 (2016): 2360–78, https://doi.org/10.1080/1369183X.2016.1205805; Kate Darian-Smith and Paula Hamilton, 'Remembering Migration', in *Remembering Migration: Oral Histories and Heritage in Australia*, ed. Kate Darian-Smith and Paula Hamilton (London: Palgrave Macmillan, 2019), 6.
8. Michael Williams, *Returning Home with Glory: Chinese Villagers around the Pacific, 1849 to 1949* (Hong Kong: Hong Kong University Press, 2018).
9. Graeme Hugo, 'Geography and Population in Australia: A Historical Perspective', *Geographic Research* 49, no. 3 (2011): 153; Lois Foster and David Stockley, *Multiculturalism: The Changing Australian Paradigm* (Clevedon, UK: Multilingual Matters, 1984), 28.
10. Ann-Mari Jordens, *Alien to Citizen: Settling Migrants in Australia, 1945–75* (Sydney: Allen & Unwin in association with the Australian Archives, 1997).
11. Byrne, 'Deep Nation'.

had been common among nineteenth-century Chinese migrants in Australia.[12] This pattern of cross-border travel is consonant with a flexible, mobile conception of belonging that eludes the category of permanence.[13]

By 1994 a total of 112 places had been listed on the Australian Register of the National Estate for their significance to migrant groups, including archaeological remains and built structures representing Chinese presence on the Australia gold-fields in the mid-nineteenth century.[14] Although comprising only 1.2 per cent of the 8,279 historic places on the register at that point, the presence of these 112 sites on the national inventory was significant in reflecting, firstly, a concerted push by a number of historians, archaeologists, and heritage experts over the preceding decade or so to document and record sites of non-Anglo migrant activity.[15] There are now many more sites listed on heritage inventories at the federal, state, and local levels of government for their association with migration. But as with the earlier-recorded sites, they are discursively framed according to a nation-bound, 'bordered' conception of post-arrival migrant existence. Like its counterparts in Canada and the United States, this framing stresses the contribution immigrants have made to the migrant-receiving nation and minimises or discursively effaces the ongoing presence so many of them have in the sending nation and their active role in pro-ducing its built environment.[16] It is a depiction that jars with the understanding, now well established in the field of migration studies, of migrants as transnational, diasporic subjects who, in Deborah Cohen's words, 'recognize themselves as par-ticipants in multiple national communities, albeit not equally or in the same way, as well as in a community that transcends the nation'.[17] The reification of the national border as a container of migrant heritage perhaps explains why points of arrival or touch-down are often celebrated as heritage sites, Australian examples being the Quarantine Station and Woolloomooloo Finger Wharf, both on Sydney Harbour, as well as the sites of the many migrant hostels across the country that in the 1950s and 1960s housed post-war immigrants until they found jobs and homes of their own.[18]

---

12. John Fitzgerald, *Big White Lie: Chinese Australians in White Australia* (Sydney: UNSW Press, 2007), 53.

13. Mimi Sheller, 'Creolization in Discourses of Global Culture', in *Uprootings/Regroundings: Questions of Home and Migration*, ed. Sara Ahmed, Claudia Castada, Anne-Marie Fortier, and Mimi Sheller (Oxford: Berg, 2003), 276–77.

14. For a summary of archaeological research on sites relating to Chinese presence in Australia, see Alister M. Bowen, *Archaeology of the Chinese Fishing Industry in Colonial Victoria* (Sydney: Sydney University Press, 2012), 7–8.

15. For the make-up of the National Estate, see R. W. Purdie, *The Register of the National Estate: Who, What, Where?* (Canberra: Australian Heritage Commission, 1997), 33.

16. See, for example, in Canada, the Museum of Migration, http://www.pier21.ca/home; and in the United States, the Angel Island Immigration Station Foundation, http://www.aiisf.org/.

17. Deborah Cohen, *Braceros: Migrant Citizens and Transnational Subjects in the Postwar United States and Mexico* (Chapel Hill: University of North Carolina Press, 2011), 5.

18. For the Quarantine Station, see http://www.quarantinestation.com.au/About-Us/; for migrant hostels in New South Wales, see http://www.migrationheritage.nsw.gov.au/exhibition/aplaceforeveryone/migrant-hostels-in-nsw/.

The narrative emphasis on settlement in Australia displaces cross-border mobility to the past: these people are construed as *once* mobile, now *settled* citizens.[19]

It is interesting to observe that Australian historians working in the field of public history who have focused on recording oral histories of migrants have, at least since the 1990s and in contrast to heritage experts and heritage agencies, adopted a more transnational orientation.[20] It is tempting to interpret this as stemming from the close contact with migrants and their descendants that they have enjoyed through oral history interviews that have revealed personal histories of cross-border mobility. This is something heritage professionals, with their focus on the materiality of sites of migration, tend to lack, arguably making them more liable to rely on the state's one-way narrative of migration history.

China: Heritage through the lens of a diaspora strategy

It is only over the last few decades that the Chinese government has been involved in recording, listing, and preserving heritage sites in China that relate to overseas migration, including the remittance houses (僑房 *kiu fong* in Cantonese) and ancestral halls discussed later in the chapter. However, this activity is strongly linked to what is known as China's 'diaspora strategy', and this has a longer history.[21] Put in place in 1949, the People's Republic of China's (PRC) diaspora strategy initially focused on promoting investment by diaspora members in the economy of their home counties and villages as part of a call to participate in the reconstruction of the homeland following the war against the Japanese (1937–1945) and the civil war between the Communists and the Nationalists (1927–1949). As Glen Peterson shows, the strategy has its roots in the diaspora outreach programmes put in place by the late Qing and Republican governments to attract remittances and investment by Chinese overseas, particularly by the large population of ethnic Chinese in Southeast Asia.[22]

Moving forward in time, during the reform era following the death of Mao in 1976, the diaspora strategy was extended to seeking the involvement of diaspora Chinese in the spheres of science and technology, education, culture, and tourism. The main institution for diaspora outreach in Zhongshan, the local branch of the government's Overseas Chinese Affairs Bureau (僑務辦公室 *qiaowu bangongshi* in Mandarin), organises tours of emigrant villages for those descendants of migrants visiting Zhongshan from America, Canada, Hawaii, Australia, and elsewhere who

---

19. Ayse Caglar, 'Still "Migrants" after All Those Years: Foundational Mobilities, Temporal Frames and Emplacement of Migrants', *Journal of Ethnic and Migration Studies* 42, no. 6 (2016): 957, https://doi.org/10.1080/1369183X.2015.1126085.

20. Darian-Smith and Hamilton, 'Remembering Migration', 6.

21. Elaine Ho, 'Leveraging Connectivities: Comparative Diaspora Strategies and Evolving Cultural Pluralities in China and Singapore', *American Behavioural Scientist* 64, no. 10 (2020): 1415–29, https://doi.org/10.1177/0002764220947754.

22. Glen Peterson, *Overseas Chinese in the People's Republic of China* (London: Routledge, 2012), 75–76.

are engaged in a form of 'roots tourism' (尋根之旅).[23] It assists some of them to locate their migrant ancestors' native village and their ancestral houses and gravesites located in the village.[24] It also publishes a magazine for circulation among the diaspora featuring stories on migration-related heritage sites in Zhongshan. Williams observes that in China since the late 1970s there has been a surge in studies of the history of China's links with the diaspora, with Chinese researchers taking the perspective 'that overseas Chinese represent a social phenomenon within China's history and society, and that their role in other countries is an aspect of China's history.'[25]

In working to reconnect overseas migrant descendants to their ancestral places in China, the government promotes the idea that their roots are in the soil of their ancestors' native place. This is not purely an invention of the post-1949 Communist state; it has an antecedent in the valorisation of native-place loyalty in traditional Chinese culture, as exemplified in the native-place associations that existed in Chinese cities in dynastic and Republican times to provide migrants from elsewhere in the country with a home away from home and to assist them to keep in touch with their origin counties and provinces.[26] Native-place discourse was brought into modern Chinese culture partly through its role as a genre in the field of folklore studies during the Republic.[27] China's current diaspora strategy is steeped in the idea of Chineseness as a genetic-cultural essence that is inalienable. The strategy's grounding in the idea of an essential Chineseness is captured in the term 'overseas Chinese' with its connotation that, though residing outside the homeland, migrants and migrant descendants continue to be members of the 'Family of China' (親情中華 qinqing Zhonghua in Mandarin).[28]

China's diaspora strategy has been criticised for invoking the idea of a Greater China and for putting coercive pressure on diasporic Chinese to retain loyalty to China and the PRC, with the two elided.[29] But as Hong Liu and Els van Dongen

---

23. Naho Maruyama and Amanda Stronza, 'Roots Tourism of Chinese Americans', *Ethnology* 49, no. 1 (2010): 23–44.
24. During the nineteenth and early twentieth centuries, the remains of Chinese migrants who died overseas were often returned to their natal village for burial in the clan cemetery, those repatriated to Zhongshan going by way of Hong Kong. See Elizabeth Sinn, *Pacific Crossing: California Gold, Chinese Migration, and the Making of Hong Kong* (Hong Kong: Hong University Press, 2013), 265–97.
24. Interviews conducted in 2017–2019 by Ien Ang, Denis Byrne, Alexandra Wong, and Christopher Cheng; see https://www.heritagecorridor.org.au.
25. Williams, *Returning Home with Glory*, 25.
26. Bryna Goodman, *Native Place, City, and Nation: Regional Networks and Identities in Shanghai, 1853–1937* (Berkeley: University of California Press, 1995).
27. Prasenjit Duara, 'Local Worlds: The Poetics and Politics of Native Place in China', *The South Atlantic Quarterly* 99, no. 1 (2000): 13–45, https://doi.org/10.1215/00382876-99-1-13.
28. Hong Liu and Els van Dongen, 'China's Diaspora Policies as a New Mode of Transnational Governance', *Journal of Contemporary China* 25, no. 102 (2016): 813, https://doi.org/10.1080/10670564.2016.1184894.
29. William A. Callahan, 'Nationalism, Civilization and Transnational Relations: The Discourse of Greater China', *Journal of Contemporary China* 14, no. 43 (2005): 269–89, https://doi.org/10.1080/10670560500065629.

argue, the diaspora is by no means a passive recipient of the strategy.[30] The diversity of positions that Chinese migrants and their descendants take up in formulating their individual identities is stressed by Ien Ang, who characterises Chineseness as a 'murky' and 'ambiguous' signifier in which a multitude of subjectivities flourish.[31] This agrees well with what Zhongshanese migrants and descendants recently interviewed in Sydney had to say on the question of identity.[32] Most situated their identity in the fluid space between China and Australia. Their various degrees of interest in and attachment to heritage sites in Zhongshan tended to be framed more in terms of family and lineage-group history than anything resembling official or professional heritage discourse emanating from either China or Australia.[33]

The Overseas Chinese Affairs Bureau in Zhongshan presents a view of homeland heritage places as being a vital constituent of the diaspora's identity and belonging. It conceives the material heritage of Chinese migration that is located overseas – gold-mining camps, market gardens, old shops, and temples, for example – as being continuous with the built heritage of the migrants' ancestral villages, including the remittance-built houses, graveyards, and ancestral halls that are present there. This pulls in the opposite direction, as it were, to the nation-centric framing of migrant heritage in destination countries such as Australia. That framing, as described earlier, posits Chinese migrant heritage in unilinear terms as representing the progressive assimilation of migrants into the geo-social corpus of their new home, their adoptive nation, which is seen to be the exclusive site of their belonging. Yet the differences between the two are less than they may seem at first glance: both are nationalist in orientation. The Chinese model, far from being internationalist, invokes a stretched version of the nation, a nation of people who, though globally distributed, remain forever essentially Chinese.

Heritage from Below: House-Hunting in Zhongshan

Much of the fieldwork carried out in Zhongshan as part of the project whose results constitute the focus of this book consisted of visiting and recording the ancestral houses of Chinese Australians.[34] In some cases this meant finding houses which were known to and had previously been visited by migrant descendants (and, in a

---

30. Liu and Van Dongen, 'China's Diaspora Policies', 280.
31. Ien Ang, *On Not Speaking Chinese: Living Between Asia and the West* (London: Routledge, 2001); Ien Ang, 'No Longer Chinese? Residual Chineseness after the Rise of China', in *Diasporic Chineseness after the Rise of China: Communities and Cultural Production*, ed. Julia Kuehn, Kam Louie, and David M. Pomfret (Vancouver: University of British Columbia, 2013).
32. Interviews conducted in 2017–2019 by Ien Ang, Denis Byrne, Alexandra Wong, and Christopher Cheng; see https://www.heritagecorridor.org.au.
33. See Chapter 3 of this volume for an extended discussion of the identity trajectories of four of our interviewees.
34. The China–Australia Heritage Corridor project, based at the Institute of Culture and Society, Western Sydney University, involved the participation of Ien Ang, Denis Byrne, Christopher Cheng, Michael Williams, and Alexandra Wong over the period 2017–2021.

few cases, first-generation migrants) living in Sydney, mostly people we had interviewed prior to our fieldwork. In the time since the reopening of China in 1978, most of these people had gone through the process – often lengthy and arduous – of discovering the location of their ancestral houses by researching immigration archives and other archival repositories in Australia, by sifting through the memories, documents, letters, and old photographs held by their own family, and by seeking help from the Zhongshan branch of the Overseas Chinese Affairs Bureau. The necessity of this work of rediscovery speaks to a loss of knowledge of the homeland stemming from the rupture in travel and communication across the China–Australia migration corridor during the Japanese occupation of Guangdong, the ensuing civil war between Nationalist and Communist forces, and the era of Mao Zedong's dominance over the People's Republic.[35] In total, this period of rupture extended from 1938 to 1976. Many Chinese in Australia lost contact with their families in China during this time, and generations of their families in Australia grew up often with only the sketchiest knowledge of their relatives in China and where they were located. Often descendants no longer knew the name or location of their ancestral village, let alone where the ancestral house had been in the village. In the case of the descendants of the earliest migrants to Australia, those who arrived in the early and mid-nineteenth century, the attrition of knowledge had often begun much earlier than 1938. Moreover, as Sophie Couchman and Kate Bagnall remind us, many of the children and descendants of those Chinese men who partnered with European or Indigenous Australians, and even many of those of 'pure' Chinese ancestry, deliberately erased their mixed-race descent as protection from the racism prevalent in Australia, particularly before the 1970s.[36]

The quest for the ancestral house in Zhongshan on the part of migrant descendants is positioned here as an act of heritage-making in which people bring old houses forward into the landscape of the present as objects that are still meaningful to them and often as objects inscribed with new meaning. This acknowledges that old things – ancient monuments, archaeological sites, buildings erected in past centuries – are not stable, static objects sequestered in the past. Rather, they are constantly being remade in the present, sometimes physically (as when they are restored, rebuilt, or repurposed) and always conceptually in the ongoing process of the reinterpretation of the material past by new generations in the present. There is a sense in which this heritage-making is a 'future-assembling' practice, an intervention that changes the trajectory of family memory by reinserting the 'forgotten' houses into family narratives that may engage future descendants who, rather than being passive receivers of

---

35. See Michael Williams, Chapter 1 of this volume.
36. Sophie Couchman and Kate Bagnall, 'Memory and Meaning in the Search for Australian-Chinese Families', in *Remembering Migration: Oral Histories and Heritage in Australia*, ed. Kate Darian-Smith and Paula Hamilton (London: Palgrave Macmillan, 2019), 335–36.

knowledge, are actors who will no doubt rework the meaning of the houses in their own terms and for their own times.[37]

During our own research in Zhongshan, on a number of occasions we attempted to locate houses that migrant descendants in Australia had never visited and had never managed to learn more about than the name of the village where they were situated. When we reached these villages, the following scene typically unfolded. On arriving at the village office and explaining what we were seeking – the ancestral house of an emigrant whose name we knew – the local officials, if the house was not already known to them, would phone an elderly villager to ask their advice, this woman or man turning up at the office shortly thereafter.[38] On one occasion, which I will describe below, the name of the pre-1949 emigrant whose house we sought was unfamiliar to both the officials and the elderly residents, prompting them to make phone calls to other villagers, or former villagers now living in apartments in Shekki (石岐, Shiqi, in Zhongshan city) or further afield. Even the elderly own mobile phones, and working-age people in this part of China usually own two, often making calls on both of them simultaneously. The result was a cacophony of conversations reaching out across space. If we only possessed a Romanised transliteration of a person's name or a place name, the discussion would focus on possible variations of the Chinese original, opening up a wider field of potential links among the pre-1949 population of the village. Animating the conversations was an obvious willingness to come up with the answer to the puzzle our inquiry posed, behind which may have been a competitiveness among those involved to display the breadth of their historical knowledge.

In November 2018, Christopher Cheng (whose PhD research formed part of our project) and I visited Ou Saek village (烏石, Wushi) in the Sanxiang (三鄉) area of southeastern Zhongshan hoping to locate the ancestral house of Cheng (Henry) Fine Chong (鄭番昌, also known as 'Ah Hing'), who had arrived in Sydney in 1877 at the age of about seventeen and went on to become a successful merchant and photographic portraitist.[39] Cheng Fine Chong's great-grandson, Brad Powe, had provided us with an early aqua-tinted photograph of the house, showing it to be a single-storey structure in the vernacular style, the façade of which had a central doorway with a shuttered window on either side, each window having a half-moon pediment featuring stucco-moulded decorations. Our photocopy of the photograph was passed around and stimulated much discussion among those gathered in the village office. Eventually we were led off to inspect an old house, located on the edge of the old core area of the village, which was thought to be a likely candidate.

---

37. For the concept of future-assembling, see Rodney Harrison, 'Archaeologies of Present and Emergent Futures', *Historical Archaeology* 50, no. 3 (2016): 170, https://doi.org/10.1007/BF03377340.

38. Alternatively, the village office would have already arranged for an elderly resident to be present, having been notified of our visit ahead of time by the staff member of the Zhongshan branch of the Overseas Chinese Affairs Office, who usually accompanied us on our fieldwork.

39. Christopher Cheng, whose family originates from Zhongshan, is no relation to Cheng Fine Chong. See https://historyandheritage.cityofparramatta.nsw.gov.au/blog/2017/01/25/cheng-fan-cheong-ah-hing-henry-fine.

Figure 9.1: The photograph of Cheng (Henry) Fine Chong's (鄭番昌) house, in the hands of an Ou Saek (烏石 Wushi) villager, November 2018. Photo by Denis Byrne 2018.

It is worth pausing here to note that like most of the old emigrant villages of Zhongshan, the residential built environment of the part of Ou Saek belonging to the pre-1949 era remains largely intact. This may be due in part to the government's return of property rights in the 1980s to diaspora Chinese who had lost these rights in 1949.[40] The effect of this has been to partially 'freeze' the built landscape of the old core area of emigrant villages because so many of the overseas owners are uninterested in redeveloping the houses, content to leave them empty (and often derelict) or rent them out unrenovated to migrant workers from other parts of China or from poorer parts of Guangdong. The relative intactness of the village core also results from the interest that the government heritage office in Zhongshan has shown over the last two decades in protecting, as heritage enclaves, these old residential areas, with their grand remittance houses and ancestral halls. Either way, the villages

---

40. Peterson, *Overseas Chinese in the People's Republic of China*, 172–73.

end up being prime terrain for the kind of heritage-making activities of migrant descendants that I describe here under the heading of 'house-hunting'.

Back in the streets of Ou Saek (烏石, Wushi), when we reached the house on the outskirts of the village, after pausing along the way to inspect the ruins of an ancestral hall that had been used as a grain store during the era of the People's Communes (1958–1983), it became obvious that the old man who occupied the house and had perhaps been allocated it during the land reform campaign of the 1950s wanted nothing to do with us and we politely withdrew. It was clear, however, that while the house was similar in style to that in our old photograph, there were enough differences, including the size and shape of the front windows, to rule it out of contention. Walking back through the village, we looked at a few other old remittance houses but their differences to the house we sought were even more marked. At one point we stopped to talk with a man on a bicycle, perhaps in his late seventies, who the village official who accompanied us thought might be able to help. The man looked carefully at our copy of the photograph but was unable to place it (Figure 9.1). He did, however, have a lot to say about the village in its former days, and moving his bicycle into the shade, he held us captive with his reminiscences.[41] As he stood leaning against his old black bike, elbow on the saddle and right foot propped on the chain guard, it was very possible to imagine him in this same easy posture talking with friends in these same streets as a youth in the 1950s (Figure 9.2).

I want to reflect briefly here on the spatio-temporal dimension of 'house-hunting'. While the relative intactness of the old core areas of Ou Saek and other emigrant villages in Zhongshan makes them ideal for the work of recovery that house-hunting represents, these core areas are surrounded by a landscape in which over the last four decades change has been immense both in scale and speed. Factories and clusters of high-rise apartment blocks now stand in what were once the rice fields of Ou Saek. The dense, low-rise village core is the still point at the centre of a wave of urban expansion that has rippled out around it, an expansion that has overflowed even the limits of the surrounding landscape. Eleven kilometres west of Ou Saek, a 2.5-kilometre-wide strip of recently reclaimed land that acts as a platform for new housing estates extends out into the Pearl River.[42] On their way to the village core areas where their migrant ancestors grew up and to which their remittance funds flowed, the house-hunters of the diaspora (or, in this case, of academic researchers) drive through zones of recent development, the landscape of

---

41. Having no Cantonese-language ability myself, his reminiscences reached me only in the form of fragments translated by those with me.

42. This reclamation is among those that comprise just the most recent iteration of a history of coastal land reclamations – previously designed to create more land for agriculture – stretching back several centuries in the Pearl River Delta. See Denis Byrne, 'Reclaiming Landscape: Coastal Reclamations before and during the Anthropocene', in *The Routledge Companion to Landscape Studies*, ed. Peter Howard, Ian Thompson, Emma Waterton, and Mick Atha (London: Routledge, 2018).

Figure 9.2: A villager in Ou Saek (烏石), reminiscing about life there in the old days. Photo by Denis Byrne 2018.

China's economic miracle. One might say they are driving through the terrain of the present to reach the terrain of the ancestral past.

Searching for ancestral houses involves some interesting temporal gymnastics. With our focus on the eighty years or so prior to the 1938 Japanese invasion of the Pearl River Delta, we jump back over the Mao era (1949–1976) to reach a time when remittances still flowed and the families of migrants still occupied the houses that remittances built. Much as the present-day visitor from the diaspora cuts through the hyper-developed landscape of present-day Zhongshan to get to the old villages, so they reach back across the Cultural Revolution, the collectivisation era, the Great Leap Forward, and the years of the land reform programme. This imaginative backtracking is not difficult, given that remarkably few tangible remains of those Mao-era events survive in the villages of today. One sees the occasional red star in moulded stucco still attached to the façade of the village office, the mouldering ruins of an expropriated ancestral hall, and sometimes remittance houses divided internally by retrofitted brick walls to accommodate the multiple families they were allocated to during land reform. But it is almost uncanny how little of this there is.

One might think that in reaching over the momentous history of the Mao era to reach the era that preceded it, visitors from the diaspora or a visitor from a foreign university, such as myself, might unsettle the village officials and the staff of the Overseas Chinese Affairs Bureau, many of whom are members of the Chinese Community Party (CCP), since it effectively effaces a large part of the history of the PRC. In fact, however, the CCP has reasons of its own for not wishing to dwell on the heritage of the Mao era, namely what it euphemistically refers to as Mao's 'mistakes', most notably those represented by the Cultural Revolution of 1965–1976 and the Great Leap Forward of 1958–1962. The latter alone resulted in the death by starvation of between thirty and fifty million people. The potential damage these disasters pose to the CCP's legitimacy has led to a concerted official effort to sanitise and suppress the collective memory of them. It has led also to an emphasis on the memory of the period preceding those events, an emphasis that amounts to a great leap backward.[43] In heritage terms, this has seen immense attention directed to sites of 'revolutionary heritage' such as those of the route of the Long March (1934–1935), the war against the Japanese, the building in Shanghai where the CCP held its first meeting, and even sites associated with land reform.[44] In Brian DeMare's words, these now represent the 'hallowed ground' of the party's legitimacy.[45] Heritage places in China that are associated with pre-1949 migration are also now considered politically safe.

We failed to find the ancestral house of Cheng Fine Chong in Ou Saek. But hundreds of migrant descendants in Australia have been more successful in their house-hunting, including members of the Mar family, whose discovery of 'their' house in the village of Sha Chong is described in Chapter 5 of this volume. Whether consciously or not, those engaging in this kind of activity are countering Australia's bordered framing of migrant heritage and the national narrative of migration that privileges histories of arrival and settlement over histories of ongoing migrant connectivity with their origin places. As Couchman and Bagnall observe of Chinese Australia family historians, 'their endeavours provide a means of overcoming national forgetting'.[46] This work of family history, which in this case sees migrant descendants retracing their ancestors' footsteps along the China–Australia migration corridor, is an example of the broader theatre of family history that Waterton and Gayo have found to be 'by far the most popular "genre" of heritage' in

---

43. See, for example, Lingchei Letty Chen, *The Great Leap Backward: Forgetting and Representing the Mao Years* (Amherst, NY: Cambria, 2020).
44. For 'revolutionary heritage', see Marina Svensson, 'Evolving and Contesting Cultural Heritage in China: The Rural Heritagescape', in *Reconsidered Cultural Heritage in East Asia*, ed. Akira Matsuda and Luisa Elena Mengoni (London: Ubiquity Press, 2016); for land reform as 'hallowed ground', see Brian DeMare, *Land Wars: The Story of China's Agrarian Revolution* (Stanford, CA: Stanford University Press, 2019), 164.
45. DeMare, *Land Wars*, 164.
46. Couchman and Bagnall, 'Memory and Meaning in the Search for Australian-Chinese Families', 333.

Australia.[47] If family history endeavours are nourished by a nostalgia for the past, the quest to track down objects and places that populated that past may be seen as an enactment of what Alfredo González-Ruibal has recently described as 'material nostalgia'.[48] Nostalgia, González-Ruibal points out, has not received a good press in recent years, being associated by some with reactionary ideology and identity politics; but for him it is a fundamental human emotion that in its material form instantiates a 'longing for the corporeal' and an insistence on material continuity between the past and the present.[49] Migrant descendants arriving at a village in Zhongshan to find their ancestral house are far from being mere spectators of the past, as Glenn and Phillip Mar show in Chapter 5 of this volume; rather, they are actively assembling a present–past–future continuum for themselves and their own descendants. It is in this respect that the kind of house-hunting discussed here is a future-assembling practice.

The Ancestral Hall as a Locus of Heritage-Making

I now turn away from the subject of ancestral houses and their rediscovery to consider the way another key site in the Zhongshan–Australia heritage corridor, the ancestral hall, has become important for the enactment of heritage-making by Chinese migrants and migrant descendants. Ancestral halls have always been a pivotal physical anchor of the lineage in southern China, and there is plentiful evidence that they continued to play that role in the 1840s to 1940s era of transnational migration. With the beginning of Deng Xiaoping's reforms in 1978, ancestral halls were returned to lineages seventy years after their confiscation.[50] They subsequently became a destination for many of the thousands of Chinese migrants and migrant descendants on visits to their home counties that became possible once again under Deng's Open Door policy. In the following pages I examine the engagement of overseas Chinese, including many from Australia, in projects to renovate or restore ancestral halls in their home villages. While this form of 'heritage from below' does not entirely bypass the official heritage management regime of county and prefectural governments in China, it can nevertheless be considered a community-based practice. First, though, it is necessary to provide some background on how the lineage is constituted.

Organised as corporate bodies, lineages in southern China comprise the males who become members of their father's lineage at birth and the women who become

---

47. Waterton and Gayo, 'The Elite and the Everyday', 76.
48. Alfredo González-Ruibal, 'What Remains? On Material Nostalgia', in *After Discourse: Things, Affects, Ethics*, ed. Bjørnar Olsen, Matts Burström, Caitlin DeSilvey, and Þóra Pétursdóttir (London: Routledge, 2021), 187–203.
49. González-Ruibal, 'What Remains?', 199.
50. Song Ping, 'The Zheng Communities and the Formation of a Transnational Community', *Journal of Chinese Overseas* 4, no. 2 (2008): 187, https://doi.org/10.1163/179325408788691372.

members of their husbands' lineage upon marriage. Lineages gained importance in southern China during the Ming dynasty (1368–1644). By the sixteenth century in the Pearl River Delta, the origin place of most of those who migrated from China to North America and Australia, lineages were deeply engaged in building up their estates.[51] Far from being compromised by the spatial dispersion of the task of keeping the lineage estate intact and in place could at times actually require dispersion.[52] As well as making financial contributions to their lineages, which were themselves major land-owning entities, the contribution migrants made to their own family's prosperity in the village was indirectly a contribution to the lineage's substance as a collective. The contributions of migrants helped lineages to build or renovate the temples, ancestral halls, and schools, which, along with their landholdings, constituted their estate. The emigrant village in southern China became a 'transnational entity'.[53] This focus on the lineage's role in migration should not, however, be allowed to eclipse other factors at least as important in explaining the movement of people from the Pearl River Delta to places such as Australia, including the region's long history of trade contact with 'Nanyang' (南陽, implying Southeast Asia), its participation from the sixteenth century in Pacific trade networks, and its proximity to Hong Kong as a key node in these networks.[54]

While ancestral halls have earned a place on government heritage inventories for their architectural and artistic significance, the buildings have little real meaning in isolation from what occurs inside them and what, indeed, they embody. On ritual occasions the lineage's ancestors are believed to take up a more substantial presence in the halls than that represented by their tablet on the altar. The halls function as liminal portals between the terrestrial and heavenly worlds, much the way graves in China are thought of as liminal gateways between the two realms.[55] While, spatially, many lineages have been stretched by transnational migration, in their temporal dimension they extend across past, present, and future generations.[56] In the rituals of ancestor worship, a lineage's membership, living and dead, is called together across time and space in a way that dissolves national boundaries and in a sense cancels out the physical remoteness of overseas migrants. The border-transcending capacity of ancestor worship is key to understanding how it has supported migration and to appreciating why homeland ancestral halls attract overseas lineage members with

---

51. David Faure, *Emperor and Ancestor: State and Lineage in South China* (Stanford, CA: Stanford University Press, 2007), 125.
52. Philip A. Kuhn, *Chinese among Others: Emigration in Modern Times* (Lanham, MD: Rowman and Littlefield, 2008), 15.
53. Adam McKeown, *Chinese Migrant Networks and Cultural Change: Peru, Chicago, Hawaii, 1900–1936* (Chicago, IL: University of Chicago Press, 2001), 75.
54. Williams, *Returning Home with Glory*, 47–49. See also Chapter 1 of this volume.
55. Jessica Rawson, 'Changes in the Representation of Life and the Afterlife as Illustrated by the Contents of Tombs of the T'ang and Sung Periods', in *Arts of the Sung and Yuan*, ed. Maxwell K. Hearn and Judith G. Smith (New York: Metropolitan Museum of Art, 1996).
56. William Lakos, *Chinese Ancestor Worship: A Practice and Ritual Oriented Approach to Understanding Chinese Culture* (Cambridge: Cambridge Scholars Publishing, 2010).

Denis Byrne

a kind of gravitational force. As a comparative aside, I note that ancestor worship in Vietnam shares many of the characteristics of its Chinese counterpart, and the global Vietnamese diaspora, believed to now number about four million people, has played a key role in rebuilding ancestral halls damaged during the 1955–1975 war and the era of hard-line Maoist Communism that preceded the 1986 market economy policies (Doi Moi). During revived rituals of ancestor worship in Vietnam, as described by Kate Jellema, the dead and the living, including those offshore, 'are urged to come home'.[57]

Traditionally the most prominent buildings in the village, ancestral halls have the high gable roofs covered with glazed terracotta tiles and the upturned eaves that we associate with traditional Chinese architecture.[58] The roof frame is supported in front by a row of granite columns, beyond which a portico leads to a large central hall, at the far end of which is an altar upon which are arranged the wooden ancestral tablets of the deceased males, often including those who died overseas. Migrant lineage members, living and dead, are also given presence in the halls by having their names inscribed in the genealogical record book and on genealogical charts that are often hung on the walls. The progressive decay of the halls, accentuated by the delta's humid subtropical climate, provides the occasion for lineage members to collaborate in undertaking restoration projects, a collective action that reinforces the lineage as a social unit.

In Mao's eyes, lineages, steeped in feudalism, were 'oppressors of the people'.[59] Following the founding of the PRC in 1949, all lineage lands were confiscated and ancestral halls were repurposed as offices, grain stores, and communal dining halls. In a sense this was a form of negative heritage management which, after 1978, lineage members at home and abroad mobilised to reverse. The religious dimension of lineages could never, however, be restored to what it was prior to 1949 since a significant proportion of lineage members had ceased to subscribe to ancestor worship as a belief system, although many still light incense and make other offerings to their ancestors as a gesture of respect. James Watson has argued that as an institution the modern lineage in southern China, especially where it has a diasporic membership, has in part become a vehicle for social and economic networking and advancement.[60] To the extent that rejection of ancestor worship might be associated with a broader embrace of modernity, we have to seek the beginnings of this shift not in Communist ideology but in an anti-superstition (迷信 *mixin*) movement among

---

57. Kate Jellema, 'Returning Home: Ancestor Veneration and the Nationalism of *Doi Moi* Vietnam', in *Modernity and Re-enchantment: Religion in Post-revolutionary Vietnam*, ed. Philip Taylor (Singapore: Institute of Southeast Asian Studies), 58.
58. Frequently the single-lineage villages of the Pearl River Delta have a principal ancestral hall, representing the lineage's main line, as well as one or more small halls representing branch lineages (whose members are also part of the 'congregation' of the main hall).
59. Ping, 'The Zheng Communities', 185.
60. James L. Watson, *Emigration and the Chinese Lineage: The Mans in Hong Kong and London* (Berkeley: University of California Press, 1975).

Chinese intellectuals and reformers that began in the late nineteenth century and which led to the destruction of many thousands of temples across China in subsequent decades.[61]

In common with other forms of modern knowledge-making with their roots in Enlightenment rationality, the field of heritage studies has shown little inclination to engage with the category of the supernatural that so informs the beliefs and practices of popular religion in Asia, including those of ancestor worship that underpin the existence of ancestral halls in the emigrant villages of Zhongshan.[62] While it is difficult to know how many in the Chinese diaspora still 'believe' in ancestor worship, we would be wise to assume that such belief can have many gradations; we should be careful not to unwittingly take on the view of those in China and the West who, since the late nineteenth century, have denigrated ancestor worship, glossed as superstition, as anachronistic and superseded by modern perspectives on filial piety.

For many present-day lineage members, particularly those based overseas, engaging in ancestral hall restoration projects is partly a matter of making a claim to having a heritage in the ancestral village and in China more generally. It is a matter, in other words, of establishing their material continuity with the homeland. This appears to have been the case with the recent restoration of an ancestral hall in Ngoi Sha (外沙 Waisha) village, situated today in the Zhuhai Special Economic Zone, an area that was originally part of the southern part of Zhongshan county. During the collectivisation period, beginning in 1958, the ancestral hall was turned into a communal dining hall. Prior to the current restoration, exhortations painted on one of the interior walls during this period were still visible, one of them announcing that meals could not be eaten early without permission, another calling on people to clean up the place after dining. When the People's Communes were disbanded in the early 1980s in favour of family farming, the hall was left in a state of dereliction. By 2014, a tree had taken root in the building and was growing through a space where the roof had fallen in.

This situation lasted until 2014 when Ronald Choy (蔡旭光), who traced his ancestry to Ngoi Sha (外沙 Waisha), visited the village for the first time and was dismayed at the state of the hall.[63] He then joined with a small number of others affiliated with the village in sending out a call for donations for the hall's restoration to lineage members living away from Ngoi Sha, many of them in Hong Kong but others in Australia and elsewhere abroad. The enthusiastic response led to a team

---

61. For the origins of anti-superstition, see Vincent Goossaert and David A. Palmer, *The Religious Question in Modern China* (Chicago, IL: University of Chicago Press, 2011), 50–55. For the destruction of temples, see Denis Byrne, 'Anti-Superstition: Campaigns against Popular Religion and Its Heritage in Asia', in *Routledge Handbook of Heritage in Asia*, ed. Patrick Daly and Tim Winter (London: Routledge, 2012), 295–310.

62. Denis Byrne, 'Divinely Significant: Towards a Post-secular Approach to the Materiality of Popular Religion in Asia', *International Journal of Heritage Studies* 26, no. 9 (2020): 857–73, https://doi.org/10.1080/13527258.2019.1590447.

63. Interview conducted with Ronald Choy in November 2019.

of professional ancestral hall and temple restorers being contracted to carry out the work (Figure 9.3). Roughly half the material fabric of the hall was replaced, including the wooden roof frame, the roof tiles, and many of the terracotta floor tiles. Salvageable woodwork was mostly refinished. The hall's wall paintings, with their depictions of gods, scenes from legendary stories, and auspicious fruit, had deteriorated badly, portions of them being so faded and exfoliated as to be barely legible. Some had been covered over with a layer of black stucco cement by iconoclastic Red Guards during the Cultural Revolution (1966–1976); parts of this layer were chipped off as carefully as possible by the restoration team to reveal the underlying paintings.

The restoration of the hall was overseen by the prefectural government's heritage experts, under the direction of whom the wall paintings were stabilised in their present state rather than repainted, as some lineage members would have wished. Exemplified here is a tension that has come to exist in many parts of Asia between heritage experts who, adopting a secular-rational approach to religious heritage, regard only the historical elements of such paintings as authentic, and local religious believers who regard the images as embodiments of deities and wish to continue the traditional practice of repainting them as an act of devotion.[64] It is a case of

Figure 9.3: A member of the restoration team inspects the newly installed stucco moulding of a shrine near the doorway of the Choy ancestral hall (蔡氏大宗祠), Ngoi Sha (外沙 Waisha) in Zhuhai. Photo by Denis Byrne 2018.

---

64. Denis Byrne, *Counterheritage: Critical Perspectives on Heritage Conservation in Asia* (New York: Routledge, 2014), 95–99.

heritage practitioners confining authenticity to the past, in contrast to true believers who locate the authenticity of the paintings in the efficacy of the deities of whom the paintings are an embodiment. The way the situation was handled in Ngoi Sha makes it clear that while it is lineages who own the ancestral halls of Zhongshan and pay for their restoration, it is the government, through its heritage agency, that has ultimate authority over their management.

Of the other ancestral halls I have visited in emigrant villages elsewhere in Zhongshan, a few had been recently restored and one, repurposed as a grain store during collectivisation, was in ruins. Most, however, were unrestored, remaining more or less in the condition they would have been at the end of the Mao era. Prior to 1949, most of them would have undergone periodic restoration at intervals ranging from several decades to a century or more. Of the halls visited, most retained the altar on which the wooden tablets of the previous few generations of ancestors would previously have been displayed, but the tablets themselves were missing; those that survived the first seventeen years of the PRC would not have survived the Cultural Revolution. Perhaps compensating for this, most of the halls display large genealogical charts of the lineage on their walls. Also commonly displayed are posed group photographs of ranks of lineage members (mostly male, but often with a few female members included), some of which date to Republican times and were taken with panorama cameras, allowing over a hundred people to be included in ranked order. A few of the halls included museum displays where old wooden agricultural tools such as hoes and rakes were preserved along with hand-operated wooden winnowing machines. One displayed a dust-covered (circa 1980s) Chang Jiang (長江) police motorbike with sidecar.

It has become common in recent decades for the village-based committees overseeing the restoration of ancestral halls and temples to circulate photos among overseas lineage members to keep them informed of progress, reinforcing the diaspora's sense of involvement in the work they are partly paying for. Copies of the photos may be kept on display on a notice board inside the ancestral hall during and after restoration. In earlier times the photos were sent by post to overseas lineage members; these days they circulate widely via the various forms of digital media that have collapsed the distance between home and away. Details of donations are also broadcast in this way and act as a cross-border accompaniment to the donor plaques that are erected at the lineage hall to permanently record the names and locations of principal donors.

Stone or wooden donor plaques have been a feature of Chinese temples since ancient times.[65] They are standard elements of the 'furniture' of ancestral halls, temples, and schools in Zhongshan that were built or restored in the nineteenth and twentieth centuries with the involvement of diaspora donors. James Watson,

---

65. Dorothy C. Wong, *Chinese Steles: Pre-Buddhist and Buddhist Use of a Symbolic Form* (Honolulu: University of Hawai'i Press, 2004).

describing the 1970s restoration of the Tin Hau temple (天后廟) at San Tin (新田), situated in the New Territories of Hong Kong, writes that over 600 emigrant members of the Man lineage (文氏) donated to the project. The names of major donors were inscribed in marble, while the names of others were displayed on sheets of red paper on show outside the temple during its reopening.[66] Donor plaques do not just memorialise the donor's financial contribution; they are long-lasting statements of their belongingness to a lineage and its ancestral hall.

By means of their participation in the restoration of ancestral halls in their home villages, diaspora members can be said to inscribe themselves in the local space of the villages. This act of inscription has not been encouraged or facilitated by the state; it is very much an example of heritage-from-below. In fact, the post-1978 restoration of ancestral halls by lineage members in China and overseas can be considered part of an effort to ameliorate or reverse the Chinese state's efforts between 1949 and 1978 to eradicate lineages from local space. According to Mayfair Yang, the Maoist state, in a concerted effort to erode place-based local cultures, set about dismantling three categories of local religious space: the ritual space of lineages, the space of the tomb, and the space of local deity cults.[67] It was part of a move by the PRC government to rebalance the allegiance of people, especially rural people, away from the local and towards the central. While it may have been implemented in a more violent manner than in many other countries, what occurred at this time in China was characteristic of modern spatial regimes everywhere whose objective has been to 'flatten' local spatial orders, ironing out local particularities and allegiances in order to make populations more legible and governable.[68]

The numerous ways in which members of the Chinese diaspora have sought to maintain or restore connections to their home villages, of which 'house-hunting' and participation in ancestral hall restoration are but two examples, can be interpreted as reflecting a desire to give substance to a translocal form of place attachment and belonging that is particular to the experience of transnational migration. Contrary to previous conceptions of migration as a one-way process which inevitably resulted in a shifting of localisation from the origin country to the destination country, research on numerous transnational migration corridors shows how common it is for migrants to be engaged in forming intensely localised ties to the latter while simultaneously keeping alive their ties to local space in the former.[69]

---

66. James L. Watson, 'Chinese Emigrant Ties to the Home Community', *New Community* 5, no. 4 (2010): 348, https://doi.org/10.1080/1369183X.1977.9975473.

67. Mayfair Yang, 'Spatial Struggles: Postcolonial Complex, State Disenchantment, and Popular Reappropriation of Space in Rural South-east China', *Journal of Asian Studies* 63, no. 3 (2004): 719–55, https://doi.org/10.1017/S0021911804000169X.

68. James C. Scott, *Seeing Like a State* (New Haven, CT: Yale University Press, 1998).

69. See, for example, Sarah Lopez, *The Remittance Landscape: Spaces of Migration in Rural Mexico and Urban USA* (Chicago, IL: University of Chicago Press, 2015); Mirjana Lozanovska, *Migrant Housing: Architecture, Dwelling, Migration* (London: Routledge, 2019).

Our use of the heritage corridor concept in this volume aims to help create a frame for thinking about how translocal placemaking plays out in the sphere of heritage.

Bibliography

Ang, Ien. *On Not Speaking Chinese: Living between Asia and the West*. London: Routledge, 2001.

Ang, Ien. 'No Longer Chinese? Residual Chineseness after the Rise of China'. In *Diasporic Chineseness after the Rise of China: Communities and Cultural Production*, edited by Julia Kuehn, Kam Louie, and David M. Pomfret, 17–31. Vancouver: University of British Columbia Press, 2013.

Bowen, Alister M. *Archaeology of the Chinese Fishing Industry in Colonial Victoria*. Sydney: Sydney University Press, 2012.

Byrne, Denis. 'Deep Nation: Australia's Acquisition of an Indigenous Past'. *Aboriginal History* 20 (1996): 82–107.

Byrne, Denis. 'Anti-Superstition: Campaigns against Popular Religion and Its Heritage in Asia'. In *Routledge Handbook of Heritage in Asia*, edited by Patrick Daly and Tim Winter, 295–310. London: Routledge, 2012.

Byrne, Denis. *Counterheritage: Critical Perspectives on Heritage Conservation in Asia*. New York: Routledge, 2014.

Byrne, Denis. 'Heritage Corridors: Transnational Flows and the Built Environment of Migration'. *Journal of Ethnic and Migration Studies* 42, no. 14 (2016): 2360–78. https://doi.org/10.1080/1369183X.2016.1205805.

Byrne, Denis. 'Reclaiming Landscape: Coastal Reclamations before and during the Anthropocene'. In *The Routledge Companion to Landscape Studies*, second edition, edited by Peter Howard, Ian Thompson, Emma Waterton, and Mick Atha, 277–87. London: Routledge, 2018.

Byrne, Denis. 'Divinely Significant: Towards a Post-secular Approach to the Materiality of Popular Religion in Asia'. *International Journal of Heritage Studies* 26, no. 9 (2020): 857–73. https://doi.org/10.1080/13527258.2019.1590447.

Caglar, Ayse. 'Still "Migrants" after All Those Years: Foundational Mobilities, Temporal Frames and Emplacement of Migrants'. *Journal of Ethnic and Migration Studies* 42, no. 6 (2016): 952–69. https://doi.org/10.1080/1369183X.2015.1126085.

Callahan, William A. 'Nationalism, Civilization and Transnational Relations: The Discourse of Greater China'. *Journal of Contemporary China* 14, no. 43 (2005): 269–89. https://doi.org/10.1080/10670560500065629.

Casey, Edward S. *Getting Back into Place: Toward a Renewed Understanding of the Place-World*. Bloomington: Indiana University Press, 1993.

Chen, Lingchei Letty. *The Great Leap Backward: Forgetting and Representing the Mao Years*. Amherst, NY: Cambria, 2020.

Cohen, Deborah. *Braceros: Migrant Citizens and Transnational Subjects in the Postwar United States and Mexico*. Chapel Hill: University of North Carolina Press, 2011.

Couchman, Sophie, and Kate Bagnall. 'Memory and Meaning in the Search for Australian-Chinese Families'. In *Remembering Migration: Oral Histories and Heritage in Australia*, edited by Kate Darian-Smith and Paula Hamilton, 331–46. London: Palgrave Macmillan, 2019.

Darian-Smith, Kate, and Paula Hamilton. 'Remembering Migration'. In *Remembering Migration: Oral Histories and Heritage in Australia*, edited by Kate Darian-Smith and Paula Hamilton, 1–14. London: Palgrave Macmillan, 2019.

DeMare, Brian. *Land Wars: The Story of China's Agrarian Revolution*. Stanford, CA: Stanford University Press, 2019.

Duara, Prasenjit. 'Local Worlds: The Poetics and Politics of Native Place in China'. *The South Atlantic Quarterly* 99, no. 1 (2000): 13–45. https://doi.org/10.1215/00382876-99-1-13.

Faure, David. *Emperor and Ancestor: State and Lineage in South China*. Stanford, CA: Stanford University Press, 2007.

Fitzgerald, John. *Big White Lie: Chinese Australians in White Australia*. Sydney: UNSW Press, 2007.

Foster, Lois and David Stockley. *Multiculturalism: The Changing Australian Paradigm*. Clevedon, UK: Multilingual Matters, 1984.

González-Ruibal, Alfredo. 'What Remains? On Material Nostalgia'. In *After Discourse: Things, Affects, Ethics*, edited by Bjørnar Olsen, Matts Burström, Caitlin DeSilvey, and Þóra Pétursdóttir, 187–203. London: Routledge, 2021.

Goodman, Bryna. *Native Place, City, and Nation: Regional Networks and Identities in Shanghai, 1853–1937*. Berkeley: University of California Press, 1995.

Goossaert, Vincent, and David A. Palmer. *The Religious Question in Modern China*. Chicago, IL: University of Chicago Press, 2011.

Harrison, Rodney. 'Archaeologies of Present and Emergent Futures'. *Historical Archaeology* 50, no. 3 (2020): 165–80. https://doi.org/10.1007/BF03377340.

Ho, Elaine. 'Leveraging Connectivities: Comparative Diaspora Strategies and Evolving Cultural Pluralities in China and Singapore'. *American Behavioural Scientist* 64, no. 10 (2020): 1415–29. https://doi.org/10.1177/0002764220947754.

Hugo, Graeme. 'Geography and Population in Australia: A Historical Perspective'. *Geographic Research* 49, no. 3 (2011): 242–60. https://doi.org/10.1111/j.1745-5871.2011.00713.x.

Jellema, Kate. 'Returning Home: Ancestor Veneration and the Nationalism of *Doi Moi* Vietnam'. In *Modernity and Re-enchantment: Religion in Post-revolutionary Vietnam*, edited by Philip Taylor, 57–89. Singapore: Institute of Southeast Asian Studies, 2007.

Jordens, Ann-Mari. *Alien to Citizen: Settling Migrants in Australia, 1945–75*. Sydney: Allen & Unwin in association with the Australian Archives, 1997.

Kuhn, Philip A. *Chinese among Others: Emigration in Modern Times*. Lanham, MD: Rowman and Littlefield, 2008.

Lakos, William. *Chinese Ancestor Worship: A Practice and Ritual Oriented Approach to Understanding Chinese Culture*. Cambridge: Cambridge Scholars Publishing, 2010.

Liu, Hong, and Els van Dongen. 'China's Diaspora Policies as a New Mode of Transnational Governance'. *Journal of Contemporary China* 25, no. 102 (2016): 201–21. https://doi.org/10.1080/10670564.2016.1184894.

Lopez, Sarah. *The Remittance Landscape: Spaces of Migration in Rural Mexico and Urban USA*. Chicago, IL: University of Chicago Press, 2015.

Lozanovska, Mirjana. *Migrant Housing: Architecture, Dwelling, Migration*. London: Routledge, 2019.

Maruyama, Naho, and Amanda Stronza. 'Roots Tourism of Chinese Americans'. *Ethnology* 49, no. 1 (2010): 23–44.

McKeown, Adam. *Chinese Migrant Networks and Cultural Change: Peru, Chicago, Hawaii, 1900–1936*. Chicago, IL: University of Chicago Press, 2001.

Muzaini, Hamzah. 'Informal Heritage-Making at the Sarawak Cultural Village, East Malaysia'. *Tourism Geographies* 19, no. 2 (2017): 244–64. https://doi.org/10.1080/14616688.2016.1160951.

Peterson, Glen. *Overseas Chinese in the People's Republic of China*. London: Routledge, 2012.

Ping, Song. 'The Zheng Communities and the Formation of a Transnational Community'. *Journal of Chinese Overseas* 4, no. 2 (2008): 183–202. https://doi.org/10.1163/179325408788691372.

Purdie, R. W. *The Register of the National Estate: Who, What, Where?* Canberra: Australian Heritage Commission, 1997.

Rawson, Jessica. 'Changes in the Representation of Life and the Afterlife as Illustrated by the Contents of Tombs of the T'ang and Sung Periods'. In *Arts of the Sung and Yuan*, edited by Maxwell K. Hearn and Judith G. Smith, 23–43. New York: Metropolitan Museum of Art, 1996.

Robertson, Iain J. M., ed. *Heritage from Below*. London: Routledge, 2016.

Scott, James C. *Seeing Like a State*. New Haven, CT: Yale University Press, 1998.

Sheller, Mimi. 'Creolization in Discourses of Global Culture'. In *Uprootings/Regroundings: Questions of Home and Migration*, edited by Sara Ahmed, Claudia Castada, Anne-Marie Fortier, and Mimi Sheller, 273–94. Oxford: Berg, 2003.

Sinn, Elizabeth. *Pacific Crossing: California Gold, Chinese Migration, and the Making of Hong Kong*. Hong Kong: Hong Kong University Press, 2013.

Smith, Laurajane. *Uses of Heritage*. Abingdon: Routledge, 2006.

Svensson, Marina. 'Evolving and Contesting Cultural Heritage in China: The Rural Heritagescape'. In *Reconsidered Cultural Heritage in East Asia*, edited by Akira Matsuda and Luisa Elena Mengoni. London: Ubiquity Press, 2016.

Waterton, Emma, and Modesto Gayo. 'The Elite and the Everyday in the Australian Heritage Field'. In *Fields, Capitals, Habitus: Australian Culture, Inequalities and Social Division*, edited by Tony Bennett, David Carter, Modesto Gayo, Michelle Kelly, and Greg Noble, 66–82. London: Routledge, 2020.

Watson, James L. *Emigration and the Chinese Lineage: The Mans in Hong Kong and London*. Berkeley: University of California Press, 1975.

Watson, James L. 'Chinese Emigrant Ties to the Home Community'. *New Community* 5, no. 4 (2010): 343–52. https://doi.org/10.1080/1369183X.1977.9975473.

Williams, Michael. *Returning Home with Glory: Chinese Villagers around the Pacific, 1849 to 1949*. Hong Kong: Hong Kong University Press, 2018.

Wong, Dorothy C. *Chinese Steles: Pre-Buddhist and Buddhist Use of a Symbolic Form*. Honolulu: University of Hawai'i Press, 2004.

Yang, Mayfair. 'Spatial Struggles: Postcolonial Complex, State Disenchantment, and Popular Reappropriation of Space in Rural South-east China'. *Journal of Asian Studies* 63, no. 3 (2004): 719–55. https://doi.org/10.1017/S002191180400169X.

Glossary

English	Character	Mandarin (Pinyin)	Cantonese
ancestral hall	祠堂	citang	chee tong
ancestral house	祖屋	zuwu	joe uk
Chinatown	唐人街	Tangrenjie	Tong yahn gaai
Chinese store (handling remittances)	金山莊	jinshanzhuang	Gam San chong
county	縣	xian	jyun
diaspora-funded school	僑捐學校	qiaojuan xuexiao	kiu gyun hok haau
dependents of *huaqiao*	僑眷	qiaojuan	kiu gyun
duplex (lit. fraternal house)	兄弟屋	xiongdiwu	heng dai uk
emigrant village	僑鄉	qiaoxiang	kiu heung
fortified (gun) tower, tower house	碉樓	diaolou	diu lau
foreign, multi-storey building	洋樓	yanglou	yeung lau
genealogy (family) book	家譜	jiapu	ka pou
genealogy (clan) book	族譜	zupu	juk pou
letters accompanying remittances	僑批	qiaopi	kiu pai
native place	故鄉	guxiang	koo heung
Overseas Chinese Affairs Bureau	僑辦	qiaoban	kiu baan
Chinese sojourner	華僑	huaqiao	wah kiu
overseas Chinese magazine	僑刊	qiaokan	kiu hon
returned Chinese migrant	歸僑	guiqiao	gwai kiu
remittance/*huaqiao* house	僑房	qiaofang	kiu fong
native-place association (lit. 'same locality club')	同鄉會	tongxianghui	tung heung wui
Southeast Asia (lit. 'South Seas')	南洋	nanyang	nam yeung
Zhongshan (Shekki) dialect	石岐話	shiqihua	Shekki waa

Place Names

Character	Mandarin (Pinyin)	Cantonese	Long Du Dialect (L) and Non-standard Romanisation
廣東	Guangdong	Kwong Tung	Canton
廣州	Guangzhou	Kwong Chou	Canton
廈門	Xiamen	Haa Mun	Amoy
中山	Zhongshan	Chung Shan	Chung Shan (L)
香山	Xiangshan	Heung San	Hsiangshan (L)
四邑	Siyi	Sze Yup	Ssu Yip
開平	Kaiping	Hoi Ping	Hoy Ping
新會	Xinhui	Sun Wui	Sun Wiy
台山	Taishan	Toi Shan	
順德	Shunde	Shuntak	Sun Duck
增城	Zengcheng	Tsang Sing	Chang Sing
東莞	Dongguan	Tung Kun	Toon Kuan
高要	Gaoyao	Ko Yiu	
石岐	Shiqi	Shekki	Shakee (L)
隆都	Long Du	Lung Dou	Loong Doo (L)
良都	Liang Du	Leung Dou	Leoong Doo
小欖	Xiaolan	Siu Lam	
沙溪	Shaxi	Sha Kay	
大涌	Dachong	Tai Chung	

Villages in Long Du district, Zhongshan

龍頭環	Longtouhuan	Lung Tau Wan	Lung Tau Won (L)
嶺後亨	Linghouheng	Leng Hau Hang	Leng Hau Harng (L)
豪吐	Haotu	Hou Tou	Ho Tu (L)
象角	Xiangjiao	Chung Gok	Cheung Kok (L)
涌頭	Chongtou	Chung Tau	Chung Tau (L)
下澤	Xiaze	Ha Zhat	Ha Kang (L)
龐頭	Pangtou	Pong Tau	Pong Tau (L)
安堂	Antang	On Tong	On Dong (L)

Villages in Liang Du district, Zhongshan

沙涌	Shachong	Sha Chong	Sarchung
竹秀園	Zhuxiuyuan	Chuk Sau Yuen	Jook So Yuen

Glossary 265

Character	Mandarin (Pinyin)	Cantonese	Long Du Dialect (L) and Non-standard Romanisation
曹邊	Caobian	Cho Bin	
渡頭	Dutou	Dou Tau	
恒美	Heng Mei	Hom Mei	
新村	Xincun	Sun Chuen	

Villages elsewhere in Zhongshan

濠頭	Haotao	Hou Tau	
(Zhuhai) 外沙	Waisha	Ngoi Sha	
(Zhuhai) 馬山	Mashan	Ma Shan	

Sites in the Zhongshan–Australia Heritage Corridor

Australia

Chung Shan Society of Australia	澳洲中山同鄉會
Chinese Presbyterian Church	雪梨華人長老會
Dixon Street	德信街
Haymarket	孖結/禧市
Heung Yup Long Du Tong Sen Tong (Long Du society)	香邑隆都同善堂
Houng Yuen & Co.	洪源
Kuomintang building	中國國民黨部大樓
Kwong War Chong	廣和昌
Yet Shing & Co.	日昇公司
Wing Sang & Co.	永生果欄

Zhongshan

Caobian School	曹邊學校
Cheuk Shan Middle School	卓山中學
Choy ancestral hall (Ngoi Sha village)	蔡氏大宗祠
Chuk Sau Yuen School	竹秀園學校
Chung Tau Kindergarten	涌頭幼兒園
Xiangshan Commercial Culture Museum	香山商業文化博物館
'Kwok Mansion'	沛勛堂
Lai Wor School (Ngoi Sha village)	禮和學校
Liangdu Church	良都堂
Ma ancestral hall (Sha Chong village)	馬氏大宗祠

'Ma (Ying Piu) Mansion'	南源堂
Mashan School	馬山小學
Sha Chong School	沙涌學校

Hong Kong/Guangzhou (Canton)/Shanghai

The 'big four' department stores	四大百貨公司
Nanking/Nanjing Road (Shanghai)	南京路
Sincere Department Store	先施百貨公司
Sun Sun Department Store	新新百貨公司
The Sun Department Store	大新百貨公司
Wing On Department Store	永安百貨公司

Contributors

Ien Ang is Distinguished Professor of Cultural Studies at Western Sydney University, where she was the founding director of the Institute for Culture and Society. Her work has focused on cultural globalisation, multiculturalism and identities, and race and ethnic representation in cultural institutions and cities, especially in relation to Chinese and Asian diasporas. Her books include *On Not Speaking Chinese: Living Between Asia and the West* (Routledge, 2001) and the co-authored *Chinatown Unbound: Trans-Asian Urbanism in the Age of China* (Rowman & Littlefield, 2019).

Denis Byrne is a professor at the Institute for Culture and Society, Western Sydney University. With a focus on Asia and Australia, he works across the fields of archaeology, critical heritage studies, and the environmental humanities, currently with a particular interest in heritage-making by recent migrants and coastal reclamations as an Anthropocene legacy. His most recent book is *Counterheritage: Critical Perspectives on Heritage Conservation in Asia* (Routledge, 2014).

Christopher Cheng is a second-generation Chinese-born Australian of Zhongshan descent. His multidisciplinary (architecture, Chinese, and anthropology) and multi-sited educational trajectory in the China–Australia Corridor (specifically Cairns, Brisbane, Guangzhou, and Hong Kong) prepared him for doctoral research on the heritage of transnational migration. His PhD research at the Institute for Culture and Society (Western Sydney University) focuses on the legacy of Chinese-Australian funded schools in the Pearl River Delta. His research appears in the *International Journal of Heritage Studies*, the *Asian and Pacific Migration Journal*, and the *Journal of Chinese Overseas*.

Glenn Mar is a Sydneysider now retired after a career in the engineering side of the water industry. A cyclist with a long-term interest in bicycles, Glenn has a particular interest in climate change policy and has a postgraduate qualification in the renewable energy/environment field. He is a committee member of the Chinese Australian Historical Society and administrator of the Chinese Australian Family History Facebook group.

Phillip Mar is an adjunct researcher at the Institute for Culture and Society, Western Sydney University. His doctoral research at Sydney University was on transnational migration between Hong Kong and Australia. His research interests include migration and affect, social contestation, cultural policy, cultural infrastructure, engagement processes in the arts, and cultural diplomacy. He has a Zhongshan lineage, his grandfather Mar Seepoy having been born in Sha Chong.

Michael Williams, adjunct professor at Western Sydney University, is a graduate of Hong Kong University, a scholar of Chinese-Australian history and a founding member of the Chinese-Australian Historical Society. He is the author of *Returning Home with Glory* (HKU Press, 2018), which traces the history of peoples from south China's Pearl River Delta around the Pacific Ports of Sydney, Hawai'i, and San Francisco. Michael has taught at Beijing Foreign Studies and Peking Universities and is currently writing a history of Chinese Australia in 88 Objects. His latest book is *Australia's Dictation Test: The Test It Was a Crime to Fail* (Brill, 2021).

Alexandra Wong is a research fellow at the Institute for Culture and Society of Western Sydney University. She holds a PhD from the University of Edinburgh, UK. Alexandra's research explores the interplay of innovation/creativity, culture, and urban theories, covering a wide range of topics such as creative cities, entrepreneurship, migration, housing, multiculturalism, education, and heritage preservation. Her latest co-authored book *Chinatown Unbound: Trans-Asian Urbanism in the Age of China* was published by Rowan and Littlefield International in 2019. She is currently working on two ARC Discovery Projects titled 'Schooling, Parenting and Ethnicity' (2020–2023) and 'Civic Sinoburbia' (2020–2024).

Index

adaptive reuse, 209, 227

affect: affective engagement with places, 107, 171–74; affective contagion, 144; affective in-between, 171; affective transmission to others, 144, 149; affectivity of remittance houses, 124, 147, 151, 172, 173; corporeality and, 172, 253; definition of, 171; and fear, 87, 180; lack of affective resonance, 124; objects and, 70, 172; shame, 172

affective relationality, 172

affective transnationality, 88, 108

agency: and building styles in colonial period, 176–78; of Chinese in migration corridor, 27–28, 48, 81; of houses, 172; of people and objects, 4

Ahmed, Sara, 64, 70, 151, 177

ancestor worship, 96, 193, 254–56

ancestral halls: and ancestor worship, 254–56; and border-transcending capacity, 254–55; cross-border distribution of photographs of, 258; donor plaques, 258–59; and heritage-making, 253–59; differing approaches to restoration of, 257–58; location in villages, 157, 255n58; repurposed in Mao era, 250, 251, 255, 256; and schooling, 192–93, 199; typical features, 255; and Vietnamese diaspora, 255; wall paintings, 257

ancestral tablets, 193, 255, 258

ancestral villages, descendants' journeys to, 94, 95–96, 112–13, 138, 142–51. *See also* villages, villages in Zhongshan

Anderson, Benedict, 79

Ang, Ien, 15, 246

Anthony Hordern & Sons department store, 136, 166

Art Deco, 167; at Kwok mansion, 166, 167 fig. 6.6, 168 fig. 6.7

Bachelard, Gaston, 152

Bagnall, Kate, 13, 247, 252

Basu, Paul, 109

Baweja, Vandana, 167–68

Bew Chip, remittances from gold fields, 43

Bew, George, 189, 228, 230, 231

Brisbane, 91, 221

Bryant, Levy, 172

California, 10, 32, 34, 44, 53, 155, 230

Cairns, Queensland, 15, 41, 44, 69, 71

Canada, 10, 85, 90, 155, 170, 243

Canton (Guangzhou): electric power plant, 162; neoclassical architecture in, 162; Zhongshan's proximity to major trading ports in, 29, 34. *See also* Pearl River Delta

Cantonese language skills, 98, 112, 114, 120, 123; lack of language skills, 90, 91, 96, 117, 134, 135, 141

'Cantonese Pacific', 48, 209

Chan, Lily, 111

Chan, Shelly, 83

Cheng, Wai-kwan, 201

Chiang, Kai-shek, 80, 218

China–Australia heritage corridor, 2, 4, 17, 75, 98, 103

China–Australia migration corridor, 4, 11, 71: circulatory flows in, 52; 240; disruption of flows in Mao era, 18, 76, 80, 81–82, 198–200, 247; district and dialect connections in, 33; importance of education for, 188, 198; meshwork theory, lines and knots in, 58–62; and opening up of China from 1978, 65, 101, 200, 208, 253, 255, 259; PRC reengagement with diaspora, 76, 92; shared temporality in, 188. *See also* identities in China Australia migration corridor

Chinatown, Sydney (Haymarket), 19, 33, 53, 89, 91, 99, 120, 135, 202, 215–37; as multi-Asian precinct, 235; multiculturalism and, 99, 220; Orientalist makeover of, 220; and transnational circulation, 222; Zhongshan merchants, 221–22. *See also* Dixon Street

Chinese Americans, 83, 93, 102, 186

Chineseness, 75–103, 134; in diaspora tourism, 117, 119, 125, 126, 127; heritage and, 245

Chinese (Xinhai) Revolution of 1911, 26, 45, 78

Chinese Republic News, 226

Chinese Times, The, 140

Chinese Youth League, 219, 220

Choi, C. Y., 216, 221

Choy, Ronald, 256

Choy Hing, James, 176, 198, 228, 230

Christianity: and Chinese Nationalist Party, 191n27; conversion in Australia, 166; and educational philanthropy, 189–91; missionary schools in China, 190

Chu, Cecilia, 176

Chu, Julie, 172–73, 179

Chun, Phillip Lee, 59, 177, 224–26, 228

Chung Shan Society, Sydney, 16, 43, 223n50, 233–34

churches in China–Australia migration corridor: Chinese Presbyterian church, Sydney, 117, 189, 195, 222; Heung San Presbyterian Self-Governance Church,

Shekki, 195; Liangdu Church, Shekki, 194 fig. 7.3, 195, 200

civil war, China, 6, 80, 218, 219, 233, 244, 247

Cohen, Deborah, 243

colonial India, 162, 174, 192

colonialism, 30–32, 48; and architectural style, 176–77, 178

colonial Malaya, 177

concrete, building material. *See* houses (remittances houses) in Zhongshan, materials

Cooktown, Queensland, 68, 224

corridor: as metaphor, 2. *See also* China–Australia heritage corridor; China–Australia migration corridor; heritage corridor; migration corridor; remittance corridor; Zhongshan–Australia heritage corridor

Corsale, Andrea, 109

Cottle, Drew, 89

Couchman, Sophie, 13, 247, 252

Cultural Revolution, 85–87, 88, 91, 97, 120, 123, 180, 199–200, 251, 257, 258

cupola: architectural element of neoclassical buildings, 196; and school buildings, 204, 205 fig. 7.6, 208

Deng, Xiaoping, 71, 76, 91, 200, 253

department stores in China, 136–37, 166, 169, 230–31. *See also* Sincere, company and department store; Wing On, company and department store; 'Four Great Companies'

diaolou. See watchtower houses

diaspora (Chinese), 9; diasporic identity, 189; 'diasporic state of mind' (Ang), 108; new Chinese diaspora, 101–2; ocean liner, resonance of, 168–69

diaspora strategies of Chinese government, 244–46

diaspora tourism, 18, 106–111; and ambivalence towards home, 109; embodied transnational approach to, 107, 123–24; and homecoming, 109,

Index 271

144; hometown visits, 107, 112–14, 117–18, 122, 138–39, 141–53; hybridity of Chinese identities in, 1, 125, 127; and identity development, 110, 127; and political and social circumstances, 123–24; 'moments of home', 110. *See also* place attachment
Dikötter, Frank, 86–87, 162, 164, 165
Dixon Street, Haymarket, 33, 59, 201, 218, 220, 223, 224, 233, 236; Dixon Street Chinese Committee, 233
dual belonging, 188

education in China: colonial India, comparison with, 192; imperial examinations, 185, 192; modern schooling, 192, 193, 196; need for educational reform, 223; in Mao era, 198–200; traditional education, 192–93; value of education in migration corridor, 19, 191
electric power: plant, Canton, 162; in Zhongshan migrant-built houses, 162, 165
emigrant villages: in Greece, 156; landholdings in Guangdong, 156–57; of Punjabi migrants in Britain, 169; as 'transnational entity', 254

families: changes in family formation, 7; 'family at both ends' in transnational migration, 6; family-like associations within corridor, 35; 'flexible kinship' in Chinese diaspora, 7; and identity, intergenerational transmission of, 111; neglect of women in Australian histories, 43–44; transnational families, 83–84, 85, 87, 101
Fiji, 202, 229, 233
Fine Chong, Cheng (Henry), 248, 252; photo of ancestral house, 249 fig. 9.1
Fitzgerald, John, 11, 62, 221, 222
Fitzgerald, Shirley, 217
Fong, King, 233–34
Fong, Say Tin, 233
Fook War Shing, 206

'Four Great Companies', 136, 166, 169–70, 230; and philanthropy, 189–90
Fujian, province: high migration levels, 30–31; house building surge with economic liberalization, 180; imported labour from, 31–32; migration to goldrushes from, 10; reinvention of tradition in Anxi, 93; remittance houses in, 155, 172

Gao, Mobo, 11
Gay, Doris, 116
Gay, George Louis, 116
Gayo, Modesto, 14, 241, 252
Glick Schiller, Nina, 9, 108, 125
Gocklock, James, 189
goldfields, Australian: and heritage registers, 243; and mobility, 52, 55; New South Wales, 32–33, 43; Victorian, 33, 189; Zhongshan participation in, 33
'Gold Mountain firms', 12, 83, 230
gold rushes, 27, 34, 48, 215; debt arrangements enabling travel to, 32; Queensland, 68, 224
Gonzalez-Ruibal, Alfredo, 253
Gregg, Melissa, 171
Guangdong: Japanese invasion and occupation of, 63, 169, 198, 247; land reform in, 179; overseas Chinese land ownership in, 84, 156–57; trade networks, 30; transnational families in, 82. *See also* Canton

Hakka people, in Zhongshan, 29, 37
Hawaii, 39, 41, 42, 116, 155
heritage: architectural significance privileged over social significance, 58; Australia's multiculturalist framing of migrant heritage, 19, 242–44; as a collective archive, 13; 'heritage from above', 240, 241–46; 'heritage from below', 240–41, 247–48, 253; invisibility of Chinese migration in, 54–57; as made or assembled in the present, 14–15, 144, 152–53, 241, 247–48,

253; Mao era, 251; and restoration to 'original' state, 57–58, 257–58; and stasis, 55–56; and state narratives, 14–15, 25, 241–46

heritage corridor, 4, 19, 25, 26, 260. *See also* China–Australia heritage corridor; Zhongshan–Australia heritage corridor

heritage-making, 13, 15, 69, 142, 151, 240–41, 247; as 'future-assembling', 247–48, 248n37, 253; and inheritance, 18, 152. *See also* heritage: 'heritage from below'

heritage of migrants (in Zhongshan), 246: ancestral halls, 253–59; built landscape, 249–50; 'house-hunting', 246–53; spatio-temporal dimension 250–51. *See also* houses (remittance houses) in Zhongshan; schools in Zhongshan, diaspora-funded; temples

heritage practitioners, 241, 244, 257–58

heritage studies, 173–74, 256; critical heritage studies, 241

home, imaginary of, 110, 151, 152

Hong, Ada, 116

Hong, Charlie, 206, 207

Hong Kong: colonial residential zoning laws, 176; firms providing services to 'smooth the movement of people' in, 12; Japanese invasion of, 137; as 'knot' in meshwork 175; lineage members in, 137; main port in Pacific migration, 34; neoclassical architecture in, 174, 176–77; racial discrimination in, 175–76; Victoria Peak (The Peak), 175, 176; Zhongshan connections to, 31–32, 41

Hosagrahar, Jyoti, 165

Houng Yuen & Co., store in Ingham, Queensland, 206

houses (built by migrants): in China, 155; in Greece, 156; in Mexico, 173; in Punjab, 169

houses (remittance houses) in Zhongshan: active waiting embodied by, 173; aerodynamic aesthetic of, 168–69;

affectivity of, 154, 171–73, 179–80; architects of, 165, 166; architectural vernacular of, 162; 'architecture of privilege', 176; Art Deco, 166, 167, 168; as assemblages of human and nonhuman agents, 178; authenticity of, 149, 150, 151; confiscation of, 84, 94, 179; as crystallisation of migrant labour, 54; *diaolou* (watchtower houses), 160, 170 fig. 6.8, 226; damage or destruction of, 67, 96–97, 117, 124; disavowal of, 94, 95; electricity, 45, 162, 165; 'gold mountain house', 96; hybrid styles, 162; interior wall paintings, 163–64, 169; in Mao era, 179–80; as material embodiment of migrants, 156; migrant descendants' visits to, 94–95, 112–13, 138–39, 146–51; migrants 'presenced' in, 156; modernity and, 155, 160–62; neoclassical style, 18, 162, 166, 174–75, 176; as placeholders, 2, 156, 169; screen walls, 158, 160, 163–65; social status and, 18, 71–72, 83, 147, 158, 162–63; typology of, 18, 156–70

houses (remittance houses) in Zhongshan, building materials: bricks, 158, 164, 172; concrete, 71–72, 164, 165, 166, 170 fig. 6.8; tiles (ceramic), 157, 160; window glass, 160–62

Huang, Wei-Jue, 110

Hunt, Harry, 119, 121, 122; Sung-Sun Hall of Learning, 65, 121 fig. 4.7, 203

Hunt, Stanley, 63–68, 64 fig. 2.1, 122, 201, 203–4. *See also* schools in Zhongshan, Mashan school

identities in China–Australia migration corridor: 'absent memory', 142; and assimilation in Australia, 8, 90, 102, 141–42, 220, 242; Australianness, sense of, 76–77, 88–91, 94, 98, 102–3, 114, 119, 127; Chineseness in White Australia, 77–81; decline of *qiaoxiang* identity, 100–101; diasporic identities, 75, 99, 107, 114, 123–24; flexible

Index

identifications, 75; historical changes in, 42–43; *huaqiao*, Chinese overseas, 78–79, 78n8; Mao years, severed links during, 81–88, 247; multiculturalism and, 90, 103, 114; national identity, as Chinese, 42–43, 78–79, 102; and opening up after 1978, 91–93; precarity of transnational identities, 98–101, 102–3; PRC promotion of *qiaoxiang*, 92–93; *qiaoxiang* identity, with village or home district, 42–43, 77, 100; and racial discrimination, 75, 79, 112, 120, 126, 189; unsettled, 75, 103

in-betweenness: of identities, 98, 99; of affective states, 171

incense, 4, 69, 255

Influx of Chinese Restriction Act 1881, NSW, 216

Ingold, Tim, 17, 58–60, 67, 69–70, 152–53. *See also* meshwork theory

Iorio, Monica, 109

Jang, Tim, 63, 68–69: grave of, 69, 71; shop of, 71; tools of, 70, 70 fig. 2.4; Zhongshan house of, 71–72. *See also* Zheng Si-Hang

Japanese: Guangdong, invasion and occupation of, 63, 169, 198, 247; Hong Kong, invasion of, 137; Pearl River Delta, occupation of, 46, 155, 251. *See also* civil war, China

Jellema, Kate, 255

Kaiping, county, Guangdong, 139, 160, 170

Keys, Angela, 89

knots. *See* meshwork theory

Kohl, David G., 17

Kuan, Seng, 174

Kuhn, Philip, 2, 77

Kuo, Mei-fen, 79, 140, 189, 229, 231

Kuomintang, 26, 42–43, 80, 81, 89, 140, 190, 226; headquarters in Sydney Chinatown, 54, 79–80, 218; Zhongshanese dominance in, 222

Kwong War Chong & Company, Dixon Street, Sydney, 44, 223–28, 225 fig. 8.1; branches in Shekki and Hong Kong, 44; building style, 177; heritage listing of, 227–28; as 'knot' in migration meshwork, 59–60; Long Du people and, 59, 223–24; market gardeners, accommodation for, 59, 225; migration services, 225; sale of building, 227, 237; and store-based remittance systems, 44; and transnational connectedness, 228

Lai, Alen, 201

Lai, Eileen, 201

Lam, Douglas, 85–87, 88, 91, 96–97, 100, 102, 107, 138, 141; ancestral house of, 96–97

Lam, Woo, 196

land reform campaign, 1949–1953, 83–85, 87, 158, 178–79

Latour, Bruno, 172

Lee, Bung Chong, 38

Lee, Chee Win, 116, 118; shop in Shekki, 118 fig. 4.5

Lee, Geoff, 118, 119

Lee, Mabel, 119–23, 119 fig. 4.6, 126

Lee, Nancy, 116–19, 123, 124, 125

Lee, Norman, 226

Lee, William, 116–19, 123, 124, 125; ancestral home of, 117

Lee Chun, Phillip, 59, 177, 224–26, 228

legacy of migration: and China Australia migration corridor, 77, 103; contested nature of, 15–16; cultural, 10, 98, 228; for descendants, 72, 98; diasporic philanthropy, 204; economic, 72; educational, 19, 68, 72, 198; and heritage classifications, 58, 241; houses, 178–80; identities evolving over time, 77, 81; 'legacy tourism', 106; 'living legacy', 17; material traces as, 1, 232–33; PRC and *huaqiao* legacy, 82; simile of heritage, 1; in Sydney, 228; and transnationalism, 11, 19, 77, 103

Leong, George, 206
Leong, Philip, 209
Leong, William, 207
Leung, Man Hon, 208–9
Levitt, Peggy, 125
Liangdu, Zhongshan district, 28, 39–41; 40 fig. 1.2; high proportion of migrants within Zhongshan from, 35, 39
Lim, Shirley, 62
lineage halls, 93, 180, 258. *See also* ancestral halls
lineage property: confiscation of, 84, 179, 255; return of, 249, 253, 255
lineages: Choy lineage, Ngoi Sha, 256; as corporate bodies, 253–54; and financial contributions, 254; Ma lineage, 169; Man lineage, 258–59; Mao, opposition to, 255, 259; migration and, 12, 246, 254; ruptured lineage, 151; single-lineage villages, 36, 145; in southern China, 29, 254; Zhongshanese merchants and, 221. *See also* ancestral halls; lineage records
lineage records, 124, 127, 138, 149
lines. *See* meshwork theory
Liu, Hong, 245–46
Long Du, Zhongshan district, 28, 39–41, 40 fig. 1.2; early diaspora-built schools in, 191; higher proportion of emigrant villages in, 35, 39
Long Du native place society, Sydney (1906–1930s), 223, 224
Louie, Andrea, 93, 102
Louie, Kam, 87–88, 99–100; ancestral house of, 97–98, 97 fig. 3.2

Ma, Denise, 111–14, 123, 124, 125; ancestral house of, 113 fig. 4.1
Ma, Joe Young (Joseph Ma), 111, 115 fig. 4.2, 137, 231; descendants of, 115 fig. 4.3
Ma, Jonathan, 112, 114, 134, 137
Ma, Wing Charn, 111, 113, 115 fig. 4.2, 189, 193
Ma, Ying Piu. *See also* Sincere; Wing Sang

Ma, Yung Joong, 112; house of, 113 fig. 4.1
Macao, 29, 34, 37–38, 47, 85, 174
MacArthur, John, 56, 57
Mao era: death of Mao, 99, 180, 244; deterioration of infrastructure in, 47; industrial growth policy, 178; migrant villages during, 47, 178, 179; repurposing of migrant-associated buildings in, 84, 169, 208, 250, 251–52, 255, 256, 258
Mar, Daisy, 137
Mar, Gordon, 79, 80, 89–90, 96, 98–99, 231; ancestral house of, 94, 95 fig. 3.1
Mar, James (Jimmy), 100, 133, 134, 135, 137: as channel for group affects, 144, 149, 150; visit to Sha Chong, 138, 141, 142, 146 fig. 5.4, 147
Mar, King-Hung, 138, 144, 146, 147, 150
Mar, Leong Wah (Harry Mar), 79–80, 81, 231
Mar, Lok Shan, 113
Mar, Raymond, 133, 134, 135, 137, 142
Mar, See Poy, 133, 136–38, 136 fig. 5.1, 140, 141, 142
Mar, See Poy, house of, 146, 146 fig. 5.4; authenticity of, 149; doubts about, 149–50, 152; material condition, 147; visit to, 138, 146–51
market gardens, market gardeners, 6, 43, 54, 55, 59–60, 61, 63, 68, 69, 71, 87, 116, 217, 219, 221, 223, 225, 246
markets, produce, Sydney: Belmore market, 217, 231; Flemington, 231, 232; Haymarket, 60, 65, 91, 217, 218
Maryborough, Queensland, 90, 91
McKeown, Adam M., 11–13, 163
meshwork theory (Tim Ingold): and Chinese migration, 58–71; dreams and imagination, 60; and flow of objects and substances, 60; and kinship, 69–70, 152; knots, 59–60, 63, 175; lifelines, 52, 59, 60, 63, 67, 175, 209, 210; lines, 58–59; as pattern meshed into other landscapes, 61–62, 156; repetition

Index

of movements forming attachments, 63–65. *See also* Ingold, Tim

Metcalf, Thomas, 174

migration corridor, 1–4, 12, 259; relation to heritage corridor, 4. *See also* China–Australia migration corridor

migration heritage in Australia: and assimilation, 242; bordered framing of, 241–42, 243; Chinese graves, 15, 63, 68–69; invisibility of, 54–58; migration sites in national register, 243–44; nationalism and, 10, 241, 243; official heritage, 241–44

migration heritage in China: and diaspora strategies of Chinese government, 244–46; management and conservation of, 209, 257; and nationalism, 10, 246; and 'native place' discourse, 245

migration studies, 7, 9; material turn in, 124; methodological nationalism in, 8; neglect of migrant agency in histories, 27, 28, 48; one-way narrative of migration in, 53, 123–24; white colonial nation-state narrative in, 25, 242. *See also* transnationalism

Miller, Daniel, 173

Ming dynasty, 30, 254; Zhongshan links in, 6, 26, 28, 30, 44

mintian areas in Zhongshan, 28–29

mobility: as challenge to heritage practices, 52; cross-border flows, 4, 6, 9, 17, 81–82, 108, 241–42, 243, 244; and hybrid sense of identity, 75; meshwork and, 58–71; migrant, ontology of, 53–54; transnational migrants as 'mobile settlers', 53

modernity: aspirational, 155; of Chinese migrants in Australia, 62; and diaspora-funded schools, 197–98, 208; infrastructural, 165–66; and light, 162; literacy and, 189; and remittance houses, 169; steamships and motor buses as emblems of, 160; and transnational Chinese migration, 53

multiculturalism: and framing of migrant heritage, 19, 242–43; and identities, 90; and neo-traditional school architecture, 202–3; and Orientalist style, 220

Museum of Chinese in Australia (MOCA), 237

Museum of Commercial Culture, Zhongshan, 114, 124

museums, 56, 114, 124, 209, 211, 227–28, 232, 237

'myth of return', 173

Nanyang (Southeast Asia), 30; labour arrangements of Chinese travelling to, 31; schools funded by returnees from, 199; trade links with, 254

nationalism: Chinese, 11, 88; long-distance nationalism, 79, 101; migrant heritage and, 246; pull of two nationalisms, 79

native place. See *qiaoxiang*

neoclassical architecture: in Australia, 174; in China, 174; colonialism and, 174–75; as floating signifier, 177–78; in Hong Kong, 175–76; hybrid version in Pearl River delta, 175; symbol of wealth and success, 176–77, 178, 179–80. *See also* houses (remittance houses) in Zhongshan; schools in China–Australia migration corridor

New South Wales Chinese Chamber of Commerce, 221

Norman, William, 110

objects: and affect, 70–71; agency of, 172; embodied memories and, 64, 114, 171–72; geographic flow of, 1–2; heritage objects, 54–55, 126–27; 'home' and, 147–49; meshwork and, 60; object relations theory, 151; role in place attachment, 124; 'things laden with capacities', 71; transnationally distributed, 60

Open Door policy of 1978, 186, 200, 253

Opium Wars, 31–32, 34–35, 98
Ou Saek, village. *See* Zhongshan, emigrant villages
overseas Chinese (*huaqiao*): capital generated by, 80, 82; confiscation of property in China, 84, 85, 94; dependents of (*qiaojuan*), 82–85, 92; land purchased by, 156–57; 'huaqiao lifestyle', 56; modernity of, 61–62; 'preferential treatment' of (1953), 84, 180; return of property in China, 92, 94, 249
Overseas Chinese Affairs Bureau, Zhongshan, 102, 244, 246, 247, 252
Oxfeld, Ellen, 109

Pearl River Delta, Guangdong, 1, 25, 27 fig. 1.1, 28, 32, 35, 45; construction labourers from, 165; diaspora philanthropy in, 192; diaspora school-building in, 186; emergent modern culture of, 168–69; emigrant counties of, 16, 17, 25; emigrant villages of, 6, 77; hybrid architectural style in, 175; Japanese occupation of, 46, 155, 251; language diversity within, 37; migration and lineages of, 254; migration into, 29; mobility of people from, 33, 52; motivations for migration from, 33–35; non-emigrant villages of, 157–58; overseas Chinese property in, 84; as 'waterworld', 62
Peterson, Glen, 6, 82, 85, 92, 100, 179, 199, 244
philanthropy, 189, 226; educational philanthropy, 65, 190–91, 195, 198, 204, 209–10, 234; philanthrocapitalism, 189–90
pilgrimage: metaphor for search of ancestral roots, 93, 109; physical and psychological journey, 142
place attachment: and authenticity, 149, 150; in diaspora tourism, 18, 107, 109–10, 124, 126, 127; and emotional colouring, 145; in heritage-making, 240

placemaking, 240; translocal placemaking, 242, 259–60; transnational placemaking, 242. *See also* heritage-making

qiaojuan, overseas Chinese dependents, 82–85, 92
qiaokan, magazines, 45, 188
qiaopi (letters accompanying remittances), 60, 188
qiaoxiang (native place) ties, 2, 12–13, 42–43, 77, 92, 221, 223, 228, 245; merchant-led *qiaoxiang* associations, 44; weakening of, 47, 101
Qing dynasty, 30, 155, 185, 192
Qinqing Zhonghua ('family of China'), 245
Quarantine Station, Sydney, 243
Queensland: Chinese stores in, 69, 206–7; Caobian-Queensland corridor, 206; as destination of Zhongshanese, 1, 16, 26; donations to Caobian school, 206, 209; remittances from, 44, 69, 206. *See also* Fook War Shing; Jang Tim
Quong Tart, 57

Ramshaw, Gregory, 110
remittance corridor, 2
remittance houses. *See* houses (remittance houses)
remittance letters. See *qiaopi*
remittances: from Australia to China, 45; as bank drafts, 156, 226; and house-building in southern China, 155; couriers, 43, 44, 83, 87; as crystallisation of sender's labour, 54; as gold, 4, 156; used for house-building and land purchase, 156–57; Japanese invasion, cessation of, 46; and meshwork, 59–60; from Queensland, 206; reduction in Mao years, 82; store-based remittance systems, 44, 206, 223–24, 225, 229; village reliance on, 45. *See also* Fook War Shing; Kwong War Chong; houses (remittance houses)
Republican era, China, 45, 78, 155, 186
Roberts, Rosie, 53

Index

277

Rookwood cemetery, 112
'roots tourism', 68, 106, 209, 245. *See also* diaspora tourism
Rowe, Peter, 174

Sam, Louisa Ellen, 140
Sandoval-Cervantes, Iván, 173
Sang On Tiy and Co., 229
schools in China–Australia migration corridor: as challenges to heritage practice, 210; construction technologies, 196, 208; decline with economic growth, 204; donor plaques in, 65, 193; earliest Australian schools, 1895, 191; early twentieth century, 191–98; and Japanese occupation, 198; memories of, 197; modernity and, 185, 189, 190, 192, 193, 196, 197, 210; and migration ecology, 19, 191; motivations of funders of, 185–88; neoclassical style of early, 196, 207; neo-traditional styles from 1978, 202–3, 203 fig. 7.4; and Open Door policy from 1978, 47, 200; peak school building periods, 186, 198, 201; PRC education policies, 198–200; school bells, 149n11, 196, 197, 204, 208; second wave of school building, 201–4, 208–9; stairs in, 197; as transnational migration heritage, 210–11
schools in Zhongshan, Australian diaspora-funded, 187 fig 7.1 (map); in ancestral hall, Sha Chong, 193, 194 fig. 7.2; Bok Oi Middle School, 201; Caobian school, 206–9; Cheuk Shan Middle School, 202; Cheun Luk Primary School, 202, 203 fig. 7.4, 234; Chuk Sau Yuen school, 198; Chung Tau kindergarten, 201; Commoners School, Longdu, 195; Lai Wor school, 198; Mashan school, 65–67, 66 fig. 2.2 and 2.3, 121 fig. 4.7, 122, 124, 201, 203–4; Owe Lerng Missionary School, 193–95, 194 fig. 7.3, 197, 200; Sai Kwong Girls' School, 195; Sha Chong primary school, 195–97, 204, 205 fig.

7.5 and 7.6; Sincere Primary School, 201; Zhongshan Overseas Chinese Middle School, 199
Seigworth, Gregory, 171
Sha Chong. *See* Zhongshan, emigrant villages
Shanghai, 26, 45, 46, 48, 54, 122: and CCP, 252; department stores, 114, 137, 169, 230–31; neoclassical buildings in, 174; Wing On Mansions in, 166
shatian (sandy fields) areas in Zhongshan, 28–29, 37
Shekki, county capital, 25n2, 37, 41, 42, 118, 156; Chinese Australians in, 38; remittance businesses in, 43, 44, 206; wealth from merchants abroad, 38
Sincere, company and department store, 111, 114, 136, 166, 176, 189, 193–95, 201, 230; model of store in museum, 114, 124
Smith, Laurajane, 240
social status, of Chinese in Hong Kong, 176; and remittance houses, 18, 72, 147, 172, 178, 179
sojourning, migration pattern, 10, 16, 28, 48, 56, 101, 202, 216, 242; as politicised term, 10–11
steamships, 55, 62, 160, 168–69
structure of feeling, 173
Sun, Yat-sen, 26, 79, 222, 226; Christian schooling, 190
Sydney, as hub for Zhongshan migration, 1, 215–16. *See also* Chinatown
Sze Yap, Guangdong region, 33, 139

Taiping rebellion, 34
Taishan (Toi Shan) county, 37, 186, 190, 221
Taiwan, 80, 92, 122, 218
technological assemblage, and emigrant village, 166
The Rocks, Sydney, 215–16, 217, 236
Thunø, Mette, 92
Tiy Sang, fruit wholesale company, 218, 228

Tölölyan, Khachig, 9
Tomkins, Silvan, 144
transnational heritage, 4, 240; as against one-way narratives of migration, 142, 241–42, 243. *See also* migration heritage in Australia; migration heritage in China
transnational household strategy, 6
transnational migration, Chinese, 1, 6, 53; and identities, 75; lineages and, 253–54; translocal place attachment in, 107, 108, 259–60; transnational migration ecology, 19, 191
Trémon, Anne-Christine, 7

van Dongen, Els, 245–46
Vertovec, Stephen, 9
Vietnam, 30, 44, 48, 255
villages. *See* emigrant villages; Zhongshan emigrant villages

Wang, Cangbai, 15
watchtower houses, 160, 170 fig. 6.8, 226
Waterton, Emma, 14, 241, 252
Watson, James L., 255, 258–59
'White Australia policy', 46, 56, 79, 136, 216, 228; and beleaguered identity, 81; Chinese population decline in Australia, 216, 219; dismantling of, 90; exemptions favouring Chinese merchant class, 236; Immigration Restriction Act, 136, 216, 221, 223; and investment in Hong Kong and China, 229; and reinforcement of transnationalism, 188; sponsorship supporting concentrations of hometowns and lineage, 221
whiteness, phenomenology of, 177
Williams, Michael, 2, 6, 11, 53, 56, 62, 77, 139, 140, 155, 190, 226, 242, 245
Wimmer, Andreas, 9
Wing Kee, George, 80–81, 90–91, 99; ancestral house of, 95
Wing On, company and department store, 44, 136, 137, 166, 189, 218, 223,

228–29, 230, 231: school philanthropy, 193–94, 195, 198
Wing Sang company and stores, 19, 89, 111, 136 fig. 5.1, 137, 189, 193, 196, 218, 228–33, 232 fig. 8.2; and remittances, 229
Wing Tiy & Co., 11, 229
Wong, Shee Ping, 139–41, 139 fig. 5.2; *The Poison of Polygamy*, 140
Woolloomooloo Finger Wharf, Sydney, 243
World War, First, 45, 80, 98
World War, Second, 46, 90, 156, 198, 218, 219, 223, 233

Xiamen, 32, 155, 174

Yee, Jonathan, 234, 235, 236
Yee, Stanley, 202, 234–35, 236; Emperor's Garden restaurant, 234, 235 fig. 8.3
Young, Koon Nuen, 44
Young Wai, John, 189, 195. *See also* churches in China Australia–migration corridor, Chinese Presbyterian Church
Yow, Cheun Hoe, 93, 101
Yu, Henry, 48n96

Zheng, Si-Hang, 15, 63, 68–72. *See* Jang Tim
Zhongshan, migration contexts: association with migrants from Dongguan and Zengcheng, 33, 223: and Communist land reform, 87, 94, 180, 250, 251; Cultural Revolution, 97, 199–200; diaspora outreach programs, 244–45; educational reform and, 185–86, 209–10; geography of, 37–38; historical context of migration from, 25–48; post-1949 communist state, 46–47; post-1978 reform era, 47; pre-modern history, 29–30; Republican era, 45; support for Sun Yat-sen, 26, 222; urbanisation and demographic change, 17, 204; variation in emigration rates within, 34
Zhongshan–Australia heritage corridor, 27, 48, 209, 253

Index 279

Zhongshan, emigrant villages, 5 fig. 0.2 (map); Buck Toy, 41, 42; Caobian, 14 fig. 0.3, 159 fig. 6.1, 161, 163 fig. 6.4, 206–9; Chuk Sau Yuen, 166, 167 fig 6.6; Chung Kok, 39; Chung Tau, 39, 201, 224, 226; Doumen, 37, 119; Dutou, 87, 97 fig. 3.2; Heng Mei, 91; Mashan, 65, 67, 68, 119, 121, 122, 123, 124, 126, 201, 203; old core areas of, 249–50; Ngoi Sha (Waisha), 198, 256, 257 fig. 9.3; Ou Saek (Wushi), 248, 249 fig. 9.1, 250; Pong Tau, 69, 70, 71; Sha Chong, 15, 18, 79, 94, 95, 100, 111, 112, 113, 114, 123, 137, 138–39, 141–52, 166, 169, 193–97, 201, 204, 205, 208, 231, 232, 252; Sun Ming Ting, 39; Xiaolan, 35, 37, 38; Xiaze, 41–42; Xincun, 116, 117, 123, 124, 125. *See also* emigrant villages in Zhongshan; Long Du; Liangdu
Zhu, Xiaoyang, 165
Zhuhai, 47, 65, 198, 201; Zhuhai Special Economic Zone, 256